Modern American Political Dynasties

Modern American Political Dynasties

A Study of Power, Family, and Political Influence

Kathleen A. Gronnerud and Scott J. Spitzer, Editors

BLOOMSBURY ACADEMIC
NEW YORK • LONDON • OXFORD • NEW DELHI • SYDNEY

BLOOMSBURY ACADEMIC
Bloomsbury Publishing Inc
1385 Broadway, New York, NY 10018, USA
50 Bedford Square, London, WC1B 3DP, UK
29 Earlsfort Terrace, Dublin 2, Ireland

BLOOMSBURY, BLOOMSBURY ACADEMIC and the Diana logo
are trademarks of Bloomsbury Publishing Plc

First published in the United States of America by ABC-CLIO 2018
Paperback edition published by Bloomsbury Academic 2025

Copyright © Bloomsbury Publishing Inc, 2025

Cover photos: Family tree. (anamad/iStockphoto); U.S. flag. (lukbar/iStockphoto)
Jacket design by Silverander Communications

All rights reserved. No part of this publication may be reproduced or
transmitted in any form or by any means, electronic or mechanical,
including photocopying, recording, or any information storage or retrieval
system, without prior permission in writing from the publishers.

Bloomsbury Publishing Inc does not have any control over, or responsibility for,
any third-party websites referred to or in this book. All internet addresses given
in this book were correct at the time of going to press. The author and publisher
regret any inconvenience caused if addresses have changed or sites have
ceased to exist, but can accept no responsibility for any such changes.

Library of Congress Cataloging-in-Publication Data
Names: Gronnerud, Kathleen A., editor. | Spitzer, Scott J., editor.
Title: Modern American political dynasties : a study of power, family, and
political influence / Kathleen A. Gronnerud and Scott J. Spitzer, editors.
Description: Santa Barbara, California : Praeger, an imprint of ABC-CLIO, LLC, [2018] |
Includes bibliographical references and index.
Identifiers: LCCN 2018023119 (print) | LCCN 2018031200 (ebook) |
ISBN 9781440854439 (ebook) | ISBN 9781440854422 (hard copy)
Subjects: LCSH: Politicians—Family relationships—United States. |
Politicians—United States—Biography. | United States—Politics and
government—20th century. | United States—Politics and government—21st century.
Classification: LCC E74 (ebook) | LCC E74 .M64 2018 (print) |
DDC 324.2092/2 [B]—dc23
LC record available at https://lccn.loc.gov/2018023119

ISBN: HB: 978-1-4408-5442-2
PB: 979-8-7651-3693-5
ePDF: 978-1-4408-5443-9
eBook: 979-8-2161-1839-8

To find out more about our authors and books visit www.bloomsbury.com
and sign up for our newsletters.

Contents

Introduction   vii
   Scott J. Spitzer

Part One	**National Political Dynasties**	1
Chapter 1	The Bush Dynasty *William Cunion*	3
Chapter 2	The Cabot Lodge Dynasty *Kathleen A. Gronnerud*	25
Chapter 3	The Clinton Dynasty *Margaret E. Scranton*	39
Chapter 4	The Gore Dynasty *Michael R. Fitzgerald*	67
Chapter 5	The Kennedy Dynasty *Barbara A. Perry*	79
Chapter 6	The Paul Dynasty *Joel F. Turner and Scott Lasley*	109
Chapter 7	The Rockefeller Dynasty *Richard Skinner*	119
Chapter 8	The Romney Dynasty *Dean J. Kotlowski*	151
Chapter 9	The Roosevelt Dynasty *Jennifer Hopper*	163
Chapter 10	The Taft Dynasty *Mindy Farmer*	189

Part Two	State Political Dynasties	209
Chapter 11	The Brown Dynasty *Ethan Rarick*	211
Chapter 12	The Byrd Dynasty *Ted Ritter*	231
Chapter 13	The Cuomo Dynasty *Saladin Ambar*	245
Chapter 14	The La Follette Dynasty *Nancy C. Unger*	259
Chapter 15	The Roberts Dynasty *Richard A. Clucas and Skyler Brocker-Knapp*	275
Chapter 16	The Simpson Dynasty *Cody J. Foster*	287
Part Three	Regional and Metropolitan Political Dynasties	295
Chapter 17	The Daley Dynasty *Larry Bennett*	297
Chapter 18	The Dingell Dynasty *Julio L. Borquez*	317
Chapter 19	The Udall Dynasty *Zachary A. Smith and Molly E. Thrash*	329

Conclusion: American Democracy and Hereditary Power in the 21st Century — 343
   Scott J. Spitzer

About the Editors and Contributors — 355

Index — 359

Introduction

Scott J. Spitzer

This study of modern American political dynasties reveals much about American political history. In these pages, we find that the historical arc of each political family—its emergence, rise, and its fading from public life—embraces centrally important features in the development of 20th-century American politics. These include: the power of the party political machines and their subsequent disruption by reforms in the early part of the century; the remarkably successful confrontation of racial hierarchy in the South by the nonviolent civil rights movement; the rise of the conservative movement in the second half of the century and its transformation of the modern Republican Party; and the modern Democratic Party's struggles to redefine its agenda, as the New Deal coalition confronted a new set of political challenges, quite different from its original agenda in addressing the economic deprivation of the Great Depression. Yet even as tracing their individual stories reveal much about the nation's political character, the very existence of these political dynasties challenges basic democratic assumptions underlying the American experiment.

The American Revolution and the Constitution

There is an unspoken tension in American democratic politics, between an emphasis on the power of everyday citizens and an appreciation of expertise and professionalism in our elected leaders. Although Americans claim nearly universal support for the democratic principle of popular sovereignty (the citizens' right to choose their leaders), the nation's political history illustrates the long-standing practice of established leadership expertise. These two are not necessarily opposed to one another—a nation can certainly have democratically elected leaders who enjoy strong support among the public and who are also refined in their political skills, possessing specialized expertise in one or more areas of relevant policy. But noteworthy tensions exist in

American politics between those who favor an unfettered democracy and those concerned with stable and experienced leadership. The American Revolution surely was animated by a commitment to the establishment of a robust democracy, epitomized in Jefferson's immortal Declaration of Independence: "We hold these truths to be self-evident that all men are created equal".[1] At the same time, the U.S. Constitution, drafted a decade later, reflects the concerns of its original framers with the destabilizing and potentially destructive power of impassioned populist movements.[2] Indeed, the difficulties that the young nation had in suppressing Shays' Rebellion, just a year before the Philadelphia Constitutional Convention of 1787, was evidence enough for the convention delegates that populism and democracy were potentially dangerous to the nation's very survival. The resulting Constitution therefore reflected both the desire for direct democratic empowerment of the public, through the elected House of Representatives, and a desire that during the debates over the Constitution the national government be directed by those with a large stake in the nation's success: elites with something to lose if the nation were to somehow fail to thrive. The latter was reflected in a Senate that would be selected by state legislatures, rather than directly elected; in the lifetime appointed terms of the federal judiciary; and in the peculiar arrangement for selecting the president, by unelected electors in each state, themselves selected by their respective state legislatures.

At the same time, the delegates to the Constitutional Convention shared with their Revolutionary brethren a fundamental commitment to popular sovereignty. The nation's leaders would be chosen in such a way that they would be ultimately accountable to the public, and the hereditary privilege of European monarchies and the upper houses of European parliaments were to be completely abolished. The Electoral College would be chosen by the elected state legislatures; U.S. senators selected by the same; and the members of the Supreme Court selected by the president and confirmed by the Senate, each of whom were to answer to the public, although indirectly. The commitment to democratic principles was so pervasive that during the debates over the Constitution the convention delegates had virtually no discussion of inherited political privilege or of the intergenerational transmission of office and power. Perhaps the framers felt that this danger to popular sovereignty had been thoroughly eradicated through the American Revolution.

In the *Federalist Papers*, widely recognized as the greatest contribution of the United States to the cannon of political philosophy, the authors—Alexander Hamilton, James Madison, and John Jay—engaged in a great deal of discussion about how the new Constitution would carefully guard against the abuse of power by those elected or selected to lead the nation. Only one paper out of the 85, however, even bothered to consider the issue of titles of nobility, and none considered the issue of hereditary transmission of power directly. In *Federalist Paper 84*, nearly as an afterthought, Hamilton wrote on

Introduction

"miscellaneous items," including "titles of nobility." On this, Hamilton was notably brief. Writing in answer to critics of the Constitution who were concerned about the lack of a Bill of Rights in the original proposed document, and comparing the New York State Constitution with the proposed U.S. Constitution, Hamilton noted that the "writ of habeas corpus, the prohibition of ex post facto laws, and of Titles of Nobility, to which we have no corresponding provision in our Constitution, are perhaps greater securities to liberty and republicanism than any it [New York's] contains."[3] On titles of nobility, in particular, Hamilton seemed to take it for granted that the American Constitution was based on popular sovereignty, barring any system of hereditary political privilege:

> Nothing need be said to illustrate the importance of the prohibition of titles of nobility. This may truly be denominated the cornerstone of republican government; for so long as they are excluded there can never be serious danger that the government will be any other than that of the people.[4]

For direct discussion of the challenges that hereditary political power posed to democratic principles in the United States, the constitutional debates are therefore not much of a guide. Instead, this was the great triumph of the American Revolution itself: to ensure that political power would be established by the people, rather than by divine right or inheritance. For example, Thomas Paine's *Common Sense* (1776), was—by contrast to the *Federalist Papers*—direct and forceful in its denunciation of hereditary political authority:

> To the evil of monarchy we have added that of hereditary succession; and as the first is a degradation and lessening of ourselves, so the second, claimed as a matter of right, is an insult and an imposition on posterity. For all men being originally equals, no *one* by *birth* could have a right to set up his own family in perpetual preference to all others for ever . . .[5]

It appears that the assumption of the constitutional framers was that this issue was settled in their revolutionary independence from England. They had broken not just from England but from the European heritage of monarchy and nobility based on birth.

At the same time, a decade after their Revolution and liberation, the new nation's leaders were thinking of how to provide for a more secure and stable governance. Rather than rely on a buoyant burst of democratic spirit from the masses, the framers of the Constitution sought instead to establish a careful architecture of government that would rely on thoughtful leadership by established elites. In the midst of this tension between a desire for elite governance and democratic legitimacy, America fell upon a new kind of inherited authority—the family political dynasty. No sooner had the Constitution been signed, then the nation's first political family legacy—the Adamses—took root. Beginning with only the nation's second presidency, the Adams family dynasty remained in power for generations, exercising political influence for one and a half centuries.[6] Since then, family political dynasties have been a steady feature of American political life. According to Stephen Hess, 44 American political families have had at least four members of the same name elected to federal office; 75 families have had at least three members in national office; and another 48 have had three or more members elected to national office who were related by marriage. Collectively, the numbers in Congress are not large relative to those who have been elected without any advantages of family connections: only 6 percent of all members elected since 1774 have been related to another member of Congress or a previous member.[7]

However, a basic count may underestimate the importance of these families, when we consider that many of these dynasties dominated the politics of a state or a region for generations, and therefore dynastic members of Congress often attained seniority and prestige within the House or the Senate, and with those resources became leaders of their respective institutions. Hess recounts, for example, the legacy of the Louisiana Longs and Senator Russell Long's chairmanship of the powerful Senate Finance Committee (Chapter 15). The prominence of family dynasties in the Congress was more pronounced in the nation's early years, when "more than 10% of Congress and more than 20% of freshmen members were related to a former member" of Congress.[8] They were most prevalent in Congress just before the Civil War, and then declined as a proportion of congressional members: 11 percent of legislators were dynastic between 1789 and 1858, but only 7 percent were dynastic since 1966.[9] Political scientist Brian Feinstein recounts that during the 110th Congress (2007–2008), 9 senators and 44 members of the House were closely related to someone who had served or who was currently serving in Congress.[10]

Although this number is certainly not dominant in the nation's politics, when one considers that more than one-fifth of all U.S. presidents have been part of prominent political families,[11] the significance of political dynasties is serious enough to warrant attention from historians and political scientists. Moreover, their significant role in American politics challenges assumptions about the openness of the democratic process and raises implicit questions about family privilege and power in American politics.

The Study of American Political Dynasties

As historians and political scientists note, the Constitution as originally ratified in 1789 was but a loose blueprint for the nation's governance. The historical unfolding of how that design would be enacted has confounded the framers' expectations in many respects. Several major features of our political system, for example, were not included in that original design: the premiere leadership of the presidency; the nation's two-party system; and an

Introduction

extensive, far-reaching federal government. These extraconstitutional developments are essential aspects of the American political system, but were unforeseen or even intentionally opposed by the framers of the Constitution. For example, the framers emphasized Congress as the centerpiece of the nation's politics and governance, and therefore failed to anticipate the 20th-century emergence of presidential leadership as the motive force in American national politics.[12] They renounced political parties, seeing them as divisive. And none would have imagined the extensiveness of the federal government and its myriad programs touching on every aspect of public life (and sometimes even private life).

Although scholars have expansively studied each of these extraconstitutional developments, the steady presence of family political dynasties throughout American political history has received scant attention. Stephen Hess's important work on American political dynasties, first published in 1966, remains the most comprehensive historical work on the subject.[13] Others have studied the prevalence of dynasties in Congress, identifying the advantages that these familial political ties confer on candidates for congressional office.[14] But for the most part, American political dynasties have received far less attention than political dynasties in other nations, such as in Japan or in the Philippines.[15]

Our study differs significantly from previous research, building on Stephen Hess's pioneering study, and extending some of the insights from quantitative studies of dynastic advantages in Congress. Most of Hess's book covers 19th-century political dynasties, whereas this volume centers on the 20th century entirely. Still, Hess's volume covers some dynasties that extend into the 20th century, and five of these six families are covered in our volume as well. Our focus, however, differs from Hess's in that this volume seeks to describe not only the history of each dynasty but also to identify the factors that explain the emergence, rise, and decline of political dynasties. In so doing, this book provides insights into the driving themes in American political development during the 20th century.

In part, our study, like the quantitative work on political dynasties in the Congress, seeks to explain how political privilege linked to family can be so prominent in a nation that simultaneously proclaims its openness to any and all political challengers. Dal Bo et al. (2009) and Feinstein (2011) each find that name recognition, political networks, and financial support provide dynasty members with important advantages in congressional elections. Likewise, the recounting of each of the histories of modern political dynasties in this volume illustrates the value of family network ties, family wealth, and the power of a brand-like name in advancing the political fortunes of politically ambitious family members. These histories, moreover, encompass a far greater diversity of political offices than the quantitative studies on political dynasties in Congress: legislators, governors, big-city mayors, powerful cabinet members, and presidents are all part of the modern political dynasties that are recounted in the forthcoming pages.

Returning to Political History

In the last several decades, a real shift has occurred in how historians study and teach U.S. history: political history, which traditionally focuses on those (most traditionally white-educated males) in positions of power, has become passé or old-fashioned. The popularity of Howard Zinn's *A People's History of the United States*, first published in 1980, signaled a conscious turn toward studying the nation's major events through the voices and contributions of those on the edges of society—the poor, laborers, immigrants, women, children, Native Americans, African Americans, and other ethnic minorities—and to look for the grassroots stories behind such events.[16] In a similar vein, the field of American studies has greatly expanded since the 1960s. When the American Studies Association began in 1951, it counted 300 members; by the end of the 20th century its membership reached more than 5,000. Many historians and American studies scholars today see the forward motion of their scholarly disciplines as challenging the long-reigning idea of American exceptionalism.[17] Often, they downplay or question "Big Man history," or "history from the top down," as too removed from the real story of America.

One of the surprising trends found in the essays compiled here, a volume dedicated to families of many such "Big Men," is how much their patterns are woven right into the country's patchwork identity. Time and again, the stories of these influential families reflect important shifts in the country as a whole—and while we might be identifying these shifts in political terms, they likewise are felt in the nation's economic and social life. Indeed, the men and women we select to lead us—as a city, state, or nation—says something about us as a collective as well. Although every vote may not seem to carry equal weight in every election, who we choose to be our "Big Men" is often reflective of significant changes taking place in our local and national landscape: changing ideas about liberalism, the proper role and size of the government; new concentrations of immigrants and their assimilation and ascent in local communities; distrust in politicians and the government they run; the influence of business industries in local and national finances and public policy decisions; and the ongoing national conversation about equality—who deserves it and how the government should appropriately promote and protect it.

In particular, there are four major thematic observations that run through the rise and fall of these dynasties and illuminate bigger themes in the nation's modern history:

- the importance of the party machines in the early part of the 20th century, and their subsequent disruption by reforms;
- the powerful racial hierarchy embedded in the Jim Crow segregated South, and the remarkably successful challenges to it by the civil rights movement in the post–World War II years;

- the rise of the conservative movement in the second half of the 20th century and its transformation of the Republican Party; and
- the New Deal Democratic Party's struggles to identify a more relevant platform for mobilizing its coalition as the Great Depression faded from memory.

Overview of the Chapters

In each of the chapters herein, the emergence of a powerful political family, and its subsequent rise to prominence and eventual loss of influence, corresponds to one of two general patterns. Either the family's cultural and political identity was a well-tailored fit for the politics of that historical moment, or they provided leadership on the cutting edge of change in that status quo. For example, the Cabot Lodge family dynasty rose to power in an era of patrician political advantage, and when immigrant political machines emerged in the early part of the 20th century, the family's influence was increasingly challenged by a new form of political power. Conversely, as the dominance of fiscal conservatism for the older Republican Party of the Eisenhower years gave way to a new party agenda including social policy conservatism, the Romney family successfully straddled these changes in Michigan and nationally, until they ultimately pushed Mitt Romney off the main stage of the party's leadership in 2016.

In selecting each of the families for this volume, our purpose was to explore the ways that modern American political dynasties bring to light important historical shifts in 20th-century American political development. We were also interested in identifying the factors that explain how political dynasties emerge in a nation committed to democratic equality, what sustains them, and what contributes to their demise. As such, this volume was never meant to be a comprehensive, encyclopedic study of all modern political dynasties. Instead, it was to be a gathering of case studies that would serve as vehicles for exploring the themes identified above.

The process for case selection was therefore one that turned to historians and political scientists across the country who were already engaged in the study of powerful members of significant 20th-century political dynasties. We sought out scholars who could think broadly about their subjects from a place of deep familiarity. We began by reaching out to historians and political scientists at universities in the home states or cities where the most powerful and well-known member of the political dynasty had risen to prominence. As scholars responded, we developed our list of contributors, always seeking to ensure coverage of a broad array of local, state, regional, and national figures, who were powerful at different periods throughout the 20th century. Our final list, we believe, provides us with a multifaceted window into the major political developments over the course of the 20th century, across the nation.

The chapters are organized into three broad sections: national political dynasties, state political dynasties, and regional and metropolitan political dynasties. National political dynasties are those that include presidents and vice presidents (Bush, Clinton, Gore, Kennedy, Rockefeller, Roosevelt, and Taft), major party presidential nominees (Romney), and nationally known candidates for the presidency (Paul). State political dynasties dominated their respective state's politics and often had national aspirations as well, including governors (Brown, Cuomo, Roberts) and senators (Byrd, La Follette, Simpson). Regional and metropolitan dynasties were more important locally or regionally and included mayors (Daley) and leaders in the House of Representatives (Dingells and Udalls). For our authors, we asked them to explore four questions in shaping their narratives:

1. To what elements or events would you attribute the start of this particular political dynasty?
2. When did the dynasty's power peak? When did its authority and influence begin to decline? Was its decline due to changing times or norms or was it a matter of personality or character?
3. Were there conflicts between generations in this dynasty that were familial in nature but also became translated into political terms? Did familial tensions bleed into politics as sibling rivalries or relationships with parents affected who continued the dynasty?
4. Why did the dynasty end? Does its ending say something important about the dynasty?

As a whole, in answering each of these questions, the chapters provide us with an exploration of some of the most important features of American political development through the lens of the political dynasty. The resulting insights into American political identity—highlighting the four major themes listed above—ironically extend from studying a feature of American politics that was, for all intended purposes, formally rejected as a violation of fundamental democratic principle. The utility of this investigation for understanding major aspects of modern American political development suggests that the tension between energized democratic mobilization and the stability of elite leadership is, in and of itself, a fundamental part of the American political character.

Notes

1. *The Declaration of Independence.* Engrossed copy of the Declaration of Independence, August 2, 1776; Miscellaneous Papers of the Continental Congress, 1774–1789; Records of the Continental and Confederation Congresses and the Constitutional Convention, 1774–1789, Record Group 360; National Archives.

Introduction

Accessed on October 15, 2017, at https://www.ourdocuments.gov/doc.php?flash=true&doc=2.

2. Robert A. Dahl, *How Democratic Is the Constitution?* 2nd ed. (New Haven, CT: Yale University Press, 2003).

3. Issac Kramnick, ed., *The Federalist Papers*. James Madison, Alexander Hamilton, and John Jay (Hammondsworth, Middlesex, UK: Penguin Classics, 1987 [1787]), 474.

4. Kramnick, ed., *The Federalist Papers*, 475.

5. Thomas Paine, *Common Sense* (New York: Penguin Books, 2005 [1776]), 18.

6. Stephen Hess, *America's Political Dynasties: From Adams to Clinton* (Washington, DC: Brookings Institution Press, 2016), Chapter 2.

7. Hess, *America's Political Dynasties*, 14.

8. Daniel M. Smith, *Dynasties and Democracy: The Inherited Incumbency Advantage in Japan* (Stanford, CA: Stanford University Press, 2018), 11.

9. Dal Bo, Ernesto Dal Bo, Pedro Dal Bo, and Jason Snyder, "Political Dynasties," *The Review of Economic Studies* (2009) 76: 115–142.

10. Brian D. Feinstein, "The Dynasty Advantage: Family Ties in Congressional Elections," *Legislative Studies Quarterly* (2010) 35(4), 571.

11. Presidents who are/have been members of political dynasties are John Adams (1797–1801); John Q. Adams (1825–1829); William H. Harrison (1841–1841); Theodore Roosevelt (1901–1909); William H. Taft (1909–1913); Franklin D. Roosevelt (1933–1945); John F. Kennedy (1961–1963); George Bush (1989–1993); William J. Clinton (1993–2001); and George W. Bush (2001–2009). Here I define political dynasties as families where multiple members have held elected office, and have exercised a significant influence over local, state, regional, or national politics.

12. Sidney M. Milkis and Michael Nelson, *The American Presidency: Origins and Development, 1776–2014* (Washington, DC: CQ Press, 2015).

13. Hess, *America's Political Dynasties*.

14. Dal Bo et al., *Political Dynasties*; Feinstein, "The Dynasty Advantage."

15. Smith, "Dynasties and Democracy"; Pablo Querubin, "Family and Politics: Dynastic Persistence in the Philippines," *Quarterly Journal of Political Science* (2018) 11(2), 151–181.

16. Howard Zinn, *A People's History of the United States: 1492–2001*, new ed. (New York: HarperCollins Press, 2003).

17. "History," American Studies Association, www/theasa.net/about/history. Accessed on September 11, 2017.

PART ONE

National Political Dynasties

CHAPTER ONE

The Bush Dynasty

William Cunion

"Don't call us a dynasty. It connotes that something is given to you."
—Jeb Bush[1]

If it were fiction, no one would believe it. Well past midnight on November 8, 2000, just hours after the polls closed, here was Republican presidential nominee George W. Bush, governor of Texas, anxiously receiving updates from his closest advisers. Everyone had expected a razor-close election, so the late night was just part of the script. In some respects, it was a scene typical of any presidential campaign on election night, with reports trickling in—mixing good news tempered with uncertainty, bad news with cautious optimism. As Governor Bush watched the pivotal state of Florida move from his opponent's column to his own, then back to undecided, he was surrounded by those who would love and support him no matter how the night turned out. In that sense, there was nothing out of the ordinary in that room. After all, what could possibly have been more normal than the candidate taking refuge with his immediate family?

It all seems perfectly normal until one reviews the roster in the room. Sitting with the candidate was his father, the 41st president of the United States, George Herbert Walker Bush, himself a son of U.S. senator Prescott Bush (who served in the Senate from Connecticut from 1952 to 1963). Also in the room was another of the former president's sons, John Ellis "Jeb" Bush, who just happened to be the current governor of the state that was already becoming the focal point of the election controversy that would soon engulf the nation for over a month. The gathering around the Republican nominee was clearly an unusual one, hardly a cross-section of America.

The old adage claims that anyone in America can grow up to become president, but with seven of the eight presidential elections between 1980 and 2004 featuring a candidate named Bush on the Republican ticket, recent facts seem to suggest that the scales are tipped toward those with some connection to the powerful already. As if to prove the point even further, it is worth adding that Bush's opponent, Vice President Al Gore, was *himself* a son of a U.S. senator. Would either of them have ever been elected to high office if they had different last names? That should not matter in the egalitarian, democratic system of which Americans are so proud.

More than two centuries after the country was founded on a rejection of nobility—firmly ensconced in the U.S. Constitution[2]—certain families are clearly far better positioned to thrive in American politics than others. This is not a new phenomenon, either; more than 50 years ago, historian Stephen Hess pointed out that "there are some families . . . who are far more equal than others at the political starting gate."[3] One could argue that the 2000 election was a tangible repudiation of the popular myth that anyone can be president. The two nominees were practically American royalty—and Vice President Gore, son of a senator, was probably the *less* well connected. This volume is dedicated to the exploration of these families—what qualities or talents they possess that others may lack, or what advantages they have that make them so much more likely to succeed than those with similar talents. Most immediately, this chapter will address the simple question of how we got to that point in November 2000: How could one family have produced so many political leaders? What do the Bushes have that the rest of us apparently do not?

Whether or not they appreciate the dynasty label, the Bush family's lengthy record of political success across generations certainly warrants attention. Perhaps more than any other family in American political history, the Bushes have effectively navigated the tension between elitism and populism by carefully crafting an image consistent with the times. During the postwar period of the 1950s, when Americans sought less partisan statesmen, Prescott Bush stepped into the role right out of central casting. When experience was in vogue, George H. W. Bush rose to the presidency in the 1980s. When the country sought a "third way," George W. Bush's moderate message of "compassionate conservatism" resonated. Similarly, in 2016, when the electorate was fed up with their elected officials and turned to outsiders, Jeb Bush was left behind. In some respects, the story of the Bush family is a story about the currents of American political life in the 20th century and beyond.

From another angle, though, theirs is very much a story about family, and the values and habits that the Bush extended family have cultivated. Their path to power has been rocky and uneven, defeat as common as victory. In both their personal and public lives, qualities like resilience and competitiveness have characterized the Bush family narrative. Each Bush family member

The Bush Dynasty

Bush Political Dynasty Family Tree

1. Prescott Sheldon Bush, 1895–1972
    U.S. Senate, 1952–1963
   Married Dorothy Wear
   Five children including George Herbert Walker

2. George Herbert Walker Bush
    House of Representatives, 1967–1971
    U.S. ambassador to the United Nations, 1971–1973
    Chairman, Republican National Committee, 1973–1974
    Director, Central Intelligence Agency, 1976–1977
    U.S. vice president, 1980–1988
    41st U.S. president, 1988–1992
   Married Barbara Pierce
   Six children including George Walker and John Ellis

3. George Walker Bush
    Governor of Texas, 1995–2000
    43rd U.S. president, 2000–2008
   Married Laura Welch
   Two children: Jenna Welch and Barbara Pierce

4. John Ellis "Jeb" Bush Sr.
    Florida secretary of commerce, 1987–1988
    Florida governor, 1999–2007
   Married Columba Garnica Gallo
   Three children: George Prescott, Noelle Lucila, and John Ellis "Jebby" Jr.

has stories that include challenges that would have destroyed many others, from tragic and unexpected deaths, to business failures, to devastating political defeats. Yet through it all, the family has kept moving forward, defining themselves by principles larger than the offices they have held.

Uncovering the inner workings of *any* family would be challenging (perhaps even from the inside), but like most political dynasties, the Bush family is an especially difficult clan to dissect and explain. Despite their decades in the public eye, they are famously guarded and private. Maybe because of that, biographies tend to fall firmly into one camp or the other. Some work is perhaps too favorable to the Bush family (e.g., Schweizer and Schweizer's *The*

Bushes: Portrait of a Dynasty), almost to the point of being promotional campaign material (e.g., Herskowitz's *Duty, Honor, Country: The Life and Legacy of Prescott Bush*). Other accounts are so critical as to border on libelous (e.g., Kitty Kelly's *The Family: The Real Story of the Bush Dynasty*) or are at least too eager to assign malevolent motives to every action (e.g., Kevin Phillips's *American Dynasty*). And because their story is still unfolding, we don't have the benefit of hindsight to smooth out these rough edges.

The evidence that we do have may well be sufficient to lay out a handful of themes characteristic of the family's "internal culture."[4] Several Bush family qualities emerge in the accounts of both supporters and critics, including:

- *High standards.* Much like the Kennedy family, expectations in the Bush family have always been extremely high. When a young George W. Bush was considering his college options, his grandfather, Senator Prescott Bush, told him bluntly that "Yale is not a choice; it is a commitment." When the dean at Andover then asked the younger Bush to list his three top choices, the future president listed Yale. Three times.[5]

- *Competitiveness.* Sports figure prominently in the Bush family narrative. Golf's Walker Cup was founded by and named for George H. W. Bush's maternal grandfather, Bert Walker, who instilled in his daughter, Dorothy, such a love of athletic competition that she placed second in a national girls' tennis championship in 1918. In turn, Dorothy then passed that spirit on to her boys. Later in life, George Bush reflected on his mother's influence in this regard: "She loved games and thought competition taught courage, fair play, and—I think most importantly—teamwork."[6] Associates of George W. and Jeb Bush have commented that they are "unbelievably fierce in competition."[7]

- *Resilience.* Until very recently, the Bush family had a perfect record of striking out in their first at-bat: each member of the Bush family, who sought public office for the first time, lost. Without exception, they all tried again and clearly, many were able to hit game-winning home runs as their career progressed.

- *Obligation to community.* Countless families are supportive and resilient, but only a few transfer those qualities into public service. For the Bushes, this commitment began with Samuel P. Bush, Prescott's father. As a business leader in Columbus, Ohio, around the turn of the 20th century, he boldly articulated a vision of the moral responsibilities of business owners to address labor concerns fairly. He did so because he believed that "it was the duty of the enlightened in the community to lead."[8] Subsequent generations took that principle much further, serving not only the local community as business leaders, but as political leaders at the state and national level. Where some families turn inward to help one another, the Bushes also looked outward.

- *Risk-taking.* One of the surprises about political dynasties in general is that these families tend to find political success across different states. Stephen

Hess found many years ago that such families have typically seen successive generations move away from "safe" locations to new pastures.⁹ The Bushes have demonstrated those same nomadic qualities, seeking new opportunities in both public service and private business ventures across the country, and subsequently holding offices in Connecticut, Texas, and Florida. Beyond their noteworthy mobility, the family also displayed an unusually high degree of ambitious risk-taking to seize opportunities quickly. There are many stories of Bushes seeking office suddenly, in special elections, or without much notice, but few of Bushes who declined an opportunity and instead waited for the "right" time.

- *Loyalty.* George W. Bush was often criticized during his presidency for excessive loyalty to his staff, and it is easy to see that he comes by this naturally. As a family, the Bushes are completely committed to one another, and every political campaign involving a Bush actually involves *all* of the Bushes. George W. once conveyed the depth of this commitment to a new consultant on his father's campaign team: "In our family, if you go to war, we want you completely on our side. If George Bush is in the room and a hand grenade rolls across the floor, we expect you to fall on it."¹⁰

The family culture has long prioritized these traits, and they all play a role in promoting political success. Even so, there are other noteworthy families who have the above traits in spades. What else do the Bushes have that sets them apart? There are at least two other qualities that seem to have helped them achieve and sustain their success:

- *The changing political climate.* The Bush family has been very fortunate to fit well with their times. Even their individual differences seem to follow the currents of the American electorate. One can hardly conceive of a more suitable Republican candidate for the growing army of evangelical Christian voters in 2000 than George W. Bush. He not only reflected their social conservatism, but he spoke their language. Unlike his father, George W. was comfortable describing himself as "born again." From a political perspective, he was simply born at the right time. That said, it is critical also to recognize that the family strategically emphasized qualities in their candidates that matched well with the times whenever they could. Like success stories of all kinds, there is both luck and skill involved in the explanation.
- *Connections and wealth.* To be sure, however important all of the above qualities have been to the Bush family, they would not be included in this book were it not for the sizable financial advantages they had long before any of them entered politics. The wealth the family accumulated over a century ago (discussed shortly) gave them a network of contacts that very few people could ever imagine. From coast to coast, and literally around the globe, the Bush family has connections that transform political dreams into realistic plans. Again, though, they bring much to the table here. The family developed

a systematic process for cultivating those contacts and the skills necessary for requesting favors when needed. Because they repay loyalty with loyalty, the Bushes have a wide network of devoted supporters. Even up to the present, the results have been obvious: In mid-2017, Jeb's son George P. Bush had already raised more than $3 million for his Texas Land Commissioner reelection campaign—which is highly unlikely to be even slightly competitive. They have been dealt a good hand, but they also play those cards very well.

There are certainly idiosyncratic factors for each successive generation that have been critical to political success, but the above list captures most of the explanation for how the Bush family has maintained their dynasty—whether they want to call it that or not.

First Generation: Before Politics

Because the Bush family can claim ancestors as far back as the *Mayflower*, it is tempting to start the story of the dynasty far too early. There were indeed notable forebears on each branch of the family tree. Through his father's side of the family, George W. Bush descends directly from the powerful early colonist Robert Livingston, while his mother shares a common ancestor with President Franklin Pierce. This history is not merely trivia. Even by the middle of the 1800s, the family had acquired status and wealth; George W.'s great-great-grandfather James Smith Bush attended Yale back in the 1840s, while another of his great-great-grandfathers, David Davis Walker, had built the largest dry goods company west of the Mississippi by the 1870s.[11]

The foundational resources were long there, but the dynasty's story really begins around the turn of the 20th century. Two generations before any Bushes moved into the White House, Samuel P. Bush and George Herbert Walker established habits and expectations that would set the dynasty in motion. They brought very different qualities to the mix: the Bushes were more duty-bound and steady, while the Walkers were risk-takers.[12] Both were highly ambitious and competitive; each believed that "to win was to be alive."[13] Together, they combined to leave a profound impression on the next generations—and subsequently on the country and the world.

S. P. Bush was born in New Jersey in 1863, son of James Smith Bush (1825–1899), a Yale-educated Episcopalian priest who fulfilled his public obligation by regularly delivering pro-Union sermons throughout the Civil War. As would happen so many times in the family, the son took a different direction than the father, though he seemed to retain his father's core values. Rather than a life of religion, and rather than attending Yale, S. P. attended the Stevens Institute of Technology to study scientific management and engineering. The decision might be seen as a safe strategy, but not one that reflected a lack of ambition. With a vision of a management career in industry, S. P. had a plan for long-term success, which he executed incredibly well. Even in college, he was competitive and driven, a standout student who was elected vice president of the student body, and who was also a member of the baseball and tennis teams. After graduating in 1884, he took positions of increasing responsibility, and by 1901, he was managing Franklin Rockefeller's Buckeye Steel in Columbus, Ohio. In just a few years, Rockefeller asked S. P. to run the company, having recognized Bush's extraordinary management skills. S. P. led Buckeye Steel for two decades and along the way added a list of notable accomplishments to his resume: he was the first president of the National Association of Manufacturers, the director of the Federal Reserve Bank of Cleveland, and during World War I, chief of the Ordinance, Small Arms, and Ammunition Section of the War Industries Board. Clearly, the decision not to go to Yale was not made out of a lack of ambition. Like the generations that would follow, S. P. Bush set extremely high standards for himself and seized opportunities throughout his career.[14]

Although there is no evidence that S. P. ever considered a career in politics, he was a strong presence in the New Jersey Democratic Party. But even more importantly, he was the type of business leader who recognized his broader obligation to community, following the practice of his father, and setting an example for future generations of Bushes. He was heavily involved in the Chamber of Commerce, but his vision for his company and its place in the civic life of Columbus went far beyond profit margins. Not only did S. P. advance the company's first philanthropic efforts, but he squarely addressed the burgeoning labor movement that affected Buckeye Steel. During a period of significant labor unrest in the 1910s, Bush took a bold public stand in defense of a far more moderate approach than most of his peers, arguing that "labor will never be reasonably contented without a living wage. . . . Everyone in a community must have decent living conditions . . . and these the average industrial community has not supplied and does not supply at the present time."[15] In the mid-1920s, he went even further and developed the housing in the African American neighborhoods near the plant, which he had described as "deplorable."[16] To be sure, his motivations were largely paternalistic, and his view of the world was more hierarchical than democratic, but his efforts came from a genuine sense of duty, which would become a hallmark of the Bush family's character.

Meanwhile, very different qualities were emerging on the other branch of the family tree. George Herbert "Bert" Walker was born in 1875 in St. Louis to a family of prominence and wealth. Even from an early age, Bert demonstrated a rebellious nature, was extremely competitive, and was probably more comfortable with risks than safety. As a student at Stonyhurst boarding school in England, Bert did well in the classroom but truly shined in athletics. He was an excellent polo player and quickly became a skilled golfer as well.

Because the game prized mental toughness, golf appealed to Bert on a fundamental level, and it was important to him for the rest of his life; he would later become the president of the USGA, and he founded the Walker's Cup, a prestigious international tournament that is still played today. But the image of a pampered, genteel young polo player and golfer belies the real Bert Walker. In fact, his best sport was boxing, and when he returned to Missouri, he promptly won the state heavyweight championship. In a sport more commonly associated with immigrants and the working poor, boxing best captured Bert's character—his competitive drive could not be overstated.[17]

Similarly, Bert was a genuine risk-taker. He was only 25 when he sold his shares in the family dry goods business to start his own investment firm; G. H. Walker and Company would be successful enough to outlive its founder. It was an ideal career path for someone with Bert's temperament. As his son Lou would later say, "The old man was a dealmaker. He *liked* taking risks."[18] By necessity, perhaps, Bert also demonstrated an exceptional measure of resilience; while S. P. Bush was slowly accumulating wealth in industry, Bert was making and losing fortunes again and again, an inevitable by-product of risk-taking. The uncertainty would occasionally produce unsettled feelings in his own family, but it did set an important example of how to bounce back. In later decades, when his descendants would have to recover from terrible personal and political struggles, they could point to Bert Walker as a role model. Notably, though, Bert was never directly involved in politics. He did promote and support numerous Republican candidates across Missouri, and he knew the importance of developing strong relationships with lawmakers. But his penchant for risk and his desire to win never translated into the political arena.

At home, Bert was not especially warm with his own sons; in fact, he preferred to spar with them (literally) than encourage them. For him, life was very competitive, and he had no tolerance for weakness. One recent author suggested that he actually "thrived on conflict."[19] Bert carried that spirit into his professional life as well, openly stating a preference to hire champion athletes over better educated applicants, as he believed deeply that the athletes had critical qualities that could not be taught.[20] Although all of his sons followed his lead and participated in sports, it was actually his daughter Dottie who learned the lessons most fully. She was unquestionably the best athlete in the group, a nationally competitive tennis player who nearly backed out of getting married in favor of playing on the circuit.

Dottie went through with the wedding and married S. P. Bush's son, Prescott, in 1921. As it happened, Prescott was quite the athlete himself, an excellent golfer who would later follow in his father-in-law's footsteps as president of the USGA. One can only speculate on the full picture that Bert had of Prescott, but authors Schweizer and Schweizer are undoubtedly correct that "what carried currency with Bert was a young man's *drive*."[21] Prescott Bush measured up; before the decade was out, he would be a vice president at Bert's investment firm. In turn, Prescott clearly admired Bert and was far closer to him than to his own father. Though they named their first son Prescott Jr., Dottie and Prescott named their second son after her father: George Herbert Walker Bush, who would draw on the qualities of both of his grandfathers, and the good fortune of their wealth and connections, and become the 41st president of the United States.

Whatever qualities George inherited, they ran through his father Prescott, who would emerge as the first in the clan to seek public office. Prescott's high standards, competitiveness, and resilience would lead him to the U.S. Senate.

Prescott Bush

Most contemporary Americans have not heard of Prescott Bush. Despite being the father of one president, and the grandfather of another, he was otherwise a somewhat obscure U.S. senator from Connecticut who served mainly during the Eisenhower years. Yet, he is the pivot in the whole story of the Bush dynasty, the one whose ambitions and sense of commitment led him into public life. Without him, this family probably would not be included in this volume. After all, there are many powerful and wealthy families in America, but only a few have ventured into politics—and fewer still have transformed it into the family business. What drove Prescott Bush, and how did it impact his children?

Prior to marrying into the Walker family, Bush had already distinguished himself as a scholar and athlete at Yale and then as a field artillery captain in World War I. He had also largely broken from his own father; whether they were fully estranged is not clear, but the fact is that S. P. did not attend Prescott's wedding to Dottie. It goes too far to suggest that Bert Walker became Prescott's surrogate father as he entered adulthood, but it is true that Prescott was very attached to his father-in-law. In 1924, Bert took over Brown Brothers Harriman, one of the largest private banks in the nation, and he immediately brought Prescott on board to run the investment side of the firm. Around the same time, Prescott also joined his father-in-law politically, and Prescott switched from the Democratic to the Republican Party.

Prescott took that political turn fully and became more directly engaged in public affairs than either his father or his father-in-law. His children would later say that the key biblical verse shared in their household emphasized their moral obligations to others: "Now it is required that those who have been given a trust must prove faithful."[22] Prescott interpreted that charge to be one of public service. Throughout the 1930s, he enthusiastically presided over the town hall meetings in Greenwich, Connecticut; the pure democracy that characterized local government in New England gave him immediate opportunities to contribute to public life. Over the next two decades, he expanded his political activity considerably, as state chair of the United Negro College Fund, as treasurer for Planned Parenthood's national fund-raising campaign, and finally as finance chair of the state Republican Party. He had even briefly given serious consideration to running for Congress in 1946, but his business partners' disapproval put an end to that plan before it even began. They believed that the office was not significant enough to justify his leaving the business. However, an open Senate seat in 1950 was too good an opportunity to resist. This would be the first time that a Bush would be on the ballot.

The whole family campaigned tirelessly for Prescott, who had cultivated a strong network of friends and associates who also joined his campaign. For the candidate, the political arena appealed to his competitive side, and the race could hardly have been any closer. When the votes were counted, Prescott came up a hair short; out of more than 850,000 votes cast, he lost by less than a thousand. The first Bush to run for office would be the first Bush to lose an election. In what would also be the first example of the family's capacity for resilience, Prescott quickly recovered, and actively sought the Republican nomination for the Senate just two years later. After losing his bid for the nomination at the party convention that summer, his political career seemed to be over before it even really began.

However, just a month later, the state's other Senate seat opened up when the incumbent senator Brien McMahon died in office. With his campaign organization still in place, Prescott Bush was able to secure the nomination quite easily, and by running openly on Dwight Eisenhower's presidential coattails, he was part of a Republican sweep across Connecticut that November. The lesson of the first Bush elected to public office is not only one of ambition and competitiveness, but also of resilience. Prescott Bush demonstrated a persistence that would be passed on to his son—and to his son's son. A political dynasty must be able to survive some setbacks.

In many ways, Prescott Bush was a low-key senator who made "little legislative mark."[23] Even his most admiring biographer concedes that he was not a significant lawmaker.[24] But he was a pragmatic voice of reason, a moderate who could reach across the aisle—and to the White House. Bush became close with President Eisenhower partly because of their similar views; both were fiscally conservative, realists in foreign policy, and supportive of civil rights. Besides their politics, Bush and Eisenhower shared a mutual love of golf, and they would play numerous rounds together during their time in Washington. Because he won his seat in a special election, Bush's first term was only four years, and his reelection bid coincided with Eisenhower's. Again, he rode the coattails of the president to a second term—the beginnings of the Bush dynasty were emerging.

To be sure, good luck was an essential contributor to Bush's political success. Would Prescott Bush have been as influential under a Lyndon Johnson presidency? He was lucky to be a member of the "right" party—and to be so proficient in the sport that President Eisenhower loved. He also had the good fortune to be in a state where his views would be politically viable: his pro-civil rights message would not have played well in Texas, for example. Beyond that, Prescott Bush was well over six feet tall and blessed with movie-star good looks; these qualities come up in every biographical treatment, so they probably should not be ignored. Evidently, factors both internal and external led to his success.

Sometimes, those qualities could cut both ways. One of the defining characteristics of Prescott Bush was loyalty, one of his core virtues—one biographer suggested that he should have had the word tattooed on his body.[25] When party leaders hesitated to support his reelection bid in 1956, he concluded that it was better to rely on family and close friends—those who would be loyal at all costs. He was so badly wounded by the party's lack of support that it may have led him to opt not to run for a third term in 1962 (a decision he later regretted). His devotion to the principle of loyalty was so great that he distanced himself from political allies (namely, Nelson Rockefeller) and even family members who were unfaithful to their spouses. Disloyalty was unforgivable, but that same principle also made Prescott Bush an incredible source of support for an aspiring politician from West Texas. When George H. W. Bush set out to follow in his father's footsteps into Congress, Prescott not only supported him in the expected ways, but also by actively calling on his contacts for special favors. Elections may be won by riding the right coattails, or by looking the part, but dynasties are built on the connections that family create over the generations.

George H. W. Bush

Perhaps no member of the Bush family better reflects the mix of qualities that have led to success than the current patriarch of the clan, George H. W. Bush, the 41st president of the United States. His story reflects the relentless pursuit of achievement, even in the face of enormous personal and political setbacks. His storied career weaved through elected office into global diplomatic work and later into a top administrative post at home—and eventually into the White House. It is tempting to characterize his as a dramatic story, but it is probably more accurate to describe it as a tale of humility. (A president without a memoir?) Though he has angrily denounced the idea that his family is a political dynasty, in ways large and small, it is George H. W. Bush that best captures that dynastic spirit.

It is fair to concede that George was a son of privilege from the beginning, but he was not a child of politics. His father would not begin his political career until George was in his late twenties, by then already married to Barbara Pierce, father of two children, a decorated combat veteran of World War II, and a graduate of Yale. There is, in fact, little or no evidence that George was particularly interested in politics in his earlier years, but there is much to

George H. W. Bush and family in Houston c. 1964. (National Archives)

suggest that his aspirations were high, and that he was willing to take enormous risks to pursue opportunity. Bush family traits were there from the start.

Prescott and Dottie sent George to Andover Academy in the fall of 1937, when George was just 13 years old. Their intention was to develop young George from a boy into a man, and by all accounts, things went according to plan. George quickly attained a reputation as a campus leader; his seriousness of purpose and competitive drive set him apart from his peers, themselves mostly quite privileged, too. Bush was the senior class president in 1941–1942, the year that the United States entered World War II.

Although the commencement speaker, Secretary of War Henry Stimson, had urged the Andover grads to go on to college to best serve the country, George was already committed—in his mind at least—to being a naval aviator, one of the most dangerous jobs in all of the armed services. Following the extremely rigorous training, Bush was commissioned as a naval ensign in June 1943. Not yet 19, he was, in fact, the youngest aviator in the U.S. Navy. Much has been made of George H. W. Bush's military career, and indeed it is a story of drama and valor, but the relevant point for our purposes is made: George H. W. Bush was a person of exceptionally high standards, open to risk, even as a young man.

That boldness would carry him throughout his career, even before politics became the family business. Upon graduating from Yale in 1948, George had an opportunity to go into investment banking with his in-laws. At the time, he expressed some reluctance to take the path already blazed for him: "I am not sure I want to capitalize completely on the benefits . . . of my social position."[26] But not long after, a family friend offered him a position with an oil company in West Texas. With his wife and newborn son, he headed to Odessa, a growing community in central Texas, just a few miles from the border of New Mexico. There, he began establishing his own reputation as a civic leader. Like his father and his grandfather, George very deliberately became his own man, reinventing himself in a new place. As his career unfolded, that willingness to take chances would lead, step-by-step, all the way to the White House.[27]

But it is perhaps his record of resilience that most notably marks the character of George H. W. Bush, and most powerfully reflects the character that has sustained the Bush family's success. In 1953, George and Barbara suffered the devastating loss of their four-year-old daughter, Robin, to leukemia. It is impossible to know how the future president managed to survive emotionally, though he acknowledged long afterward that he was unable to talk about her death for 40 years.[28] What is clear is that they persevered. One family member suggested that they kept moving forward because the "stiff upper lip" was expected: "There is a real emphasis on being and staying positive—almost to a fault, you are not to complain."[29] Alternatively, one could argue that the demands of life permitted only so much space for grief. After all, older brother George W. was only seven, and Jeb was less than a year old, and there was simply no time to be incapacitated.

George H. W. Bush would also demonstrate an ability to respond well to adversity in his public life. Like his father, he lost his first election; and like his father, it would not be his last defeat. In 1964, George ran for the U.S. Senate, but at a time when Republicans were incredibly unpopular in Texas. The GOP held just *one* out of 150 State House seats, and Democrats won all 23 U.S. House seats from Texas that November. George's 12-point loss appears strangely impressive in that light. What is truly remarkable, though, is how quickly he bounced back from the defeat. Some redistricting in 1966 had created an open seat near Houston, and Bush won that race with ease.

Bush served two terms in Congress with distinction, including a bold vote in 1968 in support of the Fair Housing Act, an unpopular decision across the conservative state. When ambition called again in 1970, that vote would haunt Bush as he lost in a second race for U.S. Senate. Two statewide political defeats in just six years would be enough for most politicians to head back to private life. Instead of retreating, however, Bush took the next decade to seize a series of unprecedented opportunities.

Several major appointments followed his Senate campaign loss in 1970. First, Bush accepted a nomination to serve as the U.S. ambassador to the United Nations. That was followed by a two-year stint as the chair of the Republican National Committee, a period that included the resignation of President Nixon following Watergate. Although Bush remained quiet publicly during that period, he privately urged Nixon to resign.[30] His integrity during that crisis kept his political career going, and he was very nearly the choice to serve as Gerald Ford's new vice president during that transition. Instead, President Ford soon asked Bush to represent the country as the official envoy to China. After holding that post for a little over a year, Bush was then appointed to be the director of the Central Intelligence Agency. As George W. Bush points out in *41*, his adoring biography of his father, George H. W. Bush is the only president in American history to hold *any* of these four posts—and he held all of them! Here is someone whose aspirations and resilience seemed to lead almost inevitably to a bid for the presidency.

Bush's 1980 presidential campaign began well, with a big win in the Iowa caucuses, narrowly edging out his competitors in a crowded six-man race. But he began to lose primaries soon after, as former California governor Ronald Reagan quickly took the lead in the race for the nomination. This time around, however, Bush was not passed over for the vice presidential nomination, and he went on to serve eight years as vice president alongside President Ronald Reagan. When Bush was elected to the nation's highest office in 1988, he became the first sitting vice president to be elected president since Martin Van Buren, more than 150 years before. In this telling, his election was a well-deserved culmination of hard work, ambition, and dedication to public service. George H. W. Bush would not be derailed by setbacks, no matter how many came along: his was not an easy path, definitely not a straight line from the bottom to the top.

However, it is important to recall that Bush did not exactly start at the bottom. Aside from having a father who had served in the U.S. Senate, Bush was also quite wealthy in his own right by the time he launched his political career in 1964. In addition to his growing network of business contacts across Texas, he had a unique capacity for bringing in the "heavy hitters" at the national level to campaign on his behalf in his first campaign, including former president Eisenhower, as well as future presidents Nixon and Ford. In addition, the well-known senator Everett Dirksen of Illinois also campaigned on behalf of the aspiring congressman. For someone who had never even *run* for office before, this support says much about the advantages of the Bush name and the Bush fortune.

Like compound interest, those advantages accrued even more steadily once Bush was elected. Looking back on his rapid rise to power in the 1970s, a critical moment came when the freshman congressman was assigned to the powerful Ways and Means Committee, an opportunity that gave him experience in working directly with congressional and party leaders. How could a first-term congressman secure such a plum assignment? His father had made some calls:

> Pres phoned his old friend and golfing partner Gerald Ford, the Republican leader in the house, and asked him to support his son's bid. Next he contacted former vice president Richard Nixon. . . . Pres then began working the other side of the aisle. As a moderate Republican, affable and reasonable, he had many friends in Democratic circles. He remained good friends with Senator William Fulbright of Arkansas. . . . Fulbright called his fellow Arkansan Wilbur Mills, chairman of the House Ways and Means Committee, and told him to expect a call from his good friend Pres Bush. . . .

Mills [talked] to Jerry Ford and by early January, George had a slot on Ways and Means.[31]

Bush became the first freshman member of Congress to serve on that committee since 1900.[32]

George H. W. Bush had the good luck to come along when he did. His particular brand of moderation resonated well with educated Republican voters in the late 1960s, as he articulated a middle ground between the conservative southerners who supported segregation and the growing power of the civil rights movement. Although he was evidently too moderate for the people of Texas, leading to his senate campaign loss in 1970, his reasonable and pragmatic approach to problem solving was a good fit for the national Republican Party of that era. Even into the 1980s, his "kinder, gentler" message struck a chord for Americans seeking a diplomatic peace at home and abroad. By contrast, imagine how poorly that message would have been received if he had been born a generation later; "a thousand points of light" would surely have fallen flat in the antiestablishment and highly partisan politics of 2016. Even by the time of his own reelection campaign in 1992, the electorate was more likely to see principled compromise as a sellout than as an admirable governing strategy. Although there were an array of reasons that Bush lost this election, an important one is that his governing style had largely fallen out of favor. Pundits largely praised him for retreating from his 1988 pledge, "Read my lips: No new taxes," but voters did not, and he won just 37 percent of the popular vote in a three-way race. Bush was fortunate to serve in public life when he did, but his luck had run out.

It is very important to close this section by pointing out that it was the *combination* of his personal qualities and his good fortune that enabled George H. W. Bush to succeed in public life. Yes, he had opportunities because of his connections that others would never have. Those opportunities did not guarantee success, however, and his track record of coming up short confirms that pretty clearly. What he did so well, though, was to cultivate those contacts in his extensive network. He learned from his father the "value of making and keeping friends,"[33] a strategy that served him well personally and politically. Perhaps it can be said that George H. W. Bush used his advantages well, drawing from his family's core values, as well as drawing from his family's vast connections. Those very same factors led his son, George W. Bush, to a successful run for the presidency.

George W. Bush

If George H. W. Bush best fits the overall narrative that explains the Bush dynasty, his somewhat prodigal son is the most difficult to explain. The ambition, maturity, and seriousness of purpose that characterized the older Bush seem wholly absent in the younger one. Even the competitive drive shared by his forebears does not appear to have been part of his formative character. Although his father and grandfather were civic leaders by their early twenties, the popular line on George W. is that he was still "partying" until age 40. Yet, this superficial picture of the 43rd president masks many underlying dynastic qualities that he inherited; beneath the surface, we see evidence of the high standards, ambition, and resilience that led the others to political success. But we also begin to see most clearly the fruits of the unearned benefits of the family name.

One author characterizes George W. Bush as "almost a caricature overcorrection of his father's political weaknesses."[34] Where Poppy could be aloof with voters, W. was endearing (perhaps more like his father's victorious opponent, Bill Clinton, than like Poppy himself). The younger Bush was able to connect personally in ways that the older Bush never could. Unlike his father, the son loved campaigning more than governing—it would be hard to see George W. Bush serving as head of the CIA, for example. Other than their names, and a general political orientation, they really have little in common—certainly far less, at any rate, than his father and grandfather shared. Perhaps this is one reason why both George Bushes dismiss talk of "dynasty."

It is also easy to question the concept of a dynasty when considering the youth of George W. Bush. He was so clearly on a different path that he was not even considered the most likely in his own *family* to follow in his father's footsteps; younger brother Jeb was generally seen as the political heir apparent. By all accounts, George's early years were aptly described as happy-go-lucky, his school days filled more with friends than with hard work. His extended adolescence, which included problems with alcohol, led to some less endearing moments as well. He was occasionally unruly and rather undisciplined well into his thirties, culminating in a tense confrontation in which the younger Bush challenged the older one to a fight—mano a mano. His rebellious streak was a far cry from the more admirable ones shared by his father and grandfather. All of them were setting out to be their own men, but George W. had so much less direction that the parallels are difficult to see.

Yet there were signs of ambition long before there was any talk of a presidential run. Although he was a mediocre student at every level, George W. Bush persisted academically, receiving an undergraduate degree from Yale, later earning an MBA from Harvard—becoming the only American president with degrees from both of these prestigious institutions. In between, he served as a pilot in the Texas Air National Guard, and he later established his own oil exploration company in west Texas. Every one of these activities remains clouded in controversy due to allegations of preferential treatment, and it is evident that Bush was not operating on a level playing field. But it is also evident that he seized those opportunities that were provided to him. As Bush later reflected, "There's a limit to the power of connections. Although they can open doors, they cannot guarantee success."[35] He may have been a child of privilege, but he was not slothful or reckless, and attempts to characterize him as such are misleading and misinformed. Nonetheless, his ambition was not nearly as clear as his father's had been—or for that matter, as his brother's.

When a congressional seat opened up in west Texas in 1978, then, it surprised everyone when George W. threw his hat in the ring. However, no one was surprised by his natural skills on the stump. He not only defeated a strong primary opponent but then ran a credible campaign in a district largely inhospitable to Republicans, losing by just six points to established, well-liked state senator Kent Hance. There were even glimpses of his competitive side in this first campaign. Years later, he would reflect on that race with some bitterness: "You don't ever get over losing."[36] He also demonstrated a kind of resilience over the next decade and a half, developing his business, starting his family, and actively supporting his father's political career. Above all, perhaps, George W. showed himself to be a risk-taker, in the true sense of the family tradition, when he arranged for a team of investors (including himself) to purchase the Texas Rangers baseball team. He became general managing partner of the team, giving him a big opportunity to become visible publicly, and most importantly, to prove that his irresponsible days were over.

He continued to have political ambitions—he even considered seriously a run for governor in 1990. But more self-aware than he had been as a younger man, he wisely passed on that election because it wasn't yet his time, and he was in no hurry. Like all of the Bushes, George has competitive qualities,[37] but this is no Bert Walker. He has never been motivated primarily by a need to be on top; he is not someone who *must* win. "I didn't *like* to lose . . . but I never feared failure."[38] His particular style of resilience has never required victory, but rather a sense of patience in moving forward, a confidence that everything would eventually work out according to plan. Some of that can be attributed to his deeply held faith, but long before he was "born again" in 1985, there were signs of this character—the resilience, the ambition, the high standards—that he drew from his family. Reflecting on that unsuccessful congressional campaign, he later said, "Thanks to my father's example, I knew life would go on after defeat."[39] Following that loss in 1978, Bush would not run again for any office until he unseated the incumbent to become governor of Texas in 1994. The Bush dynasty was fueled by ambition, competitiveness, and resilience; those same dynastic qualities were there, even if they manifested quite differently for George W. Bush than they did for previous generations.

The dynasty also succeeded based on a lot of good luck and good timing—not to mention a massive network of supporters. Within weeks of announcing his congressional run, Bush had secured donations from many powerful figures from around the country, including former president Gerald Ford and Major League Baseball Commissioner Bowie Kuhn.[40] Bush ultimately raised more than $400,000 for his campaign—a huge figure for any candidate (roughly four times the average for House candidates in 1978), but a truly staggering amount for a candidate who had never even *run* for office before![41] For decades, the Bushes had developed a vast network of supporters across the country, and Barbara Bush literally had a card file of between 8,000 and 10,000 individuals to call on for donations and support.[42] The family name would continue to pay exceptional dividends in his gubernatorial races and beyond. By September 1999, Bush had raised over $55 million for his presidential campaign; Senator John McCain was his closest Republican competitor, having raised about $7 million. In fact, his nine Republican opponents had *collectively* raised only $35 million.[43] This obviously went well beyond a card file, but it did clearly demonstrate the power of the network—and the Bush name.

Bush was fortunate in one other important respect, one that had nothing at all to do with his family connections. As a presidential candidate, George W. Bush struck a timely chord with American voters in the wake of the scandals that led to Bill Clinton's impeachment in 1998. Evangelical Christian voters were looking for a candidate who understood their moral outrage and spoke their language. Moderate Republicans were looking for someone who could work across the political aisle. In Bush, they found "a uniter, not a divider," whose message of "compassionate conservatism" was practically tailor-made for that moment in history. In more ways than one, George W. was truly a "fortunate son."

At the same time, it is worth pausing to speculate on the weight of being the son of a president. The advantages it brings may mask some pretty significant burdens, as well. In *41*, the adoring biography that he wrote about his father, George W. Bush alludes a number of times to the challenges of living—and then governing—in his father's considerable shadow. Most notably, the 43rd president discusses at length their respective confrontations with Iraq, going so far as to insist that he "was not trying 'to finish what my father had begun' as some have suggested."[44] Even so, the connection is striking, and the letters that the two presidents exchanged during that period reveal the true nature of this family's dynasty. On the day in 2003 that George W. gave the order to launch the U.S. invasion of Iraq, he wrote to his father, "I know what you went through." George H. W.'s reply was loving and supportive: "Your note touched my heart. . . . You are doing the right thing."[45] The father understood what the son had gone through, too. Whatever competition and resentment had occurred between them, lessons had been learned, values passed on.

Conclusion

Ultimately, the key to understanding a political dynasty requires an understanding of the dynamics of the family. That is no small task. In all families, the narrative thread often appears uneven when viewed up close, but often

The Bush Dynasty

becomes much clearer from a distance. Close friends probably thought that the two George Bushes had little in common, for example, but more detached observers see the parallels. Most importantly, for more than a century, the Bush family has been characterized by a common set of core values. Start with the competitive ambition and high standards, often in pursuit of public service. "To be a Bush, you had to uphold certain standards. When you disobeyed . . . you were letting down the whole family."[46] Note also that they are unafraid to take significant risks, each rebelling in their own ways against the path laid out for them. In turn, they have demonstrated an unusually high degree of resilience, undeterred by the inevitable setbacks and defeats of private and public life. The same qualities that made Samuel P. Bush and Bert Walker so prosperous have carried through the generations, resulting in perhaps the most successful political family in American history.

But many, many families share these traits. What makes the Bushes so different? In addition to possessing the requisite qualities for political success, they have also been exceptionally fortunate—both in the sense of being born into favorable circumstances and benefiting from simply being in the right place at the right time. It was good fortune that propelled George H. W. Bush into prominence in his first term in Congress; first-term members of Congress tend not to have former presidents make calls on their behalf. Similarly, George W. Bush must have been the first neophyte congressional candidate to receive a donation from a former president. This is an incredibly well-connected family, one that can turn those inherent family qualities into political reality *because* they have the good fortune to do so.

Likewise, they have been lucky to "fit" their times and their place. Could Prescott Bush, paragon of quiet moderation, have been elected to office at any time *other* than the halcyon days of the 1950s? All of the necessary qualities that he "inherited" from his father and his father-in-law would have been woefully insufficient in our own more rancorous, partisan era. It is also hard to imagine a Senator Prescott Bush from any *place* other than New England. Had his banking career taken him to, say, Alabama, a political career would have been out of the question. The very same person, with all of the same characteristics and even the same connections, would nonetheless fail without a favorable political environment. As Prescott's grandson Jeb learned so painfully in 2016, these critical qualities simply do not, ahem, trump all else.

Perhaps like all political dynasties, theirs is coming to a close. Just as we have no Byrds or Roosevelts in public office, the Bush family may soon retreat to private life. We now live in an age in which name recognition and government experience are often seen as negatives, and voters have demonstrated that they are willing to move in an entirely new direction than to stick with the tried-and-true. The family's good timing may have finally run out. Besides, George W. Bush's daughters have shown no interest in pursuing political office. Could we already have seen the conclusion of this remarkable story?

Or is there still another chapter to be written? Given the family's history of political comebacks, and the likelihood that the anti-incumbent tides will turn again, it is conceivable that Jeb Bush may yet make another run for the nation's highest office. The network of supporters is still there, along with the ambition and probably the competitive sibling rivalry. More likely, though, is that the torch has been passed to the next generation. Jeb's son George P. Bush was elected to statewide office as land commissioner of the state of Texas in 2014, becoming the first in the clan to prevail on the first try. Like the others in the family, he has already shown signs of exceptional ambition and has made excellent use of the family's powerful network of political connections. But it is his appeal as an attractive young Latino in Texas, where Hispanics now make up about 40 percent of the state,[47] that suggests that the family still has incredibly good timing.

If he ever does decide to make a run for higher office, George P. Bush will undoubtedly have the full support of the whole Bush clan. In the end, theirs is mostly a story about *family*—pooling resources from far and wide, showing unconditional loyalty to one another. Consider the moment when George H. W. Bush was officially nominated to be the candidate for president at the 1988 GOP Convention in Houston. Like the story that started this chapter, if it were fiction, no one would believe it. This gathering of Republicans from all over the country could have been mistaken for a family reunion of sorts. Jeb's wife, Columba, formally seconded her father-in-law's nomination, and that was followed by the ceremonial roll call from the states. One by one, each of George H. W. and Barbara's five children announced the support from their state delegations. Neil in Colorado, Doro in Maine, Marvin in Virginia, and, of course, Jeb in Florida. Each one of them boldly and proudly declared their state's support for Dad. Then George W. Bush, the future president, put his father over the top by casting the votes of the Texas delegation "for her favorite son and the best father in America."[48] Even 12-year-old George P. got into the act, leading the Convention in the Pledge of Allegiance. As with any successful family in any arena, the most essential quality lies within.

Notes

1. Michael Herskowitz, *Duty, Honor, Country: The Life and Legacy of Prescott Bush* (Nashville, TN: Rutledge Hill, 2003), 185–186.

2. U.S. Constitution, Article 1, Section 9, Clause 8: "No title of nobility shall be granted by the United States."

3. Stephen Hess, *America's Political Dynasties from Adams to Kennedy* (Garden City, NY: Doubleday, 1966), 2.

4. Peter Schweizer and Rochelle Schweizer, *The Bushes: Portrait of a Dynasty* (New York: Doubleday, 2004), 547.

5. Herskowitz, *Duty, Honor, Country*, 174–175.
6. Herskowitz, *Duty, Honor, Country*, 47.
7. Schweizer and Schweizer, *The Bushes*, 58.
8. Schweizer and Schweizer, *The Bushes*, 10.
9. Hess, *America's Political Dynasties*, 5.
10. Herskowitz, *Duty, Honor, Country*, 94.
11. Kevin Phillips, *American Dynasty: Aristocracy, Fortune, and the Politics of Deceit in the House of Bush* (New York: Viking, 2004), 20.
12. Schweizer and Schweizer, *The Bushes*, 24.
13. Jon Meacham, *Destiny and Power: The American Odyssey of George Herbert Walker Bush* (New York: Random House, 2015), 4.
14. Schweizer and Schweizer, *The Bushes*, 9–10.
15. Quoted in Schweizer and Schweizer, *The Bushes*, 10.
16. Schweizer and Schweizer, *The Bushes*, 11.
17. Phillips, *American Dynasty*, 20–23.
18. Schweizer and Schweizer, *The Bushes*, 26.
19. Meacham, *Destiny and Power*, 15.
20. See Schweizer and Schweizer, *The Bushes*, 29.
21. Schweizer and Schweizer, 35.
22. First Corinthians 4:2. See Meacham, *Destiny and Power*, 27.
23. Phillips, *American Dynasty*, 28.
24. See Herskowitz, *Duty, Honor, Country*, 167.
25. Herskowitz, *Duty, Honor, Country*, 90.
26. Schweizer and Schweizer, *The Bushes*, 94.
27. George W. Bush, *41: A Portrait of My Father* (New York: Crown, 2014).
28. Schweizer and Schweizer, *The Bushes*, 107.
29. Schweizer and Schweizer, *The Bushes*, 109.
30. Bush, *41*, 105–107.
31. Schweizer and Schweizer, *The Bushes*, 183–184.
32. Schweizer and Schweizer, *The Bushes*, 184.
33. Bush, *41*, 17.
34. Phillips, *American Dynasty*, 47.
35. Bush, *41*, 40.
36. Robert Draper, *Dead Certain: The Presidency of George W. Bush* (London: Simon & Schuster, 2008), 37.
37. Even when he jogs! See Draper, *Dead Certain*, 306.
38. Draper, *Dead Certain*, 36.
39. Bush, *41*, 127.
40. Schweizer and Schweizer, *The Bushes*, 259.
41. See https://www.brookings.edu/wp-content/uploads/2016/06/Vital-Statistics-Chapter-3-Campaign-Finance-in-Congressional-Elections.pdf. See especially Table 3.2.
42. See Phillips, *American Dynasty*, 86; Schweizer and Schweizer, *The Bushes*, 275.

43. See Federal Elections Commission, http://classic.fec.gov/finance/precq3.htm.
44. Bush, *41*, 207. Although the Gulf War was enormously popular at the time (1991), it did leave Saddam Hussein in power in Iraq.
45. Bush, *41*, 209.
46. Schweizer and Schweizer, *The Bushes*, 54.
47. See https://www.census.gov/quickfacts/TX.
48. Bush, *41*, 172–173.

Further Reading

Bush, George W. *41: A Portrait of My Father*. New York: Crown, 2014.

Herskowitz, Michael. *Duty, Honor, Country: The Life and Legacy of Prescott Bush*. Nashville, TN: Rutledge Hill, 2003.

Meacham, Jon. *Destiny and Power: The American Odyssey of George Herbert Walker Bush*. New York: Random House, 2015.

Phillips, Kevin. *American Dynasty: Aristocracy, Fortune, and the Politics of Deceit in the House of Bush*. New York: Viking, 2004.

Schweizer, Peter, and Rochelle Schweizer. *The Bushes: Portrait of a Dynasty*. New York: Doubleday, 2004.

CHAPTER TWO

The Cabot Lodge Dynasty

Kathleen A. Gronnerud

The Cabot Lodge political dynasty dawned with the American Revolution, rose through the Progressive era, and waned in the changing political landscape of the Cold War. Although the source of the family's multigenerational political power can be traced to both its financial and social connections, the decline of the dynasty came from the inevitable conflict between America's promise to all immigrants of wide-open opportunity and the reality of the tenacious grip that heritage and money hold on American politics. As political champions of the immigrant Irish rose to prominence in many eastern cities, they challenged the entrenched power of the colonial elite: so ran the story of the Cabot Lodges as they encountered the emerging Kennedy dynasty in the second half of the 20th century, just as they seemed to reach the pinnacle of their dynastic power.

The Cabot Lodge family first ascended to political and social prominence with George Cabot during the Revolutionary era. Although proud of his direct lineage to Anglo-Saxon settlers of the original New England colonies, Cabot supported the colonies' war for independence from Britain and went on to play key roles in the establishment of the Massachusetts state government, ratification of the U.S. Constitution, and in the early constitutional government. Cabot's personal fortune, which he amassed in the shipping industry, granted the family entry into the highest tier of Bostonian society. A series of well-made marriages by subsequent generations—such as that of George's granddaughter, Anna Sophia Cabot, to shipping magnate John Ellerton Lodge in 1842—further contributed to both the family's finances and social credentials among the small circle of Boston's most elite surnames. George Cabot's great-grandson and Anna Cabot Lodge's son, Henry Cabot Lodge, was the next political leader in the family. Henry rose to power within the Republican Party and the U.S. Senate in the early 20th century, becoming a close confidante of President Theodore Roosevelt and the first floor leader of the Senate—known today as the majority leader. In turn, Henry groomed his eldest grandson and namesake, Henry Cabot Lodge Jr., for a career in politics that led to election to the Senate, a nomination for vice president, and an appointment as U.S. ambassador to South Vietnam during the Vietnam War. Meanwhile, another grandson, John Davis Lodge, served in Congress and as governor of Connecticut.

Three times during the 20th century, members of the Cabot Lodge family faced members of the emerging Kennedy political dynasty, the most famous Massachusetts political family, in elections for the U.S. Senate. Although Henry Cabot Lodge defeated a Kennedy, Henry Cabot Lodge Jr. and his nephew, George Cabot Lodge II, lost to Kennedys in 1952 and 1962, respectively. Henry Cabot Lodge Jr. lost reelection to the Senate seat previously held by both his grandfather and great-great-grandfather in a 1952 surprise upset by John Fitzgerald Kennedy, the first of three Kennedy brothers to become U.S. senators. Although members of the Cabot Lodge dynasty continued to serve in state and national offices into the 1970s, Henry's 1952 election defeat was emblematic of a larger shift in New England and national politics. For decades wealthy, Anglo-Saxon, Protestant conservatives like the Cabots and Lodges had feared erosion of their political and economic power by more recently arrived Irish and Italian Catholic immigrants who came to cities like Boston, New York, and Chicago, built their own businesses and spheres of influence, sent their sons to Harvard, and in 1960 would see one of their own—John F. Kennedy—elected to the presidency.

George Cabot and the Founding Period of the United States of America

Born in Salem, Massachusetts, George Cabot attended Harvard College like many of the Cabot and Lodge men to follow. He then entered Boston's thriving shipping industry. George supported the American war for independence from Britain, served in the state's provincial congress in 1775 and as a delegate to the ratification convention for the Massachusetts state constitution in 1777. In 1782, he was elected to the Massachusetts Senate and served as a delegate at the Massachusetts convention considering ratification of the U.S. Constitution in 1788. In 1791, the state legislature selected him to represent Massachusetts in the newly formed U.S. Senate. Cabot was a staunch Federalist in the Senate, and both George Washington and Alexander Hamilton came to value his judgment and New England insights. In 1793, Cabot became a director of the First Bank of the United States. In 1798, President John Adams wanted Cabot to serve as the first secretary of navy, but Cabot refused to accept

The Cabot Lodge Dynasty

Cabot Lodge Political Dynasty Family Tree

1. George Cabot, 1752–1823
    Massachusetts Provincial Congress, 1775
    Massachusetts State Constitutional Convention, 1777
    Massachusetts Senate, 1783
    Massachusetts Federal Constitutional Convention, 1788
    U.S. Senate, 1791–1796
    Secretary of the navy, 1798 (declined)
Married Elizabeth Higginson
Nine children including Henry Cabot

2. Henry Cabot, 1783–1864
Married Anna Sophia Blake, 1796–1845
Three children including Anna Sophia

3. Anna Sophia Cabot, 1821–1900
Married John Ellerton Lodge, 1807–1862
Three children including Henry Cabot Lodge

4. Henry Cabot Lodge, 1850–1924
    Massachusetts House of Representatives, 1880–1881
    U.S. House of Representatives, 1887–1893
    U.S. Senate, 1893–1924
Married Anna "Nannie" Cabot Mills Davis, 1850–1915
Three children: Constance Davis, George Bay, and John Ellerton

5. Constance Davis Lodge, 1872–1948
Married Augustus Peabody Gardner, 1865–1918
    Massachusetts Senate, 1900–1901
    U.S. House of Representatives, 1902–1917
One child

5. George Bay Lodge, 1873–1909
    Poet
Married Mathilda "Bessie" Frelinghuysen Davis, 1876–1960
Three children: Helena Constance, Henry Cabot Jr., and John Davis

(continued)

Cabot Lodge Political Dynasty Family Tree (*continued*)

6. Henry Cabot Lodge Jr., 1902–1985
   Massachusetts House of Representatives, 1933–1936
   U.S. Senate, 1937–1944 (resigned to enlist in army), 1947–1953
   U.S. ambassador to the United Nations, 1953–1960
   Republican vice presidential candidate with Richard Nixon, 1960
   U.S. ambassador to South Vietnam, 1963–1964; West Germany, 1968–1969
   Special envoy to the Vatican, 1970–1977
Married Emily Esther Sears
Two children including George Cabot

6. John Davis Lodge, 1903–1985
   U.S. House of Representatives, 1947–1951
   Governor of Connecticut, 1951–1955
   U.S. ambassador to Spain, 1955–1961; Argentina, 1969–1974; Switzerland, 1983
Married Francesca Braggiotti
Two children

6. Helena Constance Lodge de Streel, 1905–1998
Married Edouard de Streel
   Belgian government official
Three children

7. George Cabot Lodge, 1927–
   Director of Information, Department of Labor, 1954–1958
   Assistant secretary of labor for international affairs, 1958–1961
Married Nancy Kundhardt
Three children

the position. By the time the national government changed hands in 1801, from Adams and the Federalists to Jefferson and a series of Democratic-Republican presidents, Cabot shunned politics for work at the helm of his shipping and mercantile business and life as a private citizen. However, like many New England Federalists over the next decade, Cabot became increasingly concerned about the adverse economic effects of the Embargo Act of 1807 and the War of 1812, and in December 1814, Cabot briefly reentered politics as presiding officer at the Hartford Convention, a series of meetings

The Cabot Lodge Dynasty

conducted by northerners determined to coordinate opposition to the policies of Republican President James Madison of Virginia. George married his cousin several times removed and had a large family, including a son named Henry Cabot, who in turn had a daughter named Anna Sophia Cabot.

Henry Cabot Lodge, the Boston Brahmins, and Power in the U.S. Senate

When Anna Sophia Cabot married John Ellerton Lodge in a lavish 1842 wedding, the two created a world of wealth and privilege for future generations that was likely envied even by other Boston elites. Having first arrived in 1700, the Lodge ancestors were latecomers to New England compared to the venerable Cabots, yet John Lodge brought to the marriage considerable wealth and business acumen as heir to his brother's shipping business. The Cabots were members of the so-called Boston Brahmins, a name given by writer Oliver Wendell Holmes in 1860 to a small circle of wealthy families that claimed roots to the first Bostonians during British rule. Although Brahmin families like the Cabots did not boast of their standing, since to do so would reek of the long despised British aristocracy, they built a world in and around Boston—in the posh neighborhoods of Beacon Hill, Beverly, and Nahant on the coast—that was distinctly British in its speech, architecture, and cultural tastes. The Brahmins were Anglo-Saxon, Protestant scions of capital, and therefore in politics they were adamantly pro-business conservatives. They sent their sons to the finest preparatory schools and Ivy League colleges; they toured Europe, attended the opera, and provided informal patronage to many New England writers and artists. This was the setting in which the Cabot and Lodge names became linked in the mid-19th century.

Two generations later Anna Cabot and John Ellerton's grandson, Henry Cabot Lodge, would follow his great-grandfather George Cabot's footsteps to Harvard,

Senator Henry Cabot Lodge of Massachusetts, between 1905 and 1945. (Library of Congress)

the Massachusetts legislature, and the U.S. Senate. He earned his law degree from Harvard as well as one of the first PhDs granted by the university, in history and government, in 1876. He remained at Harvard as an instructor in American history and published his first of many books in 1878, a volume about his great-grandfather, George Cabot. "A sentiment of respect for the memory of my great-grandfather, and a desire to rescue his name if possible from complete oblivion, induced me to undertake the work," Henry wrote in his preface to the *Life and Letters of George Cabot*.[1] He further explained that his intent was not to write a balanced history of the early nation but rather "to present one side, and that the Federalist, in the strongest and clearest light." Although Cabot Lodge went on to author and edit numerous historical publications throughout his lifetime, including biographies of Alexander Hamilton, George Washington, and Daniel Webster, it seems of particular interest that his study of his great-grandfather predates his own entry into Massachusetts and national politics.

Like his great-grandfather, Henry Cabot Lodge's first public election was to the state legislature, in which he served from 1880 to 1881 as a conservative Republican. He ran unsuccessfully for the U.S. Senate in 1882 and 1884; however, in 1886 he won election to the House of Representatives. Henry served in the House until early 1893, when he resigned to run for the Senate. Elected to the Senate that same year, Lodge went on to win reelection five times—including a close race in 1916 against John Francis "Honey Fitz" Fitzgerald, grandfather of John F. Kennedy—and served until his death in 1924. While in the Senate, Henry Cabot Lodge rose to great power. He served as the de facto Republican floor leader after 1918 (a position officially recognized today as majority leader) and as chairman of the Foreign Relations Committee. During these years, he also became a close friend and confidante to President Theodore Roosevelt.

What motivated Henry Cabot Lodge to become a politician when most of his Harvard and Boston peers looked askance at public service? As a senator, Cabot Lodge felt a sense of responsibility to protect New England industry, traditions, and values against other elements of American society—particularly against the newer Catholic immigrants who would ultimately become competitors for political power. In the 1890s, he was a strong supporter of President William McKinley, the epitome of a Republican probusiness president, and in the Senate he supported the gold standard and high tariffs. Like many Boston elites, Henry Cabot Lodge was openly mistrustful of the increasing number of Irish immigrants in Boston and their challenge to the political power and social norms of his Anglo-Saxon, Protestant circle. In the Senate, he supported curbs on immigration and called for literacy tests for potential immigrants. He opposed Progressive efforts to extend the suffrage to women and to move the selection of U.S. senators from state legislatures to popular elections. In foreign affairs, Henry Cabot Lodge agreed with President

The Cabot Lodge Dynasty

Roosevelt in support of a strong navy and the imperialistic aims of the Spanish-American War in Cuba and the Philippines. He believed in American autonomy in order to best bolster the country's economy and security and thus famously opposed President Woodrow Wilson's effort to establish the League of Nations and blocked American membership in the organization once it was established after World War I.

Although he is best known for his deft procedural maneuvering to defeat the Treaty of Versailles in the Senate and thereby deny American participation in the League of Nations, Henry Cabot Lodge is remarkable for how steeped he became in the history of the Senate and the history of New England politics. He held the same Senate seat that Daniel Webster, the "Lion of the North," once occupied. And like Webster, Cabot Lodge was a powerful voice for the interests of New England through the tenure of multiple presidents. Cabot Lodge considered the Senate the most consequential body in the federal government, and he dedicated many hours to understanding and documenting its history. In "The Senate" published in *Scribner's Magazine* in 1903,[2] Cabot Lodge wrote that "without the assent of the Senate no bill can become a law, no office can be filled, no treaty ratified. . . ." Indeed, he ascribed legislative, administrative, and judicial responsibilities to the Senate, and dedicated 32 years, most of his adult life, to service within its chamber. Time and again, political opponents in Massachusetts tried to paint Cabot Lodge as an elitist, the product of privilege and pampering, and time and again he would refuse to apologize for his lineage and wealth but rather focus on his qualifications and successes as a senator. Cabot Lodge's influence in the Senate began to fade after World War I, as domestic issues overtook international concerns and power shifted from the Foreign Relations Committee that he chaired to the Finance Committee. While he retained his leadership positions, the Republicans' unity in the Senate that Cabot Lodge had worked so hard to forge began to develop fissures, especially between agricultural and industrial interests.

Although never a viable candidate for president himself, perhaps because many of his Washington colleagues and fellow Bostonians considered him aloof and cold, Lodge was a power broker time and again within the national Republican Party. He played a decisive role in the party's convention politics during numerous elections, whether as convention chair, a nominating speaker, or an operative on the convention floor. In 1884, he fell out of favor with many Boston Republicans when he refused to back the presumptive nominee, James Blaine of Maine, for president. Instead, he led the charge for an alternative candidate at the convention, therein working alongside and befriending Theodore Roosevelt, who at the time was an ambitious young Republican from a wealthy New York family. More than a decade later, Cabot Lodge would swim against the mainstream Republican tide again, this time to encourage Roosevelt to accept the nomination as vice president on the ticket with William McKinley. When McKinley was assassinated in 1901, Vice President Roosevelt ascended to the presidency. Despite their close friendship, however, Cabot Lodge refused to follow Roosevelt out of the 1912 Republican convention in his third-party bid for president and instead supported President William Howard Taft for a second term. In 1920, Cabot Lodge, along with several other Republican senators, successfully promoted Warren G. Harding as the Republican nominee for president. Harding won in a landslide election that was seen by many as vindication for Cabot Lodge's opposition to American participation in the League of Nations. However, his stance was less popular at home, and in 1922 Cabot Lodge won reelection to the Senate by a narrow margin. In 1924, he was a delegate to the Republican Convention yet again, but unlike in past years, he was not asked to serve on the platform committee, nor was he a featured speaker.

In 1871 Henry Cabot Lodge married his distant cousin, Anna "Nannie" Cabot Mills Davis—great-granddaughter of Elijah H. Mills, former speaker of the Massachusetts House of Representatives, U.S. congressman and senator, and Federalist contemporary of George Cabot. Henry and Anna had three children: Constance Davis Lodge, George Bay Cabot Lodge, and John Ellerton Lodge. The children grew up immersed in the arts and culture as the family took trips through Europe and their parents' famous friends—Theodore Roosevelt, editor and historian Henry Adams of the Adams political dynasty, Pulitzer Prize–winning novelist Edith Wharton, and other philosophers and artists—frequented their homes in Boston and Washington. Indeed, an interest in the arts permeated all three children's lives as adults. The youngest, John, studied at Harvard and abroad and then became a curator at the Boston Museum of Fine Arts with expertise in Asian art. In 1931, John was named the founding director of the Freer Gallery of Art, part of the Smithsonian Institution in Washington.

Henry Cabot Lodge's daughter Constance contributed new wealth and ancestral clout to the family when she married Augustus Peabody Gardner in 1892 at a lavish wedding attended by Boston's finest families. Gardner's wealthy uncle and flamboyant aunt, John L. Gardner and Isabella Stewart Gardner, adopted him as a young boy after the death of both of his parents. Augustus's adoptive family was known for the extensive European art collection they amassed in their Italian-style Boston villa and for Isabella's seeming entourage of young writers and artists. Augustus attended Harvard Law School but never practiced law; instead, he served one year in the Massachusetts Senate and then in the U.S. House of Representatives, 1902–1917, where he was an early and earnest voice in support of a strong, standing military. When the United States entered World War I, Augustus enlisted and was sent to Georgia for officer training but never saw combat despite his hope for direct engagement: during a particularly harsh Georgia winter, Gardner fell ill with pneumonia and died less than a week later.

Henry Cabot Lodge's middle child, George Bay Cabot Lodge, was an aspiring poet when he died suddenly at the age of 35. Writer and family friend Henry Adams—great-grandson of President John Adams and grandson of President John Quincy Adams—accompanied the Lodge family on a trip to Europe in 1895 where he noted a naïveté in young Bay Cabot Lodge that was at once inviting and disquieting. Indeed, while Bay served for a short time as his father's private secretary after completing his studies at Harvard, he found himself at odds with the dispassion of blue-blood Boston society. He chose to return to Europe for studies at the Sorbonne and then in Berlin, and he wrote poetry that increasingly reflected his pessimism and disillusion with modern America. When Bay died of heart failure, his father—who believed Bay's talents deserved greater recognition—enlisted Adams's help to collect and publish his poems. Bay left behind his widow Mathilda "Bessie" Frelinghuysen Davis, a former Washington society belle as a member of the New Jersey Frelinghuysen political family, and their three young children: Helena Constance Lodge, Henry Cabot Lodge Jr., and John Davis Lodge.

The Lodge Brothers, the Cold War, and America's Changing Political Landscape

After Bay's death, Bessie Lodge took her children to Paris for two years. Once they returned stateside, grandfather Henry Cabot Lodge became a surrogate father figure to the young boys. Their grandfather demanded a strong work ethic and set high academic expectations for the boys, especially for Henry as the older of the two. According to historian Thomas J. Whalen, who wrote extensively about the Lodge-Kennedy political rivalry,[3] Henry Cabot Lodge Jr. recalled many evenings spent with his grandfather discussing current events, and he once told a reporter that while Henry Cabot Lodge Sr. admitted that his own sons, Bay and John, showed no interest in politics, the patriarch hoped that his namesake grandson would continue the family tradition. Both boys attended the Middlesex School, a preparatory school in Concord, Massachusetts, and then Harvard, from which Henry graduated in 1924 and John in 1925. Both would pick up the family mantle in politics; however, John would displease the family and shock the sensitivities of their elite social circle by marrying a woman from far outside the boundaries of Brahmin respectability. Meanwhile their sister, Helena, married Edouard de Streel, court secretary to the Queen of Belgium, and moved to Brussels.

John Davis Lodge graduated from Harvard Law School in 1929 and that same year married Francesca Braggiotti, a dancer from a large, colorful family of Italian performers. The couple moved to New York City for John to join a prestigious legal firm, but John was more interested in pursuing acting than the law, and he soon got a few roles on Broadway. In 1933 he had his first movie role in *Little Women*, which starred Katharine Hepburn. Over his career, he amassed 14 movie credits, often working in Europe—where he filmed *The*

Senator Henry Cabot Lodge Jr. with his family, between 1905 and 1945. (Library of Congress)

Scarlet Empress opposite Marlene Dietrich in 1934—before joining the navy in 1940 upon U.S. entry into World War II. John was decorated with the French Legion of Honor for service as a liaison between U.S. and French naval forces during the war. Once home in 1946, he successfully ran for Congress representing Connecticut's fourth district. His brother Henry, on whom their grandfather placed all expectations for political assent, successfully ran for the Senate from Massachusetts that same year.

The political power of the Lodge dynasty appeared to reach its peak in the mid-20th century with the two young brothers—heirs to a political family, Harvard educated, socially connected, and fresh out of military service—both elected to Congress. The further assent of a Cabot Lodge family member as leader of the Republican Party or president never materialized. John was reelected to Congress once and then ran successfully for governor of Connecticut, serving one term from 1950 to 1954. Connecticut had a string of Democratic governors that John broke, albeit temporarily; he was a conservative Republican, although he did support some progressive legislation including new spending for infrastructure. John lost his reelection in 1954, but the next year President Eisenhower named him as U.S. ambassador to Spain where he served until 1961. He ran unsuccessfully for the U.S. Senate in 1964, but

President Richard Nixon appointed him as ambassador to Argentina in 1969, a post he held for five years; and President Ronald Reagan selected him to be ambassador to Switzerland in 1983, where he served for two years.

According to biographer Thomas A. DeLong, author of *John Davis Lodge: A Life in Three Acts*,[4] John felt a strong rivalry with his brother that began when they were young, and which grew more acute with age. DeLong notes that while his brother Henry published two memoirs in the 1970s, John felt overlooked by his brother's accounts of their family, and their rivalry took a physical toll on him, resulting in a periodic facial tick. Over the years, John held several influential positions within the Republican Party, and he served diligently on a number of government commissions. But his national profile never reached the same level as his brother's or grandfather's.

Upon graduation from Harvard, where he was known for flaunting his family name and connections, Henry Cabot Lodge Jr. went to work as a journalist. He started as a reporter at a small Boston newspaper and then became a Washington correspondent for the *New York Herald Tribune*. In 1926, Henry married Emily Sears—daughter of a doctor and descendant of Richard Sears, one of the earliest settlers of the British colony at Plymouth: an ideal match for a Boston Brahmin about to launch a political career. In 1928, the couple embarked on a trip around the world armed with letters of introduction that led to audiences with heads of state and dignitaries. Once they returned, Cabot Lodge pivoted toward politics with a critical look at President Hoover's handling of the Great Depression. In 1932, he published his first book, *The Cult of Weakness*, a series of essays in which he echoed many the ideas of his grandfather, advocating for economic self-sufficiency, a strong military, and for a government of educated, professional politicians that would not be swayed by special interests nor distracted by minority factions.

The next year, Cabot Lodge entered the Massachusetts House of Representatives, and then in 1936 he won election to the same seat in the U.S. Senate previously held by his grandfather and his great-grandfather, George Cabot. He was reelected by a large margin in 1942 but resigned two years later to serve with the army in Africa during World War II. He was elected again to the Senate after the war in 1946 and served on the Foreign Relations Committee, like his grandfather, as a moderate Republican. Parting with his grandfather's position against U.S. membership in the League of Nations, Henry supported the United Nations and the Marshall Plan. He also publicly made the case to conservatives that the Republican Party needed to broaden its ideology and image to move beyond representing upper-class interests.

In 1952, Lodge devoted much of his time to the presidential campaign of Dwight Eisenhower. Lodge believed that the Republican Party had moved too far to the right in response to the long Democratic tenure of President Franklin Roosevelt, and he hoped that a Republican ticket with Eisenhower at the top would attract more voters than the conservative favorite, Senator Robert

Taft of Ohio—son of President William Howard Taft. Cabot Lodge began his own reelection campaign to the Senate late in the 1952 season, likely due to the attention he devoted to Eisenhower's candidacy. Having won by a landslide in the last election, Cabot Lodge likely underestimated the campaign efforts of his rival, another Harvard graduate from a connected Boston family, John F. Kennedy. In sharp contrast to Cabot Lodge's British lineage that traced back to the early American colonies, Kennedy was a descendant of 19th-century Irish Catholic immigrants who succeeded at building a better life for themselves and their offspring in Boston. Kennedy campaigned hard to unseat Cabot Lodge; he personally visited every corner of Massachusetts, and his mother and sisters helped out as highly effective campaign canvassers. Cabot Lodge lost his Senate seat to Kennedy in 1952 by only 70,000 votes in an election with more than 2.4 million ballots cast.[5] However, Eisenhower won the presidency and soon requested Cabot Lodge to serve as ambassador to the United Nations.

As U.N. ambassador, Cabot Lodge was an internationalist who pushed for the United States to develop steadfast relations with the United Nations and many Third World countries. Still, he was an ardent anti-Communist and took a tough stance against the Soviet Union. Cabot Lodge served as U.N. ambassador until 1960 when presidential nominee Richard M. Nixon tapped him to be his vice presidential running mate; it would be the second time Cabot Lodge would campaign against John Kennedy. Although Cabot Lodge was considered an effective and popular addition to the Republican ticket, he and Nixon lost in a very close race to the Kennedy-Johnson ticket—by 0.2 percent of the popular vote.[6]

In 1963, the newly elected President Kennedy appointed his former rival to be ambassador to Vietnam, a position to which President Lyndon Johnson also appointed Cabot Lodge in 1965. Initially, Cabot Lodge hoped that American support would help unify the resistance to communism in South Vietnam, but he soon became frustrated with Vietnamese President Ngo Dinh Diem. By late 1963, Cabot Lodge concluded that Diem was unpredictable and unreliable as a leader for the Vietnamese, so he signaled unstated U.S. support for a military coup—Diem was soon deposed and assassinated by a group of South Vietnamese generals, which led to a succession of even less stable governments. During his second term in Vietnam, Lodge supported President Johnson's push for increased American involvement in the Vietnam War. He believed such action was necessary to stop a communist takeover of South Vietnam, viewing such a takeover as a critical threat to U.S. interests. Cabot Lodge served as ambassador to South Vietnam until 1967, and in the following year President Nixon appointed him as ambassador to West Germany. In 1969 he led the U.S. delegation to the unsuccessful Paris Peace Talks with Vietnam. Cabot Lodge also served as an envoy to the Vatican under both Presidents Nixon and Ford before retiring from public service in 1975.

The Cabot Lodge Dynasty

Henry Cabot Lodge Jr. and his wife had two sons, George Cabot Lodge and Henry Sears Lodge. George's professional path echoed his father's in many ways, although it never led to elected office. George served in the navy in 1945–1946 and then attended Harvard, from which he graduated cum laude like his father in 1950. He worked as a reporter and columnist for the *Boston Herald* until 1954, when he became the director of information for the Department of Labor. President Eisenhower appointed him assistant secretary of labor for international affairs in 1958, and President Kennedy reappointed him to the position in 1961. Later that same year, George became a lecturer at the Harvard Business School. In 1962, he ran as the Republican candidate in a special election for the U.S. Senate seat vacated by John Kennedy when Kennedy became president—the same seat previously held by George's father, grandfather, and great-great-great-grandfather. His opponent in the election was John Kennedy's youngest brother, Edward "Ted" Kennedy, who would win and continue to serve as senator from Massachusetts for the next 47 years. In 1963, George Cabot Lodge returned to the Harvard Business School until his retirement in 1997.

"A Boston Toast," the famous satirical poem first recited by author John Collins Bossidy, an Irish Catholic surgeon, in 1910, captures the hometown power and influence that the Cabot Lodge dynasty enjoyed from the Revolutionary period through the early 20th century:

And this is good old Boston,
The home of the bean and the cod,
Where the Lowells talk only to Cabots
And the Cabots talk only to God.

However, while the Brahmin world of the Cabots and Lodges allowed access to education, culture, travel, capital, and social connections that definitely helped launch the family's political dynasty with George Cabot, such privileges alone were not enough to help its staunchly Republican members—Henry Cabot Lodge, John Davis Lodge, Henry Cabot Lodge Jr., and George Cabot Lodge—prevail in elections when the tides of the American electorate flowed decisively Democratic. In the 20th century, the Lodges were able to pull off a few key upsets, like Henry Cabot Lodge Jr.'s 1936 victory for the Senate—the same year as President Franklin Delano Roosevelt's massive landslide reelection—when he was the *only* Republican to win a Senate race for a seat previously held by a Democrat, and John Davis Lodge's victory for governor of Connecticut—a position long held by Democrats—in 1950. But in Boston and many other American cities, the first half of the 20th century brought to fruition an impeding historical shift in political and economic power from WASP elites to Irish and Italian party machines and the industrial working class—as witnessed firsthand by Henry Cabot Lodge. Although the Brahmins did not disappear, they now shared their Ivy League classrooms, prized zip codes, and charity gala guest lists with more than their own. As Oliver Wendell Holmes noted back in 1860, even in the most elite circles room exists for common country boys who gained an education. And history would prove that to be true in New England even if those boys were Catholic and of Irish lineage like John Kennedy and his brothers, Robert and Edward.

Notes

1. Henry Cabot Lodge, *Life and Letters of George Cabot* (Boston: Little, Brown, 1878).
2. Henry Cabot Lodge, "The Senate," *Scribner's Magazine*, Vol. 34 (New York: Scribner's, 1903), 541–550. Hathi Trust Digital Library. www.catalog.hathitrust.org.
3. Thomas J. Whalen, *Kennedy versus Lodge: The 1952 Massachusetts Senate Race* (Boston: Northeastern University Press, 2000).
4. Thomas A. DeLong, *John Davis Lodge: A Life in Three Acts: Actor, Politician, Diplomat* (Fairfield, CT: Sacred Heart University Press, 1999).
5. "Results of JFK's 1952 U.S. Senate Election," John F. Kennedy Presidential Library and Museum. www.jfklibrary.org.
6. "Election of 1960," The American Presidency Project. www.presidency.ucsb.edu.

Further Reading

Finger, Seymour M. *Your Man at the UN: People, Politics, and Bureaucracy in Making Foreign Policy.* New York: New York University Press, 1980.
Lodge, Henry Cabot, Jr. *As It Was: An Inside View of the Politics and Power of the 1950s and 60s.* New York: Norton, 1976.
Lodge, Henry Cabot, Jr. *The Cult of Weakness.* Boston: Houghton Mifflin, 1932.
Lodge, Henry Cabot, Jr. *The Storm Has Many Eyes.* New York: Norton, 1973.
Miller, William J. *Henry Cabot Lodge.* London: Heinemann, 1967.

CHAPTER THREE

The Clinton Dynasty

Margaret E. Scranton

The Clinton dynasty originated from William Jefferson Clinton's love of politics and his ambition to hold office in his home state of Arkansas. From humble beginnings in a state ranked poorly on personal and economic well-being and inspired by President John F. Kennedy, Clinton aimed to improve the lives of his fellow citizens. Had he not met and fallen in love with Hillary Rodham, Clinton's ambitions might have remained limited to Arkansas; however, Hillary harnessed Bill's gifts as an intellectual, speaker, and campaigner. She orchestrated his campaign and executive staffs—a significant contribution to his political victories. Likewise, had Hillary not fallen in love with Bill, she would likely be renown as a leading advocate for women and children, but she would not have become, at once, one of the most admired and most vilified women in the country. Without Bill, Hillary would not have run for the Senate or the presidency. The Clinton dynasty was born of the couple's partnership, love of politics, and shared belief that government can solve problems. The Clintons exemplified the bright, progressive, new South leaders who rose to power during the 1980s. They became each other's strongest advocates and defenders as first Bill and then Hillary were tirelessly investigated. Tormented by scandals but able to regroup and press on, the Clintons' resilience was essential to their political survival.

With Bill Clinton's election to the presidency in 1992, the Clintons became the first baby boomer generation occupants of the White House, and opponents were particularly suspicious of their motives and goals. Seen as exemplifying the activist culture at elite colleges in the late 1960s, both Clintons attracted outsized condemnation from social and moral critics; they served as lightning rods for the fears and anxieties of traditional and movement conservatives. Maps coded with red, blue, and purple states and counties documented cultural fissures in the electorate.[1] Some analysts referred to this struggle as a culture war, pitting social and economic conservatives against more progressive liberals.[2] In 1996, Clinton became the first Democratic president since Franklin Roosevelt in 1936 to win reelection. Although Hillary would win election to the U.S. Senate after her time as first lady, and then serve as U.S. secretary of state, she was less fortunate in her two runs for the presidency. In both races, new faces, Barack Obama during the primaries in 2008 and Donald Trump in 2016, were favored over Hillary, the experienced, insider candidate. After the 2016 election, Bill and Hillary invested in party renewal; she formed a fund-raising group "Onward Together" in 2017 to support anti-Trump resistance groups and recruit Democratic candidates for midterm congressional elections in 2018.

Hillary once described their unrelenting opposition's research as a "vast right-wing conspiracy."[3] As early as Bill's first term as president, hating Hillary became an industry that generated nasty campaign paraphernalia, books, videos, T-shirts, toys and games, and eventually a Facebook page.[4] The scope and intensity of anti-Clinton opinion was magnified during the 1990s by new technologies for "narrow-casting" donor appeals and "microtargeting" supporters via direct-mail fund-raising. More recently, opposition to Hillary's senatorial and presidential races was fueled by soft and dark money and rampant social media, making the 2016 presidential campaign the most angry, acrimonious, and viciously personal episode in recent memory.

Both of the Clintons have human failings that time and again have temporarily derailed their political projectory. Both have made political and personal mistakes that contradict their intelligence and political acumen. Hillary, famed for carefully calibrated messages, can also lapse into comments that offend supporters and opponents, such as her infamous comment about preferring to pursue her profession rather than baking cookies, not just "standing by her man," and her reference to Donald Trump's supporters as a "basket of deplorables." When charged with wrongdoing, by preferring to defend her position rather than admit a mistake that enemies might exploit, Hillary has appeared untrustworthy. Bill, known for prioritizing his "political viability," engaged in risky relationships with women—the most famous of which led to impeachment proceedings in the Senate in 1999. Nonetheless, the Clintons have persisted to come back politically from presumably disqualifying events. Both Clintons have exhibited high resilience to setbacks and deep determination to move on, to accomplish more. Such resilience, determination, and an unwavering commitment to public service are attributes at the heart of the founding and continuation of the Clinton political dynasty.

As policy wonks addressing complex, controversial issues, Bill and Hillary were often caught between making promises that embodied "best"

Clinton Political Dynasty Family Tree

1. William Jefferson "Bill" Clinton, 1946–
   Attorney general of Arkansas, 1977–1978
   Governor of Arkansas, 1979–1981, 1983–1992
   Chair, Democratic Leadership Council, 1990–1991
   Chair, Southern Growth Policy Board, 1985–1986
   Chair, Education Commission of the States, 1986–1987
   Chair, National Governor's Association, 1986–1987
   Chair, National Governor's Association Task Force on Child Care, 1990–1991
   42nd president of the United States, 1993–2001
Married Hillary Rodham Clinton
One child: Chelsea Victoria

1. Hillary Rodham Clinton, 1947–
   First lady of the U.S., 1993–2001
   U.S. Senate, 2001–2009
   Secretary of state, 2009–2013
   Democratic Party candidate for president, 2016

2. Chelsea Victoria Clinton, 1980–
   Vice chair of the Bill, Hillary & Chelsea Clinton Foundation
Married Marc Mezvinsky
Two children: Charlotte Clinton and Aidan Clinton

---

solutions and compromising or even breaking campaign pledges to enact legislation. The ongoing debate over the long-term significance of the Clinton dynasty centers on whether Bill and Hillary tried hard enough to pass what they promised, were sufficiently willing to challenge powerful interests, and whether scandals will fade or overshadow the programs they enacted. If subsequent Republican presidents overturn or roll back their programmatic achievements, they will be transitional figures in a series of swings between Democratic and Republican presidents. If their grounding philosophy provides a base for a new majority party, they will be seen as laying the foundation for Democrats to replace the outworn New Deal.

Presently, Bill and Hillary Clinton have long-term goals based on the premise that a lasting governing majority requires an electoral realignment that expands party loyal voters and elects enough candidates to control Congress over time. Achieving such a seismic shift in the electorate requires a message that resonates with moderates and independents, groups that outnumber strong party identifiers. Achieving those goals depends on whether their philosophy and "Clintonism" as a third-way political strategy turn into a winning formula for upcoming elections, as opposed to shifting the party more to the left. Beyond electoral and party politics, the Clintons continue to advocate policies and promote their ideas through the Bill, Hillary & Chelsea Clinton Foundation in New York City and the University of Arkansas (UA) Clinton School of Leadership in Public Service in Little Rock. At present, Chelsea Clinton's role as dynastic successor is materializing.

Bill Clinton's Formative Years

Bill Clinton was born in Hope, Arkansas, just three months after his father, William Jefferson Blythe III, drowned after his car crashed into a ditch while he was returning home from Chicago. Bill's mother, Virginia, asked her parents to care for her baby boy while she went to New Orleans to train as a nurse-anesthetist. Although Bill grew up in a poor, rural state, his grandparents valued education and kept current on the news; they proudly claimed that Bill was an avid newspaper reader by the age of six. When Virginia returned to Arkansas, she married Roger Clinton, and the family moved to the spa and horse-race resort of Hot Springs, a town known for bars, gambling, and the occasional gangster. Bill's early years and adolescence were peppered with the affection of caring, kind grandparents, but were also hurt by Roger Clinton's drinking and abusive behavior toward Virginia, Bill, and his younger brother, Roger Jr. Bill became the soother of family tensions, and at age 14 felt compelled to physically intervene to protect his mom and brother. Still, when he turned 16, Bill formally changed his name to Clinton.

In Arkansas, Bill developed friends who would support his political ambitions over many decades. Obviously smart and an avid learner, Bill also was a popular leader in the many groups he joined. Classmates predicted he would one day run for office. In 1963, Clinton was elected to represent Arkansas at Boys' Nation in Washington, DC. While there, he met President John F. Kennedy at a Rose Garden reception at the White House. That experience in Washington convinced Bill to devote his life to public service through elective office. Clinton attended Georgetown University. While still in college, he gained campaign experience in Arkansas as he worked for Frank Holt's unsuccessful campaign for governor. Clinton learned about Washington politics while working part-time for Senator J. William Fulbright (D-AR). While at school in Washington, Bill clerked for the Foreign Relations Committee's hearings on the war in Vietnam; during his summers in Arkansas, he served as Fulbright's driver through cities and small towns, where he met local leaders whom he would later mobilize into an effective campaign organization. From 1968 to 1970, Clinton networked and studied as a Rhodes scholar at

Oxford in England. While there, Bill applied for a Vietnam War draft deferment—a calculated decision that would cause controversy in his first presidential campaign. Even more harmful than the accusation of being a draft dodger was criticism of the reason he gave, the need to preserve his political viability.

Clinton came to national attention as a Rhodes scholar and Yale law school graduate who returned to Arkansas to run for Congress. Throughout his university years, Clinton engaged in campus politics, read extensively, debated issues, and developed a network of friends and professional contacts. Upon graduation from Yale at the age of 28, he returned to Arkansas to teach law at the University of Arkansas, Fayetteville (UAF), and launch his first political campaign to challenge Republican Congressman John Paul Hammerschmidt's bid for reelection.

Hillary Rodham's Formative Years

Hillary Diane Rodham was born in Chicago, Illinois, and grew up during the 1950s in the middle-class neighborhood Park Ridge, a suburb known for excellent public schools. Her parents, Hugh E. and Dorothy Howell Rodham, instilled in their daughter a deep commitment to serve others and a determination to succeed in academics and sports. Her father, a small businessman, was politically conservative and regularly led vigorous dinnertime discussions of politics. Her mother held more liberal views and encouraged Hillary to aim for any career and excel at every opportunity. A bright, engaged student, Rodham thrived academically while participating in student government and academic organizations. In her initial foray into politics, she campaigned in 1964 as a "Goldwater Girl" for presidential candidate Barry Goldwater (R-AZ).

A youth minister at the family's Methodist church,

President Bill Clinton, Hillary Clinton, and Chelsea Clinton walk Buddy the dog on the South Lawn of the White House, July 24, 1998. (William J. Clinton Presidential Library and Museum)

Reverend Don Jones, influenced Rodham's social outlook through speakers, like Martin Luther King Jr., and meetings with residents of minority neighborhoods. Rodham's faith embraced a strong service orientation and her church's "university of life" program provided her with volunteer opportunities in diverse neighborhoods and exposure to conditions that enveloped the disadvantaged.

At Wellesley College, where the motto is "not to be ministered unto but to minister," Rodham found more opportunities for community service and leadership. She emerged as a student leader during her sophomore year, 1967, in conjunction with her shift in political views from Goldwater conservatism to liberal reformism. She campaigned for Democratic presidential candidates in the 1968 primaries. Her political activism reached beyond campus politics to include outreach to young students in poor neighborhoods around Boston. In her honors thesis, Rodham evaluated the effectiveness of Chicago community organizer Saul Alinsky's method of achieving change, "action through agitation." She concluded that this strategy, while effective at times, was not sustainable and not as likely to effect change as work done from within the system and the use of "normal" channels like political parties.

In campus organizations and student politics, Rodham developed a consensus-building leadership style. She worked with college president Ruth Adams and mobilized classmates to reform from within—to modernize the curriculum with more choices among required courses and to reduce social restrictions governing student conduct. After Martin Luther King Jr.'s assassination, Rodham collaborated with President Adams to meet demands from the few black students then enrolled at Wellesley, who called for immediate changes in roommate assignments and affirmative action in both faculty and staff hiring and student recruitment. In the span of only one year, the college created a Martin Luther King lecture series, an African American studies program, and provided a home on campus for minority organizations and programming. The administration hired several more African American faculty and staff members and launched a campaign to recruit many more African American students, making Wellesley a national model for racial progress. These events reinforced Rodham's convictions that listening, consensus building, and working within an institution could result in significant progress.

In 1969, when President Adams agreed to students' demands for having a student speak at commencement, Rodham came to national attention for the first time. Selected by her classmates to represent their views, Rodham canvassed the senior class for ideas to include in her speech. Before making her prepared remarks, Rodham commented on the official speaker's address. Senator Edward Brooke (R-MA) delivered a critique of student protests and a defense of President Richard Nixon's programs, which shocked and angered many of the graduates. Speaking for "the 400 of us," Rodham described the transformation she and her classmates experienced during their four years at

Wellesley: "We arrived not yet knowing what was not possible. Consequently, we expected a lot."[5] She reflected that "every protest, every dissent, whether it's an individual academic paper or Founder's parking lot demonstration, is unabashedly an attempt to forge an identity in this particular age." Consequently, considering "that for too long our leaders have viewed politics as the art of the possible," Rodham voiced the challenge facing her classmates: "to practice politics as the art of making what appears to be impossible possible." Throughout her career, Rodham would achieve some seemingly impossible goals and break barriers to once impossible outcomes, but she also would repeatedly be constrained by the possible. In her commencement address, Rodham expressed ideas that would in the 1980s be labeled the New Democrat philosophy: to build community, to take responsibility, and, through politics, to open up more opportunities. Rodham's address prompted a seven-minute standing ovation from the graduates, but many parents and alumnae were shocked and offended. Nonetheless, *Life* featured excerpts from her address, along with statements from other student commencement speakers whom the magazine identified as representative of their generation.

Choosing Yale rather than Harvard Law School, Rodham aimed for a career in which she could investigate social problems and advocate for remedies. She gained additional national attention for speaking out about peaceful ways to counter injustices at a national convention of the League of Women Voters. As a participant on a panel about women and human rights chaired by Marian Wright Edelman, Rodham advocated for the use of economic leverage to oppose corporations that conducted business in countries known for human rights abuses. Networking with Edelman, Rodham obtained a summer congressional internship; she was assigned to a Senate subcommittee investigation of conditions for migrant laborers and their children. Rodham's field research, which built on her high school volunteer work with Hispanic laborers near Chicago, honed her method for diagnosing a problem and advocating solutions: begin with site visits and direct observation of conditions, connect personally with the people experiencing the problem, synthesize those observations into a technical report, and then formulate possible political and legal remedies.

Rodham met Bill Clinton at Yale early in 1971, and the couple became known for constantly debating how to solve pressing issues.[6] Both worked as field coordinators for Senator George McGovern's presidential campaign in 1972, where they gained practical experience in the registration and mobilization of voters and learned lessons about articulating campaign messages. Rodham spent an additional year at the Yale Child Study Center studying legal conditions of women and children, a cause she would champion throughout her lifetime. After graduation, Rodham worked with Edelman's Children's Defense Fund and for the Carnegie Council on Children. She was hired to serve on the impeachment inquiry staff of the House Judiciary Committee, and when the investigation terminated after President Nixon's resignation in August 1974, Rodham made the life-changing decision to join Bill Clinton in Arkansas.

The Clintons in Arkansas

Bill and Hillary became political partners when she moved to Fayetteville in 1974 and jumped into his flagging congressional campaign. Rodham taught criminal law classes at the UAF School of Law and ran the behind-the-scenes management of Clinton's campaign. This marked the first time they worked together as campaign partners: Hillary worked inside to orchestrate and discipline the staff work; Bill performed outside to exert personal charm through his trademark, friends-and-neighbors style of relating to voters. In his grass roots campaign, Bill followed the local custom of driving into town to meet and greet leaders and constituents, and spending time with anyone willing to talk. Although victory over such a strong incumbent was unlikely, Clinton narrowed Representative Hammerschmidt's victory to only 51.5 percent, which impressed Democratic Party power brokers and positioned Clinton for a statewide race in 1976.

Initially conflicted over whether she should marry Clinton and stay in Arkansas, Hillary accepted Bill's third proposal of marriage, an offer that also included a house in Fayetteville that she admired. They were married on October 11, 1975, with a reception that doubled as a campaign rally for his candidacy to be state attorney general. The Arkansas Republican Party was weak at that time and declined to field candidates for many higher offices; Bill won the Democratic primary easily, which guaranteed him a general election victory. When Bill took office in 1977, the Clintons moved to Little Rock; Rodham continued to teach, now at the UA Bowen School of Law, and joined the prestigious Rose Law Firm. That same year, President Jimmy Carter asked Hillary to serve a two-year term on the Legal Services Corporation, an appointment based on Rodham's experience creating legal services clinics at both university law schools in Arkansas.

As attorney general, Bill advocated consumers' interests, fought against utilities, and reduced prison overcrowding through work release programs, which garnered him attention throughout the state and the region. In 1978, an opening in the next gubernatorial race appeared when Governor David Pryor opted to run for Congress rather than reelection. Bill easily won the Democratic nomination and became, at age 32, the youngest governor in the nation. This made the Clintons a rising power couple in the region and on the national stage. As first lady of Arkansas, Rodham was the first governor's wife in state history to pursue a profession while she occupied the governor's mansion. Especially during Bill's first term, Hillary's priority was to build her legal practice and financial position. Despite their intensive work together in both the 1976 and 1978 campaigns, Hillary and Bill expected to pursue their individual vocations as young professionals, with Hillary in the private sector and Bill in public office. One lesson both Clintons learned from Bill's reelection defeat in 1980 to Republican Frank White was that their partnership needed to operate on a full-time basis.

One way that dynasties fail at the fledgling stage is to underestimate political resistance and overestimate their appeal. During his first term, Bill aimed to transform Arkansas into a more modern and prosperous state, to overcome the influence of timber and agricultural interests, and to make investments in social policies. Institutionally, with the help of "outsider" professional staff members, he was also determined to modernize state government. After only two years in office, this acclaimed new leader became the youngest *former* governor in the country. This outcome prompts important questions that resurface during Clinton's years in the White House. Why did this politically astute campaigner, famous for listening attentively to voters and their concerns, think that his state was ready for large rather than incremental change? And how, after suffering an embarrassing defeat, was he able to recast his agenda, rebound into office in 1982, and then rally voters for reelection? As president, Bill repeated this error when he and Hillary attempted to reform health care in opposition to powerful medical and insurance interests; and, just as he reconfigured his agenda and political strategies in Arkansas, he had to learn and rebound as president. The Clintons' abilities to diagnose political mistakes, reframe their agendas, and devise more effective strategies saved the dynasty from an early downfall.

Bill's first term as governor is puzzling. He already was intensely familiar with Arkansas's small towns and political culture, having been a campaign driver for Senator William J. Fulbright in the 1960s. Plus, he had ample personal experience based on his own campaigns and serving as attorney general during the governorship of the politically savvy David Pryor. He witnessed the Arkansas legislature's folkways and was close friends with the state's best political analysts. And Clinton had a deep personal sense of small town Arkansas from childhood hours spent in his grandfather Cassidy's store in Hope. Yet this contextual knowledge was not on display during his first term; instead Clinton's elite-educated, policy wonk persona was dominant, as if he had theorized the programmatic achievements his first term should yield without any assessment of whether he had a mandate for change. He staffed the governor's office with smart public administration professionals who were convinced they knew how to fix Arkansas's long-standing problems and push the state forward. Clinton's first-term initiatives drew opposition from economic interest groups and legislative leaders. Most controversial, due to its widespread impact on voters, was Clinton's decision to fund highway improvements with user fees rather than cuts to social and education programs, a choice necessitated because Arkansas law requires a balanced budget.

Clinton chose to raise vehicle registration fees, title transfer fees, and taxes on tires and gas, and he doubled the cost of car and truck license tag renewals. Apparently, Clinton failed to develop a communications plan to justify these fees and advertise the benefits that would result from more than 1,000 improvement projects. Anger over the fees created an opportunity that Frank White seized to challenge Clinton in 1980. Although White's victory was buoyed by Ronald Reagan's presidential coattails, the election was clearly a referendum on Clinton's first term. Two additional issues contributed to Clinton's defeat. In May 1980, President Jimmy Carter chose Arkansas as a relocation center for Cubans from the Mariel boat lift, sending 18,000 refugees to Ft. Chafee. Although many refugees were resettled elsewhere, widely publicized escape attempts and riots raised fears and spiked gun sales in western Arkansas as news reports described the area as a war zone.[7] Frank White responded with a new campaign slogan, "Cubans and Car Tags," and faulted Clinton for failing to stand up to President Carter. In fact, Clinton objected fiercely to receiving an additional 10,000 refugees; having managed Carter's 1976 campaign in Arkansas, Clinton expected some consideration for his political interests, but Carter insisted.

The third factor contributing to White's 1980 victory was "the Hillary factor." Criticism of Hillary began with Rodham's decision to retain her maiden name even after the birth of the Clintons' daughter. Critics noted her personal style, nontraditional image, and the perception that she was a part-time first lady who prioritized her legal career. At this juncture, Rodham was not criticized for being too powerful; instead, she was faulted for being too liberal, too feminist, and failing to appreciate her position as the state's first lady.

To overcome these factors, Bill and Hillary planned a comeback strategy with significant input from pollster Dick Morris and McGovern campaign organizer Betsey Wright.[8] Morris's surveys identified policy priorities and personal characteristics that respondents found off-putting or attractive; Wright built a database for mobilizing voters and fund-raising. Bill sported a shorter haircut and occasionally campaigned in a plaid flannel shirt with a pickup truck in the background. He and Hillary visited every county, spending time with local politicians to build up a statewide organization. Since no refugees remained at Ft. Chaffee by February 1982, the rebound strategy addressed other issues. Bill's second-term agenda would be about Arkansans: improving education, creating jobs, and curbing utility rates. Hillary began using Clinton as her last name, underwent a style makeover, and planned a policy initiative for improving the state's public schools.

Although critics charged that the Clintons abandoned their values in lieu of polling for popular positions, these changes can also be assessed as realistic adjustments required to regain office. Bill learned to limit his advocacy to what was politically possible, concluding that he tried too much too soon. He realized that he had failed to communicate his vision and the benefits his programs would bring; partly he blamed himself, but he put much of the onus on the media. The lesson the Clintons learned were to cultivate pundits and to instantaneously counter opposition attacks and negative coverage; immediate counter-messaging became a standard operating procedure. As the 1982 campaign season opened, Bill apologized humbly for his mistakes and vigorously challenged Governor White's record. The strategy worked: Clinton won back the governorship with 52 percent to White's 45 percent.

As his most significant and productive period as governor, Clinton's second term paralleled the efforts of other New South governors in Texas and Tennessee, who aimed to transform their states through education reform and economic development. Clinton's challenge was to move Arkansas from the bottom of the national rankings on quality of life, and the first target was education. Hillary spearheaded a task force that proposed K–12 reforms for Arkansas's public schools.[9] To investigate problems in the schools and solicit recommendations, Hillary pioneered a political strategy that became a signature move in her senatorial and presidential campaigns—she undertook a "listening tour" of the state's 67 counties. She testified effectively at legislative hearings to explain and advocate for the Education Standards Task Force recommendations, which prompted one member to comment that the state "elected the wrong Clinton" as governor. This successful initiative expanded the Clinton partnership into policy making and served as the precedent the Clintons hoped to repeat in 1993 when they set health care reform as a presidential first-year priority. Governor Clinton won reelection three more times.[10] He considered running for president in 1988, but decided not to due to possible scandals; he captured national attention, if not acclaim, for making a long, primetime address to nominate Michael Dukakis at the Democratic convention. Bill displayed good humor as well as musical talent, when he appeared on the Johnny Carson *Tonight Show* just two nights after his convention gaffe; his performance charmed the host and gained public and pundits' approval. Year by year, the Clintons gained national prominence and recognition as pragmatic progressives; in 1991, Bill was ranked by fellow governors as "the most effective governor in the nation."[11] The networking vehicles that the Clintons chose to join were the National Governors Association and the Democratic Leadership Council (DLC); the latter used extensive polling to identify potential party identifiers and to move the party toward a centrist and progressive party platform based on New Democrat principles.

During the 1980s the Clintons' policy concerns broadened to encompass national issues and how to build the Democratic Party to majority status by appealing to potential identifiers in the center/moderate zone of the political spectrum. The Democratic Party was long overdue for realignment in terms of historical trends, but the number of strong identifiers remained in the mid-30 percentage range. Both Clintons had worked in McGovern's and Carter's campaigns. From McGovern's loss and Carter's victory, they learned to plan to amass convention delegates as well as primary and caucus victories. They also expanded on Carter's use of Peanut Brigades, volunteers who traveled from Georgia to early primary states to vouch personally for the candidate, creating a corps of "Arkansas Travelers." They also appreciated Rosalynn Carter's central role as a campaign partner, media spokesperson, and as a program-oriented first lady model for Hillary.

Going National: The 1992 Campaign

With incumbent President George H. W. Bush running again as Ronald Reagan's Republican successor, Bill Clinton was poised to be a counter candidate, representing youth and a new generation of progressive governors. Bill launched his presidential campaign from the Arkansas Statehouse on October 3, 1991. Compared to fellow Democrats, Clinton was a populist from a small, southern state, rather than a northern, more traditional, liberal Democrat. His main competitors for the nomination were Senator Tom Harkin (D-IA) and former senator Paul Tsongas (D-PA), who won, respectively, the Iowa caucuses and New Hampshire primary. As the documentary *The War Room* faithfully portrays, the Clinton campaign recovered from two ostensibly lethal scandals—allegations against Bill for draft dodging and a longtime affair with a woman from Arkansas, Gennifer Flowers—due largely to Hillary's fierce defense of her husband. The film also documents innovative aspects of Clinton's Arkansas-based campaign that contributed to his victory: a horizontal campaign staff structure, opposition research and rapid response to any negative claims, deployment of home state volunteers, and a strong partnership between the candidate and future first lady. Bill won the election largely due to the Clinton's employment of talented staff specialists on media and messaging, vigorous mobilization of voters, and tireless effort. As a campaign surrogate, Hillary spoke as a policy advocate for the progressive, centrist New Democrat principles; as her husband's most effective defender, she was credited with saving the campaign during the primaries, particularly with her strong defense of Bill during an interview on the CBS program *60 Minutes*. Like many of Hillary's strong statements, her assertion that she was "not just standing by" her man ignited both fervent approval and outrage. After weathering scandals in New Hampshire, Clinton won primaries in most of the southern states, Illinois, New York, Michigan, Pennsylvania, and California. The three-candidate structure of the general election facilitated Clinton's victory (Texas billionaire Ross Perot ran as an Independent candidate), but denied him a mandate for governing. Voters, despite concerns about Clinton's character and inexperience, blamed President Bush for a weakening national economy and growing national debt; Perot also called attention to these economic concerns.[12] Nonetheless, by winning only 43 percent of the popular vote and voters casting ballots against a second term for Bush, Clinton entered the presidency without a mandate for his platform.[13]

Clinton used his nomination acceptance speech, first inaugural address, and every State of the Union address to articulate a broad political platform designed to appeal to both his base and more centrist voters. At the party's National Convention he called for a New Covenant rather than just a variation on the New Deal or President Lyndon Johnson's New Society; his aim was to forge "a solemn agreement between the people and their government based not simply on what each of us can take but what all of us must give to our nation." Countering Republican charges against welfare liberalism, Clinton offered "a new choice based on old values. We offer opportunity. We demand responsibility. We will build an American community again." He explained, "The choice we offer is not conservative or liberal. In many ways it's not even Republican or Democratic. It's different. It's new. And it will work. It will work because it is rooted in the vision and the values of the American people." Strategically, Bill's challenge in 1992 and Hillary's in 2008 and 2016 were due to their party's shrinking base of strong identifiers and the resulting growth of independent voters. Each of their presidential campaigns had to incorporate nonpartisans, who by definition and inclination did not share the policy preferences of the liberal base, but still keep the loyalty of strong party identifiers. (Bernie Sanders's insurgent presidential candidacy in 2016 reflected the persistence of this challenge.) Their party stuck in minority status made winning elections more difficult for the Clintons and carried over into governance challenges. Once in office, President Bill Clinton could not rely on party unity votes for his legislative initiatives; instead, he had to build ad hoc coalitions in support of each one.

Clinton Presidency

Given the centrality of policy solutions to the Clinton dynasty, the programs and rationales put in place during President Clinton's two terms may outlast Bill and Hillary's careers. Domestically, Clinton enacted the Family and Medical Leave Act, welfare reform, and expanded local police forces.[14] He left office not just having balanced the budget, a long-standing goal of both parties, but also with a budget surplus. Internationally, Clinton articulated choices that continue to challenge presidents: whether to take on a selective leadership role he described as engagement, or to withdraw from pacts and agreements, and thereby move toward isolationism and protectionism. President Clinton dealt with issues that remain on the country's agenda 20 years later: how to navigate the pros and cons of globalization, respond to ethnic conflict and genocide overseas, best combine diplomacy with military force, and create trade agreements to avert unfair practices and foster beneficial competition. The alternative, which Clinton rejected, was to turn inward and reduce defense spending in favor of a peace dividend.

In foreign policy, Clinton asserted U.S. leadership through partnership, NATO expansion, and promoting of democracy, particularly in Eastern

Europe. The underlying premise was that a new, post–Cold War order needed to be constructed; the challenge, in the absence of threats from a powerful adversary state, was how to prioritize scarce resources and differentiate among threats. Clinton officials used the analogy of the United States having slain a great dragon at the gate only to be surrounded by countless poisonous snakes nipping at its heels. Clinton set forth a rationale and road map for promotion of U.S. interests in a new era of economic interconnectedness and security threats resulting from the weaknesses of failed and outlaw states—terrorism, illegal trafficking in material and persons, piracy, and ethnic conflict.

Clinton articulated two significant national security doctrines. The first clarified criteria for intervention at a time of U.S. military preponderance, answering how the United States could refrain from becoming "the world's 911." These ideas were systemized in the 2000 National Security Strategy, which defined U.S. national security interests below the level of "vital." Using language similar to Senator Fulbright's hierarchy of interests as vital, important, or convenient, Clinton sought to define the two lower levels. "Important interests" became those that affect "our national well-being and the character of the world in which we live" and arise from economic interdependencies, climate issues, refugees, and ethnic conflicts. Clinton defined "discretionary interests" as those where "our nation may act because our values demand it," such as responding to horrific natural disasters and violations of human rights and supporting democratization and the rule of law.[15]

The second doctrine specified criteria for humanitarian intervention. In remarks made in San Francisco in February 1999, President Clinton articulated the dilemma confronting the United States: resisting the traditional pull of isolationism and the lure of investing a peace dividend at home versus taking on the modern pull of "the inexorable logic of globalization—that everything, from the strength of our economy to the safety of our cities, to the health of our people, depends on events not only within our borders, but half a world away."[16] The latter includes examples that, while only emergent in 1999, became action items for President George W. Bush's agenda after 2000: regional wars, proliferation of weapons of mass destruction, and terrorism. The task Clinton articulated was for the United States to "lead with confidence in our strengths and with a clear vision of what we seek to avoid and what we seek to advance."[17] Subsequently, Presidents Bush and Obama would pursue national security strategies that continued to elaborate ways to realize desired outcomes and meet emerging threats.

Hillary prepared for her role in the White House by reading biographies of former first ladies. She identified with the activism of Eleanor Roosevelt and embraced Rosalynn Carter's precedents of actively investigating and advocating mental health reform and her strong political partnership with the president. Right away, Hillary cochaired a health care reform task force that produced a 1,000-plus-page bill; although she testified effectively before several congressional committees and held over 175 private meetings with senators and representatives, her efforts were rebuffed by Democrats as well as Republicans. Hillary was criticized, as Rosalynn Carter had been, for acting as an unelected policy maker and transgressing the boundaries of appropriate first lady behavior. Hillary challenged another traditional norm as she kept an office in the West Wing as well as the first lady's traditional East Wing domain. Ready for the challenge of finding other ways to be an effective policy advocate, Hillary hosted White House conferences on children and women's health; spoke at international conferences, most notably in Beijing where she asserted that "human rights are women's rights and women's rights are human rights once and for all"[18]; and worked to pass legislation on adoption and foster care.[19]

Despite investigations into the Clinton's Arkansas-era finances dubbed the Whitewater matter, the failure of their health care reform initiative, the crippling sweep of Republicans' midterm election victories in 1994, and a government shutdown, Bill won reelection in 1996. Key to his reelection success and continued public popularity was his willingness to compromise to gain partial victories. Still, the president's legacy was marred by details of his affair with White House intern Monica Lewinsky, accusations of perjury, and impeachment by the House of Representatives.[20] The impeachment trial in the Senate reflected deep rifts in America's culture as the five-week trial culminated with impassioned speeches by Chief Prosecutor Henry Hyde (R-IL) and former senator Dale Bumpers (D-AR). Their rhetoric reflected the ongoing culture wars and the "values divide" separating proponents and opponents of impeachment, in Congress and America at large. The Senate acquitted Clinton of charges of perjury and obstruction of justice, which gratified those who detested Independent Counsel Kenneth Starr's long and costly investigation, and also energized a hard-right movement to win the presidency in 2000 and bring their conservative values to power.

The Whitewater investigation and repeated claims of Bill's extramarital indiscretions posed a lethal threat to the survival of the Clinton dynasty. Hillary initially adopted her fierce defender role; but after Bill confessed to improprieties with Lewinsky, Hillary faced a turning point: to dissolve the partnership and move forward on her own or to reconcile and keep her partnership and marriage. Her decision achieved both; she kept the family intact and struck out on her own quest for elected office. Clinton's decision to move to New York and run for the Senate marked the first time that a first lady would run for office. It also reversed the Clintons' campaign partnership, with Bill in the surrogate role, a challenging experience for the veteran campaigner.

Two times during their political careers the Clintons competed for the highest office against members of the Bush family. Bill defeated President George H. W. Bush in 1992, marking a handoff from a World War II veteran to the first president who had not served in the military, and who had opposed the Vietnam War. In 2000, the Clintons hoped to cement their legacy through the election of Clinton's two-term vice president, Al Gore, who lost in a historically close and contested election to the son, George W. Bush.

Opinions about Bill and Hillary Clinton are inextricably linked to a longer term, post-Watergate trend, declining trust in government.[21] For the dynasty to succeed politically, the Clintons' premise that government can do good must gain public acceptance, measured in responses to survey questions asking whether officials can be trusted to "do the right thing all or most of the time." At the start of Clinton's first term, only 25 percent of respondents in surveys analyzed by the Pew Research Center agreed with the two higher levels of trust; six months later the trend bottomed out at a 50-year low of only 19 percent. Unlike previous post-Watergate presidencies, however, and despite scandals and controversies, responses to the trust question rose to 38 percent near the end of Clinton's second term. The trend for Presidents Carter, Bush '41, Bush '43, and Obama was an overall decline punctuated by occasional upswings; only Reagan and Clinton left office with higher trust in government levels than when they took office.[22]

Bill Clinton's Postpresidency

Clinton began his postpresidency at a young age, at 55. He continued his policy work from his Foundation Headquarters in the Harlem district of New York City and through his Presidential Library and Museum in Little Rock. He maintained an extensive speaking schedule and wrote a lengthy biography, *My Life*. As a convener of fund-raisers, foundation leaders, and policy activists at annual meetings of the Clinton Global Initiative, along with cohorts of students and graduates from the Arkansas-based Clinton School of Leadership in Public Service, Bill explored global problems and orchestrated investments in solutions throughout the world. Similar to President Jimmy Carter's postpresidency, Clinton used his foundation, books, and speeches to continue his diagnosis of social, political, and economic ills and to initiate practical solutions. Whereas Carter's presidential center works directly on problems, the Clinton Foundation operates more as a convener and catalyst, building public/private partnerships that connect donors with field organizations and using his celebrity status to bring together international experts to coordinate and collaborate.

The hallmark of the Clinton political dynasty is that the Clintons are idea merchants. Bill's postpresidency includes mentoring hundreds of graduates of the UA Clinton School of Public Service, which teaches policy diagnosis, program development, and community building skills in line with the school's mission statement: the belief "in the right of all individuals, without exclusion, to participate fully and democratically in the social, cultural, economic and political systems that affect their lives . . . and to reach their full potential and to embody the spirit of democracy."[23] Founded to promote development in Arkansas and communities wherever Clinton school students conduct fieldwork, the school trains graduates "to understand, engage and transform these complex systems to ensure equity, eliminate injustice and effect positive social change."[24] Bill Clinton interacts regularly with students in Little Rock and at the annual meetings of the Clinton Foundation's Global Initiative.[25]

Hillary Clinton in the Senate, as Secretary of State, and Her Presidential Campaigns

Hillary began her Senate campaign in 1999 with a listening tour, in which she drove throughout the state in a Ford van, stopping to chat with New Yorkers about their concerns and respond in person to charges that she was an opportunistic carpetbagger—Clinton moved to New York State after long-time senator Patrick Moynihan announced his retirement. In her speeches and debates with Republican rivals Mayor Rudy Giuliani and then Rick Lazio, she referenced constituent interests and local issues, naming people and places she had visited. The Clintons bought a home in Chappaqua in 1999, and Bill announced his postpresidential headquarters would be in Harlem. In November, Hillary restricted her White House duties and relocated to New York; first daughter Chelsea, then 20 years old, stepped in to host social functions and traveled with her dad on presidential trips abroad. During the summer, Chelsea began campaigning in New York for her mom; she took a leave from her studies at Stanford University during the fall to be full-time campaign partner with Hillary and to serve as first daughter in the White House. Beyond substantive duties, Chelsea formed a supportive partnership with each parent, easing the loneliness of campaigning for her mom and providing a poised hostess and an enthusiastic intellectual companion for her dad.

Senator Clinton took office in January 2001 and served two terms; she served on the Armed Services and Budget Committees, among others, and cosponsored almost 75 bills, many with Republicans.[26] As a senator, Hillary deliberately took the role of a workhorse rather than show horse, investing in committee work and constituent service, and she cooperated with both fellow Democrats and Republicans. She voted for the Patriot Act and the war in Afghanistan and invasion of Iraq.

She decided to run for president in 2008, beginning the campaign as the Democratic frontrunner. The election of George W. Bush in 2000 set up a dynastic rivalry that some hoped would culminate in a contest between President Bush and Hillary in 2004 or Bush's successor and Hillary in 2008. Instead, Hillary's first quest for the White House was derailed by the candidacy of Barack Obama, at a historical moment when change in Washington was more appealing to voters than the possible election of the first woman president. Prospects for a future run at the presidency were kept alive when President Obama asked

Hillary to serve as secretary of state, an opportunity for her to gain significant executive management experience and foreign policy expertise.

As secretary of state, Clinton became the first former first lady to hold a cabinet position. During her tenure from 2009 to 2013, her approach—similar to President Bill Clinton's engagement strategy—revived U.S. leadership in traditional international institutions, added "smart power" to supplement the use of force, and used social media to promote U.S. values abroad. Hillary put special emphasis on programs for women, children, and girls. She successfully transitioned into the role of team player within Obama's national security team and established a productive working relationship with Secretary of Defense Robert Gates, as they both tried to increase diplomatic and foreign assistance to supplement military action.

A very different social tide dashed Hillary's hopes for victory as President Obama's successor in the presidential election of 2016; angry, alienated, economically deprived voters on one hand, and Hillary's inability to reconstitute the Obama electoral coalition on the other, doomed her second presidential campaign. Although she captured the Democratic nomination and was favored in most national polls, on election night her Republican rival, real estate mogul and television reality star Donald Trump, was able to win the Electoral College votes of enough states to beat Hillary, even though she won more of the overall popular vote.

Second Generation: Chelsea Victoria Clinton

Chelsea Victoria Clinton was born on February 27, 1980, in Little Rock, Arkansas. As governor, Clinton breakfasted with his daughter every morning; and as she grew up, he supervised her homework at a small desk in his office. Chelsea sometimes kidded that her dad was the primary homework helper because her mom had a busier schedule. Both parents attended her softball games so regularly that ballparks became a venue for contacting the governor and first lady.

Just as their parents propelled them to succeed through academic achievement, Bill and Hillary urged Chelsea to challenge herself and excel. Raised in a home where political issues were nightly fare, Chelsea came of age surrounded by politics, campaigns, and media intrusions on the family's private lives. Her parents took her along on campaign swings throughout Arkansas and to annual political events like the Jefferson-Jackson Day Dinner and the Gillette Coon Supper. Like her parents, Chelsea readily excelled in school, achieving academic distinctions while participating in many and varied activities. Just as previous parents in the White House shielded their children from media scrutiny, the Clintons used media ground rules to protect their daughter and provide private space for her and her friends, like sleepovers and movie nights at the White House.

During the White House years, Clinton attended the prestigious, private Sidwell Friends' School in Washington where her favorite subjects were history, science and math, and international relations. She continued taking ballet, studying at the Washington School of Ballet. Chelsea Clinton occasionally traveled abroad with the first lady and the president, including a well-publicized trip to India in 1995, during which she was interviewed about her impressions. Chelsea graduated from high school in 1997, and in contrast to her parents' college choices, she selected a West Coast school, Stanford University in northern California. Her initial academic interest was medicine, perhaps to become a pediatric cardiologist; unlike her parents again, Chelsea eschewed student government, perhaps due to her determination to blend into campus life and minimize media attention. The Monica Lewinsky scandal and impeachment proceedings culminated during her sophomore year at Stanford. Chelsea visited Washington to support her parents and hold the family together, exemplified by the iconic photo of her walking toward Marine One between her parents, holding hands with each of them.

At Stanford, Chelsea participated in community service as a tutor and volunteered at Children's Hospital. Chelsea switched her major from chemistry to history in her junior year and wrote a 167-page honors thesis on the peace process in Northern Ireland, a signal achievement of her father's presidency. Beyond consultation with her father and administration officials as sources, Clinton interviewed political leaders and participants in the peace talks that led to the 1998 Good Friday Agreement. Like Hillary Rodham's investigation of overcoming community conflicts in Chicago for her college thesis, Chelsea analyzed how to bring people together to solve their problems and how best to engage leaders in a conflict resolution process.

Chelsea remained involved in her parents' careers, taking time off to participate in Hillary Clinton's 2000 senatorial campaign and to live with them in the White House during the final months of the Clinton presidency. She returned to Stanford in 2001 and completed her thesis, graduating with highest honors in 2001; former President Clinton was the commencement speaker. After graduation, Chelsea initially chose to work in the private sector in New York, specializing in finance; her rationale was to round out her education with practical experience on Wall Street. She spent three years at McKinsey & Company consulting firm and three more years at the global investment firm Avenue Capital. Concurrently, she served a three-year stint as a special correspondent for the NBC news series, "Making a Difference," where she shared examples of solution-based advocacy at home and abroad, about people overcoming struggles and programs that work—such as canine therapy for soldiers, the Maya Angelou Academy, and foster grandparents—aimed to empower others to act.

On July 31, 2010, Chelsea married Marc Mezvinsky, son of former congresswoman Marjorie Margolies-Mezvinsky (D-PA), whom Chelsea met at a

Renaissance Weekend when she was 12 and Marc was 15. Chelsea and Marc became friends during the Clinton presidency as both families participated in Democratic retreats and regularly attended Renaissance Weekends. Entering Stanford University, a year prior to Chelsea, Mezvinsky graduated in 2000 with a major in philosophy and religious studies. The couple began dating in 2005 and announced their engagement in 2009. Mezvinsky attended the University of Oxford and earned an MA in politics, philosophy, and economics. He then worked as an investment banker at Goldman Sachs; subsequently, he cofounded the hedge fund Eaglevale Partners where he worked until the firm closed in December 2016.

Chelsea initially declined stepping into leadership of the Clinton Foundation as a legacy position and instead honed her skills in organizational management and project evaluation. Clinton completed a master of public health at Columbia University's Mailman School. She taught graduate courses at Mailman School beginning in 2012. Concurrently, she served as an assistant vice provost for the Global Network University of New York University (NYU). After beginning a PhD program at the Wagner School of Public Service at NYU, Chelsea transferred to Oxford to continue working with her adviser; she earned a PhD in 2014. (Like her undergraduate honors thesis, Chelsea Clinton's dissertation, "The Global Fund: An Experiment in Global Governance," is not publicly available.[27]) Building on her graduate research, Chelsea coauthored with Devi Sridhar *Governing Global Health: Who Runs the World and Why?*[28] The broader significance of her dissertation is that it represents her training in evaluation research and her talent for synthesizing complex, varied performance indicators, exactly the skills that she would use as vice president of the Clinton Foundation. Chelsea's policy skills equal those of her parents: she combines Bill's capacity to synthesize voluminous details to diagnose a situation and Hillary's ability to cut to the core to make practical recommendations for change.[29]

During the mid-2010s Chelsea began working as vice chair of the Clinton Foundation, which then became the Bill, Hillary & Chelsea Clinton Foundation. Heretofore, she had taken independent pathways as an academic researcher, as an assistant professor of public health, as a news reporter/interviewer, and as a financial analyst. When she became vice chair, she brought to the job policy expertise, analytical skills in project evaluation research, and a global network of her own connections. At the foundation, her work spans a range of projects: expanding the Day of Action (where Clinton Global Initiative students "give back locally" to their communities); the Alliance for a Healthier Generation and Clinton Health Matters Initiative, which connects to her ongoing work on global health, particularly preventing childhood obesity, HIV and AIDS, and childhood diarrhea; and No Ceilings: The Full Participation Project, an empowerment initiative for women and girls. In the future, the foundation is a base from which she, and at some point perhaps one of her children, can pursue public service and become a successor to the Clinton dynasty.

During Hillary's 2016 presidential campaign, Chelsea maintained a full campaign schedule of speeches and press gaggles, even though she was expecting her second child. As a speaker, Chelsea's style is more like Hillary's: she is poised and composed, consistently on message, but still passionate about her concerns. Like her parents, she uses stories and humor to illustrate policy problems; she shares with them the ability to translate complex issues into lucid, graspable terms. More recently, she maintains a public presence by tweeting about issues, supporting her causes, criticizing President Trump, and inviting her followers to join in and speak out.

Chelsea authors books to empower girls and young people. She has published two books, *It's Your World: Get Informed, Get Inspired & Get Going!* and *She Persisted: 13 American Women Who Changed the World*. The former tells kids how to investigate concerns in their communities, learn more about issues, and put solutions into action; the latter narrates the lives of women, including Oprah Winfrey and Sonia Sotomayor, who would not "take no for an answer" until they reached their goals.[30] Whereas her parents worked for change directly within political institutions and the Democratic Party, Chelsea's public service path is outside of Washington. Chelsea insists, when asked about a possible run for office, that her life is centered in New York with her family.

Legacy

The Clinton dynasty operates like a brain trust consisting of a small, highly educated family augmented by networks in the United States and abroad of political friends, issue experts, project stakeholders, and activists attracted to the Clintons' ideas and their pragmatic, centrist approach to governing. Despite their intellectual abilities, Bill and Hillary could not consistently convert expertise into electoral success. They won first-term elections when their philosophy resonated with many and varied voters, and when they represented change rather than continuity. They won by deploying innovative campaign strategies, a strong ground game, and appealing sound bites, like "it's the economy, stupid." They lost when their strategies miscalculated or failed to activate targeted voters.

The Clinton dynasty is built on intellectual capital; Bill, Hillary, and Chelsea lead through rhetoric and networking. All three Clintons use public service and media to advocate pragmatic solutions to complex problems. They write books, make speeches, tweet, and convene meetings of experts to explore solutions to local, national, and global problems. Rhetorically, each Clinton uses stories, humor, and personal examples to invite audiences to appreciate complex linkages. Stylistically, each has a different voice: Bill has the more charismatic style, a studied yet off-hand, folksy delivery; he is characterized by friends and foes as a natural campaigner who radiates empathetic listening and heart-felt responses. Hillary uses a more technical, legalistic delivery to explain issues, plans, and consequences; she is portrayed as more preachy and professorial in public but funny and engaging in small group settings. When addressing public audiences, Chelsea uses restrained conversational tones, jokes about her parents to build rapport, and then makes coherently structured arguments to explain her message.

The Clintons not only propose programs but also reiterate a grounding philosophy, based on the New Democrat principles dating from the 1980s: expanding opportunity, taking personal responsibility, and building community. Accepting the party's nomination in 1992, Bill proposed "a solemn agreement between the people and their government based not simply on what each of us can take but what all of us must give to our Nation."[31] These principles undergird the programs and priorities of his presidency. They framed every one of his state of the union addresses, beginning in 1993: "I believe we will find our new direction in the basic old values that brought us here over the last two centuries: a commitment to opportunity, to individual responsibility, to community, to work, to family, and to faith. We must now break the habits of both political parties and say there can be no more something for nothing and admit frankly that we are all in this together."[32] This statement proclaims the New Democrat principles plus a political strategy: rejecting zero-sum partisan conflict in favor of triangulating toward a center by appealing to centrist partisans, independents, and moderates. Unfortunately for the president, few Democrats in Congress during 1993–1994 embraced New Democrat principles.

Clinton's hopes to build a philosophical foundation for a durable Democratic majority were also challenged by the rising leader of the Republicans in the House of Representatives. In 1994, Speaker Newt Gingrich (R-GA) proposed a Contract with America to create a Conservative Opportunity Society (COS) to displace the traditional Democrat's liberal welfare state. The contract called for some similar principles: taking personal and fiscal responsibility, creating jobs and higher wages, restoring national security, and taking back our streets.[33] Gingrich and the Clintons were trying to grow their parties by recasting their platforms and, more fundamentally, redefining the role of government to be sustainable financially in the 1990s and beyond.

This ideological competition continues into the present: neither party has united its factions nor significantly expanded its base. Thus far, the Bush dynasty has also failed to reframe Republicanism. President George W. Bush promoted "compassionate conservatism" in 2000; he won a second term but failed to enlarge the Republican base. Jeb Bush could not translate his brand of governing into a popular concept in his 2016 bid for the presidency, perhaps because he was "a non-grievance candidate in a grievance year."[34] Hillary's presidential campaigns in 2008 and 2016 updated New Democrat appeals in terms of inclusivity. Accepting her party's nomination for president in 2016, she framed voters' choices as having "to decide whether we will all work together so we can all rise together," and she repeated the message from her book *It Takes a Village*, "None of us can raise a family, build a business, heal a community or lift a country totally alone." She hoped to lead toward a "country where all our children can dream and those dreams are within reach, where families are strong, communities are safe and, yes, where love trumps hate."[35] Building upon Bill's policies on trade and international order building, Hillary advocated positive response to the challenges of globalization, promotion of engagement rather than the "America First" withdrawals promoted by candidate Trump. However, confronted with an electorate more divided than ever, her appeals fell short. Hillary failed to expand the Clinton base into a majority despite winning the popular vote. Her slogan "Stronger Together" echoed Bill's rejection of zero-sum partisan politics, but in 2016, opponents' antielitist, anti-Washington, and exclusionist bids were more popular than Clinton's appeals.

Chelsea also frames her messages in New Democrat terms. In her book for young people, she tells her own story of getting involved in community service and urges children to take responsibility for making a difference in their communities.[36] The Mezvinskys have two young children, Charlotte and Aidan, who like their parents, are being raised in an actively political family and a policy-infused environment. Whether they, too, will feel called to public service cannot yet be known.

Notes

1. Recent and older maps are available from the University of Michigan at http://www-personal.umich.edu/~mejn/election/2016. For historical context on the emergence of red versus blue America, see Toni Monkovic, "50 Years of Electoral College Maps: How the U.S. Turned Red and Blue," *New York Times*, August 22, 2016; available at https://www.nytimes.com/2016/08/23/upshot/50-years-of-electoral-college-maps-how-the-us-turned-red-and-blue.html?mcubz=0&_r=0.

2. John Kenneth White, *The Values Divide* (Washington, DC: CQ Press, 2003).

3. Compare, e.g., David Brock's anti-Hillary book *The Seduction of Hillary Rodham* (New York: Free Press, 1996) versus his confessional *Blinded by the Right: The Conscience of an Ex-Conservative* (New York: Crown, 2002). For investigations in Arkansas, see *The Encyclopedia of Arkansas History & Culture* entry on "Arkansas Project," available at http://www.encyclopediaofarkansas.net/encyclopedia/entry-detail.aspx?entryID=5378.

4. See, e.g., the Facebook page, https://www.facebook.com/ihatehillaryclinton. The historian Henry Louis Gates wrote a lengthy analysis, "Hating Hillary:

Hillary Clinton Has Been Trashed Right and Left—but What's Really Fueling the Furies?" for *The New Yorker*, February 26, 1996; available at http://www.newyorker.com/magazine/1996/02/26/hating-hillary; accessed March 12, 1998. Just before the 2016 election, *The Economist* published an update, analyzing Clinton's years as a senator and as secretary of state, "Hating Hillary: America's Probably Next President Is Deeply Reviled. Why?" October 22, 2016; available at http://www.economist.com/news/united-states/21709053-americas-probable-next-president-deeply-reviled-why-hating-hillary; accessed November 1, 2016.

5. Hillary Diane Rodham, "1969 Commencement Address," Wellesley College, May 31, 1969. Subsequent quotes from the address are also from this source; available at http://www.wellesley.edu/events/commencement/archives/1969commencement/studentspeech#dx7yZubG2BEitMJ0.99; accessed June 15, 2013.

6. Bill Clinton gave a moving account of meeting Hillary in his speech to the Democratic National Convention on July 26, 2016, recalling seeing her in their class on political and civil rights and describing how she looked (thick blond hair, big glasses, wore no makeup, and she had a sense of strength and self-possession that I found magnetic") and recounting how she made the first move, introducing herself to him in the Yale library. "Clinton Speech" available at *Newsweek*, July 27, 2016, at http://www.newsweek.com/full-transcript-bill-clintons-speech-democratic-convention-484326; accessed May 19, 2017.

7. For details, see "Cuban Refugee Crisis," *Encyclopedia of Arkansas*; available at http://www.encyclopediaofarkansas.net/encyclopedia/entry-detail.aspx?entryID=4248; accessed May 1, 2017.

8. Dick Morris recounts these events and his subsequent work with the Clintons in *Rewriting History*, a book he wrote to counter Hillary's *Living History* (New York: HarperCollins, 2004).

9. For details, see Margaret E. Scranton, "Hillary's Arkansas Comeback: Achieving Education Standards Reform," in *Hillary Rodham Clinton and the 2016 Election*, ed. Michelle Lockhart and Kathleen Mollick (Lanham, MD: Lexington, 2015), 15–40.

10. For details about Clinton's terms as governor, see "Bill Clinton," *Encyclopedia of Arkansas History and Culture;* available at http://www.encyclopediaofarkansas.net/encyclopedia/entry-detail.aspx?entryID=95.

11. Peter Applebome, "Clinton Record in Leading Arkansas: Successes, but Not without Criticism," *The New York Times*, December 22, 1991; available at http://www.nytimes.com/1991/12/22/us/clinton-record-in-leading-arkansas-successes-but-not-without-criticism.html?pagewanted=all&mcubz=0; accessed May 21, 2017.

12. Perot, crusading as a deficit hawk, initially appeared to pose a significant challenge to Clinton because he also targeted moderates disenthralled with democratic and republican platitudes; he dropped out of the race temporarily, and when he resumed his campaign he was unable to regain momentum, finishing in third place in the general election.

13. Clinton promised to reduce national debt and lower taxes on the middle class and the poor while raising taxes on the top 2 percent, relying on economic growth to reduce the deficit; he called for advanced public works projects like high-speed rail, repairing the nation's infrastructure, and for a national computer network. He promised national health insurance, financial aid for qualified college students, and welfare reform.

14. For an overview and details of Clinton's domestic policies and programs, see the University of Virginia, Miller Center essay, based on oral history interviews with numerous administration officials, "Bill Clinton: Domestic Affairs"; available at https://millercenter.org/president/clinton/domestic-affairs.

15. The White House, "A National Security Strategy for a New Century," December 1, 1999, 1–2; available at http://nssarchive.us/national-security-strategy-2000-2; accessed April 1, 2017. Quotations are from pp. 1–2.

16. William J. Clinton, "Remarks by the President on Foreign Policy," delivered at San Francisco on February 26, 1999; available from The American Presidency Project at http://www.presidency.ucsb.edu/ws/?pid=57170; accessed April 1, 2017.

17. Ibid.

18. The speech is featured at American Rhetoric as one of the top 100 speeches; the site contains a transcript and video of her address; available at http://www.americanrhetoric.com/speeches/hillaryclintonbeijingspeech.htm.

19. The National First Ladies Library offers a detailed biography of Hillary Clinton with archival images and videos of her speeches and congressional testimony; available at http://www.firstladies.org/biographies/firstladies.aspx?biography=43.

20. For details on the impeachment process, charges, and evidence, see the *Washington Post*'s site "Clinton Accused: Special Report"; available at http://www.washingtonpost.com/wp-srv/politics/special/clinton/stories/impeach122098.htm.

21. Pew Research Center, "Public Trust in Government: 1958–2015," November 23, 2015; available at http://www.people-press.org/2015/11/23/public-trust-in-government-1958-2015; accessed April 24, 2017.

22. Pew Research Center, "Public Trust in Government: 1957–2017"; available at http://www.people-press.org/2017/05/03/public-trust-in-government-1958-2017.

23. University of Arkansas Clinton School of Public Service, "Mission, Vision & Values"; available at http://clintonschool.uasys.edu/about/vision-mission-values; accessed January 29, 2017.

24. Ibid.

25. Bill Clinton, "Graduation Address," Little Rock, Arkansas, May 15, 2016; available at https://www.clintonschoolspeakers.com/content/2016-clinton-school-graduation.

26. A list of bills and an analysis of Senator Clinton's votes that compares her ideologically to other senators is available at https://www.govtrack.us/congress/members/hillary_clinton/300022.

27. Chelsea Clinton, "The Global Fund: An Experiment in Global Governance," PhD Dissertation, University of Oxford, United Kingdom, 2014. Document URL:

http://74.217.196.173/docview/1683352?accountid=14482. At present, Oxford declines interlibrary loan requests, stating that the author controls access to the document.

28. Published by Oxford University Press, 2017; Sridhar is a professor of global public health at the University of Edinburgh Medical School. The book assessed the public/private partnerships sponsored by the Global Fund and the GAVI Alliance and compared their effectiveness to programs sponsored by two traditional international organizations, the World Bank and World Health Organization. A presentation of their findings with a question and answer session is available at https://www.lshtm.ac.uk/newsevents/news/2017/governingglobalhealthwhorunstheworldandwhy and at https://www.c-span.org/video/?424618-2/chelsea-clinton-devi-sridhar-discuss-governing-global-health.

29. To illustrate the intellectual approach she takes, one can read the memorandum she wrote to "Dad and Mom" about the Clinton Foundation's work in Haiti, a hacked unclassified U.S. Department of State document published in WikiLeaks in 2016. Chelsea combines analytical language with firsthand personal urgency: "To say that I was profoundly disturbed by what I saw—and didn't see—would be an understatement. The incompetence is mind numbing. . . . If we do not quickly change the organization, management, accountability and delivery paradigm on the ground, we could quite conceivable confront tens of thousands of children's deaths . . . in the near future." Since the memo is seven pages long, she puts in bold the ideas "I think most important" so her parents can quickly absorb her takeaways, connecting directly to their key interests, writing about "mental health in settlements and beyond" where "clear people are thinking about this now—largely because Dad asked about it and made it prominent. . . ." In the context section at the end of the memo she reports on the sources she consulted and the places she observed during her four-day site visit. The document reads like an after-action report by an official delegation, documenting official meetings, informal encounters with people on the streets, and visits with military and civilian service providers. Beyond her professional training, this memo evidences the full array of Chelsea Clinton's personal skills: how to conduct a "listening tour" as her Mom used in her campaigns, the official visitor and the rapporteur skills she polished on foreign travels with President Clinton and Secretary of State Clinton, along with her ability to engage any and everyone attending a rally. The memo is "HAITI," From: Chelsea Clinton To: Bill Clinton Date: 2001-01-01 03:00. Subject: *HAITI.* UNCLASSIFIED U.S. Department of State. Case No. F-2014-20439. Doc No. C05774218. Date: 08/31/2015. Available at https://wikileaks.org/clinton-emails/emailid/410; accessed May 1, 2017.

30. Chelsea Clinton, *It's Your World: Get Informed, Get Inspired & Get Going!* (New York: Philomel, 2015) and *She Persisted: 13 American Women Who Changed the World* (New York: Philomel, 2017), illustrated by Alexandra Boiger. *It's Your World* has a companion multimedia, kid-friendly website at http://www.itsyourworld.com.

31. William J. Clinton, "Address Accepting the Presidential Nomination at the Democratic National Convention in New York," July 16, 1992; available at

The American Presidency Project, http://www.presidency.ucsb.edu/ws/?pid=25958; accessed March 25, 2017.

32. William J. Clinton, "Address before a Joint Session of Congress on Administration Goals," February 17, 1993; The American Presidency Project, available at http://www.presidency.ucsb.edu/ws/?pid=47232; accessed March 25, 2017.

33. Armey Gingrich, Dick Armey, and Newt Gingrich, Contract with America, Republican National Committee, December 26, 1994. The text of the contract is also available at the U.S. House of Representatives archive at https://web.archive.org/web/19990427174200/http://www.house.gov/house/Contract/CONTRACT.html.

34. Molly Ball, "There's Nothing Better Than a Scared, Rich Candidate," *The Atlantic*, October 2016, p. 57.

35. Hillary Clinton, "Address Accepting the Presidential Nomination at the Democratic National Convention in Philadelphia, Pennsylvania," July 28, 2016, The American Presidency Project; available at http://www.presidency.ucsb.edu/ws/index.php?pid=118051; accessed March 25, 2017. Hillary Rodham Clinton, *It Takes a Village* (New York: Simon & Schuster, 2006).

36. Chelsea Clinton, *It's Your World: Get Informed, Get Inspired & Get Going!* (New York: Philomel, 2015); the most insightful interview with Chelsea Clinton, based on months of being embedded with her staff during 2012 is by Jonathan Van Meter, "Waiting in the Wings: An Exclusive Interview with Chelsea Clinton," *Vogue Magazine*, August 13, 2012; available at http://www.vogue.com/article/waiting-in-the-wings-an-exclusive-interview-with-chelsea-clinton; accessed May 1, 2017.

Further Reading

Bernstein, Carl. *A Woman in Charge*. New York: Vintage, 2007.
Clinton, Bill. *My Life*. New York: Knopf, 2004.
Clinton, Hillary Rodham. *Hard Choices*. New York: Simon & Schuster, 2014.
Clinton, Hillary Rodham. *What Happened*. New York: Simon & Schuster, 2017.
Gillon, Steven M. *The Pact: Bill Clinton, Newt Gingrich, and the Rivalry That Defined a Generation*. New York: Oxford University Press, 2008.
Harris, John F. *The Survivor: Bill Clinton in the White House*. New York: Random House, 2005.

CHAPTER FOUR

The Gore Dynasty

Michael R. Fitzgerald

The story of the Gore dynasty in Tennessee is a tale of the rise of the New South, its shifting politics, and a dream unfulfilled. Its rise began during the Great Depression, flourished during the mid-20th century, and waned in the early 1970s. It soon rebounded and enjoyed power for another three decades, ending suddenly in 2000. Its reign encompassed the economic, social, and political changes that transformed the American South from President Franklin D. Roosevelt's New Deal, through the civil rights and countercultural revolutions, into the Internet age. The family's rise to political power emanated from two remarkable and highly ambitious individuals, Albert Gore Sr. and Pauline LaFon. Within a year of their marriage in 1937, Albert won a coveted seat in Congress from which two generations of political power emanated. The dynasty ended, paradoxically, at the apex of its influence.

The arch of the Gore family story reflects the 20th-century transformation of southern politics. Twice the family found that the liberalism of the national Democratic Party could not be reconciled with Tennessee conservatism. It was perhaps to their credit, but at their cost, that Albert Gore Sr. and his namesake son found their principles at odds with Tennessee voters at critical points in their careers. Albert lost his Senate seat in 1970. Al Gore Jr. lost Tennessee in his 2000 presidential election, which dramatically ended with a recount in Florida. The Gore dynasty contributed much to the political and economic transformation that brought the South closer to the American mainstream. However, at the turn of the 21st century the family lost its Tennessee political base and none of its third generation endeavored to maintain the dynasty.

Albert Gore Sr., Founder

Albert Gore Sr. was born in 1907 and grew up on a family farm near Carthage in Smith County, Tennessee. His ancestors were early Scotch-Irish settlers who migrated from Virginia to the Upper Cumberland region of Tennessee after the Revolutionary War. The Gore family owned a small farm, practiced the Baptist faith, and were respected citizens.

After graduating from high school in 1925, Albert worked his way through college by teaching in rural public schools. Filled with political ambition, he became active in local Democratic politics and at the tender age of 25, he ran for the office of Smith County school superintendent. Gore lost that race to the popular incumbent, but later was appointed to the post when the incumbent suddenly died. While serving as superintendent, Gore drove back and forth to Nashville to attend YMCA night law school. In a coffee shop in Nashville, he met Pauline LaFon who was working as a waitress to pay for law school at Vanderbilt. In 1936, Pauline graduated and moved to Arkansas to practice law, but she returned to Tennessee a year later to marry Albert. They had two children, Nancy born in 1938 and Albert Jr. born in 1948. Pauline would serve as a close adviser to her husband throughout his career in government. A formidable political strategist and campaigner, she was an integral part of every Gore family election campaign.

Appointed to the post of state commissioner of labor in 1937, Gore was a progressive administrator who fought powerful old guard politicians to bring Tennessee into line with national labor standards. After mortgaging the family farm to fund his campaign, Gore was elected to Congress in 1938. In a congressional career spanning 32 years in the House and then Senate, Albert Gore served in the populist mode of his hero Andrew Jackson, while his perspective as an internationalist was inspired by his admiration of Woodrow Wilson. Gore was mentored early in his career in practical politics and government, by fellow Tennessean Cordell Hull. Hull was a childhood friend of Gore's father and uncles, and Albert took great pride in winning the House seat Hull had once occupied.

A reliable congressional supporter of the New Deal, Gore maintained close ties to his constituents. He allied with the rising generation of Tennessee politicians who fought the powerful Crump Democratic machine in Memphis. He helped end the machine's dominance in the Democratic Party and its stranglehold on Tennessee politics and government. Except for a brief stint with the army in Europe in 1945, Gore spent World War II in Congress. His expertise and reputation for integrity led to Gore's appointment to a small secret committee charged with oversight of the Manhattan Project to build the atomic bomb. After the war, Gore defended President Roosevelt's New Deal legacy and supported President Harry Truman's domestic and foreign policy initiatives. In

The Gore Dynasty

Gore Political Dynasty Family Tree

1. Albert Arnold Gore Sr., 1907–1998
   County superintendent of education of Smith County, TN, 1932–1936
   Tennessee commissioner of labor, 1936–1937
   Member of U.S. House of Representatives, 1939–1953
   U.S. senator, 1953–1970
Married Pauline LaFon Gore, 1912–2004
Two children: Albert Jr. and Nancy

2. Albert (Al) Gore Jr., 1948–
   Member of U.S. House of Representatives, 1977–1985
   U.S. senator, 1985–1993
   Vice president, 1993–2001
Married Mary Elizabeth (Tipper) Aitcheson
Four children: Karenna, Kristin, Sarah, and Albert III

Karenna Gore Schiff, 1973–
Born August 6, 1973

Kristin Gore Kulash, 1977–
Born June 5, 1977
Daughter of Al Gore Jr. and Tipper Aitcheson Gore
Granddaughter of Albert Gore Sr. and Pauline LaFon Gore

Sarah Gore Maiani, 1979–
Born January 7, 1979
Daughter of Al Gore Jr. and Tipper Aitcheson Gore
Granddaughter of Albert Gore Sr. and Pauline LaFon Gore

Albert Gore III, 1982–
Born October 19, 1982
Son of Al Gore Jr. and Tipper Aitcheson Gore
Grandson of Albert Gore Sr. and Pauline LaFon Gore

1946, Gore campaigned for Democratic candidates during the midterm election. Breaking with many southern Democrats, he supported President Truman's reelection and worked hard for progressive Democratic candidates in Tennessee. Four years later, Gore upset the six-term incumbent in the Democratic primary election. Gore's victory signaled the end of the Crump political machine's control of Tennessee state politics. Gore easily defeated his Republican opponent in November.

In the Senate, Gore joined a bloc of southern progressives, including Lyndon Johnson of Texas and William Fulbright of Arkansas. His major accomplishments included blocking Republican proposals to privatize the Tennessee Valley Authority, strong support for bipartisan foreign and national defense policy, and the promotion of initiatives in education, housing, taxation, and economic development. Gore prided himself in being a populist defender of the common people against policies that benefited corporations and the wealthy at the expense of the working class and poor. He cultivated an image as a legislative maverick willing to go his own way when political principles were at stake. Gore was a vocal critic of the Republican Eisenhower administration. Whenever its legislative proposals benefited his state and region, Gore would cooperate. Thus, he cosponsored the legislation proposed by President Eisenhower for the creation of the interstate highway system, which linked Tennessee to the rest of the nation.

As a southerner, Gore appreciated the explosive social and political implications of race relations in postwar America. Because only a small percentage of African Americans lived in Gore's House district, local civil rights issues were subdued there. Most white citizens in Tennessee held traditional southern attitudes in favor of racial segregation. Well aware of this, Gore took a moderate approach to race relations and civil rights in Congress. He was appalled by the most blatant racists and racist practices which, he believed, served an oppressive white elite at the expense of the common people of all races. As a southern progressive he publicly recognized that discrimination existed and avoided race baiting during his campaigns for office. Gore mostly avoided the subject whenever possible. Gore did stand out among southern senators, in calling for peaceful compliance with federal court orders for the desegregation of public schools.

At the Democratic Conventions in 1956 and 1960, hoping to gain a path to the White House, Senator Gore unsuccessfully sought the vice presidential nomination. Gore successfully defended his Senate seat in 1958, conducting a traditional southern-style campaign where the candidate, family, and friends traversed the state by automobile. In the Democratic primary, Gore faced a segregationist opponent who attacked his moderation on civil rights and race relations. With difficulty, Gore withstood the primary challenge and then easily defeated his Republican opponent.

The early 1960s brought change to Tennessee politics, and the Democratic Party's dominance diminished. As the national Democratic Party became more liberal on civil rights and other cultural issues, Tennessee voters increasingly were drawn to the Republican Party, which threatened Gore's reelection prospects. Most especially, as race relations approached the boiling point in 1964, a growing number of white Tennesseans were disenthralled with the senator's civil rights record, even though he voted against the 1964 Civil Rights Act. This did little to placate disgruntled whites in middle and west Tennessee, but it reduced his support among black voters. In 1964, Gore found it more difficult than in 1958 to defeat another race-baiting primary opponent. He was attacked for refusing to join other Tennessee politicians in condemnation of federal efforts to desegregate public schools in the South. Gore's positions on race relations, arms control, school prayer, and gun control, while more moderate than those of many Senate Democrats, nevertheless rendered him increasingly vulnerable in Tennessee. After surviving the primary, he narrowly defeated a relatively unknown but well-financed Republican who accused Gore of abandoning traditional Tennessee values for those of northern liberals.

Events following the 1964 election exacerbated differences between Democratic voters in Tennessee and their national counterparts. Gore's support for the Voting Rights Act of 1965 restored his standing with black voters but distanced him further from white Democrats who were moving toward the Republican Party. The election of Republican Howard Baker Jr. to the Senate in 1966 presaged Richard Nixon's victory in Tennessee during the 1968 presidential race. After Nixon's election, Gore became a prominent critic of the Nixon administration's domestic, national security, and foreign policies. The enmity between Senator Gore and President Nixon was bitter, deep, and personal. The senator's opposition to the Vietnam War infuriated the president, as did Gore's opposition to the conservative southern judges Nixon nominated for the Supreme Court.

For Nixon's White House and the Republican National Committee, Tennessee was ground zero in 1970 and Gore was the target. As part of their southern strategy to win a majority in Congress, the Republicans exploited differences between Gore and his constituents. Gore's Republican opponent benefited greatly from White House support and he ran a media savvy, well-financed campaign effectively exploiting Nixon's popularity in Tennessee. Gore was tagged as a member of the Democratic liberal establishment who had betrayed his southern roots and was out of touch with Tennessee values. His long-distinguished career in Congress ended in November 1970 when Gore was decisively defeated. The loss of the patriarch's Senate seat imperiled the potential for a Gore dynasty. Albert and Pauline pinned their hopes on their son, whom they'd groomed for political greatness.

Senator Al Gore Sr. speaking at the Democratic Convention, August 28, 1968. (Library of Congress)

Al Gore Jr., Heir

Al Gore Jr. attended exclusive private schools in Washington, but every summer returned to Carthage to work on the family farm. When he entered Harvard in 1965, he thrived in its liberal social and political environment. Al often differed with his more conservative father on social, cultural, and economic issues. Al opposed the Vietnam War, but he avoided antiwar demonstrations. He knew that protesting Vietnam would damage his father's career because the majority of Tennessee voters supported the war. As college graduation approached, Al confronted the issue of military service. Unlike the sons of many prominent politicians, Al did not use his connections to avoid the draft. He enlisted in the army in 1969 upon finishing at Harvard. In May 1970, Al married Mary Elizabeth "Tipper" Aitcheson. During his father's reelection campaign the message was conveyed in appearances and advertising: the senator's son was performing his patriotic duty. After the election, Al volunteered for duty in Vietnam.

Disillusioned by his father's defeat, and dispirited after his return from Vietnam in 1971, Al spent the next several years contemplating his future. Rather than attending law school, which his parents urged as a path to politics, Al enrolled at Vanderbilt University's Divinity School. He also worked nights for *The Tennessean* newspaper as an investigative reporter. In 1974, having left divinity school, he took a leave from the newspaper to attend Vanderbilt Law

School. Al left law school to run for the vacant congressional seat once held by his father.

Following victory in a closely contested primary, Gore easily defeated his Republican opponent. To establish his own identity, Al kept his father in the background during his campaign, but his mother and sister were active. After Al entered Congress, Tipper worked as a freelance photographer, eventually publishing several photography books. She became a public figure in her own right during Gore's time in Congress. She led a campaign against pornographic lyrics in rock music and organized groups advocating for children, families, the homeless, and those suffering from mental illness.

In Congress, Al focused on issues of science, technology, and national security. He was a proponent for strengthening national defense, which sat well with his Tennessee constituency. Gore was cautious on environmental issues. He strove to balance support for environmental protection with the opinions of constituents and the economic interests of his state. A supporter of legislation providing federal funds for developing high-speed computing, he worked hard to secure the funding research that produced the Internet. Gore assiduously studied complex and highly technical issues, which made him a congressional leader in areas such as weapons development, deployment, and arms control.

Al's sister Nancy greatly influenced his life. She was 10 years old when Al was born in 1948. During her teen years, while the senator and Pauline were occupied with social activities and public affairs, Nancy served as a surrogate mother to her younger brother. In 1984, after years of heavy smoking, Nancy succumbed to lung cancer. Her premature death at the age of 49 deeply affected the Gore family. The Gores abandoned tobacco growing, and Al became a leader in the movement against smoking and the tobacco industry. Nancy and her husband, Frank Hunger, had worked hard for the family in every election campaign. After Nancy's death, Hunger remained close to the Gore family and played instrumental roles in Al's presidential campaigns as a friend and adviser.

Al Gore was a reliable but not doctrinaire Democrat. Unlike his father, who relished taking independent stands, Al accommodated rather than confronted party leaders. On issues where the national party was particularly liberal, Gore took a low profile—hewing as closely as possible to more moderate positions. This frustrated many liberals but solidified his political base in Tennessee. Always mindful of his father's defeat due to perceptions that Albert Sr. had lost touch with Tennessee voters, Al emphasized constituent service. He returned to Tennessee almost every weekend to meet his constituents and nurture statewide political contacts. When Republican senator Howard Baker announced his retirement in 1984, Al announced his candidacy for the seat. Dynasty redemption was sweet when, at only 38 years of age, Al Gore won a lively Democratic primary and easily defeated his Republican opponent for his father's old Senate seat.

Two years later in 1987, strongly encouraged by his father, Al ran for the Democratic nomination for president. Dynasty dreams of winning the White House were dashed when Al decisively lost the nomination to Governor Michael Dukakis of Massachusetts. The Gore family moved past the defeat and campaigned hard for the Democratic ticket, but to no avail. George H. W. Bush won Tennessee easily on his way to national victory and the presidency.

Family plans for another presidential bid were set aside when tragedy struck in 1989. Al and Tipper's youngest child, Albert Gore III, nearly died in an auto accident. The family, especially Tipper, struggled through a private crisis in the aftermath. Meanwhile, Al was arguably the most popular public figure in Tennessee. Against token opposition, he easily won reelection to the Senate in 1990, taking 70 percent of the vote.

Safely reelected, with his presidential aspirations on hold, Al resolved to make more of his public office. Previously, Gore was a quiet proponent of legislation to mitigate the deleterious effects of environmental degradation. In 1992, he proclaimed alarm about the threat of greenhouse gas emissions to the Earth's ecosystem in a best-selling book, *Earth in the Balance*. An environmental call to arms, the book established Al as a preeminent actor in the deepening contest between environmental groups and the fossil fuel industry. During his national tour promoting the book, Gore announced that he would not be a candidate in the upcoming presidential election.

Al Gore's national reputation as a Democrat strong on national defense issues, including the use of military force, grew dramatically during the Persian Gulf War of 1991. Gore broke with party leaders and voted to authorize the use of military force in response to Iraq's invasion of Kuwait. In early 1992, incumbent President Bush's reelection appeared certain. Bush's popularity for winning the Persian Gulf War and ending the Cold War deterred the most prominent Democratic office holders from entering the primaries. Al Gore's decision not to run opened the way for another "New South" candidate, Governor Bill Clinton of Arkansas. Clinton, despite questions about extramarital affairs and shady business deals, won the Democratic nomination by focusing on domestic rather than international issues. Instead of balancing the ticket geographically and ideologically, Clinton asked fellow southern moderate Al Gore to join him as his running mate. As a Vietnam veteran, strong on defense, and experienced in international affairs with an insider's knowledge of how things worked in Washington, Gore possessed strengths to balance Clinton's vulnerabilities. In accepting the vice presidential nomination, Gore set aside previous misgivings about subjecting his family to the ordeal of another presidential campaign so soon after the trauma of his son's near-fatal accident. The Clinton-Gore team won the election, and during the transition they set terms for an innovative governing partnership, which granted the vice president an unprecedented role in policy and administrative matters.

Vice President Gore was loyal to President Clinton and in turn enjoyed extensive influence in international, defense, and environmental affairs. The most dramatic example of Vice President Gore's importance was the critical role he played in negotiating the Kyoto protocol to reduce global warming pollution in 1997. The Clinton-Gore team won reelection in 1996. Gore's loyalty to Clinton ran deep but was sorely tested during the second term. Whatever his personal misgivings, Gore refused publicly to distance himself from the president through the scandals, involving Clinton's affair with a White House intern, that culminated in Clinton's impeachment by the House and subsequent trial in the Senate.

The closest thing to a scandal in Al Gore's career arose from campaign fundraising as vice president. He was accused of violating federal restriction on fund-raising when, going into the reelection campaign, he made telephone solicitations for contributions on behalf of the Democratic National Committee from his White House office. Gore was also implicated in activities associated with illegal Chinese government donations to the reelection campaign. But investigations by the Department of Justice and Congress did not produce charges against him.

Albert Gore Sr. died just before his 91st birthday in 1998. In a moving eulogy, Al Jr. praised his father as an exemplar of public service and an inspiration to the rising generation that was building a New South. Two years later, Al brought the dynasty to the precipice of fulfilling the late patriarch's greatest dream: the presidency. Because of his success in raising money for the party and the ticket, the vice president became the front-runner for the Democratic nomination in 2000.

The politics and policy that made Gore an asset to the Clinton presidency and secured him the Democratic Party nomination caused him problems back in Tennessee. Gore's connection to his home state diminished during his eight years as vice president. Time spent in the state was largely limited to fund-raising trips and campaigning for Clinton's reelection. The family returned to the Carthage for holidays and special occasions, but the dynasty's third generation—Karenna, Kristin, Sarah, and Albert III—did not establish Tennessee roots. By the 2000 campaign, the Gore family's political base was in Washington, not the volunteer state. That November, Al Gore lost Tennessee to former Texas governor George W. Bush, the son of President George H. W. Bush. A victory in his home state would have made Gore president. Instead, the election was settled in Florida where Bush prevailed by the smallest of margins after a disputed recount and where Bush's brother, Jeb, was governor.

The 2000 campaign was the high-water mark of the Gore family dynasty. Defeat left the family without a secure political base from which to launch a comeback. The death of Gore's mother in 2004 took away its indomitable matriarch. Political dynasties require generational continuity, something that eluded the Gore family at the turn of the century.

Vice President Al Gore speaks at the dedication of the FDR Memorial in Washington, DC, May 2, 1997. (Library of Congress)

After the 2000 election defeat, Tipper and Al left Washington to live in Nashville where Al pondered his future and taught at local colleges. In 2002, Al ended speculation about a rematch with Bush by declaring unequivocally that he would not seek the presidency in 2004. Gore continued fund-raising for favored causes and candidates, but his political career ended. In 2007, he published *An Inconvenient Truth*, calling for comprehensive action to confront the threat of climate change. This best-selling book and its companion Oscar-winning documentary opened a new career as a passionate activist for domestic and global action on climate change. Gore won international acclaim and a Nobel Peace Prize, while his work also made him a lightning rod for global warming and climate change skeptics. Undeterred, Gore continues the crusade for international action to mitigate global warming nearly 20 years later.

In 2010, after 40 years of marriage, Al and Tipper announced their separation and thereby ended an extraordinary partnership. Tipper moved to California to focus on her photography, and Al remained in Nashville to continue work as an environmental activist and business entrepreneur. Their four children took up lives on the East and West Coasts.

Of the next generation, it seemed that Karenna, the eldest, was the Gore dynasty's heir apparent. She spent summers working on the farm in Carthage under the tutelage of her grandfather, who taught Karenna about family traditions and her Tennessee roots. Following graduation from Harvard in 1995,

Karenna completed law school at Columbia. She worked on her father's vice presidential campaigns and delivered a nominating speech for him at the 2000 Democratic Convention. During his presidential campaign, she directed the youth outreach program. The rough campaign and its bitterly disappointing result turned Karenna from electoral politics, and she chose not to pursue public office. After two generations of preeminence, no Gores were left in Tennessee nor willing to run for public office.

Further Reading

Gore, Albert, Sr. *Let the Glory Out: My South and Its Politics.* New York: Viking, 1972.

Longley, Kyle, and Albert Gore Jr. *Senator Albert Gore, Sr.: Tennessee Maverick.* Baton Rouge: Louisiana State University Press, 2004.

Maraniss, David, and Ellen Y. Nakashima. *The Prince of Tennessee: Al Gore Meets His Fate.* New York: Simon & Schuster, 2001.

CHAPTER FIVE

The Kennedy Dynasty

Barbara A. Perry

When Irish immigrant Patrick Kennedy landed in Boston, an impoverished refugee from the devastating potato famine of the 1840s, no one could have predicted that he would sire the most powerful and prolific political dynasty in American history. His son, Patrick Joseph (P.J.) Kennedy, formed the foundation for the family's financial and political fortunes, moving squarely into Boston's middle class as a tavern owner and community bank officer. An unpretentious ward heeler,[1] P.J. served in the Massachusetts legislature, but preferred to wield his influence behind the scenes. His Harvard-educated son, Joseph P. Kennedy, built on his father's savings by serving as president of his dad's bank, shrewdly trading stocks, and becoming a Hollywood producer. By the end of the Roaring Twenties, he was a multimillionaire.

Joseph P. Kennedy Sr.

Besides independent wealth, a key to launching the Kennedy political dynasty was Joe Kennedy's marriage to Rose Fitzgerald, debutante daughter of former congressman and Boston mayor John F. (Honey Fitz) Fitzgerald. Joe and Rose produced nine children, who would form the nucleus of the family's political dynamo, including John, Robert, and Edward Kennedy. That trio would constitute the dynasty's apogee in 1963, with John as president, Robert his attorney general, and Edward in the U.S. Senate. In turn, Joe and Rose's children would foster two additional generations of politicians and public servants.

Married in 1914, Joe and Rose welcomed their first child, Joe Jr., just 10 months after their wedding. His brother John (Jack) Fitzgerald Kennedy, named for his maternal grandfather, arrived barely two years later, followed in close succession by four sisters (Rosemary, Kathleen, Eunice, and Patricia). Brother Robert (Bobby) joined the brood in 1925 and his sister Jean two years later. The last child, Edward (Teddy), born in 1932, became the adored baby of the family.[2]

Joe Sr. started married life as the president of a modest East Boston bank, where he remained until the United States entered World War I in 1917. He then became assistant general manager of the Bethlehem Ship Building Corporation's Fore River plant, overseeing production of naval vessels for the U.S. war effort and making his first contacts with the young navy assistant secretary, Franklin D. Roosevelt.[3]

When Armistice Day ended the "Great War" in November 1918, Kennedy became a Boston stockbroker and began to play the market systematically in the precrash decade, before the federal government intervened to regulate it.[4] Wall Street maneuvering prompted him to move his growing family in 1927 to a Manhattan suburb. Kennedy hoped the relocation would help his family escape Boston's provincialism and set his children on a course to avoid the Boston Brahmins' religious and ethnic bigotry.[5] Maintaining their Bay State roots, however, Joe rented, and then in 1928 bought, a summer home at Hyannis Port that would become the centerpiece of the family's storied Cape Cod compound.

Yet, no sooner had Mrs. Kennedy moved her seven children to the Empire State, than her husband headed west to California, determined to rise from a minor East Coast movie entrepreneur to a Hollywood mogul. Combining two smaller movie businesses into RKO, he would emerge from his years as a film producer a multimillionaire.[6]

With his newfound millions and media experience, which he would later use to launch his family's political careers, Kennedy returned to New York and settled the family in the upscale suburb of Bronxville, about 15 miles north of midtown Manhattan. In a mere dozen years, the Kennedys had moved from middle-class Brookline, Massachusetts, to the opulence of Bronxville, New York. Their fortune multiplied during the Great Depression. Kennedy had pulled his investments out of the stock market prior to the 1929 crash and used the economic downturn to acquire bargains, like the family's Palm Beach, Florida, estate.[7]

Deciding to support Democratic New York governor Franklin D. Roosevelt in his 1932 presidential campaign, Kennedy raised nearly $300,000 (nearly $5 million in 2017) in donations and loans. He contributed $25,000 (more than $400,000 in 2017) and loaned the campaign an additional $50,000 (more than $800,000 in 2017). His funding earned Joe a spot on FDR's transcontinental campaign train. Kennedy attracted supporters from the movie industry, assisted with campaign speeches, and linked FDR's camp to the press corps. When Roosevelt defeated incumbent President Herbert Hoover, Joe sponsored a

Kennedy Political Dynasty Family Tree

1. John Francis "Honey Fitz" Fitzgerald, 1863–1950
    U.S. House of Representatives, 1895–1901
    Mayor of Boston, 1906–1908, 1910–1914
   Married Josephine Hannon
   10 children including Rose Elizabeth

1. Patrick J. Kennedy, 1858–1929
    Massachusetts legislature, 1884–1895
   Married Mary Augusta Hickey
   10 children including Joseph Patrick

2. Joseph Patrick Kennedy Sr., 1888–1969
    U.S. ambassador to United Kingdom, 1938–1940
   Married Rose Elizabeth Fitzgerald
   Nine children: Joseph P. Jr., John Fitzgerald, Rosemary, Kathleen, Eunice, Patricia, Robert, Jean, and Edward

3. John "Jack" Fitzgerald Kennedy, 1917–1963
    U.S. House of Representatives, 1947–1952
    U.S. Senate, 1953–1961
    35th president, 1961–1963
   Married Jacqueline "Jackie" Lee Bouvier
   Four children: Arabella, Caroline Bouvier, John F. Jr., and Patrick Bouvier

4. Caroline Kennedy, 1957–
    U.S. ambassador to Japan, 2013–2017
   Married Edwin Arthur Schossberg
   Three children: Rose, Tatiana Celia, and John Bouvier

3. Eunice Mary Kennedy, 1921–2009
    Founder, Special Olympics
   Married Robert Sargent Shriver Jr., 1915–2011
    Director, Peace Corps, 1961–1966
    Director, federal Office of Economic Opportunity, 1964–1968
    U.S. ambassador to France, 1968–1970
   Five children: Robert Sargent III, Maria Owings, Timothy Perry, Mark Kennedy, and Anthony

(continued)

Kennedy Political Dynasty Family Tree (continued)

4. Robert Sargent "Bobby" Shriver III, 1954–
   Santa Monica, California City Council, 2004–
Married Malissa Feruzzi
Two children

4. Mark Kennedy Shriver, 1964–
   Maryland House of Delegates, 1995–2003
Married Jeanne Eileen Ripp
Three children

3. Robert Francis "Bobby" Kennedy, 1925–1968
   U.S. attorney general, 1961–1963
   U.S. Senate, 1964–1968
Married Ethel Skakel
11 children: Kathleen Harrington, Joseph P. II, Robert F. Jr., David Anthony, Mary Courtney, Michael LeMoyne, Mary Kerry, Christopher George, Matthew Maxwell Taylor, Douglas Harriman, and Rory Elizabeth Katherine

4. Kathleen Kennedy Townsend, 1950–
   Massachusetts lieutenant governor, 1995–2003
Married David Lee Townsend
Four children

4. Joseph P. Kennedy II, 1952–
   U.S. House of Representatives, 1987–1999
Married Sheila Brewster Rauch
Two children: Matthew Rauch and Joseph P. III

5. Joseph P. Kennedy III, 1980–
   U.S. House of Representatives, 2013–

3. Jean Kennedy Smith, 1928–
   U.S. ambassador to Ireland, 1993–1998
Married Stephen Edward Smith Sr.
Two children

(continued)

Kennedy Political Dynasty Family Tree (*continued*)

3. Edward Moore "Ted" Kennedy, 1932–2009
 U.S. Senate, 1962–2009
Married Virginia Joan Bennett, then Victoria Anne Reggie
Three children: Kara Anne, Edward M. Jr., and Patrick J. II

4. Edward M. Kennedy Jr., 1961–
 Connecticut state Senate, 2014–
Married Katherine Anne Gershman
Two children

4. Patrick J. Kennedy II, 1967–
 U.S. House of Representatives, 1995–2009
Married Amy Savell
Two children

---

celebration for the president-elect's family and friends.[8] He hoped that President Roosevelt would offer him a government position. Joe coveted the treasury secretary post, but FDR awarded it to two other successive candidates (Henry Morgenthou Jr. and Frederick Vinson). Kennedy bided his time and was delighted when the president invited Rose and him to stay at the White House in the spring of 1934.[9]

Three months after the Kennedys' White House visit, FDR appointed Joe as chairman of the new Securities and Exchange Commission (SEC). What better person to rein in Wall Street's excesses than the very man who had skillfully maneuvered through them prior to the crash? Joe left Bronxville for Washington, moving to a 125-acre Maryland estate, where he entertained FDR and his brain trust—his closest advisers—as well as the president's secretaries/mistresses.[10]

Meanwhile, Jack, noted for his leadership of student shenanigans but named "most likely to succeed," graduated from Choate prep school in 1935. He hoped to copy Joe Jr.'s experience studying at the London School of Economics before enrolling in college. Rose and Joe Sr., who resigned from the SEC once the commission was under way, accompanied Jack abroad. After settling him in London, Joe and Rose visited Winston Churchill at his country estate. Suffering from chronic undiagnosed ailments, Jack returned home, where he enrolled at Princeton. But ill health again intervened and landed him in a Boston hospital. After two months' hospitalization, and still no definitive diagnosis, Jack left Boston for Arizona's dryer, warmer climate. However, by 1936 both Joe Jr. and

Jack were attending their father's alma mater, Harvard. Every Sunday they lunched with their grandfather Honey Fitz, who regaled them with stories of Boston politics and history.[11]

Joe Sr. spent considerable time, energy, and money working for FDR's 1936 reelection. Shortly after his second inauguration, attended by the Kennedy children, Roosevelt again asked Kennedy to join the administration, this time as head of the new Maritime Commission. Kennedy was now among the highest-ranking Catholics in the administration, yet he coveted a more exalted position. As 1937 drew to a close, FDR finally offered a plum position: the ambassadorship to the Court of St. James's. Kennedy would become the first Irish American to serve as the U.S. representative to Great Britain.[12]

"The Kennedy Family: Nine Children and Nine Million Dollars," *Life* magazine proclaimed in December 1937.[13] "Big, rich, good-looking families always beguiled *Life*'s attention back in 1937 when the magazine was only a year old," explained editor Philip B. Kunhardt Jr.

> The variety of their [the Kennedys'] activities and their sumptuous settings and life-styles were ideal for pictures. In addition, the Kennedy children had a shrewd, outspoken father who wielded enormous power in financial circles, had a glamorous background in Hollywood filmmaking. . . . And there was mother Rose, the lovely daughter of a storied mayor of Boston—stylish, reverent, eloquent in her own cool way—the ideal mother. The four sons seemed dashing and athletic. The five daughters pretty and competitive. The settings were usually Palm Beach or Cape Cod. Politics was on the horizon. How could a fledgling magazine ask for more![14]

At the White House on February 18, 1938, Supreme Court Justice Stanley Reed swore Joe in as ambassador to Great Britain. Having climbed the ladder from famine Irish to lace curtain Irish in narrow-minded Boston, the Kennedys had achieved money, power, and celebrity in cosmopolitan New York. They would soon conquer the international scene in England.[15]

Arriving in London, the family proceeded directly to the embassy. The seven Kennedys in London (Joe Jr. and Jack stayed at Harvard, and two of their sisters remained at American schools) marched arm in arm into the embassy's private garden. A scrum of some 20 photographers snapped away at Britain's newest media sensation. Comparing the family to Canada's celebrated Dionne quintuplets, *Life* magazine covered the Kennedy invasion of Britain. Yet the magazine proclaimed, "There are only five Dionne Quints and the Kennedy kids are nine . . . ." It named Joe and Rose's brood "the most politically ingratiating family since Theodore Roosevelt's."[16] If Joe Kennedy reached the pinnacle of his short political career as U.S. ambassador to Britain, Rose's experience in England created a bridge in her long public life from the young daughter of Boston's mayor to a political matriarch: she had become a celebrated spouse on an international and historic stage. Honing her social skills in courtly prewar London, Rose's experiences would form the core of her early campaign speeches for John F. Kennedy during his first forays into the political arena.[17]

A mere three weeks had passed before Joe and Rose were driven to Windsor Castle for a weekend with King George and Queen Elizabeth. The trip took less than an hour, but it represented a journey back through centuries of British history for the enthralled Kennedys. Forever after, Mrs. Kennedy loved to quote her husband's pithy summary of the royal scene: "Rose, this is a helluva long way from East Boston."[18] In the reception room the Kennedys chatted with Prime Minister Neville Chamberlain, and at dinner Ambassador Kennedy sat with the queen while Rose took her place next to the king.[19]

In late August 1938 Ambassador Kennedy met at 10 Downing Street with Prime Minister Neville Chamberlain to discuss Nazi Germany's aggressive move to annex Czechoslovakia's Sudetenland. Joe's aversion to war began to attract rebukes from President Roosevelt and Secretary of State Cordell Hull. A few days later, Adolf Hitler convened the annual Nazi Party conference in Nuremberg, Germany, featuring especially strident tirades against the Czechs. As the world hurtled toward war, the Kennedys spent time with heads of state and government, members of Parliament, and visited Rome for the installation of Pope Pius XII. The new pope offered young Teddy his First Communion, a rare honor.[20]

On August 24, 1939, Germany and the Soviet Union signed a nonaggression treaty, but Hitler invaded Poland a week later. British Prime Minister Chamberlain and Ambassador Kennedy had earned considerable enmity for their "appeasement" of the Germans, among British and American proponents of stopping the Nazi war machine. Now their best efforts to avoid war had come to nothing. In fact, worse than nothing; their policy of placating Hitler only emboldened him. Rose defended her husband, writing later that he was one of many statesmen who urged a peaceful solution to Hitler's aggression. Joe Kennedy knew that the United States was unprepared for war, and he was understandably reluctant to expose his fortune and two oldest sons to the ravages of war.[21]

Within a month, all of the Kennedys had returned home, save Joe Sr. and Rosemary, who suffered from what was then labeled "retardation" and who was thriving at a convent school in the British countryside. The Kennedys refused to institutionalize their beloved daughter and tried to give her as normal a life as possible, but they dared not disclose her condition publicly in an era of discrimination against such conditions.[22]

Back in the states, the two oldest sons returned to Harvard—Joe Jr. to start law school and Jack to complete his undergraduate degree and write his senior thesis on Britain's failure to prepare for war, based on research he had gathered during his six months in Europe. Using his father's influence and with editing assistance, Jack published his thesis as his first book, *Why England Slept*.[23]

Isolated from his family, and facing professional uncertainty as his differences with Roosevelt over the war became more pronounced, Joe Sr. spent the fall of 1939 in deep melancholia. Some American reporters still touted him as a potential 1940 presidential nominee. Publicly, Joe always claimed no interest, but it's hard to believe he would have turned down a nomination should FDR have not run for a third term.[24] Joe braced for the upcoming Battle of Britain, a deadly air offensive by the Nazis. He had consistently given Britain long odds against Germany, predicting a "dictated peace" in which the Nazis would get the British Navy, "and we will find ourselves in a terrible mess."[25] This defeatism spilled out publicly when an American reporter quoted the ambassador's pessimism in what he thought was an off-the-record interview. Joe's political career was over.[26] Now he would place all his hopes in his number 1 son, Joe Jr.

The eldest of Rose and Joe Kennedy's children, Joe Jr., was their golden child. Handsome, intelligent, responsible, and athletic, he seemed to them destined for greatness. After his father's self-inflicted political wound, the family believed that Joe Jr. would become the first Catholic president of the United States. As a Harvard Law student, young Joe became a delegate to the 1940 Democratic National Convention and demonstrated his independent streak by casting his vote for Postmaster General James Farley, rather than FDR. But World War II intervened, and both Joe Jr. and Jack enlisted in the navy, becoming junior officers. Joe trained as an aviator, Jack as a PT-boat skipper.[27]

When Jack, who always played second fiddle and the clown to Joe's responsible big brother persona, earned military honors for saving his crew in the South Pacific after a Japanese destroyer collided with his boat, Joe volunteered for a dangerous mission to bomb Nazi megaweapon sites in France. Shortly after takeoff from a British landing strip in August 1944, Joe's plane, packed with explosives, blew apart, killing him and his copilot.[28]

Once the initial shock and grief of Joe Jr.'s death subsided, the Kennedy family founded a charitable foundation in his name. At first focused on underprivileged children, it eventually turned its attention to the mental disability that had limited sister Rosemary's life. Joe had misplaced his hope in a new procedure, the lobotomy, which Rosemary underwent in 1941; but the invasive brain surgery went terribly wrong, undoing all of the family's schooling and care for their beloved daughter and sister. Rosemary now required constant monitoring, and the family could no longer avoid institutionalizing her. The Joseph P. Kennedy Jr. Foundation expanded its mission to include research and efforts to prevent the causes of what was then called mental retardation, as well as to educate and inspire through athletics children and adults with intellectual challenges, an effort that launched the Special Olympics.[29]

John F. Kennedy

Former Ambassador Kennedy now shifted his dreams for the family's political success to Jack. Returning from the South Pacific to nurse his back, which was injured in the PT-boat collision, and to recover from malaria, JFK pondered his future. Perhaps he would become a journalist; he covered the United Nations conference in San Francisco for the Hearst newspapers in 1945. But the call of the Fitzgerald-Kennedy incipient dynasty proved seductive, and Jack would rather make news than report on it. By 1946 JFK was running to represent the 11th District of Massachusetts in the U.S. House of Representatives, where he hoped to follow in Grandpa Fitzgerald's footsteps. "I had in politics, to begin with, the great advantage of having a well-known name and that served me in good stead," JFK later commented.[30] With his mother and sisters drawing record crowds to Kennedy tea parties, and his father providing strategic planning, unlimited funds, and public relations resources (including publication of Jack's war record), the young veteran swept to victory in the Democratic primary and won the general election with 73 percent of the vote.[31] The centerpiece of the Kennedy political dynasty was now in place.

Congressman Kennedy found the routine of a freshman representative uninspiring and set his sights on moving up to the Senate as soon as possible. Again, behind the scenes, Joe Kennedy promoted his son's name throughout the Bay State and ensured that funds were available for extra staff in the congressman's Washington and Boston offices. His dad also pressured Democratic congressional leader John McCormack from Massachusetts to appoint Jack to the House Education and Labor Committee, which he used as a springboard to debate policies related to schools and unions. He secured membership on the Veterans' Affairs Committee and its subcommittee on veterans' housing, allowing him to address issues that concerned his fellow vets. Yet the minutiae of public policy bored Jack, and he admitted that his family was more interested "in the mechanics" of the political process than its outcomes.[32]

Congressman Kennedy combined the procapitalism, inherited from his father, with what Professor James MacGregor Burns labeled "bread-and-better" liberalism. Thus, JFK hewed to fiscal conservatism, except when supporting social programs for housing, minimum wage, immigration, and education that benefited his constituents.[33] In foreign affairs he exhibited the Cold Warrior traits typical of his era and supported the containment of communism through the Truman Doctrine, Marshall Plan, and NATO. He criticized his own party's presidents, Roosevelt and Truman, for the loss of China to the Communists, and he spoke out against Communist infiltration of labor unions. Nevertheless, JFK provided a reliable vote for labor's interests against management, evidenced by his opposition to the Taft-Hartley bill in 1947.[34]

On education policy, Kennedy tried to straddle the line between church and state on the question of federal aid to parochial schools. He followed the Supreme Court's 1947 ruling that government funds can support "child benefit" services, such as bus fare for students attending religious schools. Representing a majority Catholic district, he wished to placate constituents, but he knew very well that being too closely tied to his faith could become a political handicap for his future aspirations, as American voters had never before elected a Catholic as president.[35]

During his first congressional term, he made a sentimental journey to Ireland to visit his favorite sister Kathleen (Kick), who had married into British and Anglican nobility in 1944, only to become a war widow three months later. The trip ended abruptly in London when JFK once more fell victim to a mysterious illness, finally diagnosed by a British physician as Addison's disease, an incurable adrenal insufficiency that typically proved fatal by exposing its sufferers to deadly infections. A new treatment developed in 1949, using synthetic cortisone, proved successful in saving Jack's life, though future surgeries on his chronically unstable and painful back brought him near death. Worries over his health were only eclipsed in 1948 when Kathleen perished in a plane crash while flying with her new fiancée to the Riviera. Once more the Kennedy family faced unbearable tragedy.[36]

After winning reelection in both 1948 and 1950, Congressman Kennedy began expanding his portfolio with extensive trips abroad as he looked toward a 1952 Senate run. The first journey included stays in England, France, Spain, Yugoslavia, Turkey, and Italy, where he had a private meeting with Pope Pius XII. His next trip proved more ambitious and included his brother Bobby and sister Pat. The trio flew around the world, visiting Israel, Iran, Pakistan, India, Singapore, Thailand, South Korea, and Indochina, and met with public officials, politicians, ambassadors, reporters, and citizens in each country. In Vietnam Kennedy formed strong impressions of France's attempts to reassert its colonial dominance over a native independence movement led by Communist revolutionary Ho Chi Minh. JFK returned home determined to move up in Congress and tackle international issues that he found more interesting than local politics.[37]

By December 1951, Jack had decided to challenge incumbent Henry Cabot Lodge Jr. for his Massachusetts U.S. Senate seat. Lodge was preoccupied with General Dwight Eisenhower's 1952 presidential campaign, having persuaded the war hero to run as the GOP candidate. The Kennedys mounted a statewide juggernaut campaign in Lodge's absence. "In 1952 I worked a year and a half ahead of the November election, a year and a half before Senator Lodge did," JFK recalled in 1960.[38]

> I believe most aspirants for public office start much too late. When you think of the money that Coca-Cola and Lucky Strike put into advertising day after

day, even though they have well-known brand names, you can realize how difficult it is to become an identifiable political figure. The idea that people can get to know you well enough to support you in two months or three months is wholly wrong. Most of us do not follow politics and politicians. We become interested only around election time. For the politician to make a dent in the consciousness of the great majority of the people is a long and laborious job. . . .[39]

JFK's stunning win over the venerable Lodge, heir to another Massachusetts political dynasty, despite Ike's landslide defeat of Democrat Adlai Stevenson (including in Massachusetts), was by a slim 70,737-vote margin. As in 1946, Joe Kennedy remained offstage, but he played a crucial role by writing checks, drafting 26-year-old Bobby as campaign manager, and promoting journalistic support for Jack.[40] Joe credited Rose for her expanded participation in the family's campaign machine. "[Y]ou would have been very much surprised and pleased to have seen the wonderful television programs that Rose and the [Kennedy] girls put on for Jack and the remarkable speeches Rose made," he wrote to a British friend.[41] But perhaps most persuasive was Lodge's labeling "those damn tea parties" as the reason for his defeat.[42]

Rose played a particularly crucial role in reaching women voters because Jack remained unmarried, even as he approached his midthirties. Although Jack's bachelor status might attract young female votes, in the family-centered culture of the 1950s, he needed a spouse and children to remain a viable political figure. Journalist and Kennedy friend, Charles Bartlett, played matchmaker by introducing Jack to Jacqueline Bouvier, a budding *Washington Times-Herald* columnist and photographer, in 1951; but no romantic sparks flew, so Bartlett's wife invited them both to another dinner party a year later. The newly elected Massachusetts senator asked Bouvier to attend a presidential inaugural ball with him in January 1953. When she left for London that spring to cover Queen Elizabeth's coronation, Kennedy missed her. On her return, he presented Jackie with an engagement ring.[43]

Bouvier's mother wanted no reporters at the wedding, but the groom's father insisted that media cover the nuptials.[44] St. Mary's Catholic Church in Newport, Rhode Island, only held 750 congregants, but Hammersmith Farm, home of Jackie's wealthy stepfather, and site of the reception, was plenty spacious. Joe supervised invitations for 1,400. Another 3,000 spectators surrounded the church to catch a glimpse of America's newest celebrity couple on September 12, 1953.[45] Jacqueline Bouvier Kennedy would become the queen of the political dynasty.

By 1953 Jack's chronic back pain flared so badly that he could barely walk. Following the best medical advice available, he decided to undergo a delicate procedure, in October 1954, to fuse his lumbar and sacroiliac. If the operation failed, Senator Kennedy might be confined to a wheelchair. At the very least, his Addison's made him vulnerable to life-threatening postoperative infections. But he told his father that he would rather die than hobble on crutches and suffer paralyzing pain.[46]

The surgery went badly from the start; an infection set in, nearly killing the comatose patient. Yet Jack rallied, and two months later his physicians released him to be flown to Palm Beach for Christmas. Still barely able to sit, stand, or walk, he spent much of his time confined to bed. His gaping surgical wound, around the steel plate implanted in his back, would simply not heal.[47]

Kennedy's lengthy absence from Capitol Hill allowed him to skirt one of the most divisive conflicts of the era: Wisconsin senator Joseph McCarthy's Communist witch hunts. The Kennedy family had a long relationship with the Catholic senator. Joe Kennedy supported him, JFK sister's Pat dated him, and brother Bobby worked briefly on his staff and chose McCarthy as his firstborn child Kathleen's godfather.[48] But by late 1954 the alcoholic senator's egregious violations of civil rights and liberties prompted the Senate to censure him. Jack remained in Palm Beach on his sickbed and missed one of the most visible political and moral debates of the decade. Democratic stalwarts, like Eleanor Roosevelt, would never forgive him or the Kennedy family for their failure to oppose McCarthy and his odious anti-Communist witch hunt.

By February 1955, so little progress had been made in Jack's condition that he decided to undergo yet another surgical procedure—this time a spinal bone graft and removal of the troublesome metal plate. The third incision on his vertebrae finally healed, providing some relief. Even so, all winter and spring Jack convalesced at Palm Beach, where he began his second book, *Profiles in Courage*, aided by a battery of researchers and writers.[49] It would win the 1957 Pulitzer Prize and burnish Kennedy's résumé for his ultimate campaign to become the nation's first Roman Catholic president.

Jack returned to the Senate in May 1955 and, although still underweight, he was well enough by the summer of 1956 to seek the Democratic vice presidential nomination at the Chicago convention. Kennedy burst on the national political scene with a refreshing charisma. He narrated the convention's film on the Democratic Party's history and delivered a stirring nomination speech for Adlai Stevenson. The *New York Times* captured Kennedy's essence: "Senator Kennedy came before the convention tonight as a photogenic movie star."[50] Joe opposed the gamble, reasoning that if Stevenson lost, Jack's Catholicism would be blamed, barring him from a future presidential run. Joe was relieved when the vice presidential slot went to Tennessee senator Estes Kefauver instead.[51]

Meanwhile, Bobby was making a name for himself as a hard-nosed Senate committee staff lawyer and strategizing with Joe on Jack's steps toward the presidency. Jack moved toward his 1958 Senate reelection campaign and developed plans to run nationally in 1960, hiring pollster Louis Harris to assist

The Kennedy Dynasty

in determining how and where to campaign most effectively.[52] But first Jack had to win reelection to the Senate. The family now turned to the novel technology of television to spread their message. "At Home with the Kennedys," a live 30-minute television program, aired a week prior to the 1958 Senate election. Joining Rose around a cozy living room set were Jackie, Eunice, and Jean. The elder Mrs. Kennedy led a discussion among the women. Jackie observed that Teddy was serving as Jack's campaign manager when he could spare time from his final year at UVA's law school. Rose then introduced and narrated a video featuring Eunice, Bobby, and Pat with their spouses and children. Senator Kennedy joined the midmorning show asking women viewers for their vote. He displayed a firm command of policy details and a ready wit. He thanked his sisters and his mother, particularly for her support of Honey Fitz's and Joe's public service. As a heart-warming conclusion, Jack joined Jackie on the couch and introduced their one-year-old daughter Caroline.[53] Here was a vintage Kennedy performance in a new medium that brought three generations of the famous family into voters' living rooms. Just as Joe and Rose had utilized print and newsreels to presenting their young brood to the voting public, now television would launch Jack and Jackie as political celebrities.[54] Left unstated was JFK's desire to demonstrate overwhelming popularity as he prepared for a bold run at the Democratic presidential nomination two years later—he would be just 42 years old. No Roman Catholic had run for president since Al Smith's 1928 shellacking by Herbert Hoover. Jack's final poll results in 1958 didn't disappoint; he won 73.6 percent of the votes, the largest winning margin in Massachusetts history and the second largest among all 1958 Senate candidates.[55]

JFK's Senate career, from 1953 to 1961, was marked by a number of guideposts that would lead him to the White House. He hired Theodore Sorensen, a brilliant young lawyer from Nebraska, who would become his "intellectual blood bank." A wordsmith of the highest order, Sorensen would produce the soaring themes and phrasing of JFK's speeches. Not a natural orator, Kennedy continued to improve his speaking style until he perfected a compelling, dramatic, yet accessible, technique for reaching audiences. His clipped New England brogue would always mark him as a native Bostonian, but it made him unique and rendered his keen wit even more charming. The product of a Unitarian father and Jewish mother, Sorensen also helped develop Kennedy's public positions on church and state that stressed Jeffersonian separationism.[56]

Sorensen's progressivism, along with that of the professors whom Kennedy would call upon for policy prescriptions, dovetailed with JFK's promises to jumpstart the Massachusetts economy, which was already showing signs of decline due to the post–World War II manufacturing boom in the South. Kennedy proposed bills to expand New England's economy, but Massachusetts viewed one of his positions as a threat to Boston's port. Kennedy decided to support construction of the St. Lawrence Seaway (SLS) that would connect northern Canada with the Great Lakes, through a system of rivers, channels, and locks. Voting for the SLS bill gave him national stature as a lawmaker who was not simply interested in his state's constituencies.[57] As a senator looking toward a future national campaign, Kennedy searched for a midpoint between the northern pro–civil rights Democrats and southern segregationist Democrats as they debated the 1957 Civil Rights Act.[58] His votes on its various provisions reflect a purely pragmatic (some might say opportunistic) mix of conservatism and liberalism.[59]

In foreign affairs Senator Kennedy, who relished his assignment to the Foreign Relations Committee, reasoned that he could take a bolder stand. Applying the lessons he learned from his 1951 visit to Vietnam, he wrote and spoke out against the French colonial war to subdue another independence movement, this time in Algeria, in northern Africa. "The most powerful single force in the world today is neither communism nor capitalism, neither the H-bomb nor the guided missile—it is man's eternal desire to be free and independent," Kennedy observed in the introduction to his 1957 Senate floor speech on the North African country.[60] Distribution of the speech to major newspapers and publication in well-regarded periodicals led to an invitation from *Foreign Affairs* to contribute an article, "A Democrat Looks at Foreign Policy."[61] Kennedy was distinguishing himself from potential adversaries for the 1960 Democratic presidential nomination.

Meanwhile, Kennedy crisscrossed the country, sometimes with Jackie, more often with alter ego Ted Sorensen. The 1960 Democratic presidential nomination contest featured only 16 primaries. JFK decided to focus on New Hampshire, Wisconsin, Indiana, West Virginia, Nebraska, Maryland, and Oregon. He couldn't secure the nomination by winning primaries in these states, but victories in most of them would demonstrate his electability.[62] In addition, he spent several years building organizations of Democratic activists, office holders, and union rank and file across the nation who would support him in those states that selected pledged delegates via conventions, rather than primaries.[63]

Kennedy officially announced his candidacy for president in Washington on January 2, 1960. New Hampshire was first among the primaries, known for rewarding candidates who spent endless hours crisscrossing the Granite State and mingling with the voters. The Kennedy clan fanned out across the state, and Jack received 85 percent of the New Hampshire vote.[64]

Wisconsin was next, where JFK battled regional favorite, Minnesota senator Hubert Humphrey. Except for enclaves of Catholic voters in a few large cities, Kennedy faced Protestant strongholds. A credible showing might weaken the religion argument against his candidacy. Jack won Wisconsin's April 5, 1960, primary, carrying 56 percent of the votes and 6 out of 10 congressional districts. For his part, Humphrey would fight on in the West

Virginia primary in May. Jack scored a major victory over Humphrey in West Virginia, proving that a Catholic could carry an overwhelmingly Protestant state. The win also eliminated one of his key opponents for the nomination—short on money and organization, Humphrey couldn't mount a viable response to the Kennedy family machine. Meanwhile, Senators Adlai Stevenson of Illinois and Lyndon Johnson of Texas waited in the wings, refusing to participate in the primaries but sending signals that they would accept the Democrats' nomination. Jack's campaign now moved on to Maryland and Nebraska, where he would win with 89 and 70 percent of the vote, respectively.[65]

The Kennedy family headed to Los Angeles for the 1960 Democratic Convention. (Jackie, four months pregnant, stayed behind in Hyannis with two-year-old Caroline.[66]) Jack had compiled seven primary victories across the country, yet the nomination wasn't assured. Some delegates supported Stevenson, the unsuccessful nominee in 1952 and 1956, who had the backing of Eleanor Roosevelt, no admirer of Jack or his father. Senator Johnson, who detested the thought of young Jack Kennedy coming out on top, was launching a last-minute effort to rally support. His camp spread word about Jack's Addison's disease, which the Kennedys hadn't publicized and denied when asked about the malady. Jack defeated Johnson on the first ballot, 806 to 409. He chose LBJ for the vice presidential slot to secure Texas's 24 electoral votes and remove Lyndon from his Senate power base as majority leader. Kennedy's acceptance speech coined the term "new frontier" to embody his commitment to "get the country moving again" and "leadership for the '60s."[67]

The Kennedy family, minus its patriarch, fanned out across the country, to campaign for Jack, with Bobby leading the team. By now, the clan included in-laws married to the Kennedy siblings, who also joined in the endeavor. Several turning points marked the 1960 race to the White House between JFK and his former colleague from the House and Senate, incumbent Vice President Richard Nixon. For the first time in presidential history, the candidates agreed to a series of four debates to be carried live on the new medium of television. The Kennedy family's mastery of television's visual impact ensured that Jack looked perfect in black and white, with his tan complexion, perfectly coiffed hair, dazzling smile, professional makeup, blue shirt, and natty dark suit. Unfortunately for Nixon, who had more debating experience, an infection had landed him in the hospital the week before the first debate, and he appeared wan, pale, and perspired. His decision to forgo a camouflage of his perpetual five-o'clock shadow proved costly. Combined with his dark darting eyes, Nixon's face was a portrait in discomfort, confirming his image as an untrustworthy politician. He had portrayed himself as the experienced right-hand man to President Eisenhower, but Kennedy appeared the calm, unflappable, fluent statesman.[68]

Kennedy, however, faced mounting opposition based on his religion. His campaign had hoped to avoid the issue, although they were never averse to campaigning in cities with high Catholic populations. JFK's strategy was to attract as many of his coreligionists as possible, while avoiding the 1928 Al Smith presidential trouncing in which the Democratic presidential candidate lost most of the Bible Belt's southern states. Nevertheless, by late summer, it appeared that the Protestant attacks on him were gaining momentum. The Kennedy campaign decided to take the issue head-on with a speech in Texas to the Greater Houston Ministerial Association. Borrowing from his wordsmith Ted Sorensen's Unitarian lexicon, JFK focused on the Jeffersonian separation of church and state. To a rapt audience of World War II vets, Kennedy recalled that no one asked him his religion when he volunteered for service in the South Pacific, nor did anyone ask his brother his beliefs before he gave his life for his country in the European Theater. The senator assured the ministers that he would be guided by the Constitution, not the Vatican, in public policy decisions. Likewise, he argued that clerics should not dictate to their flocks for whom they should vote. Kennedy concluded with a compelling reference to Texas iconography, the Alamo, observing dramatically that those who gave their lives there for the Lone Star State's independence fought to the death without regard to the religious affiliations of their comrades in arms.[69] Nationwide, JFK would attract about one-third of Protestants to his candidacy.

Ultimately, Kennedy needed every ballot, winning the popular vote tally by only two-tenths of a percent; although, by claiming the electoral votes of Texas and Illinois, he ended with a comfortable margin of victory in the Electoral College (303–219 votes). The outcome was unclear until Nixon conceded in the early hours of the next morning. At the Kennedy compound in Hyannis Port, the family gathered around Joe and Rose's hearth for a historic portrait with the new president-elect.[70]

Robert F. Kennedy

On January 20, 1961, Joseph Kennedy's first piece of the ultimate political dynasty fell into place, as he and Rose watched Jack take the presidential oath of office on a frigid day in the nation's capital. Also on the viewing stand sat the nominee for attorney general, Robert Kennedy. He had hoped to return to private life after seeing Jack ensconced in the Oval Office, but their father insisted that Bobby should assist his older brother by heading the Justice Department. Recognizing the nepotism charge that circulated in the press, JFK quipped to a friend that he would like to announce the nominee by opening the door of his Georgetown home at 2 a.m. and whispering, "It's Bobby." When the new president told an Alfalfa Club dinner that the Kennedys didn't see anything wrong in giving 35-year-old Bobby "a little legal experience before he went out to practice law," the nominee was not amused.[71] Bobby had earned a law degree from the University of Virginia, but other than his stint on Capitol Hill as a Senate committee counsel, he had virtually no experience as an attorney. Now he was to be the top law enforcement officer in the land.

The Kennedy Dynasty

The Kennedy brothers: Attorney General Robert F. Kennedy, Senator Edward M. Kennedy, and President John F. Kennedy outside the Oval Office, August 28, 1963. (National Archives)

The Kennedy administration faced its first crisis fewer than 100 days in office, when the president allowed the Eisenhower-planned invasion of Cuba to move forward. Prior to leaving the presidency, Ike had approved the mission to overthrow Communist Cuban leader Fidel Castro, using CIA-trained Cuban freedom fighters. Who was Kennedy, a lieutenant in World War II's Pacific Theater, to question the decision of the former supreme allied commander and five-star army general? However, Kennedy made several crucial errors in moving forward with the plan. First, he changed the location of the landing to the treacherous waters of the Bay of Pigs, not accounting for the swampland that surrounded it; second, he mistakenly believed that the plan remained secret; and finally, he did not provide sufficient air cover for the invaders. Fiasco is the label most often applied to the failed effort. JFK accepted culpability in a press conference several days after the operation. "I'm the responsible officer of the government," the president observed.[72] His approval rating spiked even higher: 11 points up, from 72 percent, already a very high level of public approbation as he had entered office in January.[73]

The president's father, who spoke by phone nearly every day to his son in the White House, tried to bolster Jack's spirits after the disaster, but the former ambassador told Rose that he was "dying" over JFK's pain from the debacle.[74] Joe suggested that Jack bring Bobby even closer to his decision-making apparatus because the president believed that the CIA and Joint Chiefs of Staff had misled him in approving the Cuban invasion. Jack took his father's advice and included the attorney general in foreign policy decisions.

Cuba again became the focus of world attention in October 1962, after American reconnaissance aircraft discovered the placement of Soviet nuclear missiles aimed at the United States on the Communist island, just 90 miles from Florida. JFK formed the Executive Committee ("Ex Com") of the National Security Council, which included the attorney general. For 13 days and as many sleepless nights, Kennedy huddled with Cabinet secretaries, military leaders, intelligence directors, the vice president, Ted Sorensen, and his brother Bobby to find a peaceful end to the Cuban missile crisis. Aggressive tactics suggested by the hawkish generals included bombing the missile sites, followed by an invasion of Cuba; but the president refused to precipitate a nuclear conflagration. Instead, while Attorney General Kennedy worked back channels with the Kremlin, the president ordered a naval quarantine of Cuba, turning back any ships carrying offensive weapons. The maneuver succeeded, allowing Kennedy to assure his Soviet counterpart, Nikita Khrushchev, that the United States would not invade the island nation and would quietly remove American obsolete missiles, aimed at the USSR, from Turkey.

Jack and Bobby made an effective team in addressing civil rights, too. Initially, they maintained the cautious approach of Jack's Senate career. During his first two years in the White House, the president refused to send any sweeping civil rights proposals to Congress for fear that the southern Democrats would not only defeat them but also stall his other New Frontier policies. Still, JFK did use executive action to address equal opportunity in federal employment and in contracts let by the federal government.[75] For example, Kennedy observed no black members among the Coast Guard Academy cadets marching in the inaugural parade, and one of his first actions as president was to ask the academy to remedy that fact.

Yet the last thing the Kennedy administration wanted was to provoke southern segregationists. Thus, the so-called Freedom Riders, young black and white college student activists, who boarded Greyhound buses in the North and headed south to challenge Jim Crow laws in public transportation, vexed the Kennedys during the first year of Jack's presidency. The Kennedy brothers called on the organizers of the Freedom Riders to rein in their participants in order to avoid violent clashes in the erstwhile Confederacy. But the protesters refused to relent. Eventually, Attorney General Kennedy, to protect his brother from direct involvement, deployed U.S. marshals in an unsuccessful effort to keep the peace. The Kennedy administration relied on incremental law enforcement and policy approaches rather than bold legislative action and refused to follow civil rights leaders' requests to label their cause a moral one.[76]

Efforts to desegregate the flagship universities of Mississippi and Alabama, however, heightened the pressure on the Kennedy administration. When

James Meredith, a slave's grandson, applied to Ole Miss in 1961, the avowedly segregated institution rejected the 28-year-old Air Force veteran. Thus began his odyssey through the federal courts, led by the NAACP's Legal Defense and Educational Fund. The Kennedy Justice Department filed briefs supporting Meredith's suit. After the U.S. Fifth Circuit of Appeals continued to stay orders to desegregate the University of Mississippi, Meredith appealed to the U.S. Supreme Court. Justice Hugo Black ordered Ole Miss to admit the plaintiff for the 1962 fall term, and the U.S. District Court drew up the necessary edict.[77]

Still reluctant to write off the South, both in Congress and for his 1964 reelection, JFK tried to thread the needle of performing his constitutional duty while not provoking violence or Mississippi governor Ross Barnett's wrath. In a phone call with the governor, Kennedy explained his predicament over Meredith: "Listen, I didn't put him in the university, but on the other hand, under the Constitution . . . I have to carry out the orders. . . . I don't want to do it in a way that causes difficulty to you or to anyone else. But I've got to do it. Now, I'd like to get your help in doing that."[78] Barnett's help was anything but forthcoming. His defiant recalcitrance in support of Mississippi's "sovereignty," along with his demagogic rallies for preserving Mississippi's "customs," whipped town and gown into a frenzy. Court-sanctioned attempts to lead Meredith on campus, accompanied by U.S. Justice Department officials, were met by thousands of angry protesters. Finally, President Kennedy had to send in U.S. troops, but not before two bystanders were shot to death and scores of injuries resulted from the vigilantism. As troops began to calm the campus, Meredith finally registered, becoming the first African American to thwart Jim Crow at Ole Miss under a federal court order.[79]

The summer of 1963 gave every indication that it would be as volatile as the previous fall. Now the flashpoint was Birmingham, Alabama, where Dr. Martin Luther King Jr. had decided to bring his civil disobedience campaign to bear on the city's entrenched segregationist power structure. As black civil rights advocates took to the streets, Bull Connor, the city's commissioner of public safety, turned police dogs and water hoses on the peaceful protesters, many of whom were young students. The vicious attacks on nonviolent African Americans simply exercising their First Amendment right to assemble flashed around the world. President Kennedy was personally horrified by Connor's response, but he also knew that such images damaged the United States' reputation abroad.[80] How could he convince Third World countries, many of which had black and brown populations, to side with the "free world" in the Cold War when the United States clearly denied the benefits of full citizenship to American Negroes?

Once again a university campus became a battlefield for the clash between state-sponsored segregation and the federal Constitution's requirement of equal protection of the laws in state institutions. Vivian Malone and James

Hood, two unsuccessful black applicants, received in the summer of 1963 a U.S. District Court ruling ordering the University of Alabama to admit them. This time the recalcitrant segregationist governor was George Wallace. Robert Kennedy's Justice Department took every measure to avoid the violence that had engulfed Ole Miss the previous year. The DOJ won a federal court injunction against Wallace's effort to block Malone and Hood from enrolling. Not wanting to provoke the violent protests produced in Mississippi, for fear the Kennedys would imprison him, Wallace chose the symbolic act of standing in the schoolhouse entrance. President Kennedy, rather than mustering regular army troops, as he had in Mississippi, federalized the Alabama National Guard and threatened to send them to the Tuscaloosa campus to enforce the federal order. Wallace staged one more solo protest before yielding to Malone and Hood, accompanied by Assistant Attorney General Nicholas Katzenbach. With that, the U.S. government rolled over the Crimson Tide, and the University of Alabama became the nation's last racially segregated state university.[81]

After two and a half years of self-imposed political incrementalism, JFK determined that he had to take a moral stand on civil rights. On June 11, 1963, the president decided to deliver a televised speech, so hastily prepared by Ted Sorensen that it lacked a conclusion as the broadcast began. Its most memorable declaration echoes into the 21st century: "We are confronted with primarily a moral issue. It is as old as the scriptures and it is as clear as the American Constitution."[82] In his extemporaneous coda, Kennedy cited the famous dictum from U.S. Supreme Court Justice John Marshall Harlan, whose dissent in *Plessy v. Ferguson*, the 1896 ruling upholding Louisiana's racial segregation of rail cars, declared that the Constitution was "colorblind."[83]

Abandoning his passivity, by which he had tried to mollify the southern caucus in Congress, the president now announced that he would propose legislation to ban segregation in hotels, restaurants, theaters, stores, and other private businesses. Because they were not state institutions, the Fourteenth Amendment's Equal Protection Clause did not apply; but the Kennedy administration argued that Congress should pass this new civil rights law under its authority to regulate interstate commerce, in which such businesses engaged.[84]

Despite Kennedy's new sense of urgency, he was too late to stem the tide of protests for civil rights. On August 28, 1963, some 200,000 people (black and white) converged on the nation's capital for the March on Washington for Jobs and Freedom, culminating in Dr. Martin Luther King's historic "I Have a Dream" speech: a clarion call for color blindness. Fearing violence, the Kennedy administration amassed unprecedented law enforcement and military presence in and around Washington. Relieved that no violent outbreaks occurred, and genuinely impressed with King's oratory, JFK welcomed the civil rights leader and his compatriots to the Oval Office for an exchange of pleasantries.[85]

After JFK's first year in the White House, one Kennedy was no longer available to provide advice to the president. Joe had suffered a massive stroke in December 1961, and, until the end of his life eight years later, could not speak coherently.[86] But before his disability, the Kennedy patriarch had made one more crucial decision for the dynasty, encouraging youngest son Teddy to run for Jack's Senate seat in a special 1962 Massachusetts election.

Edward M. Kennedy

Like Bobby, Teddy possessed Harvard undergraduate and University of Virginia Law School degrees. After learning Massachusetts politics from his Grandpa Fitzgerald on weekly childhood visits with the Irish pol, Teddy readied himself for his eventual mastery of Bay State politics by serving as Jack's campaign chairman for his 1958 Senate reelection. In that role he could learn from the seasoned veterans of his brother's campaigns. Just after Jack's successful 1958 campaign, Teddy married Joan Bennett, whom he had met at his sisters' alma mater, Manhattanville College.[87]

Fresh from law school, Teddy plunged into presidential politics when Jack asked him to campaign in the western United States during his 1960 campaign for the White House. With Honey Fitz's flair for grassroots politicking and a natural exuberance, the candidate's kid brother was an enthusiastic stand-in for Jack. After serving as an assistant prosecutor in Boston, Teddy tossed his hat into the ring for the 1962 Senate race. Having one brother in the White House and another in the Cabinet proved both a blessing and a curse. Teddy naturally benefited from the family's varied political experience, unlimited resources, and knowledgeable advisers. Yet opponents accused him of playing off the Kennedy name. Nevertheless, Teddy won the nomination and went on to defeat another scion of Massachusetts politics, Republican George Cabot Lodge II, whose father had lost the same seat to John Kennedy 10 years earlier.[88]

Only a few weeks beyond the constitutionally mandated age of 30 for assuming a Senate seat, Edward Kennedy happily accepted appointments to the immigration and constitutional rights subcommittees of the Judiciary Committee. Performing his legislative homework each night, he also made sure to attend meetings for his other assignment on the Labor and Public Welfare Committee. As a junior senator, Teddy was presiding over the chamber during a routine debate, on November 22, 1963, when an aide dashed in to tell him that the president had been shot while riding in a Dallas motorcade.[89] The attorney general had been lunching at home with colleagues when FBI Director J. Edgar Hoover phoned to tell him the shocking news. Not long after the first call, Bobby received word that the president was dead.[90] The attorney general fell into a deep depression, unable to comprehend how his brother had been taken in the prime of life, with so much yet to accomplish. A few months later he resigned from the Cabinet, finding it impossible to serve the new chief executive, Lyndon Johnson, whom he detested.[91]

The next November, Teddy ran in the regularly scheduled 1964 Senate election. Having suffered a broken back in a private plane crash on the way to the Massachusetts Democratic Party convention that past summer, he had to campaign from his hospital bed through surrogates, namely his wife and mother. He returned to the Senate in January 1965, just in time to welcome the new junior senator from New York, Robert F. Kennedy.[92] RFK had handily defeated incumbent republican Kenneth Keating, overcoming charges of "carpetbagging" because of the Kennedy family's long ties to Massachusetts. Bobby's mother, Rose, campaigned extensively for her son and emphasized that the family had settled in New York not long after his birth.

The two Kennedy brothers now joined forces in the Senate on issues of health care, jobs, housing, education, and poverty. In 1967 Bobby made a fact-finding tour of the Mississippi Delta, where circumstances stunned him as he saw children starving in substandard housing. He returned to Washington determined to find federal solutions for Third World problems in his own country.[93] He also learned about César Chávez's association of migrant farm workers and their movement to earn a living wage and improve employment conditions.[94] Though he despised President Johnson, Robert Kennedy joined forces with him to promote gun-control legislation. Bobby and Teddy looked on approvingly as LBJ signed comprehensive immigration reform in 1965, on New York's Liberty Island.[95] The junior senator from New York also traveled abroad to continue the work of his fallen brother in spreading democracy. Bobby's 1966 trip to South Africa made headlines for his bold and eloquent declarations against racial apartheid. Closer to home, RFK assisted poverty-stricken African Americans with redevelopment programs in Brooklyn's Bedford-Stuyvesant neighborhood.[96]

By 1968 Bobby Kennedy's passionate crusade to fight poverty and his growing opposition to the Vietnam War, as well as LBJ's decision not to run, prompted RFK's entrance into the race for the Democratic presidential nomination. He swept the Indiana and Nebraska primaries before becoming the first Kennedy to experience an electoral defeat, in the Oregon contest, won by Senator Eugene McCarthy of Minnesota. But after declaring victory in early June's California primary, Bobby fell victim to assassination. "It seemed impossible that the same kind of disaster could befall our family twice in five years," the senator's bereft mother thought.[97] "If I had read it in fiction, I would have said it was incredible."[98]

Equally devastated was the last surviving son of Joe and Rose Kennedy. Bobby's assassination piled new responsibilities on 36-year-old Edward Kennedy. He became a surrogate father to his older brothers' combined 13 children, in addition to watching over his own 3—Kara, Teddy Jr., and Patrick. An assassination nightmare haunted him,[99] and he turned to alcohol for solace.[100]

The Kennedy Dynasty

In July 1969, Teddy retreated to Martha's Vineyard for the annual Edgartown sailing regatta and a nostalgic party for several young women who had labored in Bobby's ill-fated 1968 campaign. "Chappaquiddick," the one-word code for Senator Kennedy's personal and political fall from grace in the wake of Mary Jo Kopechne's death, which he caused in a late-night car crash into an inlet on the New England island, would haunt him for the rest of his life. Despite pleading guilty to leaving the scene of an accident involving a personal injury, he clung to his Senate seat, after Massachusetts voters responded 10 to 1 in favor of his staying in office. Tragedy continued to befall his family, when in 1973, Teddy Jr. underwent surgery to remove his cancerous right leg and endured two years of debilitating, experimental chemotherapy. Senator Kennedy stayed by the boy's side throughout the ordeal, and Teddy Jr. survived. For his father, the experience prompted the public policy battle of his life to expand health coverage for all Americans.[101]

By 1980 Senator Kennedy bowed to pressure from the liberal wing of the Democratic Party to challenge incumbent President Jimmy Carter for the party's nomination. Teddy pursued his presidential candidacy all the way to the convention, but won only a third of the delegates. Yet he dominated the convention with his eloquent concession speech, concluding to thunderous applause, "For me, a few hours ago, this campaign came to an end. For all those whose cares have been our concerns, the work goes on, the cause endures, the hope still lives, and the dream shall never die."[102]

Senator Kennedy's marriage to Joan ended in divorce two years later. Aware of his personal shortcomings, in 1991 Kennedy delivered a public lecture at Harvard, accepting responsibility for his shortcomings. In the audience as Teddy's special guest was Victoria Reggie, a successful Washington attorney, who one year later would become the senator's wife. In 1994, Teddy defeated Mitt Romney for his sixth Senate term. By the dawn of the 21st century, Senator Kennedy had produced an admirable legislative record: expansion of civil rights, lowering the voting age to 18, abolition of poll taxes, fighting for universal health care, ending the draft, support for peace initiatives throughout the world, expansion of education opportunities, establishment of public service projects, and leading the charge against conservative judicial appointees. He also assisted his sister Jean Kennedy Smith, named U.S. ambassador to Ireland by President Bill Clinton, in facilitating the 1998 Good Friday Irish peace accords.[103]

No wonder Adam Clymer of the *New York Times* deemed Edward Kennedy "the leading senator of his time" and "one of the greats in history, wise in the workings of this singular institution, especially its demand to be more than partisan to accomplish much." In 2008 Teddy anointed his young Senate colleague, Barack Obama—junior senator from Illinois—as the rightful heir to Jack's and Bobby's legacies. From the chamber he loved, Kennedy labored over President Obama's domestic centerpiece, the Patient Protection and Affordable

Care Act, until brain cancer overtook the 77-year-old senator from Massachusetts on August 25, 2009. Edward was laid to rest near his brothers, Jack and Bobby, at Arlington National Cemetery, overlooking the nation's capital, where the trio had experienced the apogee of the Kennedy dynasty nearly a half-century earlier.[104]

Passing the Torch to New Generations

Rose and Joe Kennedy's offspring produced 29 grandchildren and scores of great-grandchildren, many of whom have gone into politics or other public service. President Kennedy's daughter Caroline served as the U.S. ambassador to Japan during the Obama administration. Bobby's eldest child, Kathleen, was the lieutenant governor of Maryland, and her brother Joseph P. Kennedy II won six terms in the U.S. House of Representatives, where his son, Joe Kennedy III, is now a congressman from Massachusetts's 4th district. Robert F. Kennedy Jr. is an environmental activist, and his brother Christopher ran for the Democratic nomination for Illinois governor in 2017. Teddy's eldest son, and namesake, serves in the Connecticut state legislature, and brother Patrick had eight terms in the U.S. House of Representatives, where he worked to pass legislation for aiding Americans with mental illness and substance addiction.[105] Eunice Kennedy Shriver's children have followed in her footsteps by directing the Special Olympics and advocating for children and adults with intellectual challenges, and Robert Shriver III served on the city council in Santa Monica, California. Brother Mark Shriver was a Maryland state legislator; sister Maria Shriver forged a successful broadcasting career and became California's first lady in 2003 when husband Arnold Schwarzenegger was elected governor. (They separated in 2011.)

Eunice's husband, R. Sargent Shriver Jr., was the most politically prominent of the Kennedy in-laws. After directing the family's main investment property, Chicago's Merchandise Mart, he worked in the 1960 presidential campaign for his brother-in-law Jack Kennedy, who appointed him the founding director of the Peace Corps. Under Lyndon Johnson's presidency, Sargent Shriver headed the Office of Economic Opportunity. LBJ appointed him U.S. ambassador to France in 1968. Shriver ran unsuccessfully as the Democratic vice presidential nominee on the 1972 George McGovern ticket.

A month before his assassination, President Kennedy teased his brother Teddy, the junior senator from Massachusetts, at a fund-raising dinner for the Democratic Party in Boston: "Teddy has been down in Washington, and he came to see me the other day, and he said he was really tired of being referred to as the younger brother of the president, and being another Kennedy, . . . and that he was going to break loose and change his name. He was going out on his own. Instead of being Teddy Kennedy now, he is changing his name

The Kennedy Dynasty

to Teddy Roosevelt." The quip brought peals of laughter from the partisan audience. The president speculated that his last campaign, the 1964 reelection race, was approaching, but that "Teddy is around and, therefore, these dinners can go on indefinitely."[106] JFK wouldn't live to run again, but his brothers, sisters, and their progeny would carry on the name and public service of one of America's most powerful dynasties, which would define a political and cultural era still known as Camelot.

Notes

1. A ward is a voting district within an urban area. Ward heelers assisted political machines in turning out the vote and offering assistance to immigrant populations, in return for electoral support.

2. For a complete family tree, see Robert Sullivan, ed., *The Kennedys: End of a Dynasty* (New York: LIFE Books, 2009), 8–9.

3. Doris Kearns Goodwin, *The Fitzgeralds and the Kennedys: An American Saga* (New York: St. Martin's Press, 1991), 369–371.

4. Ibid.

5. Robert Dallek, *An Unfinished Life: John F. Kennedy, 1917–1963* (Boston: Little, Brown, 2003), 29. JFK's Grandfather Fitzgerald recalled "No Irish Need Apply" signs in Boston businesses, demonstrating the rampant discrimination against immigrants who had fled by the thousands from Ireland during the Great Famine of the 1840s. Rose Kennedy described the complete segregation of Irish Catholics and Protestant Yankees that Boston society imposed well into her young adulthood. Barbara A. Perry, *Rose Kennedy: The Life and Times of a Political Matriarch* (Norton, 2013), 31.

6. Edward M. Kennedy, *True Compass: A Memoir* (New York: Twelve, 2009), 37; David Nasaw, *The Patriarch: The Remarkable Life and Turbulent Times of Joseph P. Kennedy* (New York: Penguin Press, 2012).

7. Perry, *Rose Kennedy*, 81–82.

8. Amanda Smith, ed., *Hostage to Fortune: The Letters of Joseph P. Kennedy* (New York: Penguin Books, 2001), 66.

9. Perry, *Rose Kennedy*, 85–86.

10. Ibid., 86–87

11. Ibid., 87–92.

12. Ibid., 93–94.

13. "Life on the American News Front: The Kennedy Family: Nine Children and $9,000,000," *Life*, Dec. 20, 1937, pp. 18–19.

14. Philip B. Kunhardt Jr., *Life in Camelot: The Kennedy Years* (Boston: Little, Brown, 1988), 5.

15. Ibid., 96–98.

16. Ibid., 99; Will Swift, *The Kennedys amidst the Gathering Storm: A Thousand Days in London, 1938–1940* (New York: Smithsonian Books, 2008), 35.

17. Perry, *Rose Kennedy*, 100.

18. Rose Fitzgerald Kennedy, *Times to Remember* (New York: Doubleday, 1974), 221.

19. Perry, *Rose Kennedy*, 102.

20. Ibid., 111–113, 134–135.

21. Ibid., 144–146.

22. Ibid., 147, 149–150.

23. John F. Kennedy, *Why England Slept* (New York: Wilfred Funk, 1940).

24. Perry, *Rose Kennedy*, 151.

25. Joseph Kennedy to Rose Kennedy, May 20, 1940, in Smith, *Hostage to Fortune*, 432–433.

26. Perry, *Rose Kennedy*, 158.

27. For a full-length biography of Joe Jr., see Hank Searls, *The Lost Prince: Young Joe, the Forgotten Kennedy* (New York: NAL Book, World Publishing, 1969).

28. Perry, Rose *Kennedy*, 180–181.

29. Ibid., 164–65, 184; Edward Shorter, *The Kennedy Family and the Story of Mental Retardation* (Philadelphia: Temple University Press, 2000).

30. "John F. Kennedy on Politics and Public Service," White House Tapes, Presidential Recordings Program, Miller Center, University of Virginia, http://archive.millercenter.org/presidentialrecordings/jfk-db-39.

31. Dallek, *An Unfinished Life*, 133.

32. Ibid., Chap. 5; "John F. Kennedy on Politics and Public Service."

33. James N. Giglio, *The Presidency of John F. Kennedy* (Lawrence: University Press of Kansas, 1991), 8.

34. Dallek, *An Unfinished Life*, 145–146.

35. Ibid., 146–147.

36. Michael O'Brien, *Rethinking Kennedy: An Interpretive Biography* (Chicago: Ivan R. Dee, 2009), 63–66.

37. Ibid., 67–69.

38. "John F. Kennedy on Politics and Public Service."

39. Ibid.

40. Dallek, *An Unfinished Life*, 174–175, 171–172.

41. Joseph P. Kennedy to Sir James Calder, Dec. 31, 1952, in Smith, *Hostage to Fortune*, 661.

42. Gloria Negri, "Pauline Fitzgerald: The Force behind JFK Tea Parties." *Boston Globe*, Feb. 18, 2008, http://archive.boston.com/bostonglobe/obituaries/articles/2008/02/18/pauline_fitzgerald_the_force_behind_famed_jfk_tea_parties.

43. Barbara A. Perry, *Jacqueline Kennedy: First Lady of the New Frontier* (Lawrence: University Press of Kansas, 2004), 32–36.

44. Rose Kennedy, interview by Robert Coughlan, Jan. 19, 1972, Box 10, Rose Fitzgerald Kennedy Papers, John F. Kennedy Library.

45. Perry, *Jacqueline Kennedy*, 37.

46. Dallek, *An Unfinished Life*, 195–196.

47. Perry, *Jacqueline Kennedy*, 44–45.

48. O'Brien, *Rethinking Kennedy*, 72–73.

49. Perry, *Jacqueline Kennedy*, 44–45.

50. Ibid., 47.
51. Rose Kennedy, interview by Coughlan, Jan. 21, 1972.
52. Thomas Oliphant and Curtis Wilkie, *The Road to Camelot: Inside JFK's Five-Year Campaign* (New York: Simon & Schuster, 2017), 131.
53. "At Home with the Kennedys," Oct. 28, 1958, IFP 156, John F. Kennedy Library.
54. Perry, *Rose Kennedy*, 229.
55. Dallek, *An Unfinished Life*, 225.
56. See Barbara A. Perry, "Catholics and the Supreme Court: From the 'Catholic Seat' to the New Majority," in *Catholics and Politics: The Dynamic Tension between Faith and Power*, Mark Rozell et al., eds. (Washington, DC: Georgetown University Press, 2008).
57. Dallek, *An Unfinished Life*, 183.
58. Nick Bryant, *The Bystander: John F. Kennedy and the Struggle for Black Equality* (New York: Basic Books, 2006), 66.
59. Giglio, *The Presidency of John F. Kennedy*, 13.
60. Oliphant and Wilkie, *The Road to Camelot*, 95.
61. John F. Kennedy, "A Democrat Looks at Foreign Policy," *Foreign Affairs*, Oct. 1957, https://www.foreignaffairs.com/articles/united-states/1957-10-01/democrat-looks-foreign-policy.
62. Perry, *Jacqueline Kennedy*, 56.
63. See Oliphant and Wilkie, *The Road to Camelot*, and Helen O'Donnell, with Kenneth O'Donnell Sr., *The Irish Brotherhood: John F. Kennedy, His Inner Circle, and the Improbable Rise to the Presidency* (Berkeley, CA: Counterpoint, 2015).
64. Perry, *Rose Kennedy*, 232.
65. Ibid., 232–237.
66. Ibid., 237–228.
67. Ibid., 239–240.
68. Ibid., 240–243.
69. Theodore C. Sorensen, ed., *"Let the Word Go Forth": The Speeches, Statements, and Writings of John F. Kennedy, 1947–1963* (New York: Delacorte Press, 1988), 130–136.
70. Perry, *Rose Kennedy*, 244.
71. Arthur M. Schlesinger Jr., *Robert Kennedy and His Times* (New York: Ballantine Books, 1978), 246–255.
72. Harold W. Chase and Allen H. Lerman, eds., *Kennedy and the Press: The News Conferences* (New York: Thomas Y. Crowell, 1965), 70.
73. Gallup, "Presidential Approval Ratings—Gallup Historical Statistics and Trends," http://www.gallup.com/poll/116677/presidential-approval-ratings-gallup-historical-statistics-trends.aspx; Jeffrey M. Jones, Gallup, "Obama's Approval Ratings in Historical Context," Jan. 26, 2009, http://www.gallup.com/poll/113968/obama-initial-approval-ratings-historical-context.aspx.
74. Perry, *Rose Kennedy*, 252.
75. For JFK's record on civil rights, see Barbara A. Perry, "John F. Kennedy," in *The Presidents and the Constitution*, Ken Gormley, ed. (New York: New York

University Press, 2016). Barbara A. Perry, *The Michigan Affirmative Action Cases* (Lawrence: University Press of Kansas, 2007), 6.

76. Dallek, *An Unfinished Life*, 283–88; Schlesinger, *Robert Kennedy*, 317.

77. Bryant, *The Bystander*, 331–33; Jonathan Rosenberg and Zachary Karabell, eds., *Kennedy, Johnson, and the Quest for Justice: The Civil Rights Tapes* (New York: Norton), 32–33.

78. Timothy Naftali and Philip Zelikow, *The Presidential Recordings, John F. Kennedy: The Great Crises*, Vol. 2 (New York: Norton, 2001), 233.

79. Bryant, *The Bystander*, 332–350.

80. Perry, *The Michigan Affirmative Action Cases*, 9.

81. Bryant, *The Bystander*, 417–420.

82. Ibid., 422–423.

83. Ibid. and *Plessy v. Ferguson*, 163 U.S. 537.

84. Perry, *The Michigan Affirmative Action Cases*, 10–13.

85. Ibid., 11–12.

86. Perry, *Rose Kennedy*, 260–261.

87. Barbara A. Perry and Robert A. Martin Jr., *Edward M. Kennedy Oral History Project* (Charlottesville, VA: Miller Center Foundation and Edward M. Kennedy Institute for the United States Senate, 2015), 9–10.

88. Edward Kennedy, *True Compass*, 184–186.

89. Perry and Martin, *Edward M. Kennedy Oral History Project*, 10.

90. Schlesinger, *Robert Kennedy*, 655.

91. Edward Kennedy, *True Compass*, 210, 226.

92. Perry and Martin, *Edward Kennedy Oral History Project*, 10.

93. Larry Tye, *Bobby Kennedy: The Making of a Liberal Icon* (New York: Random House, 2016), 348–353.

94. Ibid., 358–360.

95. Perry and Martin, *Edward M. Kennedy Oral History Project*, 28.

96. Tye, *Bobby Kennedy*, 353–358.

97. Rose Kennedy, *Times to Remember*, 475.

98. Rose Kennedy, "Diaries 1968," Box 4, Rose Fitzgerald Kennedy Papers, John F. Kennedy Library.

99. Perry and Martin, *Edward M. Kennedy Oral History Project*, 10.

100. Edward Kennedy, *True Compass*, 184.

101. Perry and Martin, *Edward M. Kennedy Oral History Project*, 10.

102. Ibid.

103. Ibid., 10, 53–71.

104. Ibid., 10.

105. See Patrick J. Kennedy and Stephen Fried, *A Common Struggle: A Personal Journey through the Past and Future of Mental Illness and Addiction* (New York: Blue Rider Press, 2015).

106. John F. Kennedy, "Remarks in Boston at the 'New England's Salute to the President' Dinner," Oct. 19, 1963. Online by Gerhard Peters and John T. Woolley, *The American Presidency Project*, http://www.presidency.ucsb.edu/ws/?pid=9484.

Further Reading

Dallek, Robert. *An Unfinished Life, John F. Kennedy, 1917–1963.* Boston: Little, Brown, 2003.

Kennedy, Edward M. *True Compass: A Memoir.* New York: Twelve, 2009.

Perry, Barbara A. *Rose Kennedy: The Life and Times of a Political Matriarch.* New York: Norton, 2013.

Tye, Larry. *Bobby Kennedy: The Making of a Liberal Icon.* New York: Random House, 2016.

CHAPTER SIX

The Paul Dynasty

Joel F. Turner and Scott Lasley

The Paul family political dynasty is notable largely due to its unorthodox development. It is perhaps more accurate to view the rise of the Paul family as part dynasty and part movement, with the Pauls capitalizing by operating as political entrepreneurs. The major players in this family dynasty, patriarch Ron and son Rand, respectively secured House and Senate seats and launched presidential campaigns, while largely working outside of the traditional political party structure. Both were able to successfully utilize national strategies to support their campaigns, an approach that flies in the face of the conventional "all politics is local" wisdom. Additionally, the Paul family has turned their devotion to this movement, and the devotion of their supporters, into a cottage industry as Ron and, to some extent Rand, have created a variety of organizations to further their political cause.

The Patriarch

Ron Paul's political career emerged from his early work as a physician. After graduating from Duke University Medical School and completing his residency, he worked as a flight surgeon in the Air Force and the Air National Guard. Upon leaving the military, Paul entered private practice in obstetrics and gynecology in Texas. This is an important era in Paul's political development because during this time he became interested in economic policy, particularly the work of libertarian leaning economists such as Hayek and Rand.[1] Specifically, he developed an affinity for the gold standard. When the United States ultimately decided to end its association with the gold standard, Paul decided to enter politics.[2]

Paul's first foray was unsuccessful, as he was defeated by Democrat Robert Casey in Texas's 22nd Congressional District in 1974. Following Casey's appointment to the Federal Maritime Commission, Paul won a special election in April 1976, but narrowly lost that November to Robert Gammage. Paul defeated Gammage for the seat in 1978, and he was reelected in 1980 and 1982. According to Gammage, Paul's occupation served him well in the district, as he quipped that Paul was popular because he and his partner delivered all the babies in Brazoria County.[3]

During Paul's first term in the House, he would form the Foundation of Rational Economics and Education (FREE), the first of several successful nonprofit think-tank operations that have helped characterize his political career. Ron used FREE to help promote himself as well as his beliefs on noninterventionism and free markets. Paul resigned from the House of Representatives in 1984 to run for the U.S. Senate, where he lost in the Republican primary to Phil Gramm. During that same year, he was appointed as leader of another group that allowed him to spread his political message, Citizens for a Sound Economy (CSE), an organization funded by the Koch brothers with the mission of extolling the virtues of limited government. Much like FREE, CSE continues to have political influence today, eventually splitting into two groups (FreedomWorks and Americans for Prosperity), which became leaders in the Tea Party movement.

Following his 1984 loss to Gramm, Ron turned his attention to presidential politics, competing in the 1988 presidential election as a libertarian. Paul finished third in the popular vote, and despite the long odds saw out the election to the end because it presented him with an opportunity to promote his libertarian ideals to the country.[4] After endorsing, and working for, Pat Buchanan in the 1992 election, Paul attempted a return to the House of Representatives, winning the seat for Texas's 14th Congressional District in 1996, a seat that he held until he retired from the House to run for president in 2012.

The unique niche that he carved out for himself within the Republican Party helped Ron build a passionate national following. His ardent followers would show up at town hall meetings across the country pressing members of Congress on issues that were important to them. He used this broad base of national support to launch another presidential bid. The national pinnacle of his political career occurred during the presidential election of 2008. Despite being largely ignored by the traditional news media early on, Paul was able to attract a loyal following of grassroots supporters mostly via social media platforms. Following an impressive debate performance, interest in him generally, and his devoted following specifically, increased. Paul was able to capitalize on this financially, generating huge fund-raising dollars heading into the Iowa Caucuses. However, despite this increased popularity and fund-raising success, Paul was unable to translate this into an electoral victory. Paul also ruffled feathers among Republicans by refusing to endorse the

Paul Political Dynasty Family Tree

1. Ron Paul, 1935–
   U.S. Congress, 1976–1977, 1979–1987, 1997–2013
   Presidential candidate, 1988, 2008, 2012
   Married Carolyn Wells
   Five children including Rand and Lori

2. Rand Paul, 1963–
   U.S. Senate, 2011–
   Presidential candidate, 2016
   Married Kelley Ashby
   Three children

2. Lori Rand Pyeatt, 1961–
   Vice president and treasurer of Foundation of Rational Economics and Education (FREE)
   Married Tom Pyeatt
   Five children including Valori

3. Valori Pyeatt, 1985–

3. Married Jesse Benton, 1977–
   Campaign manager for Rand Paul, 2010
   Campaign manager for Mitch McConnell, 2014
   Trump "Great America" Super PAC
   One child

Republican nominee John McCain, while expressing support for several third-party candidates.

Ultimately, he was able to gain more political traction because of this showing, with his followers getting more involved than ever before in party politics at the state and local levels, and by him translating these newfound supporters and popularity into the Campaign for Liberty.[5] Campaign for Liberty was established as a 501(c)(4) organization in June 2008. According to Ron, the purpose of this organization was to continue to advance the principles he advocated during the 2008 presidential primary that caught on among his most fervent followers. Most notably, this group is a strong advocate of auditing the Federal Reserve, which is consistent with Ron's longstanding libertarian approach toward monetary policy. While the Republican National

Convention was meeting in Saint Paul, Ron Paul and his Campaign for Liberty held their own event across the river in Minneapolis.[6] The Rally for the Republic sold out and brought Ron Paul disciples from across the country together.

Paul ran for president again in 2012. Despite reasonably strong showings in Iowa and New Hampshire, his candidacy failed to generate the momentum of his 2008 effort, and he dropped out in May of that year, once again ultimately refusing to endorse the eventual Republican nominee, Mitt Romney. Ron Paul supporters from around the country again ensured that the movement would not exit quietly. His supporters were able to take control of several state Republican parties, which helped complicate Romney's presidential hopes. In Nevada, the Republican National Committee established a shadow organization to bypass the state Republican Party when setting up their get-out-the-voter operation for the presidential election. Again, Ron Paul held his own rally during the week of the Republican National Convention drawing 10,000 supporters to the University of South Florida Sun Dome.[7]

Dropping out of this campaign, combined with his retirement from the House of Representatives, ended his career as an elected official. However, it did not end his political involvement, as it led to the creation of this most recent political venture, the creation of the Ron Paul Institute for Peace and Prosperity. This institute, a project of his larger FREE venture, advocates a noninterventionist foreign policy and the protection of civil liberties, two positions that again are largely in line with his libertarian leanings.[8] Ron Paul also continues to speak out, both in paid speeches across the country and in radio and television appearances.

The Son

Rand Paul followed a similar-physician-turned-politician-track to his father. After graduating from Duke University School of Medicine, he settled in Bowling Green, Kentucky, where he was a practicing ophthalmologist. Perhaps following family tradition, Rand's entry into Kentucky politics was a bit unconventional. Generally, he rejected overtures to become active in more formal state and local party organizations. Just as his Dad had done previously, Rand carved out his own political niche by emerging as an antitax crusader when he founded Kentucky Taxpayers United. In reality, Kentucky Taxpayers United is more accurately described as a personal vehicle for Rand to advocate his small government, antitax positions rather than an organization.[9] Rand also remained active in his father's political career during this time and managed his 1996 congressional campaign. Although he frequently spoke on behalf of Ron and went door to door for him in the 2008 presidential election, Rand maintained a relatively low profile until a series of national and state events

The Paul Dynasty

made his improbable election to the U.S. Senate almost seem inevitable. Ultimately, he was able to capitalize on the experience he gained working behind the scenes on his father's campaigns and as an antitax crusader to help ease his transition into being the candidate.

Rand's initial foray into electoral politics involved running for Senate in Kentucky. In 2009, there was a movement among Paul supporters to draft him to run for the seat held at the time by embattled senator Jim Bunning. Paul, a friend of Bunning, indicated he was interested in running, but only if Bunning decided not to seek reelection. Ultimately, Bunning decided to retire, and Rand Paul entered the race.[10] On the surface, Rand's first run for office looked like a long shot. In the Republican primary he faced Kentucky secretary of state Trey Grayson. Grayson, seen as a protégé of Senator Mitch McConnell, was a well-liked and well-known commodity in Kentucky politics and considered to be the favorite. However, Rand was able to mitigate many of the advantages Grayson was thought to have, using Grayson's experience against him by pitching him as a "career politician." Although the son of a sitting member of Congress, Rand was able to pitch himself as a political outsider and was able to capitalize on voter discontent with "establishment" politicians who had supported bailout and stimulus legislation. He was able to form a symbiotic relationship with upstart Tea Party organizations. Paul gave the Tea Party movement a champion of smaller government and lower taxes, while the Tea Party gave him a forum for drawing public support and media attention.[11]

Like most scions of political families, Rand was able to use the Paul brand to bring attention and legitimacy to his candidacy. He successfully used his father's national and fervent following to raise enough money to compete with Grayson. Like his father, Rand was able to use grassroots fund-raising strategies like "money bombs" to help raise over $3 million during the primary campaign.[12] Rand also reached out to his father's faithful following by trying to reach them where they were. During the primary he made multiple appearances on the show of controversial talk radio provocateur Alex Jones. His appearances on the *Alex Jones Show* led to a flood of contributions to Paul's website. Not only did Paul rely on a national network for fund-raising, but his campaign made the explicit decision to make the election a referendum on national politics. Rand Paul coasted to an easy primary victory, which led his proponents to coin the term "Randslide."

While the Kentucky Senate primary was a vintage outsider campaign, the general election veered from the familiar Paul family script and almost immediately shifted to more conventional electoral politics. Following the primary, the Paul campaign replaced its campaign manager, Tea Party activist David Adams, with Jesse Benton. Benton is married to Ron Paul's granddaughter and cut his political teeth working for a variety of conservative causes including Ron's 2008 presidential effort and the Campaign for Liberty. Much to the chagrin of some of his most ardent supporters, Rand Paul also formed a somewhat uneasy but overall mutually beneficial partnership with Senator McConnell. Following the rough start to the general election campaign, Paul ran a relatively low-key race and coasted to victory over Democratic attorney general Jack Conway in November.

Rand's Senate victory illustrated a few interesting political points. First, it highlighted that his candidacy was not bound by geography, as he was able to tap into his father's nationwide network of supporters to aid his campaign. Second, it reinforced his image as an "nontraditional" type of politician. Things that would have torpedoed typical campaigns, such as the civil rights remarks and the association with Alex Jones, did not hinder his candidacy.[13] Although there are many similarities between Rand and Ron Paul, some key differences did emerge during the campaign. Most notably, Rand's ability to play nice and work with the establishment to achieve his electoral goals is a key difference. It also signaled the beginning of a balancing act that he continues to perform with varying degrees of success.

Rand was ultimately able to parlay the success of his Senate candidacy and leader of the Tea Party movement to generate national attention. He was a sought after speaker on the Lincoln Day Dinner circuit and made frequent appearances in Iowa, New Hampshire, and other states that play a key role in the presidential nomination process. Unlike his father, he endorsed Republican nominee Mitt Romney in the 2012 presidential race and spoke at the Republican National Convention in Tampa. He delivered the Tea Party response to President Obama's State of the Union speech in 2013 and also served as a featured speaker at both CPAC and the GOP Freedom Summit in 2014. These appearances helped lay the foundation for Rand's campaign for the Republican nomination for president in 2016.

Rand's presidential campaign was markedly different than those run by his father. The elder Paul was open about the long shot nature of his candidacy, publicly stating that he focused on college campuses with a hope to reach young people and change their political attitudes going forward. Rand actually wanted to be president and thought he had a viable path to victory. This campaign was also made all the more interesting from Rand's perspective because it occurred during the same year that he would be up for reelection for his Senate seat, and Kentucky state law prevented him from being on the ballot for both races. This legal roadblock was circumvented by a rule change made by the Republican Party of Kentucky, which resulted in, for the first time ever, the party using a caucus rather than a primary.[14] The rule change turned out to be unnecessary, however, as Rand's candidacy featured a series of hiccups that resulted in him dropping out following a fifth place finish in the Iowa Caucuses and before the Kentucky Caucuses even took place. The emergence of Donald Trump and the success of Ted Cruz effectively blocked Paul's path to victory as he failed to reach the level of support his father had received in previous Iowa Caucuses. Rand, at the conclusion of the campaign, unlike his father, chose to endorse the Republican nominee. Despite this national failure, Rand continued to be a popular commodity in the Commonwealth, as he easily defeated Lexington mayor Jim Gray in his Senate reelection bid.

Other Family Members

Although Ron and Rand Paul have been the most visible of the Paul political brand, other members of the family have had a hand in building the brand, albeit often playing less visible and more limited roles. Ron's wife Carol has frequently served as an officer for FREE and Ron Paul Jr. served as vice president of the Campaign for Liberty. Ron Paul's daughter, Lori Pyeatt, has played a more active role and has served, at different times, as the vice president and treasurer for FREE. She has frequently played an advisory role within the organization. Kelley Paul, Rand's wife, has often served as a partner in his political career. At one point, she was employed by The Strategy Group for Media where Ted Cruz was one of her clients. It is not uncommon for her to serve as a stand-in for her husband at fund-raisers and other political functions. She has largely been seen as an asset for Rand's political career.

Ultimately, it is Pyeatt's son-in-law Jesse Benton that has gained the most notoriety of the next generation of the Paul brand. Benton is married to Valori Pyeatt. They met during their work on Ron Paul's 2008 presidential campaign. Benton established his reputation as a grassroots organizer. After successfully managing Rand Paul's Senate election in 2010, he joined Ron Paul's 2012 presidential effort before signing on to manage Senator Mitch McConnell's 2014 reelection campaign. Benton's time as McConnell's campaign manager highlights the politically expedient relationship forged between Paul and McConnell. Benton's tenure as McConnell's campaign manger came to a controversial end when he was accused of bribery for his role in allegations of trying to buy an Iowa politician's support for Ron Paul in the 2012 presidential election. Benton was eventually indicted and sentenced to probation for his role in the scandal.[15] During the 2016 election cycle, Benton resurfaced and was hired to work on a pro-Trump super PAC.

The Dynasty Going Forward

The future of the Paul brand going forward is not entirely clear. Rand Paul remains one of the most visible members of the U.S. Senate where he can be a thorn the side of his fellow senator from Kentucky, Majority Leader Mitch McConnell. Paul frequently takes a contrarian position from Senate leadership. He coasted to an easy win in his 2016 reelection bid and is unlikely to face a serious threat if he chooses to run for reelection in 2022. It is unclear if a second presidential bid is in his future.

Another interesting question is what type of legislative legacy the Pauls will leave from their time in Congress. Although both have been leading voices in advocating limited government and noninterventionist foreign policy, tangible legislative accomplishments have been few and far between. Supporters see their antiestablishment positions as taking a principled stand. Paul critics take a more cynical view. Jonah Goldberg, for instance, has accused the Pauls of taking the path of political expediency rather than taking principled stands.[16] For example, Ron Paul would frequently stuff spending bills with earmarks and then vote against them, already certain they would pass. As he starts his second term in the U.S. Senate, Rand Paul has emerged as a leading opposition voice against things he deems to be "government overreach," such as Obamacare and intrusions into American's civil liberties, but has yet to pass what would be perceived as his signature piece of legislation. However, in Rand's case, he still has time to accomplish this in his career.

At the end of the day, the Paul family is a unique American political dynasty. Both father and son have worked outside of the traditional party structures to achieve significant electoral success. Because they have approached campaigning and governing in such a unique way, they have been able to successfully parlay their approach into a cottage industry by which they reach their followers to help spread the message of the Paul family in a way that has not been seen before in American politics. This makes them one of the most interesting, and arguably one of the most frustrating, political dynasties in American history.

Notes

1. Taylor, Jay. 2000. "Interview with Ron Paul: In Defense of our Unalienable Rights." *J. Taylor's Gold and Technology Stocks Newsletter.*

2. Gwynne, S. C. 2001. "Dr. No." *Texas Monthly.*

3. Goodwyn, Wade. 2007. "Paul Has Long Drawn Support from Unlikely Places." *NPR: The '08 Candidates' First Campaigns.*

4. Rosenthal, Andrew. 1998. "Now for a Real Underdog: Ron Paul, Libertarian, for President." *The New York Times.*

5. Preston, Mark. 2008. "Paul Suspends Presidential Campaign; Forms New Organization." *cnn.com.*

6. Keck, Kristi. 2008. "Thousands Rally at Ron Paul Convention." *cnn.com.*

7. Steinmetz, Kay. 2012. "Ron Paul in Tampa: A GOP Outsider's Last Hurrah." *Time Magazine.*

8. Wyler, Grace. 2013. "Ron Paul Is Launching His Own Foreign Policy Institute." *businessinsider.com.*

9. Blackmon, Douglas. 2010. "Rand Paul's Antitax Group Has Been Inactive for Years." *The Wall Street Journal*.

10. Giroux, Greg. 2009. "Rand Paul Declares Candidacy for Kentucky Senate Seat." *CQ Politics*.

11. Turner, Joel, and Scott Lasley. 2012. "Randslide: TEA Party Success in the Establishment's Backyard." in *Key States, High Stakes: Sarah Palin, the TEA Party, and the 2010 Midterm Elections*, ed. Charles Bullock (Lanham, MA: Rowman and Littlefield).

12. Lizza, Ryan. 2014. "The Revenge of Rand Paul." *The New Yorker*.

13. Thompson, Krissah, and Dan Balz. 2010. "Rand Paul Comments about Civil Rights Stir Controversy." *The Washington Post*.

14. Scott, Eugene, and Tai Kopan. 2015. "Rand Paul Win: Kentucky GOP Switch to Caucus." *cnn.com*.

15. Weigel, David. 2016. "Trump Super PAC Strategist Found Guilty of Campaign Finance Violations." *The Washington Post*.

16. Goldberg, Jonah. 2017. "Is Rand Paul's Opposition to the GOP Health Bill Principled, or Cynical?" http://www.latimes.com/opinion/op-ed/la-oe-goldberg-rand-paul-20170718-story.html.

Further Reading

Paul, Rand. *Taking a Stand: Moving beyond Partisan Politics to Unite America*. New York: Center Street, 2015.

Paul, Ron. *The Revolution: A Manifesto*. New York: Grand Central Publishing, 2009.

CHAPTER SEVEN

The Rockefeller Dynasty

Richard Skinner

To call the Rockefellers a political dynasty is to actually understate their influence. Although comparisons across times and cultures are challenging, they are probably the wealthiest nonroyal family that has ever existed. They created Standard Oil, one of the signature corporations of the Industrial Revolution. The Rockefellers also built one of the first major philanthropic foundations and endowed one of the nation's leading research universities, the University of Chicago. The Rockefellers defined over a century of American life. John D. Rockefeller Sr., the father of the family fortune, became a leading symbol of the Gilded Age and the greatest villain of the Progressive era. John D. Rockefeller Jr. used the "scientific charity" of the Progressive era to remake the family reputation. John D. Jr.'s five sons—the so-called brothers—embraced the optimism of what Henry Luce, publisher of *Time* and *Life*, in 1941 called "The American Century," imagining that business, government, and philanthropy could together solve any problems facing the United States. The Rockefeller family thus exemplified a mingling of private and public power that alarmed both the Left and the Right. The great fortune that the Rockefellers accumulated through business, made them giants in philanthropy, and gained them entry to politics. But that wealth was not able to overcome suspicions of centralized power that run deep in American life.

Although the Rockefellers would go on to loom large in public life, they only embraced elective politics after achieving prominence in business and politics. John D. Rockefeller Sr. distrusted politicians, especially those who attacked his business practices while taking his contributions. John D. Rockefeller Jr. gave lavishly to the Republican Party, but thought politics an unsuitable endeavor for someone with so controversial a surname. But two of Rockefeller Jr.'s five sons embraced public life. Nelson Rockefeller was the first in his family to enter into national politics, serving in appointive positions under three consecutive presidents, was elected to four terms as governor of New York, and served as vice president. After an unlikely midlife move to Arkansas, Winthrop Rockefeller was elected twice as governor. Both men could point to great accomplishments in office, but their careers ended in frustration. Nelson openly sought the presidency twice, and flirted with running two other times, but never captured his prize in large part because of an incompatibility with his own political party. Winthrop was brought down by his own personal demons. In the following generation, John D. (Jay) Rockefeller IV was elected as governor and senator by the people of West Virginia despite his own shallow roots in the state. Win Paul Rockefeller served more than a decade as lieutenant governor of Arkansas and was about to seek his father's office as governor when he fell victim to cancer. Once Jay Rockefeller retired in 2015, the nation lacked a Rockefeller in elected office for the first time in more than a half century.

The Founder: John D. Rockefeller Sr.

John D. Rockefeller was certainly the wealthiest American of his time, probably the wealthiest American of *all* time, and very likely the wealthiest person who ever lived. Rockefeller was the principal founder of Standard Oil, which dominated the marketing and refining of petroleum in the United States from the 1870s until its breakup in 1911 due to an antitrust case. Due to his great wealth and his perceived ruthlessness in acquiring it, John D. Rockefeller was perhaps the most despised man of his era.

Perhaps the quintessential figure of the Gilded Age, Rockefeller became arguably the principal villain of the Progressive era. The power of Standard Oil helped make the distrust of big business a highly salient issue in the 1880s and 1890s, leading to the passage of the Sherman Antitrust Act. Revelations of the vast sums given by Standard Oil to the Republican Party helped spark the first movement for campaign finance reform. Ida Tarbell's *The History of the Standard Oil Company* (1904), an expose of Rockefeller's business methods, was the quintessential "muckraking" work of the Progressive era.

Rockefeller supported the Republican Party for his entire adult life—he cast his first vote for president in 1860 for Abraham Lincoln. Rockefeller's strong convictions against slavery and in favor of temperance were only strengthened by his marriage to Laura Spelman, whose parents were abolitionists involved with the Underground Railroad. The couple remained loyal to their chosen causes, becoming the leading supporters of the Anti-Saloon League and prominent funders of African American education initiatives. Rockefeller made his first financial contribution to a Republican presidential candidate in 1880,

Rockefeller Political Dynasty Family Tree

1. John Davidson Rockefeller Sr., 1839–1937
    President and founder of Standard Oil, philanthropist
Married Laura C. Spelman
Six children including John D. Rockefeller Jr.

2. John D. Rockefeller Jr., 1874–1960
Married Abby Greene Aldrich (daughter of Senator Nelson W. Aldrich), then Martha Baird Allen
Six children including John D. Rockefeller III, Nelson, and Winthrop

3. Nelson A. Rockefeller, 1908–1979
    Governor of New York, 1959–1973
    Vice president, 1974–1977
Married Mary Todhunter Clark, then Margaretta Large Fitler
Seven children

4. Winthrop Rockefeller, 1912–1973
    Governor of Arkansas, 1967–1971
Married Barbara Sears, then Jeannette Edris
One son: Winthrop Paul

5. Winthrop Paul Rockefeller, 1948–2006
    Arkansas lieutenant governor, 1996–2006
Married Deborah Cluett Sage, then Lisenne Dudderar
Eight children

5. John "Jay" D. Rockefeller IV, 1937–, son of John D. Rockefeller III
    West Virginia House of Delegates, 1967–1969
    West Virginia secretary of state, 1969–1973
    Governor of West Virginia, 1977–1985
    U.S. Senate, 1985–2015
Married Sharon Percy
Four children

when he backed James Garfield. He remained a loyal donor to the GOP for the remainder of his life: President William McKinley was a favored recipient of contributions (his campaign manager Mark Hanna had attended high school with Rockefeller).

But Rockefeller overall did not care much for politicians. Standard Oil had long kept many of them on its payroll, and Rockefeller sometimes complained that politicians often took his money and then denounced him to win votes. Rockefeller had contributed to the campaigns of Theodore Roosevelt, but as president, Roosevelt repaid his generosity by initiating the lawsuit that dissolved Standard Oil. Unlike some of his political rivals, Roosevelt was not uniformly hostile to big business. He preferred the regulation of trusts versus breaking them up, and voluntary constraint versus long, costly court cases. However, by November 1906, Standard Oil vice president John D. Archbold (by then the company's de facto chief executive, given that the aging Rockefeller now devoted himself primarily to philanthropy) managed to alienate the president through his inflexibility and heavy-handed tactics. In an era where Americans had become suspicious of the power of big business, Standard Oil had made itself an obvious target.

The Justice Department initiated antitrust proceedings against Standard Oil. The case would drag on for nearly five years. Roosevelt's successor, William Howard Taft, had a friendlier relationship with the Rockefellers. But that did not make him any less committed to the Standard Oil prosecution. In May 1911, the Supreme Court ruled that Standard Oil had violated the Sherman Antitrust Act and ordered that it be broken up into 34 separate companies. Ironically, the breakup made John D. Rockefeller even wealthier, given that the combined net worth of the new companies soon far exceeded that of Standard Oil.[1] Rockefeller not only helped create the modern corporation with Standard Oil, but he also created modern philanthropy. As his fortune exploded in the 1880s and 1890s, Rockefeller became concerned with finding more systematic ways of giving it away. He disliked "handouts" to the less fortunate and had grown weary of being dunned for contributions by potential recipients. Frederick T. Gates, secretary of the American Baptist Education Society, shared many of Rockefeller's concerns. He became Rockefeller's principal philanthropic and business adviser. They began shifting Rockefeller's giving away from one-time gifts to specific recipients toward broader efforts at social reform, particularly focused on education and public health.

After the turn of the century, Rockefeller and Gates, now joined by John D. Rockefeller Jr., began to envision a charitable foundation of unprecedented scale. In 1913, the Rockefeller Foundation was chartered under New York State law. If John D. Rockefeller Sr. was the principal villain of the Progressive era, the foundation he created nevertheless was a quintessentially Progressive enterprise: technocratic, impersonal, optimistic, and aimed at social reform without threatening the status quo. Gone was the era of episodic charity aimed at the donor's pet causes; the age of "scientific" philanthropy administered by experts had arrived.

The Philanthropist: John D. Rockefeller Jr.

Aside from contributing enormous sums to the Republican Party, John D. Rockefeller Jr. (known as Junior within the family) was not involved deeply in politics.[2] Still, Junior was central to the rise of expertise in American life, an evolution with profound consequences for government. He funded pioneering think tanks such as the Brookings Institution, the Council on Foreign Relations, and the National Bureau for Economic Research. He followed his father in pursuing "scientific charity," building the Rockefeller Foundation into a model for other philanthropic endeavors.

In 1914, national guardsmen massacred about two dozen people at a miners' encampment in Ludlow, Colorado; the victims were striking against Rockefeller-owned Colorado Fuel & Iron. The incident sparked wide outrage against the family, arguably surpassing even the decades of resentment of the power of Standard Oil. John D. Rockefeller Jr. worked with labor relations expert W. L. Mackenzie King (later prime minister of Canada) to develop a new management scheme for Colorado Fuel & Iron. This began a long interest in labor relations by the Rockefeller family. Junior also sparked the clan's interest in conservation issues, helping to establish Acadia, Grand Teton, and Great Smoky Mountains National Parks. The Rockefeller Foundation funded the Bureau of Social Hygiene, which supported research on birth control and sex education, foreshadowing John D. Rockefeller III's role in advocating population control. The statistician Beardsley Ruml used Rockefeller funds to build the Social Science Research Council. The Rockefeller Foundation was also involved in education, public health, and the arts.

Junior did much to rehabilitate the family image. It is difficult to imagine his children and grandchildren pursuing political careers without his efforts to make the Rockefeller name synonymous with good works rather than with greed. But commentators noted that Junior pioneered corporate public relations as well as organized philanthropy. Not only did the Rockefeller charities promote good will for the family, but they rarely seriously threatened the status quo. The combination of vast wealth, political connections, scientific expertise, and savvy public relations could be simultaneously exciting and threatening; populists of both the Left and the Right tended to suspect the Rockefellers of dark doings.

The Brothers' Generation

By the 1940s, Junior's five sons (known as the "brothers") were ready to take over the family institutions. (Their sister, Abby Aldrich Rockefeller, mostly

John D. Rockefeller and John D. Rockefeller Jr., c. 1915. (Library of Congress)

stayed aloof from family affairs.) Early on, Nelson established himself as the dominant brother, shoving aside his reserved older brother John D. III and humiliating his troubled younger brother Winthrop. Laurance was always the brother most loyal to Nelson, while youngest child David established himself as the family intellectual, earning a PhD in economics. With the Rockefeller Foundation under the management of philanthropic professionals, the new generation created the Rockefeller Brothers Fund in 1940 to coordinate their own giving.

The brothers were not always close, but they did present a shared worldview that contrasted to their father's Victorian caution. They were quintessential figures of the "greatest generation" and of the Cold War. They displayed a faith in American global leadership, grounded in a confidence in the nation's institutions that now seems quaint. In contrast, they also displayed deep concern about threats facing the nation, whether posed by communism, by the "population explosion," or the "revolution of rising expectations" in the developing world.[3] More than their conservative father, they embraced activist government, especially in partnership with business. But they carried on Junior's confidence in "scientific" expertise and his preference for orderly methods of social change.[4]

If their father avoided overt political involvement, the brothers embraced public life. Nelson and Winthrop spent much of their adult lives in government, both in appointed and elected office. David turned down repeated offers to hold public office but was engaged in political affairs behind the scenes for decades, serving as an informal adviser to presidents and chairing the Council on Foreign Relations for a decade and a half. John D. III and Laurance kept lower profiles, but their philanthropy made them experts in their fields to an extent that several presidents sought their opinions. All remained at least nominal Republicans but often found themselves ill at ease with their party's rising right wing.

As the brothers returned from wartime service in 1945, they began to assert themselves against their father's control. Nelson remodeled their wing of the family offices on the 56th floor of 30 Rockefeller Plaza. Showing his father around the new space, Nelson asked him, "Isn't this impressive?" His father supposedly responded, "Nelson, whom are we trying to impress?"[5] The brothers were in a hurry to impress the world. They soon assumed control of the family enterprises, and the brothers became an object of popular fascination, emblematic of the optimism of postwar America and the confidence that, with enough money and blue-ribbon commissions, all social problems were solvable.

Perhaps no enterprise more typified the Rockefeller brothers than the Special Studies Project, launched by Nelson Rockefeller after he left the Eisenhower administration in 1956. Meant to define the problems and opportunities facing the United States and to formulate a national purpose, the project was composed of seven blue-ribbon panels featuring such luminaries as *Time/Life* founder Henry Luce, RCA founder David Sarnoff, and retired general Lucius D. Clay, as well as brothers John D. III and Laurance. Henry Kissinger (future national security adviser and U.S. secretary of state), already emerging as a foreign policy intellectual in his midthirties, served as director. The findings were published in 1958–1960.[6,7] Not surprisingly, the project called for the United States to play a more active role in foreign affairs, to embrace economic globalization, and to increase assistance to the developing world. In domestic policy, the study called for the federal government to increase its management of the economy and to improve the nation's educational system.

But the study is best remembered for its recommendations for military policy, which were rushed to publication three years earlier, following the Soviet launch of the satellite *Sputnik*. Reflecting the worldviews of both Henry Kissinger and Nelson Rockefeller, the report urged huge increases in military spending in order to match the Soviets. It also promoted a doctrine of "counterforce" that broke with the policy of "massive retaliation" backed by Secretary of State John Foster Dulles. Rather than responding to every Soviet encroachment by threatening complete annihilation, the United States could employ a range of options, including intervening in regional conflicts and engaging in "limited" nuclear war. The panel's recommendations were widely seen as a criticism of President Dwight Eisenhower's cautious foreign policy, including his unwillingness to boost military spending if it risked larger budget deficits. The study influenced both parties' platforms in 1960 and helped shape the foreign policy of the Kennedy and Johnson administrations.[8,9]

Nelson Rockefeller Goes to Washington

Nelson Rockefeller burst onto the public stage in the 1930s, through his work on the iconic family properties of the era in New York City: the Museum of Modern Art (his mother's pet project) and Rockefeller Center (his father's). In 1939, he assumed the presidencies of both entities, landing him on the cover of *Time* at the age of 30. His involvement with the family investments in Mexico and Venezuela fueled a lifelong passion for Latin America. After France fell to Germany in June 1940, concern grew over the Axis Powers' influence in the Western Hemisphere. Rockefeller proposed creating a presidentially appointed position to orchestrate U.S. policy in Latin America. President Franklin D. Roosevelt named Rockefeller as coordinator of Inter-American Affairs in August 1940. Rockefeller quickly used his connections, political skills, and fortune to turn an ill-defined position into a center of power in wartime Washington. Aware of his vulnerability to bureaucratic rivals elsewhere in the federal government (particularly in the State Department), Rockefeller assembled a legion of patrons who ran the ideological gamut from Vice President Henry Wallace on the Left to FBI Director J. Edgar Hoover on the Right. His ties to media figures such as Luce and CBS president William S. Paley also served him well. Rockefeller attracted numerous young and able subordinates willing to work punishing hours.[10,11]

While the coordinator's position was initially justified by the need to fight Axis economic influence in Latin America, the office soon became most identified with American propaganda efforts. The coordinator's office produced *En Guardia*, a propaganda magazine for a Latin audience. Leading film and music stars toured Central and South America. The popular newsreel series *The March of Time* began a Spanish-language edition. Most famously, at Rockefeller's behest, Walt Disney produced two cartoons set in Latin America.

After Pearl Harbor, Rockefeller expanded his activities to include the Institute of Inter-American Affairs. The new project engaged in joint projects with Latin American governments to pursue ventures in agriculture and public health. Both the isolationist Right and the fellow-traveler Left (even in the era of the U.S.-Soviet alliance, he could barely disguise his militant anticommunism) treated Rockefeller with suspicion, but his reputation in Latin America swelled. A network of coordination committees made up of U.S. expatriates gave Rockefeller eyes and ears in every Latin American capital and only further annoyed the diplomatic corps.

After FDR's reelection in November 1944, Edward Stettinus replaced Cordell Hull as secretary of state. Hull had been a fierce bureaucratic rival of Rockefeller, but Stettinus complied with FDR's wish that Rockefeller be named assistant secretary of state for Latin America. In his new post, Rockefeller was consumed by a drive to build a regional security alliance in the Western Hemisphere, a project distrusted by those who preferred the global arrangements epitomized by the nascent United Nations. He also found himself preoccupied with the United States' complicated relationship with Argentina, which had remained neutral for most of the war and was widely seen as being sympathetic to the Axis Powers. His endless machinations at the inaugural United Nations Conference, held in San Francisco in 1945, annoyed many of his colleagues at State, who found him obsessed with Latin American opinion, and too willing to accept Argentina's repressive military regime as a partner against communism. But Rockefeller did win a provision in the U.N. Charter that allowed for regional security alliances and was later used as a justification for NATO. His time at the State Department was running short, however. FDR's death meant that Rockefeller lost a longtime patron. When President Harry Truman replaced Stettinus with James Byrnes in August 1945, the new secretary of state quickly pushed out Rockefeller.[12]

Nelson's return to New York after the war marked his establishment as the dominant figure in the Rockefeller family. Not only did he assume control of the family institutions, he emerged as a leading citizen of New York City. Most notably, he was deeply involved in the effort to win the competition for the location for the headquarters of the newly founded United Nations. Nelson Rockefeller returned to public life in 1950 when President Truman named him chairman of the International Development Advisory Board, which supervised a new program of assistance to the developing world. But Rockefeller found his opinions ignored and was outmaneuvered in bureaucratic warfare by his friend and fellow plutocrat W. Averell Harriman. Rockefeller resigned in the fall of 1951.

Nelson Rockefeller and Dwight Eisenhower

In 1952, a group of East Coast moderates organized to draft General Dwight Eisenhower for the Republican presidential nomination.[13] Nelson Rockefeller was personally close to many figures involved in the Citizens for Eisenhower movement, most notably his uncle Winthrop Aldrich, president of the Chase National Bank. But Rockefeller was slow to publicly identify himself with Dwight Eisenhower; when Rockefeller finally offered his services after the Republican Convention, New York governor Thomas Dewey froze him out of any meaningful role in the campaign. (Dewey was often skeptical of Rockefeller's political ambitions; when consulted about a possible gubernatorial run, he offered to help Rockefeller become postmaster in New York City.) After the election, President Eisenhower named Rockefeller chairman of the President's Advisory Committee on Government Organization. PACGO made a series of recommendations, most notably suggesting that the hodgepodge of entities that composed the Federal Security Agency be turned into a cabinet-level Department of Health, Education, and Welfare (HEW).

After Eisenhower signed legislation creating HEW, he appointed Oveta Culp Hobby, a Houston newspaper publisher and prominent supporter, as its

New York governor Nelson Rockefeller campaigning for the Republican presidential nomination, July 11, 1968. (Library of Congress)

first secretary. Hobby asked Rockefeller to serve as her undersecretary. She had limited expertise in her department's policy areas, and Rockefeller was widely seen as HEW's dominant figure. Eisenhower also lacked interest in or knowledge of domestic social policy, allowing Undersecretary Rockefeller to play a role far greater than his title would suggest. Still, he often found himself squeezed between a Right that thought he was going too far and a Left that thought he was too cautious. Thwarting the wishes of the Republican Right, Rockefeller managed to persuade Eisenhower to approve an expansion of Social Security. But a scheme to expand private health insurance ran into steep opposition from both ends of the ideological spectrum.[14] It did not take long for Nelson Rockefeller to realize that HEW was a backwater in an administration focused on foreign policy. In the fall of 1954, he joined the Eisenhower White House in a position as an administrative assistant on foreign policy. This vaguely defined position fit Rockefeller's tendencies toward the optimistic and the nebulous, but not surprisingly led him into frequent conflict with Secretary of State John Foster Dulles. Rockefeller sponsored two gatherings of leading Cold War thinkers at the marine corps base in Quantico, Virginia, which urged much greater military spending, and thereby annoyed the many fiscal conservatives in the administration. Although Eisenhower proposed his "Open Skies" initiative at the Geneva superpower summit (Khrushchev rejected it), Rockefeller's year as a foreign policy strategist proved frustrating, and he resigned in December 1955.

Rockefeller's experience in the Eisenhower administration resembled his two previous forays into federal service. He could attract talented subordinates, often with an academic pedigree, to his service (his ability to place some of them on the family payroll did not hurt). But observers often thought that Rockefeller was using his fortune and connections to make up for his own intellectual shortcomings. Eisenhower quipped that "he is too used to borrowing brains instead of using his own."[15] Rockefeller had an affinity for broad, dreamy concepts but lacked the ability to implement them effectively or to sell them to the skeptical. Eisenhower said of Rockefeller, "He has one hundred ideas. One of them may be brilliant . . . it's worthwhile to have him around because that one idea is worth the ninety-nine that aren't."[16] Rockefeller was often intrigued by schemes for business-government cooperation that the Left thought too friendly to business and the Right thought constituted too much "big government." During World War II, Rockefeller often confronted opposition from a Left that thought he was too obsessed with communism, but his major opposition in the Eisenhower years usually came from a Right that perceived him as free-spending and utopian.[17]

During his years under Franklin Roosevelt, Rockefeller's good ties with the White House often helped him triumph in bureaucratic warfare, but he never established quite the same relationship with Eisenhower, despite repeated exercises in blatant sycophancy. He worked better with Vice President Richard Nixon, who shared his desires for a more aggressive foreign policy and a more pragmatic domestic policy.

Governor Rockefeller

Rockefeller's frustrating sojourns in three consecutive presidential administrations convinced him of the need to seek elective office on his own terms. In the mid-1950s, leading New Yorkers sought to recruit him to run for mayor, governor, or U.S. senator. One of those New Yorkers was state Republican chairman Judson Morhouse. After Rockefeller told him he had no interest in serving in the Senate, Morhouse began to lay the groundwork for a gubernatorial bid in 1958. Every 20 years, New York State voters got to decide whether to call another constitutional convention. Governor Averell Harriman (D), a friend and sometimes rival of Rockefeller, agreed to appoint him as chairman of a temporary commission to consider issues that might face such a convention. The commission itself turned out to be for naught, since New Yorkers rejected a convention in a November 1957 vote. Still, Rockefeller used the commission to educate himself on state issues, to assemble a knowledgeable policy staff, and to elevate his public profile.

Although Rockefeller lacked ties to the county bosses who dominated the New York Republican Party, Morhouse and Assemblyman Malcolm Wilson (who would go on to be Rockefeller's lieutenant governor) were happy to put their own extensive networks to work on his behalf. Wilson and Rockefeller launched a memorable tour of upstate New York in the summer of 1958, where the Fifth Avenue plutocrat proved to be a smashing success on the region's main streets. Meanwhile, many leading Republican moderates in New York City began to rally behind Rockefeller. His main opponent, former Republican National Committee chairman Leonard Hall, was initially seen as Eisenhower's choice. But both Eisenhower (privately) and Nixon (publicly) encouraged Rockefeller to run.

Many Republican insiders were happy to back Rockefeller without much thought to what kind of governor he might be. They assumed that he would lose: with the country mired in recession, 1958 was shaping up to be a Democratic year. Although the Republican legislature had blocked most of his proposals, Harriman was a popular, if uninspiring, governor. He had sought the Democratic presidential nomination in 1952 and 1956, and most assumed he would run again in 1960. If Republican prospects looked grim, a Rockefeller at the top of the ticket would at least guarantee an adequate campaign budget. Moreover, Rockefeller's riches and connections did not hurt in wooing the GOP's county bosses and small-town gentry. His opponents quit the race before the state convention, and Rockefeller was nominated by acclamation.

If the Republican Convention was a lovefest, the Democratic Convention descended into factional warfare. In New York City, a long-running battle between the party bosses and liberal reformers was nearing its peak. Harriman found himself caught between the factions, forced to accept boss-chosen candidates for senator and attorney general. Liberals were enraged, while many machine politicians were less than smitten with the aristocratic Harriman. Harriman's wife Marie commented on the Tammany triumph by declaring, "They gave ole Ave a real Philadelphia rat-f***ing."[18] Despite his own backing by machine bosses like J. Russell Sprague of Nassau County, Rockefeller attacked Harriman as a tool of party politics.

Rockefeller ran an intense, high-energy campaign that contrasted sharply with Harriman's low-key style. Donations from Rockefellers and Rockefeller associates swelled his campaign war chest to bursting, allowing him to greatly outspend the Democrats. Rockefeller followed a centrist path, playing down his Republican label, and reaching out to traditionally Democratic minority groups. Harriman eventually turned to tying Rockefeller to the decreasingly popular President Eisenhower, who was at his public nadir in the midst of a recession, and especially to the disliked Vice President Nixon. When Nixon came to New York to stump for Republicans, Rockefeller appeared to distance himself, before finally appearing in person with him at the end of his visit. As a result, the then-liberal *New York Post*, whose owner Dorothy Schiff was personally close to Rockefeller, endorsed Harriman. But when the governor appeared to imply that Rockefeller, a loyal supporter of Jewish causes, was

The Rockefeller Dynasty

unsympathetic to Israel, the *Post* took back its endorsement in a front-page editorial by Schiff. Even as Democrats triumphed nationwide, Rockefeller won in a 10-point landslide, performing unusually well for a Republican in New York City, and with African Americans and Jews. The Rockefeller name had finally been redeemed by the voters.[19,20]

Rockefeller eventually won the governorship four times. His campaigns proved highly influential and memorable. This scion of wealth, whose life had been spent at great remove from most citizens, turned out to be a natural campaigner. He was a master of both the "old" politics of streets and backrooms, and of the "new" politics of money and television. Rockefeller's personal campaigning excited frenzies comparable to that experienced by pop stars, whether he was visiting small-town diners, marching in ethnic parades, or chomping blintzes in a Lower East Side restaurant. His shouts of "Howaya" and "Hiya, fella" quickly dispelled voters' suspicions that he was an aloof aristocrat. Meanwhile, he ran the New York Republican Party as an absolute monarchy, using money (his and the state's) and patronage to win the loyalty of the state's clubhouses. His friendly relationships with union leaders and Democratic pols often made them less-than-enthusiastic supporters of Rockefeller's opponents. But Rockefeller ruled the state's living rooms as well as its backrooms. His vast campaign spending overwhelmed the Democrats. He was one of the first state-level politicians to embrace the modern techniques of polling and television advertisements. (Perhaps his most memorable spot featured talking fish praising his efforts to clean up the state's waterways.)

Rockefeller took to life as governor as happily as he embraced the campaign trail. He proved to be a natural at the wheeling and dealing of the legislative process, working well with both Democrats and Republicans. He was fortunate to govern mostly in a time of prosperity, when an economic boom was sending a flood of revenue into the state treasury. Among his achievements were:

- A vast expansion of the State University of New York;
- The nation's most generous Medicaid program;
- The nation's first state department of environmental conservation;
- The Pure Waters Act, a pioneering effort at water pollution control;
- The nation's first state arts council;
- The first state-level minimum wage; and
- A major expansion of the state park system.

But his long list of accomplishments loomed less lustrous by the mid-1970s, when both the city and state of New York fell into deep fiscal trouble.

Nelson Rockefeller's First Flirtation with the White House

Richard Nixon appeared to be the overwhelming frontrunner for the Republican presidential nomination in 1960. His leading rival, Senate Republican Leader William Knowland, destroyed his political career in 1958 through an ill-conceived race for governor of California. But Rockefeller's triumph in an otherwise Democratic year made him an instant rival to Nixon. There was also much speculation about a potential Nixon-Rockefeller ticket. The national media, much of it based in New York, and eager for a contested GOP race, also hyped Rockefeller's chances. In late 1959, Rockefeller made the rounds of Republican events around the nation, in what was widely seen as a prelude to a presidential campaign. He was received politely, but no more. Nixon had spent eight years wooing the Republican base, while Rockefeller lacked the same grounds for loyalty. He was also already seen as a liberal, out of step with the party faithful. On December 26, Rockefeller announced that he would not seek the presidency. He made it clear that he had no interest in the vice presidency either.

In the spring of 1960, Rockefeller's interest in the national stage revived. The economy had slipped into recession. The "sit-in" movement was pushing civil rights to the forefront of national attention. (Rockefeller had long been an advocate for a more vigorous role for the federal government in managing the economy. Following his family's tradition, Rockefeller backed civil rights legislation with great intensity.) The U-2 incident embarrassed Eisenhower.[21] Rockefeller began to toy with the idea of a presidential draft, even though his advisers told him that he had almost no chance of winning the nomination, especially given that Nixon had swept the primaries. He called Eisenhower's foreign policy excessively cautious, even though that put him at odds with the nation's most popular Republican. (Rockefeller introduced the idea of a "missile gap," that the United States was falling behind the Soviet Union in the nuclear arms race. John F. Kennedy embraced this theme in his own presidential campaign, despite it not being supported by the evidence.)

On June 8, Rockefeller issued a "statement of conscience." He called for much more spending on both the military and on civil defense. He said that Republicans needed to more clearly embrace the civil rights movement. He also proposed a greater federal role in health care and education. Not surprisingly, this statement annoyed Eisenhower and Nixon, although they kept their doubts private. Rockefeller supporters prepared to launch a draft effort at the convention. The vast majority of delegates were committed to Nixon, but Rockefeller backers thought that they could be persuaded that only the New York governor could win in November. Nixon did not actually think Rockefeller had a chance of winning the nomination, but he increasingly feared a divisive convention that would embarrass him.

On July 22, Rockefeller warned that he might launch a floor fight at the convention if the platform was not changed to fit his demands. Fearing a damaging civil war among Republicans, former Attorney General Herbert Brownell arranged for Nixon and Rockefeller to meet immediately. At Rockefeller's insistence, the gathering took place over dinner at his Fifth Avenue apartment. Eager to win Rockefeller's support, Nixon flew to New York from Washington, without consulting with his advisers. After trading Washington stories over lamb chops, Nixon offered Rockefeller the vice presidency. Once again, Rockefeller turned down the offer, saying that he did not want to serve as standby equipment. They then reviewed the proposed Republican platform, as well as Rockefeller's suggested changes. Their policy differences on civil rights and health care were not great; both men were stronger backers of civil rights than was Eisenhower and both men were comfortable with an activist federal government. Nixon was more reluctant to call for a huge increase in defense spending, not out of principle, but because he did not want to break publicly with Eisenhower. But at midnight, the two men called platform committee chairman Charles Percy in his Chicago hotel room and gave him the altered platform language. In the morning, Rockefeller's press office announced the meeting and declared that it had been Nixon's idea. To the casual observer, Nixon looked like he had begged for Rockefeller's support.

Eisenhower felt insulted by the proposed platform changes, which implied that he had let his fiscal conservatism damage America's national security. Conservatives and southerners were also upset, especially by the new civil rights language. If journalists dubbed the meeting "The Compact of Fifth Avenue," Barry Goldwater called it a "Republican Munich," recalling the prewar appeasement of Adolf Hitler. When the platform committee rejected the Nixon-Rockefeller language, the two men lobbied the committee fiercely. The battle over the civil rights plank, which pitted southerners like Senate candidate John Tower against Rockefeller's New Yorkers, prefigured the divisions of 1964. Although Nixon and Rockefeller mostly won the battle over the platform, conservatives were left feeling betrayed. The growing number of southern Republicans would forever see Nelson Rockefeller as their confirmed enemy. Many conservatives groused later that Rockefeller did too little to help Nixon to win in the fall. Rockefeller himself blamed Nixon's loss on spending too much time courting white southerners.

Rockefeller's experience in 1960 reflected many of the factors that would keep him from winning the presidency. He showed little connection to the Republican grassroots, particularly movement conservatives. He alienated people who had showed him some good will, particularly Eisenhower and Nixon, who both seemed to desire a Nixon-Rockefeller ticket. He seemed unable to either fully commit to a presidential run or to abandon it.[22,23,24,25]

Rockefeller the Front-Runner

Despite his tense relationships with other leading Republicans, Nelson Rockefeller became the party's front-runner for the 1964 presidential nomination. Indeed, the first two years of the Kennedy administration marked the only period of his career when Rockefeller appeared likely to be the GOP's standard bearer. Even though his policy differences with John F. Kennedy were small, Rockefeller took on the role of Republican attack dog. An even more ardent Cold War warrior than the man in the White House, Rockefeller called for more civil defense measures precisely so that the United States could more credibly threaten to use nuclear weapons. Even though Rockefeller's record in New York did not give him credibility as an economic conservative, he nonetheless advocated tax cuts bigger than Kennedy's, and he warned that JFK's proposed Department of Urban Affairs would concentrate too much power in Washington. But Rockefeller seemed most convincing in attacking Kennedy for inaction on civil rights. The Rockefeller family had advocated for African American rights for decades, while John F. Kennedy was a relative newcomer to the issue. Nelson Rockefeller had warmer relations with both Martin Luther King Jr. and Jackie Robinson than Kennedy did. He could boast of pushing for stronger antidiscrimination laws in New York State, while bashing Kennedy for coddling southern Democrats.[26,27,28]

Rockefeller tried to speak as a leader of the entire Republican Party. He played down his real differences with the GOP Right. He had regular breakfasts with Senator Barry Goldwater, who told his ideological comrades that Rockefeller was more conservative than they thought. But movement conservatives continued to distrust the New York governor. His big-taxing, big-spending, big-borrowing record in office certainly gave them reason for skepticism. If Rockefeller's anticommunism was as fervent as that of any *National Review* writer, he also had a penchant for dreamy internationalism that made him the subject of right-wing conspiracy theories. But perhaps it was Rockefeller's passionate support for civil rights that most annoyed the Right. Most conservative thinkers saw the future of the GOP in the South and were happy to have Democrats embrace racial integration if it drove Dixie closer to the Republicans.

A Battle for the Soul of the GOP

The spring and summer of 1963 marked the end of Rockefeller's rein as GOP front-runner and perhaps of his plausibility as a Republican nominee under any circumstances. Rockefeller and his first wife had divorced in March 1962, after years of unhappy wedlock (and obsessive womanizing on his part). It created a public outcry, but Rockefeller's political standing recovered before long. But in May 1963, he married Margaretta Fitler "Happy" Murphy, a onetime assistant and family friend. She was more than two decades younger than Rockefeller, had divorced her husband recently, and had given up custody of her children to her husband. The condemnation of Rockefeller's remarriage crossed partisan and cultural lines but seemed especially intense among the GOP rank and file. He lost his previous polling lead over Barry Goldwater. Even though Rockefeller did not abandon his campaign (he formally announced his candidacy in November 1963), party moderates began to look elsewhere. Richard Nixon, 1960 vice presidential nominee Henry Cabot Lodge, Pennsylvania governor William Scranton, and Michigan governor George Romney were all subject to speculation as the GOP candidate. Any of these figures could plausibly win the support of Dwight Eisenhower, who made it clear he had little use for either Rockefeller or Goldwater.

Other events also diminished Rockefeller's chances at the Republican nomination. On June 11, John F. Kennedy announced his support for what would become the Civil Rights Act of 1964. This followed several months when Kennedy was increasingly seen as a champion of racial integration. Rockefeller had long criticized Kennedy for moving too slowly on civil rights. This critique of Kennedy was no longer politically viable. Increasingly, Republicans saw more advantage in attacking national Democrats for moving too fast. African Americans were now part of the Democratic base, and even a longtime civil rights champion like Rockefeller was not likely to pull them away. Not coincidentally, the conservative movement within the GOP was growing rapidly. Following a year and a half of covert organization, the National Draft Goldwater Committee went public on April 8. Goldwater supporters increasingly dominated Republican gatherings. Encouraged by party liberals, Rockefeller delivered a fiery address on July 14. He called conservatives a "radical, well-financed, and highly disciplined minority" that appealed to racism. The address backfired, ending his relationship with Goldwater and other conservatives, without winning over moderates. Rockefeller no longer appeared a plausible unifying figure for Republicans. He was now a leader of a faction—a faction that increasingly seemed like a minority.

Arguably, Rockefeller was now a liability to Republican moderates. Unlike figures like Lodge or Scranton, he appeared unacceptable to conservatives. His remarriage made him personally offensive to millions of Republican voters. But Rockefeller continued to seek the nomination. He campaigned enthusiastically in New Hampshire, giving voters in the Granite State a taste of the handshaking and backslapping New Yorkers had experienced. Huge spending (mostly fueled by family money) made his ads inescapable on local television. But a visibly pregnant Happy accompanied him on the campaign trail, reminding voters of his remarriage. Fortunately for Rockefeller, Barry Goldwater proved to be a gaffe machine, issuing alarming statements on topics ranging from Social Security to nuclear war. Many New Hampshire Republicans found themselves wishing for another choice. A group of Boston-based operatives launched a write-in campaign for Henry Cabot Lodge. Lodge was half a world away, serving as ambassador to South Vietnam, but he did nothing to discourage the effort. The Lodge team pulled off a shocking upset, winning 35 percent to Goldwater's 22 percent, Rockefeller's 21 percent, and 16 percent for Nixon as a write-in. Suddenly, Lodge was hailed as the front-runner, despite not having announced his candidacy.

Armed with a massive campaign staff and an advertising budget to match, Rockefeller fought on. With many moderate Republicans, Oregon looked like an inviting target. Lodge and Nixon were both on the ballot and had informal campaign apparatuses, despite not being technically in the race. Goldwater barely visited the state. But Rockefeller barnstormed throughout Oregon, giving rise to his slogan, "He Cares Enough to Come." Rockefeller won in Oregon, effectively ending Lodge's undeclared campaign. Meanwhile, Goldwater continued to roll up huge margins among delegates chosen in nonprimary states.[29]

Both Rockefeller and Goldwater understood that California was likely to be a key primary. Goldwater had a large enough lead among delegates chosen in nonprimary states, that a California win would probably lock up the nomination. A Rockefeller win would mean a deadlocked convention that might select another moderate such as Nixon or Scranton. Goldwater benefited from a fervent base of conservative volunteers. Early polls showed him with a clear lead over Rockefeller. But Rockefeller had his huge financial resources, which allowed him to hire Stu Spencer and Bill Roberts, California's top Republican consultants. He enjoyed the support of the state's business and political establishments, and the endorsements of nearly all the state's newspapers. The campaign turned nasty, with Goldwater volunteers making violent threats against Rockefeller, and the Rockefeller campaign issuing literature warning that Goldwater could not be trusted with nuclear weapons. But Rockefeller refused to run a TV documentary, produced by Spencer and Roberts, that associated Goldwater with right-wing extremism. His advisers convinced him that the program was too intense and would backfire.[30]

Showing his typical indecision, Eisenhower issued a statement that appeared to oppose Goldwater, but then said he did not mean to single him out. Rockefeller's vast resources allowed him to dominate the airwaves, but the campaign decided to ease off spending in the last days, given that Rockefeller had jumped to a lead in polls. Meanwhile, Goldwater launched a last-minute ad blitz. That may have made the difference as Goldwater edged out Rockefeller, 51 percent to 49 percent. But some political observers preferred another explanation: Happy giving birth to Nelson Rockefeller Jr. just three days before the primary.

With his defeat in California, Rockefeller's chances of winning the nomination evaporated. He joined moderates in seeking to stop Goldwater somehow, but the Arizona senator's delegate lead made that improbable. Goldwater's decision to vote against passage of the Civil Rights Act of 1964 increased moderate determination to fight his nomination but did not make the mathematics any easier. Scranton, so hesitant about entering the race that wags dubbed him the "Hamlet of Harrisburg," finally announced his candidacy a month before the convention. Rockefeller transferred to him his campaign organization (but not his delegates). He allied with Scranton in pushing for three platform planks: one supporting the Civil Rights Act of 1964, one declaring that only the president could order a nuclear attack, and one denouncing extremism on both the Left and Right. Rockefeller spoke to the convention in support of the antiextremism plank. The delegates responded with boos and chants of "We Want Barry." All of the planks backed by Scranton and Rockefeller failed. In the end, the atmosphere was so poisonous that Goldwater refused to accept Rockefeller's phone call congratulating him on winning the nomination. Rockefeller hedged on backing Goldwater in the general election, finally endorsing him in an unenthusiastic joint appearance in September.

Rockefeller's political career would always be defined by the 1964 campaign, marking him as a symbol of the defeat of moderates within the GOP. His actions during the campaign, the convention, and afterward further deepened conservatives' distrust. By contrast, Nixon, who shared Rockefeller's views on most issues, and who was also eager to deny Goldwater the nomination, accepted the conservative triumph. He not only campaigned for Goldwater, but he stumped for Republicans of all stripes, who would remember his help in the hour of need.[31,32]

Rockefeller's failure in 1964 had multiple fathers. The scandal of his divorce and remarriage alienated many rank-and-file Republican voters. His moderate-to-liberal record in New York State appealed to many swing voters, but not the party base. Throughout his two decades of seeking the GOP presidential nomination, he never showed much affinity for Republican activists outside the Northeast. Before the spring of 1963, when Rockefeller appeared to be a consensus front-runner, the GOP faithful might have begrudgingly accepted him as the nominee. But after Rockefeller stumbled, they saw little reason to help him regain his footing. Dwight Eisenhower did not want to see Barry Goldwater as the nominee. But Rockefeller's years of criticism of Ike's record in the White House made it difficult for the ex-president to back him for his old office. The constituencies that were friendliest to Rockefeller—organized labor, the national media, the civil rights community—were either outside the Republican Party or opposed to it.

But Rockefeller's biggest obstacle was the rising conservative movement. Thousands of activists were willing to work to claim the GOP for Barry Goldwater. Strategists like F. Clifton White and William Rusher were able to wrest control of the nomination apparatus from the Republican establishment. Far more than any other moderate Republican, Nelson Rockefeller served as a demon figure for the conservative movement. He taxed, spent, and borrowed. He embraced the civil rights movement. He supported the United Nations.

He pursued a scandalous personal life. He lived on Fifth Avenue. He even liked modern art. If Nelson Rockefeller didn't exist, the conservatives of the South and West would have had to invent him. Meanwhile, the "Eastern Establishment" that had backed Dewey and Eisenhower had lost its grip on the GOP.

At the Center of a Tumultuous Year

Goldwater's nomination remade the GOP in a fashion that marginalized Rockefeller. Movement conservatives were now central to the party's identity. White southerners seemed like the GOP's future. African Americans deserted the Republicans nearly entirely. Richard Nixon was not a movement conservative or a southerner, but he was willing to appease these groups, and he no longer had much hope for the GOP's prospects among black voters.

In the aftermath of the 1964 election, Rockefeller declared that he had no interest in running for president again. Instead, he backed Michigan governor George Romney for the nomination in 1968. Romney lacked Rockefeller's personal baggage (indeed the devout Mormon struck many journalists as self-righteous), but his relationships with movement conservatives were not much warmer. Although most savvy observers doubted Rockefeller had completely given up his desires for the White House, his abandonment of national politics stood in sharp contrast to the endless hours Nixon spent on the rubber-chicken circuit.

Even as Lyndon Johnson pursued a Great Society in Washington, Nelson Rockefeller built his own version in Albany. Having forsaken the pursuit of the Republican presidential nomination, and with the Johnson landslide having given Democrats temporary control of the New York State legislature, two important constraints had come off Rockefeller's big-spending habits. He imposed New York's first sales tax. Spending on welfare and public housing soared. Most consequently, New York adopted an especially generous and expensive Medicaid program that would bust state budgets for decades to come.

As the 1966 election approached, Rockefeller looked like an underdog for reelection. Prominent Democrats led him in polls, and some Republicans looked around for possible replacements at the top of the ticket. Conservatives were still annoyed by Rockefeller's treatment of Goldwater in 1964 and by his divorce and remarriage. Liberals thought his spending programs did not go far enough and felt his law-and-order approach to the problems of crime and drug abuse was simple-minded. Newly elected New York mayor John Lindsay challenged him for leadership of moderate and liberal Republicans. The two men, not terribly far apart on policy substance, had dramatically different political styles, and feuded frequently. New Yorkers of all stripes were annoyed by his breaking of a no-tax-increase pledge and by his continuing flirtations with the White House.

Rockefeller responded to these challenges in his usual big-spending, ideologically ambiguous, fashion. When polls found that New Yorkers were unaware of his accomplishments as governor, but were weary of his larger-than-life personality, the campaign launched a series of television ads entitled "Governor Rockefeller for Governor." These touted his achievements in areas from highway construction to environmental protection, but never showed Rockefeller himself. He pounded away at Democratic nominee Frank O'Connor, telling liberals he was a machine hack, while warning conservatives that the former prosecutor was actually soft on crime. Rockefeller beat O'Connor by a 45 percent to 38 percent margin, his closest race as governor, with significant votes going to minor-party candidates.

The national Republican wave in 1966 created optimism about the party recapturing the White House, as well as excitement about a new set of GOP stars. California governor Ronald Reagan replaced Goldwater as the leader of the conservative movement. Several newly elected Republicans challenged Rockefeller for the leadership of the party's moderate-to-liberal wing: Lindsay, Senator Charles Percy (R-IL), Senator Mark Hatfield (R-OR), Maryland governor Spiro Agnew. But Romney, once the GOP frontrunner, saw his support sag. Comfortable with domestic issues, Romney often seemed out of his depth on foreign policy, especially the Vietnam War. In an interview on a Detroit TV show in August 1967, Romney explained his increasing dovishness by saying he had experienced a "brainwashing" by the military brass during a visit to Vietnam. Romney was almost laughed out of the race, and his withdrawal in February 1968 seemed anticlimactic, given Nixon's massive polling lead.

To the surprise of few, Rockefeller's interest in the presidency revived in 1967. Most savvy observers thought his backing of Romney had always been more strategic than sincere. Republican governors—most of them relatively moderate—looked for a champion as Romney's fortunes waned. Nixon was branded as a "loser," while Reagan was tied to an ideology that many though had been discredited by Goldwater's defeat. None of the new breed of moderates was able to establish himself as a front-runner. Rockefeller seemed an appealing alternative. Savvy observers talked of a Rockefeller-Reagan ticket, despite the two men having little in common except an expressed lack of interest in the vice presidency.

Romney's withdrawal from the race created an opportunity for Rockefeller to announce his candidacy. While Nixon was dominating the primaries, Rockefeller and his circle thought that he could still win the nomination at the convention, in part by arguing for his greater electability. (It had worked for Dwight Eisenhower in 1952 and for Wendell Willkie in 1940.) But a meeting with Republican members of Congress seems to have convinced Rockefeller that party regulars mostly wanted him to run in order to heighten the effect of any Nixon primary victories. A poll in Oregon—again a key primary state—showed Nixon leading. (Nixon himself was more worried about Reagan, since he was confident that Rockefeller could not win the nomination.) On March 21, Rockefeller announced he would not seek the presidency, shocking the press, and humiliating Agnew. The Maryland governor had asked local journalists to join him in watching what he had assumed would be the kickoff to a campaign that would feature him as a key supporter. (Before long, Agnew would be lunching with Nixon, complaining of his maltreatment by Rockefeller.) Many moderate Republicans decided that Nixon was both inevitable and acceptable, and switched their allegiances to him.

Just like eight years before, Rockefeller experienced second thoughts about not running. Lyndon Johnson urged him to seek the presidency, even promising him that he would not campaign against him should he become the Republican nominee. He seems to have been genuinely concerned that Nixon could not win a general election, and if he did, would be a poor president. Rockefeller saw Nixon as a shallow opportunist bereft of a policy vision; Nixon, in turn, perceived Rockefeller as a self-absorbed elitist unwilling to be a team player.

On April 30, Rockefeller announced that he had changed his mind and he *was* going to run for president after all. That same day, he won the Massachusetts primary as a write-in. Despite this win, his campaign got off to a poor start. Rockefeller was more interested in the details of public policy than in the mechanics of delegate selection. If he had understood the nomination process better, he might have realized that it was much too late to stop Nixon. After Robert Kennedy's assassination in June, Rockefeller gained a new sense of mission, but one that did little to help him win the nomination. He identified himself with the slain senator's cause and gained the support of some of his backers; indeed, he made a special effort to reach out to African Americans, many of whom indeed admired both RFK and Rockefeller. But most Republican voters and activists were less concerned with fixing the problems of the ghettoes than with maintaining law and order. A lifelong hawk, Rockefeller attempted to embrace the antiwar movement. As a result, Rockefeller saw his support rise among Democrats and Independents—but fall among Republicans. It did not help that he seemed to spend more time attacking Nixon than the Democratic administration.

Ronald Reagan was conducting his own presidential campaign, though without actually entering the race. Despite the two men's obvious differences on issues, savvy members of both teams understood that their only hope was to work together to keep Nixon from winning on the first ballot. Each candidate appealed to groups that had little use for the other. Reagan had an especially strong bond with southern Republicans; Nixon feared this challenge, leading him to make assurances to Senator Strom Thurmond (R-SC) that he would not pursue civil rights enforcement too vigorously.

When they arrived in Miami Beach for the Republican national convention, the Rockefeller campaign's main message was "Rocky Can Win," which was supported by months of survey data. But a new Gallup Poll showed Nixon performing better than Rockefeller against the most likely Democratic nominees. The delegate math looked difficult for the Rockefeller-Reagan coalition. But Rockefeller thought that "favorite sons" would hold several northern states against Nixon. Reagan, who was finally officially in the race, aimed to win over southern delegates, many of whom privately preferred him to Nixon. But Senator Thurmond told them of Nixon's promises to him and warned, "a vote for Reagan is a vote for Rockefeller." In the end, Nixon's southern support held fast, while Rockefeller's "favorite son" strategy collapsed when some New Jersey and Pennsylvania delegates backed Nixon. Nixon won on the first ballot and picked Agnew, so humiliated by Rockefeller, as his running mate. Even if the alliance with Reagan had succeeded in blocking Nixon, Rockefeller's path to the nomination remained difficult. Conservatives might grudgingly accept Nixon, but they still despised Rockefeller. Moderates might distrust Nixon, but they generally could live with him as the nominee. Rockefeller also lacked the relationships with Republican politicians and the respect of the Republican grassroots that Nixon had developed over two decades of relentless politicking. Rockefeller left the convention feeling embittered, but overcame his anger enough to stump for Nixon with far more enthusiasm than he had ever shown for Goldwater.

Rockefeller and Nixon: Allies at Last

Despite their mutual disdain, Rockefeller developed a working relationship with Nixon during the Californian's time in the White House. Rockefeller increasingly understood that his own Oval Office ambitions could only be realized by cultivating the good will of the new president. In turn, Nixon respected Rockefeller's political acumen and his power in New York State. Although Nixon passed over Rockefeller for his cabinet, he nonetheless appointed numerous Rockefeller loyalists in key positions. Henry Kissinger became national security adviser. John N. Mitchell, Nixon's law partner and campaign manager, but also a longtime Rockefeller ally, became attorney general. Nixon's speech-writing staff included William Safire, who had worked for Rockefeller in 1964, and Raymond Price, last editorial page chief for the always Rockefeller-friendly *New York Herald Tribune*. New York's education commissioner, James Allen, took a similar post under Nixon. Nancy Hanks, a longtime Rockefeller protégé (and onetime mistress), took over the National Endowment for the Arts. Nixon's generally centrist domestic policy often followed Rockefeller's lead: the Environmental Protection Agency owed much to New York's Department of Environmental Conservation.

In turn, Rockefeller allied himself closely with Nixon. Shedding his brief guise as a dove, Rockefeller was a loyal supporter of Nixon's foreign policy (much of it devised by his longtime sidekick Kissinger). He took on a lengthy mission to his longtime stomping ground of Latin America in May and June 1969. If the trip sometimes subjected Rockefeller to criticism for his coziness with authoritarian regimes, it certainly showed his willingness to be a team player at last. Rockefeller's political strategies paralleled Nixon's. Both backed crackdowns on crime, drugs, and campus unrest. Rockefeller's successful 1970 reelection campaign rested on winning blue-collar Catholics; Nixon did the same in 1972.

Fiscal pressures on New York, in part due to Rockefeller's own programs, pushed the governor to embrace Nixon's "New Federalism." Rockefeller was especially enthusiastic about block grants and "revenue sharing," two schemes to give states more access to federal funds. Pressure from conservative Republicans in the state legislature pushed Rockefeller to the right on spending and welfare reform. But he was still willing to break with conservatives on some issues: in 1970, Rockefeller signed a liberalized abortion law. Two years later, he vetoed an attempt to overturn it.

The reconciliation between Nixon and Rockefeller culminated in the president's 1972 campaign. Rockefeller lent staff to Nixon, placed his name in nomination at the Republican Convention, and controlled the president's organization in New York State. For the first time in three presidential campaigns, Nixon carried New York, winning an impressive 59 percent of the vote. Surely, now that Rockefeller had showed his loyalty to the GOP and his willingness to accommodate conservatives, he had won the right to the presidential nomination.

As Rockefeller wooed the Right, however, he lost the admiration he once enjoyed from liberals. The antiwar movement saw little to admire in the patron of Henry Kissinger. Baby boomers who rebelled at hierarchy distrusted Rockefeller's authoritarian style, which got crankier and more inflexible as he aged. His increasingly hard line on crime and welfare lost him much of the affection he had once enjoyed from the civil rights movement. In September 1971, prisoners seized control of the Attica Correctional Facility in western New York and took 42 officers and civilians hostages. After four days of negotiation, Rockefeller ordered the state police to seize the prison. Twenty-nine prisoners and 10 guards died in the ensuing battle. In January 1973, Rockefeller, always concerned about drug abuse, called for sentencing dealers in hard drugs to lengthy sentences in prison. After months of heavy lobbying, Rockefeller's proposal became law in May. The state's prison population exploded. Subsequent governors rolled back the law's penalties, and for later generations the "Rockefeller law" became synonymous with a draconian, inflexible approach to the drug problem.

After Nixon's reelection triumph, Rockefeller appeared to be one of the four leading contenders for the 1976 Republican nomination, along with Reagan, Agnew, and former treasury secretary John Connally (Nixon's favorite, but still a nominal Democrat). Nixon appointed Rockefeller to head the National Commission on Critical Choices for Americans (yet another high-minded blue-ribbon commission) and the National Commission on Water Quality. Rockefeller was tired of the governorship, ready to focus on his next presidential run, and wanted to give the long-serving Malcolm Wilson a head start on the 1974 election. In December 1973, Rockefeller announced that he was quitting the governorship in order to chair the two commissions.

Vice President Rockefeller

By this point, Nixon was deep into the Watergate scandal. Rockefeller was publicly supportive of Nixon, while privately he felt his longstanding doubts about the president had been vindicated. When Vice President Agnew resigned in October 1973 due to an unrelated scandal, there was speculation that Rockefeller would be appointed to replace him as vice president. But conservative skepticism made that unlikely, and Nixon instead chose House Republican Leader Gerald Ford. On August 17, eight days after Nixon's resignation, Ford offered the vice presidency to Rockefeller. Against the advice of some of his aides, Rockefeller accepted the offer. Ford had promised Rockefeller that he would play a role in domestic policy comparable to Kissinger's in foreign policy. Instead, the vice presidency would mark the end of Rockefeller's political career.

Rockefeller's ability to alienate both the Left and the Right appeared once again. Conservatives were enraged especially since Ford had not yet said he would run for president in his own right. A Vice President Rockefeller might have the inside track for the GOP nomination in 1976. His confirmation hearings held by a Democratic Congress proved more confrontational than expected. After he finally took office, Rockefeller soon discovered that his long lack of interest in the vice presidency had real justification. White House Chief of Staff Donald Rumsfeld soon emerged as Rockefeller's rival, blocking his access to Ford and winning battles over staff. Rockefeller offered a wide variety of ideas on jobs, health care, and energy. He even suggested buying Greenland from Denmark for its supposed mineral riches. But Ford and Rumsfeld were more interested in holding down government spending.

New York City's fiscal crisis heightened the conflict between Rockefeller and the rest of the Ford administration. To conservatives like Treasury Secretary William Simon, Rockefeller was a symbol of an out-of-control, fiscally reckless liberalism. Echoing his experiences under Eisenhower, Rockefeller found himself out of step with a basically conservative administration. He fought with the Right on Capitol Hill as well, where as president of the Senate, Rockefeller helped enact filibuster reform and a strong renewal of the Voting Rights Act, causes backed by liberals in both parties.

By the summer of 1975, talk was growing that Rockefeller would be dropped from the ticket. Ronald Reagan was gearing up to challenge Ford for the nomination from the Right. In July, Ford's campaign manager declared Rockefeller to be Ford's leading political problem. Polls showed Rockefeller hurting Ford with many Republican voters. On October 28, Ford asked Rockefeller to withdraw. Although Rockefeller would provide some assistance to Ford's winning the nomination, his political career was essentially over.

After he returned to New York in January 1977, Rockefeller made it clear he had lost all interest in politics. His efforts to assert dominance over the family philanthropies led to conflict with his brother John III and a new rising generation of Rockefellers. Nelson Rockefeller died suddenly on January 26, 1979. Tributes to his years of public service and contemplations of his leadership of GOP liberals turned into sniggers when it was revealed that he had died in the intimate company of a young female assistant.

Winthrop: The Ozarks Rockefeller

Winthrop emerged early as the "black sheep" of the Rockefeller brothers. As a young man, he felt more comfortable working as an oil field roughneck or commanding troops in the South Pacific than serving in the family enterprises. Winthrop was best known for a hedonistic lifestyle that included womanizing, heavy drinking, and an expensive and high-profile divorce. He certainly did not fit in with his father's Puritanism or with his brothers' world of philanthropy and power.

In 1953, a visit to an army friend in Arkansas changed Winthrop's life. He soon moved to the state, where he established Winrock Farms, a cattle ranch that gained world renown. In 1955, Governor Orval Faubus named him as the first chairman of Arkansas Industrial Development Commission. Winthrop courted industry vigorously for his impoverished new home state, while his philanthropy gained him the respect he had previously lacked.

Winthrop found himself turning against his patron Orval Faubus. The governor's vehement defense of racial segregation clashed with the Rockefellers' long support for civil rights. Winthrop's loyal Republicanism led him to seek to bring two-party politics to staunchly Democratic Arkansas. In 1964, Winthrop challenged Faubus for reelection; the incumbent governor beat the Yankee billionaire by 57 percent to 43 percent—but that was still the best performance by a Republican in an Arkansas gubernatorial election since Reconstruction.[33]

Two years later, Winthrop defeated segregationist Democrat Jim Johnson to be elected Arkansas's first Republican governor in nearly a century. Facing a legislature both conservative and almost entirely Democratic, Winthrop was often frustrated as governor. But he nonetheless produced numerous accomplishments: reform of the state's notorious prison system, a freedom of information law, a state minimum wage, and improved insurance regulation. His staunch support for civil rights made for a stark contrast with Faubus's segregationism. Winthrop was the only southern governor to hold a public ceremony to mourn Martin Luther King Jr.'s death. His governorship was seen by many as the point when Arkansas joined the "New South."

Winthrop won reelection in 1968, against Marion Crank, a rural-based conservative Democrat. But his second term was unproductive, and his increasingly visible alcoholism and the public breakdown of his second marriage appeared to distract him from official duties. In 1970, he was defeated for reelection by Dale Bumpers, a Democratic lawyer new to politics and free from segregationist baggage. Winthrop Rockefeller died of pancreatic cancer in February 1973, but his family philanthropy continues to benefit Arkansas.

David Rockefeller

Although he briefly worked for New York mayor Fiorello LaGuardia, David Rockefeller spent his professional life in finance, rising to be president (1961–1969) and chairman (1969–1981) of Chase Manhattan Bank. (When he joined Chase, it was headed by his uncle Winthrop Aldrich; it also had long ties to Standard Oil and to the Rockefeller family more broadly.) But even as he built a career in banking, he also became a force in foreign affairs, serving on the boards of think tanks, and welcome in the offices of heads of states. He served as chairman of the Council on Foreign Relations for 15 years.[34] Three times David was offered the position as secretary of the treasury, and his brother Nelson once offered to appoint him to the U.S. Senate to fill a vacancy. He turned down all these proposals. His influence arguably peaked during the Nixon and Ford administrations, assisted by the family's long relationship with Henry Kissinger, who had been Nelson's longtime foreign policy adviser, and served in the same role to Nixon and Ford. David's contacts around the world, particularly in the Middle East and Latin America, made him a valuable partner for the White House. His relationship with President Jimmy Carter was cooler. Carter was a self-proclaimed outsider, while David was a quintessential enough insider to have founded the Trilateral Commission.[35] The fraught state of the relationship between the two men was exemplified by David's repeated attempts in 1979 to help bring the disposed Shah of Iran to the United States for medical treatment. When the Shah was finally admitted, Iranian students seized the U.S. Embassy in Teheran, precipitating the crisis that would dominate the rest of Carter's presidency. After David's retirement in 1981, he spent three decades as an elder statesman, welcome in presidential palaces and executive suites around the world.[36]

The Other Brothers

Although he was overshadowed by his younger brother Nelson, eldest son John D. Rockefeller III nonetheless made his mark as the leading philanthropist among the brothers. John III chaired the Rockefeller Foundation for 20 years, served as a leading spokesman for the nonprofit sector, and sought to strengthen U.S.-Asian relations. He also served as a leading figure behind the construction of the Lincoln Center cultural complex in New York City, which helped make him a prominent voice for arts funding. But he did not attract wide public attention until he became a vocal advocate of population control in the 1960s and 1970s, when Lyndon Johnson and Richard Nixon appointed him to chair commissions on the issue. John III was emerging as the most liberal of the brothers, and the only one with much sympathy for the spirit of the Age of Aquarius. This sometimes led to conflict with the Nixon White House, and with his brother Nelson. After Nelson left public life, his attempts to establish total control of the Rockefeller Brothers Fund confronted fierce resistance from John III. The fraternal battles only ended with the sudden deaths of both men in the late 1970s.

Laurance S. Rockefeller, the youngest of the brothers, devoted his life to investing and to conservationism, sometimes advising Nelson as well as several presidents on environmental issues. But his most important role was as the longtime president of the Rockefeller Brothers Fund, in which capacity he loyally served Nelson.

The Cousins

By the late 1960s, the next generation of Rockefellers (often known as "the cousins") was coming of age. In sharp contrast to the Rockefeller brothers, about two-thirds of the two dozen cousins were female, and many of them rebelled against the family's patriarchal culture. Several Rockefeller women embraced the 1960s counterculture, funding New Left institutions such as Students for a Democratic Society and the magazine *Ramparts*, and questioning their family's investments in defense contractors and polluting industries. Many cousins of both sexes felt ambivalent toward the Rockefeller legacy. Not surprisingly, relations between the two generations of Rockefellers turned ugly. Although some cousins entered the business world, more chose less lucrative careers, in academia, journalism, and the caring professions. As tensions relaxed after Nelson's death, the cousins assumed roles in the family businesses and philanthropies. But few sought the world-spanning roles played by the Rockefeller brothers.

Unlike most other Rockefellers of his generation, John D. Rockefeller IV (usually known as "Jay") chose a life in the public spotlight. Jay graduated from Harvard University in 1961. After serving in minor posts in the Kennedy

The Rockefeller Dynasty

administration, Jay Rockefeller came to West Virginia as a VISTA volunteer in 1964. Two years later, he was elected to the West Virginia House of Delegates (as a Democrat) and was elected secretary of state in 1968. Rockefeller turned down an offer from his uncle Nelson to be appointed to fill the vacancy created by the assassination of Senator Robert F. Kennedy. Instead, he chose to continue building his political career in West Virginia. In a state with a long history of political corruption, he cracked down on vote-buying and other electoral fraud. He developed an enemy in the coal industry when he announced his opposition to strip mining. Many observers saw him as presidential material, perhaps in 1976.

Rockefeller challenged Republican governor Arch Moore for reelection in 1972. Moore portrayed Rockefeller as a wealthy dilettante out of touch with the humble lives of most West Virginians. He warned that Rockefeller would destroy the state's coal industry. Hearkening back to earlier generations, Moore charged that Rockefeller was part of a ruthless clan of robber barons. Moore also ran a memorable advertisement that featured New Yorkers being asked about electing a West Virginian as governor. One responded, "That makes as much sense to me as having the next Governor of West Virginia be a New Yorker." Signs appeared around the state that simply declared, "Remember Ludlow," recalling the 1915 massacre of coal miners in Colorado. Saddled with George McGovern heading the Democratic ticket, Rockefeller lost to Moore, 55 percent to 45 percent, a humiliating defeat for a man who had seemed destined for the White House.

Still, Rockefeller remained in the state and was elected governor in a landslide just four years later, in 1976. Serving as governor of West Virginia was less glamorous than his uncle Nelson's tenure in Albany. He abandoned his previous opposition to strip mining. A deep recession gave West Virginia the nation's highest unemployment rate. Rockefeller gained a reputation as an able and honest governor who was nonetheless beset by problems beyond his ability to overcome. After leaving the governor's seat, Jay was elected to the U.S. Senate in 1984, spending $12 million of his own money, a formidable sum in a small state.

Rockefeller gained a reputation in the Senate as a liberal who had a special interest in health care policy, and as a "workhorse" willing to master unglamorous issues relevant to West Virginia. He considered running for president in 1992, probably the only time when he could have realistically won the White House, but decided against it. He continued working on health care, coauthoring the Children's Health Insurance Program and backing a public option as part of the Affordable Care Act. As chairman of the Senate Intelligence Committee, he was a prominent critic of the Iraq War. Facing a challenging reelection campaign in an increasingly Republican state, and enduring increasing health problems, Senator Rockefeller announced his retirement in January 2013.

Winthrop Paul Rockefeller (known as "Win Paul"), Winthrop's only child, was the only other Rockefeller cousin who won public office. After spending two decades managing the ranch and investments he inherited from his father, Win Paul Rockefeller was elected lieutenant governor of Arkansas in 1996. A decade later, he was preparing to seek the state's governorship. But he was diagnosed with a rare blood disorder and died in July 2006.

Alida Ferry Rockefeller Messinger, sister of Senator Jay Rockefeller, has been a leading donor to progressive causes and the Democratic Party. She was married to Mark Dayton, a retailing heir who has served as a U.S. senator and as governor of Minnesota. Although they divorced in 1986, she has remained a Minnesotan and a supporter of Dayton's political career. The next generation (the "second cousins" perhaps) has not yet produced any elected officials, but Jay's son Justin is a politically engaged philanthropist, and Win Paul's son Will has been mentioned as a possible Republican candidate in Arkansas.

Conclusion

The Rockefeller family, so prominent in 20th-century America, does not play the same role in this century. That shift is partially due to predictable changes. As the family has grown with each generation, the fortune has become more fragmented. If the Rockefeller brothers embraced public life, the following generations have mostly chosen to keep a low profile. New technologies have produced new billionaires. Perhaps the late 21st century will see Bezoses and Zuckerbergs in high office? But the decline of the Rockefellers also may reflect broader shifts in American life. The Rockefellers were identified with the rise of large bureaucratic organizations—in business, government, labor, academia, and philanthropy. These organizations were staffed by experts applying the latest "scientific" techniques. There was a time when Americans had faith in bureaucracies and experts. That time has passed.

Notes

1. Ron Chernow. 1998. *Titan: The Life of John D. Rockefeller, Sr.* New York: Vintage Books, 556.

2. He did marry Abby Greene Aldrich, daughter of Senator Nelson W. Aldrich (R-RI). She was mostly known for her support for modern art, but her extroverted personality had a profound impact on her children, particularly Nelson.

3. For discussions of Nelson's militant anticommunism, see Cary Reich. 1996. *The Life of Nelson A. Rockefeller: Worlds to Conquer, 1908–1958.* New York: Doubleday, xvi–xvii, 335–336, 448–449, 554–555; Rick Perlstein. 2001. *Before the Storm: Barry Goldwater and the Unmaking of the American Consensus.* New York: Perseus Books, 77; Peter Collier and David Horowitz. 1976. *The Rockefellers: An American Dynasty.* New York: Holt, Rinehart, and Winston, 325–330; for John III's concerns

about overpopulation, see John Ensor Harr and Peter J. Johnson. 1991. *The Rockefeller Conscience: An American Family in Public and in Private*. New York: Scribner's, especially 158–179, 395–442; "the revolution of rising expectations" is a major theme of Rockefeller Brothers Fund. 1961. *Prospect for America: The Rockefeller Panel Reports*. New York: Doubleday; also see John Andrew III. 1998. "Cracks in the Consensus: The Rockefeller Brothers Fund Special Studies Project and Eisenhower's America." *Presidential Studies Quarterly*, 535–552.

4. Perlstein 2001, 77–78, Collier and Horowitz 1976, 325–330; for Junior's trust in expertise in pursuit of essentially conservative projects of reform and uplift, see Collier and Horowitz 1976, 139–145; Chernow 1998, 637–647; Reich 1996, 11–12; Smith 2014, 33–34.

5. Cary Reich. 1996. *The Life of Nelson A. Rockefeller: Worlds to Conquer, 1908–1958*. New York: Doubleday, 380.

6. Rockefeller Brothers Fund. 1961. *Prospect for America: The Rockefeller Panel Reports*. New York: Doubleday.

7. John Andrew III. 1998. "Cracks in the Consensus: The Rockefeller Brothers Fund Special Studies Project and Eisenhower's America." *Presidential Studies Quarterly*, 535–552.

8. Richard Norton Smith. 2014. *On His Own Terms: A Life of Nelson Rockefeller*. New York: Random House, 262.

9. Andrew 1998.

10. Smith 2014, 138–164.

11. Reich 1996, 165–264.

12. Smith 2014, 186–188.

13. Eisenhower had previously served as supreme allied commander in Europe, army chief of staff, and NATO supreme commander.

14. Smith 2014, 229–234.

15. Reich 1996, 650.

16. Smith 2014, 220.

17. Reich 1996, 609–617.

18. Smith 2014, 280.

19. Smith 2014, 264–291.

20. Reich 1996, 669–769.

21. In May 1960, the Soviet Union shot down a U-2 spy plane, which was overflying its territory, and captured its pilot. The Eisenhower administration initially stuck to its cover story that the Soviets had shot down a weather plane, but was eventually forced to concede that the U-2 was on an espionage mission. A superpower summit in Paris collapsed. The incident was widely seen as embarrassing to Eisenhower, especially since he had appeared to have been untruthful.

22. Smith 2014, 321–348.

23. Geoffrey Kabaservice. 2012. *Rule and Ruin: The Downfall of Moderation and the Destruction of the Republican Party, from Eisenhower to the Tea Party*. New York: Oxford University Press, 26–31.

24. Theodore H. White. 1961. *The Making of the President, 1960*. New York: Atheneum House, 79–92, 216–247.

25. Rick Perlstein. 2001. *Before the Storm: Barry Goldwater and the Unmaking of the American Consensus.* New York: Perseus Books, 53–57, 76–95.

26. Richard Reeves. 1993. *President Kennedy: Profile of Power.* New York: Simon & Schuster, 465, 468.

27. Smith 2014, 371–373.

28. Perlstein 2001, 136.

29. At the time, most convention delegates were not selected by primaries and primaries did not always bind delegates to candidates. It was common for presidential candidates to wait until the convention to enter the race.

30. Smith 2014, 439–447.

31. Smith 2014, 417–457.

32. Perlstein 2001, 269–389.

33. "Winthrop Rockefeller, 1912–1973." The Rockefeller Archive. http://rockarch.org/bio/winthrop.php. Accessed December 16, 2017.

34. Founded in 1921, the CFR is the leading think tank devoted to foreign policy.

35. The Trilateral Commission is devoted to improving dialogue among the leaders of the United States, Europe, and Japan.

36. David Rockefeller. 2002. *Memoirs.* New York: Random House.

Further Reading

Collier, Peter, and David Horowitz. *The Rockefellers: An American Dynasty.* New York: Holt, Rinehart, and Winston, 1976.

Harr, John Ensor, and Peter J. Johnson. *The Rockefeller Conscience: An American Family in Public and in Private.* New York: Scribner's, 1991.

CHAPTER EIGHT

The Romney Dynasty

Dean J. Kotlowski

The Romney dynasty spans Republican Party politics from 1962 to the present day. Its principal members include George Wilcken Romney, who served as governor of Michigan, and his son, Willard Mitt Romney, who was governor of Massachusetts. Both father and son ran for president: George in 1968 and Mitt in 2008 and 2012, when he received the Republican Party's nomination but lost the general election to President Barack Obama. In 2017, the dynasty's national reach extended to a third generation, when President Donald J. Trump named Ronna Romney McDaniel, George's granddaughter and Mitt's niece, as chair of the Republican National Committee (RNC). The political aspirations of other family members have gone unfulfilled, however, and they remain lesser figures. Ronna Romney McDaniel's mother, Ronna Stern Romney, served in the administrations of Ronald Reagan and George H. W. Bush and became active in the RNC. She twice sought a U.S. Senate seat from Michigan, losing the Republican primary to Spencer Abraham in 1994 and the general election to Democratic senator Carl Levin in 1996. In 1998, Ronna Romney McDaniel's father (and George Romney's elder son), G. Scott Romney, lost a race to be Michigan's attorney general. Earlier, in 1970, George Romney's wife, Lenore LaFount Romney, failed in her bid to unseat Democratic senator Philip A. Hart of Michigan. The rise, achievements, and setbacks of the Romneys reflect the evolution of the Grand Old Party (GOP), from the moderation of Dwight D. Eisenhower and Richard Nixon to the conservatism of Ronald Reagan and George W. Bush to the populist nationalism of Donald Trump. The dynasty also exemplifies many voters' fondness for civic-minded business leaders and the growing visibility of The Church of Jesus Christ of Latter-day Saints (the Church).

George Romney founded the dynasty, which revolved around private sector success, traditional morality, Mormonism, voluntarism, political independence, state-level reform, and presidential ambition. Romney was born in Colonia Dublán, Mexico, where his grandparents had fled to evade American laws against polygamy. Romney's parents, Gaskell Romney and Anna Amelia Pratt Romney, did not practice polygamy, which the Church prohibited in 1890. In 1912, the Mexican Revolution forced Gaskell, Anna, and their seven children to return to the United States. Financially strapped, the family eventually settled in Salt Lake City in 1921. By then, George was in high school, working as a plasterer and exhibiting "determination" and "persistence," according to his brother Maurice.[1] In 1931, following a prolonged courtship, George married Lenore LaFount, the daughter of a wealthy family and an aspiring actress. Before marrying Lenore, Romney completed two years of Mormon missionary work in Great Britain, then attended the University of Utah and George Washington University (from which Lenore graduated in 1929) without earning a degree. He also worked in Washington for Democratic senator David I. Walsh of Massachusetts. Romney's good manners, diligence, competence, and political connections impressed leaders of the Aluminum Corporation of America and Aluminum Wares Association, both of which employed him as a Washington-based lobbyist between 1932 and 1938.

Romney ascended steadily in the private sector. In 1939, automobile executives tapped him to run the Detroit branch of the Automobile Manufacturers Association. Three years later, he became general manager of the association, serving until 1948. During World War II, he testified before Congress on production and labor-management relations in the automotive industry and warned against the power of unions. United Automobile Workers leader Victor Reuther characterized Romney as "a zealous salesman and largely a promoter."[2] Such traits, among others, worked to Romney's advantage. Experience in the auto industry enabled him to become special assistant to the head of the Nash-Kelvinator Corporation in 1948. Six years later, after Nash-Kelvinator and the Hudson Motor Car Company formed the American Motors Corporation (AMC), Romney became AMC's second president. He made the company profitable by pushing the compact Nash Rambler as a fuel-efficient alternative to "the large, chromium-laden cars produced by Ford, Chrysler and General Motors." He once blamed a traffic jam on the gigantic vehicles clogging the roadways, asserting that such problems could be averted if people would "try a Rambler."[3] He assailed big cars as "gas-guzzling dinosaurs" and compared AMC to a tiny elephant among the three "mastodons" of Ford, General Motors, and Chrysler.[4] By challenging both big business and big labor, Romney won praise as a "fresh breeze from the West."[5]

Romney adhered to core principles and displayed a forceful persona. He followed Mormon practices by tithing, respecting the Sabbath, and

Romney Political Dynasty Family Tree

1. George Wilcken Romney, 1907–1995
   Delegate to the Michigan State Constitutional Convention, 1961–1962
   Vice president (one of three) of the Michigan State Constitutional Convention, 1961–1962
   Governor of Michigan, 1963–1969
   Candidate for the Republican Party's presidential nomination, 1967–1968
   Secretary of Housing and Urban Development, 1969–1972
   Married Lenore LaFount, 1908–1998
     Republican nominee for the U.S. Senate from Michigan, 1970
   Four children including Willard Mitt and G. Scott

2. Willard Mitt Romney, 1947–
   Republican nominee for the U.S. Senate from Massachusetts, 1994
   President and chief executive officer of the Salt Lake Organizing Committee for the 2002 Winter Olympics, 1999–2002
   Governor of Massachusetts, 2003–2007
   Chair of the Republican Governors Association, 2005–2006
   Candidate for the Republican Party's presidential nomination, 2007–2008
   Republican nominee for president of the United States, 2012
   Married Ann Davies
   Five children

2. G. Scott Romney, 1941–
   Republican nominee to be Michigan attorney general, 1998
   Married (later divorced) Ronna Stern Romney, 1943–
     Member of the Republican National Committee, 1984–1992
     Commissioner of the President's National Advisory Council on Adult Education, 1982–1985
     Chair of the President's Commission on White House Fellowships, 1989–1993
     Candidate for the Republican nomination for the United States from Michigan, 1994
     Republican nominee for the U.S. Senate from Michigan, 1996
   Five children including Ronna Romney McDaniel

3. Ronna Romney McDaniel, 1973–
   Chair of the Michigan Republican Party, 2015–2017
   Chair of the Republican National Committee, 2017–
   Married Patrick McDaniel
   Two children

abstaining from tobacco, alcohol, and caffeine. He served as president of the Detroit Stake of the Church in the 1950s, but opposed the exclusion of African Americans from the Church clergy. At home, Romney loved his daughters Margo Lynn and Jane, sons Scott and Mitt, and wife, even though he and Lenore frequently quarreled. As a business leader, he shielded AMC from corporate raiders and achieved financial security for his family and, to some extent, for others. "He was on a great mission with American Motors to build innovative cars so that people could save money and fuel, and have better lives," Mitt later explained.[6] Devoted to the wider community and to voluntary service, Romney served on a committee to reform Detroit's schools during the late 1950s and spearheaded Citizens for Michigan, a grassroots campaign to rewrite the state constitution. The new constitution, drafted in 1962, garnered support from business and civic leaders and lifted Romney's prospects in that year's gubernatorial race. Romney's squeaky-clean image, public weariness with politics-as-usual, and the voting strength of Detroit's suburbs further boosted his campaign. Lenore stumped for her husband, whose "tall, graying, athletic-looking" appearance suggested distinction and dynamism.[7] One observer remembered Romney campaigning "on the run with his right arm outstretched to give any potential voter a friendly handshake."[8] On Election Day, he beat incumbent John Swainson to become Michigan's first Republican governor since 1949.

Governor Romney emerged as a leading GOP moderate. He extolled nonpartisanship, won ratification of the Michigan's new constitution, and secured tax increases to steady the state's finances. He approved measures to raise the minimum wage and increase unemployment benefits. Romney also participated in a protest against discrimination in housing, implored President Lyndon B. Johnson to send troops to quell racial unrest in Detroit in 1967, and warned Republicans against sacrificing "the rights of others" in a bid for white racist votes.[9] He denounced the militantly anti-Communist John Birch Society, and in 1964 he opposed the presidential bid of Republican senator Barry M. Goldwater of Arizona, who he found too conservative, especially on civil rights. Romney considered running against Goldwater in "a 'crusade' for moderate Republican principles."[10] In the end, he refused both to run and to endorse Goldwater in the general election—a stand that alienated the party's right wing. Following Goldwater's defeat, a few Republicans grumbled about Romney being frustratingly independent, fiscally liberal, "short-fused," humorless, and overly pious.[11] Yet he proved popular in Michigan, where a booming economy eased his reelection in 1964 and 1966. And he remained, as President Eisenhower remarked, "a man of integrity and character and a great deal of ability."[12] Early in 1967, odds put Romney at "even money" to win the party's presidential nomination in 1968, and GOP governors deemed him their "natural candidate," especially after New York's Nelson A. Rockefeller declined to run.[13] Such prognostication overlooked a nationwide reality, headlined by the *Los Angeles Times* in 1967: "Nixon '68 Choice of Local GOP Leaders."[14]

Romney's presidential campaign flopped. One newspaper editor lamented that he was "running too fast and too soon."[15] He spoke out forcefully, often before thinking through his positions. With respect to the Vietnam War, as the historian Andrew Johns observed, "Romney demonstrated no indication of expertise or even competence."[16] In April 1967, he rejected an American withdrawal. Four months later, however, he dubbed the war a "tragic mistake."[17] Eisenhower regretted Romney's "jumping all around the lot" on Vietnam, and veteran political reporter Jack Germond longed for a typewriter capable of instantaneously producing the phrase "Romney later explained."[18] Especially damaging was a televised interview in which Romney remarked that the diplomatic corps and military brass had given him "the greatest brainwashing that anybody can get" during a 1965 visit to Vietnam.[19] Use of the word "brainwashing" sparked ridicule, even though Americans would later learn that the U.S. government had misled them about the war. The *New York Times* bemoaned Romney's "crippling lack of agility and verbal precision."[20] "Watching George Romney run for the presidency," Republican governor James Rhodes of Ohio quipped, "was like watching a duck try to make love to a football."[21] Plummeting in the polls, Romney exited the race before the New Hampshire primary. As the journalist Theodore H. White reflected, he seemed to be "an honest and decent man simply not cut out to be president."[22]

Romney endured a tense relationship with the party's eventual nominee, Richard Nixon. At the Republican National Convention, Romney declined to release his delegates from Michigan and Utah, and he agreed to be nominated for vice president against Nixon's choice, Governor Spiro T. Agnew of Maryland, who won on the first ballot. Following the election, Nixon reached out by naming Romney secretary of Housing and Urban Development (HUD). Yet, Romney's independent streak and fondness for government action annoyed White House officials. At HUD, he strove to increase the availability of low- and medium-income housing, backed federal aid to cities, and pushed for racial integration of suburbs, without first seeking presidential approval. He believed that a little "disagreement would sharpen Nixon's decision making."[23] But dissension irritated the president, who angled to force Romney's resignation. Indeed, Lenore Romney's 1970 Senate bid originated in a Nixon-inspired plot to induce George Romney to leave HUD and challenge Phil Hart. Instead, Lenore ran for the Senate in George's place.

Lenore Romney's campaign, observed the *Washington Post*, "never really got off the ground."[24] She faced several obstacles: "anti-Romneyism" among conservative Republicans in Michigan; uproar over her husband's recent push to integrate an overwhelmingly white Detroit suburb; and a popular, antiwar incumbent.[25] Operating within her family's political traditions, Lenore blended conservative values (upholding traditional morality) with progressive positions (opposition to the Vietnam War). Yet instead of independence, she projected confusion and inexperience. The conservative *Detroit News* found her speeches "vague, insubstantial and contradictory."[26] And the *Wall Street Journal*

Governor George Romney of Michigan speaks at the Republican National Convention in San Francisco, July 14, 1964. (Library of Congress)

lampooned her campaign film as having "no more substance than a blob of cotton candy."[27] Lenore's call for withdrawal from Vietnam impressed few war-weary Michiganites. One voter told her: "We didn't hear from you in two years. Where were you? Were you brainwashed like your husband said he was on the war?"[28] She refused to respond. In the end, Hart won by a landslide.

George Romney resigned from HUD after Nixon's reelection in 1972, but he remained politically active. In 1974, he weighed, then ruled out, running for the U.S. Senate from Utah. In 1992, Romney founded "Americans for America," an outfit that exhorted citizens to refrain from voting on the basis of "partisanship or economic interest."[29] Two years later, he stumped for his son Mitt, when he sought to unseat Democratic senator Edward M. Kennedy of Massachusetts. George shared ideas with Mitt, assailed anti-Mormon prejudice, and attracted attention almost everywhere he went. "Life on the Romney campaign," Mitt's biographers observed, "was never dull with George around."[30] When Romney died a year later, the dynastic torch passed to Mitt.

Mitt Romney idolized, and even resembled, his father. "I thought everything he said was interesting," Mitt recalled.[31] Even when Mitt was a boy, the pair conversed as peers about their love of cars and politics. When George launched his campaign for governor in 1962, an enthusiastic, 14-year-old Mitt "created a minor problem" by telling reporters that his dad had informed the family of his decision to run abruptly—at 3:30 a.m.![32] Mitt campaigned for his father's election. By then, the Romneys had started to look alike, with their thick hair, lean frames, and square jaws. Both married their high school sweethearts, after two years as missionaries in Europe. Ann Davies, who Mitt married in 1969, was, like Lenore Romney, "beautiful, smart, and independent-minded."[33] Yet Ann, unlike Lenore, had converted to Mormonism. Service to the church assumed a larger role in the life of Mitt, who spent his early years in Michigan (where few Mormons lived), than that of George, who had resided in heavily Church-populated Utah. There were other differences as well. Unlike his father, Mitt grew up in affluent surroundings, attended private schools, and earned a bachelor's degree from Brigham Young University in 1971 and a juris doctor/master of business administration degree from Harvard University in 1975. In 1977 Mitt joined Bain & Company, a Boston-based consulting firm, and in 1984 he cofounded Bain Capital, an investment company. When William Bain interviewed Mitt Romney, he noted that "he very strongly resembles his father."[34] George Romney rejected the comparison. "He's better than a chip off the old block," George stated, during Mitt's Senate bid. "No. 1, he's got a better education. No. 2, he's turned around dozens of companies while I turned around only one. And No. 3, he's made a lot more money than I have."[35]

Mitt Romney differed from his father in two key respects. First, he experienced competing political pressures. While George came of age during the heyday of American liberalism and Republican moderation, Mitt from his youth sensed the GOP's growing conservatism. He witnessed the culture wars of the 1960s from a safe niche at BYU, "which prohibited many rock-and-roll bands, liberal speakers and student organizations, and even long hair on male students."[36] At a time when moral values were being liberalized in ways unknown to a young George Romney, Mitt and Ann maintained a traditional family that included sons Taggart, Matthew, Joshua, Benjamin, and Craig and involved devotion to the Church. Yet George's support for civil rights had impressed Mitt, who initially adopted liberal positions on some social issues before disposing of them later on. At his core, Mitt was more pragmatic than idealistic, the second major way he diverged from his father. He coolly analyzed data, then deployed it to advance his financial and political fortunes. As Mitt's biographers noted, "George did what he felt was right, and if the torpedoes came, the torpedoes came." In contrast, Mitt maneuvered "to identify the consequences he wants, then figure out how to get there" via methods that "varied depending on the race."[37] The result was an awkward amalgam of moral conviction and political opportunism, somewhat reminiscent of his mother's Senate campaign.

Mitt Romney cut his teeth in Massachusetts politics. He had established himself as the chief executive at Bain Capital, presiding over the rescue of some companies, the emergence of others (like Staples), and the closure or downsizing of still others. Although enormously wealthy, Romney proved restless. "I thought of my dad," he said, as he entered public service.[38] Romney's first race in 1994 was against the scion of another dynasty: Senator Ted Kennedy. As a wholesome, energetic newcomer, Romney easily cast Kennedy "as an obsolete, out-of-touch politician." Kennedy, in turn, portrayed his challenger "as a job-slashing corporate raider."[39] On social issues, however, Romney could not match Kennedy in such a strongly liberal state. Romney backed nondiscrimination in employment for gays and lesbians but opposed same-sex marriage. He favored a woman's right to have an abortion, but insisted that states not be required to pay for such operations. Following a sluggish start to the campaign, Kennedy performed well in the televised debates and prevailed on Election Day, winning 58 percent of the vote.

Romney gained national attention for giving Kennedy the closest race of his career; such exposure helped him become head of the Salt Lake Organizing Committee for the 2002 Winter Olympics. Beginning in 1999, Romney rescued the Games from a cash shortfall and the taint of scandal. He enlisted corporate sponsors, trimmed the budget, and promoted patriotic pride in the highly symbolic international event. Political self-interest as well as civic-minded altruism influenced Romney because, as his biographers explained, "if he could turn the Games around, it would be the perfect bridge to elective office."[40] His strategy worked. In 2002, Massachusetts voters elected Romney governor, after a campaign in which he ran as "a fiscal conservative with moderate views on such issues as abortion, gay rights, guns, and the environment."[41] Governor Romney shored up the state's finances and won passage of a bill that required most residents of Massachusetts to purchase health insurance or pay a penalty. The health care law presaged President Barack Obama's Affordable Care Act (2010), although it did not assure Romney's political future in Massachusetts. Determined to run for president and doubtful about winning reelection in a heavily Democratic state, Romney retired after one term as governor.

Romney both inspired and unsettled Republicans when, 40 years after his father ran for president, he entered the race for the GOP nomination in 2008. He announced his candidacy in Michigan—with a Nash Rambler behind him. On the surface, his résumé, good looks, and faultless personal life made him an appealing candidate. Yet, most conservatives deemed him too moderate, and many Evangelicals disliked his Mormon faith. Other Republican candidates despised his unrestrained ambition, his recent switch to a pro-life position on abortion, and his unleashing of vitriolic television ads against them. Arizona senator John McCain, the eventual nominee who went on to lose the general election against Barack Obama, thought him a "phony."[42] Romney won 11 state contests, second only to McCain, making him a favorite for the GOP presidential nomination in 2012. By then, America's lackluster recovery from the recession of 2008–2009 seemed to demand a president with Romney's "formidable intellect, economic expertise, problem-solving know-how, and patriotic zeal."[43] Unfortunately, large numbers of Republicans only saw "a flip-flopping Mormon" who had laid the groundwork for Obamacare, anathema to the GOP's right wing.[44] Nevertheless, according to political scientist Barry C. Burden, Romney benefited from his experience as a presidential candidate, "superior funding and organization," and "air of electability that none of the other Republican contenders could match."[45] Slashing attacks on illegal immigration and gay marriage, a field of uninspiring rivals, and the party's history of nominating an established, senior figure—which had worked against his father—propelled Romney to the Republican nomination.

Romney's prospects against President Obama peaked immediately following the first televised debate, where he appeared sharper and more assertive than the president. However, prior to the debate, release of an unauthorized video that captured Romney's closed-door remarks at a fund-raiser, in which he disparaged 47 percent of the electorate for being dependent on federal programs, reinforced his reputation for elitism. Decrying the gaffe as millionaire-talk, the conservative columnist David Brooks likened Romney to Thurston Howell III, the shipwrecked tycoon on the sitcom *Gilligan's Island*. Peggy Noonan, another conservative columnist, pronounced the Republican campaign "incompetent," and such criticism brought to mind the worst aspects of George Romney's presidential quest.[46] Also damaging was Mitt's opposition to a 2009 bailout of the automobile industry, voiced in a *New York Times* editorial titled "Let Detroit Go Bankrupt."[47] Perceptions that Romney lacked the common touch; a steadily improving economy in Detroit and elsewhere; and a masterfully designed and executed Obama campaign, together sank the GOP nominee. The president won 51 percent of the popular vote to 47 percent for Romney, who took 206 electoral votes against 332 for Obama.

The Romneys remain a nonpresidential dynasty situated on the ideological fault lines of the Republican Party. As Trump's populist/nationalist presidential campaign gathered steam in 2016, Mitt Romney resisted calls from mainstream Republicans to enter the GOP primaries. He instead denounced Trump for his dishonesty, vulgarity, vanity, volatility, avarice, misogyny, and ignorance of foreign affairs.[48] Such remarks, and Romney's refusal to endorse Trump in the general election, paralleled George Romney's principled stand against Goldwater's candidacy in 1964. Following Trump's election, however, Romney set aside past differences and agreed to be considered for secretary of state. After being passed over for that position, he next pondered running in 2018 for the U.S. Senate from Utah, a state long associated with his family and uneasy with Trump's presidency. Romney weighed entering that race in the spring of 2017—as President Trump's approval ratings nosedived and investigators probed ties between his presidential campaign team and Russian agents. Romney's possible role in the Trump era remains uncertain. The same may be said for his niece, RNC chair Ronna Romney McDaniel, especially given Trump's propensity to jettison subordinates he thinks insufficiently loyal or effective. The Romneys are thus a dynasty of the past, the present, and, perhaps, the future.

Notes

1. Clark R. Mollenhoff, *George Romney: Mormon in Politics* (New York: Meredith Press, 1968), 33.

2. Mollenhoff, *George Romney*, 88.

3. Bart Barnes, "George W. Romney Dies at Age 88; Michigan Governor, HUD Secretary," *Washington Post*, July 27, 1995, p. C5.

4. David S. Broder, "George Romney's Republican Party," *Washington Post*, July 30, 1995, p. C9 (first quotation) and Mollenhoff, *George Romney*, 127 (second quotation).

5. Mollenhoff, *George Romney*, 156.

6. Michael Kranish and Scott Helman, *The Real Romney* (New York: HarperCollins, 2012), 16.

7. "George Romney," *Current Biography Yearbook 1958* (New York: H. W. Wilson, 1958), 368.

8. Godfrey Sperling, "The George Romney We Missed Out On," *Christian Science Monitor*, August 22, 1995, p. 19.

9. T. George Harris, *Romney's Way: A Man and an Idea* (Englewood Cliffs, NJ: Prentice-Hall, 1967), 195.

10. Memorandum on "the events that preceded and took place at the Cleveland Governor's Conference," undated (1964), folder: memoranda—others, box 1, Leonard Garment Papers, Manuscript Division, Library of Congress, Washington, DC.

11. News clipping, "Republican Regulars Reluctant on Romney," undated (1967), folder: Romney, George 1967 (4), box 18, Special Names Series, Dwight D. Eisenhower Post-Presidential Papers, Dwight D. Eisenhower Library (DDEL), Abilene, Kansas.

12. Dwight D. Eisenhower to Barry Leithead, March 24, 1967, folder: Romney, George 1967 (4), box 18, Special Names Series, Eisenhower Post-Presidential Papers, DDEL.

13. Theodore H. White, *The Making of the President 1968* (New York: Pocket Books, 1970), 63 (first quotation) and 46 (second quotation).

14. George Gallup, "Nixon '68 Choice of Local GOP Leaders," *Los Angeles Times*, April 16, 1967, p. G3.

15. "Nixon to Beat Romney, Editors Feel," *Pontiac Press*, April 21, 1967, folder: Richard M. Nixon, box 363, George W. Romney Gubernatorial Papers, Michigan Historical Collections, Bentley Historical Library, University of Michigan, Ann Arbor.

16. Andrew L. Johns, *Vietnam's Second Front: Domestic Politics, the Republican Party, and the War* (Lexington: University Press of Kentucky, 2010), 134.

17. Michael Nelson, *Resilient America: Electing Nixon in 1968, Channeling Dissent, and Dividing Government* (Lawrence: University Press of Kansas, 2014), 114.

18. Eisenhower to Willard J. Marriott, January 3, 1968, folder: Romney, George 1968, box 18, Special Names Series, Eisenhower Post-Presidential Papers, DDEL (first quotation) and Nelson, *Resilient America*, 113 (second quotation).

19. Mollenhoff, *George Romney*, 292.

20. Johns, *Vietnam's Second Front*, 163.

21. White, *The Making of the President 1968*, 65.

22. White, *The Making of the President 1968*, 74.

23. Dean J. Kotlowski, *Nixon's Civil Rights: Politics, Principle, and Policy* (Cambridge, MA: Harvard University Press, 2001), 53.

24. "Democrats Win Key Midwestern Senate, Governor Races," *Washington Post*, November 4, 1970, p. A7.

25. Laurence O'Donnell, "Political Trouble Hits the Romneys," *Wall Street Journal*, August 4, 1970, p. 14.

26. "Detroit News Rejects Hart, Mrs. Romney," *Washington Post*, October 24, 1970, p. A6.

27. Fred L. Zimmerman, ". . . As Practiced in a Film Called 'Lenore,'" *Wall Street Journal*, June 23, 1970, p. 16.

28. "First Lady Helps Mrs. Romney," *New York Times*, October 20, 1970, p. 35.

29. Maralee Schwartz and David S. Broder, "Nonpartisan Citizen Romney Returns," *Washington Post*, February 22, 1992, p. A8.

30. Kranish and Helman, *The Real Romney*, 188.

31. Kranish and Helman, *The Real Romney*, 18.

32. Mollenhoff, *George Romney*, 173.

33. Kranish and Helman, *The Real Romney*, 27.

34. Kranish and Helman, *The Real Romney*, 130.

35. Kranish and Helman, *The Real Romney*, 188.

36. Kranish and Helman, *The Real Romney*, 89–90.

37. Kranish and Helman, *The Real Romney*, 6 (all previous quotations).

38. Kranish and Helman, *The Real Romney*, 165.

39. Sara Rimer, "'Perfect Anti-Kennedy' Opposes Senator," *New York Times*, October 25, 1994, p. A1.

40. Kranish and Helman, *The Real Romney*, 206.

41. Kranish and Helman, *The Real Romney*, 229.

42. John Heilemann and Mark Halperin, *Game Change: Obama and the Clintons, McCain and Palin, and the Race of a Lifetime* (New York: HarperCollins, 2010), 294.

43. John Heilemann and Mark Halperin, *Double Down: Game Change 2012* (New York: Penguin Press, 2013), 5.

44. Heilemann and Halperin, *Double Down*, 5.

45. Barry C. Burden, "The Nominations: Ideology, Timing, and Organization," in *The Elections of 2012*, ed. Michael Nelson (Washington, DC: Sage, 2014), 43.

46. Heilemann and Halperin, *Double Down*, 403.
47. Heilemann and Halperin, *Double Down*, 94.
48. "Mitt Romney's Full Speech against Donald Trump," March 3, 2016, *New York Times* online video, accessed August 15, 2017, https://www.nytimes.com/video/us/politics/100000004249503/mitt-romneys-full-speech-against-donald-trump.html.

Further Reading

Bonastia, Christopher. *Knocking on the Door: The Federal Government's Attempt to Desegregate the Suburbs.* Princeton, NJ: Princeton University Press, 2008.

Hetherington, Marc J. "The Election: How the Campaign Mattered." In *The Elections of 2012*, edited by Michael Nelson, 47–72. Washington, DC: Sage, 2014.

Lamb, Charles M. *Housing Segregation in Suburban America since 1960: Presidential and Judicial Politics.* New York: Cambridge University Press, 2005.

Nesmith, Bruce, and Paul J. Quirk. "The Presidency: No Exit from Deadlock." In *The Elections of 2012*, edited by Michael Nelson, 173–202. Washington, DC: Sage, 2014.

Plas, Gerald O. *The Romney Riddle.* Detroit: Berwyn, 1967.

Romney, Mitt. *No Apology: The Case for American Greatness.* New York: St. Martin's Press, 2010.

Romney, Mitt, and Timothy Robinson. *Turnaround: Crisis, Leadership, and the Olympic Games.* Washington, DC: Regnery, 2004.

Scott, Ronald B. *Mitt Romney: An Inside Look at the Man and His Politics.* Guilford, CT: Lyons Press, 2012.

White, Theodore H. *The Making of the President 1964.* New York: Mentor, 1966.

CHAPTER NINE

The Roosevelt Dynasty

Jennifer Hopper

The Roosevelt family in America descended from two founding brothers, Johannes and Jacobus, who embarked on two different paths in 18th-century New York. This divide produced factions within the family separated by geography, party affiliation, and views on who could rightfully lay claim to the powerful legacy the Roosevelts would create in U.S. politics. The dynasty was first established with the remarkable rise of Theodore Roosevelt to the presidency at the turn of the 20th century, reached its height with his cousin Franklin Delano Roosevelt's groundbreaking and transformative 12 years in the presidency as he grappled with the Great Depression and World War II, and continued with First Lady Eleanor Roosevelt's activism on women's rights and humanitarian causes following her husband's death. In the mid-20th century, with the children of these three giants unable or unwilling to follow in their formidable footsteps, the rise of new liberal causes and leaders, and an eventual conservative turn in American politics, the Roosevelt dynasty came to an end, though U.S. governance and public policy continue to reflect its deep influences to the present day.

Distant cousins Theodore and Franklin Roosevelt could both trace their lineage back to Claes van Rosenvelt, an immigrant from the Netherlands who arrived in New Amsterdam in the 1650s. Of his two grandsons, Johannes and his descendants would set up residence in Long Island, eventually settling in Oyster Bay. Johannes's great-great-grandson was Theodore Roosevelt Sr., the first President Roosevelt's father. Theodore Sr.'s niece, daughter of his brother Elliott, was Anna Eleanor Roosevelt, the future first lady. By contrast, the heirs of van Rosenvelt's other grandson, Jacobus, resided in upper Manhattan and established farms in the Hudson Valley area of Hyde Park, a family ancestry line that produced Franklin after his father James married Sara Delano in 1880. Franklin and Eleanor, sixth cousins, wed in 1904, joining the two wings of the family in marriage. But the Oyster Bay and the Hyde Park Roosevelts continued to be split, not only by geography but by politics. In the early years of the country's history, the Roosevelts affiliated with the Federalist Party and later the Whigs. When the Whig Party gave way to the Republicans shortly before the Civil War, the Oyster Bay Roosevelts supported the new party because of its antislavery position. The Hyde Park Roosevelts, meanwhile, backed the Democrats and Franklin's father James voted against Republican candidate Abraham Lincoln in the elections of 1860 and 1864.

Roosevelts in both branches of the family enjoyed every advantage in terms of wealth, education, and social standing. They attended the most prestigious schools, were financially secure, and associated with other elite families. Yet the political dynasty that emerged from the family's ranks would be linked to sharp critiques of those who held economic and political power as well as to efforts to help more vulnerable groups in society. At the onset of the Roosevelt dynasty, the privileged class to which the family belonged was insular and shunned politics. Theodore, Franklin, and Eleanor Roosevelt rejected the conventions of the wealthy and instead identified with the needy and advocated for progressive reform. Though all three grew up largely shielded from the horrors of poverty, their early encounters with such conditions as experienced by others indelibly shaped their views on the central role government should take in addressing such hardships. Further, their personal lives were marked by a determination to overcome adversity, whether it was Theodore's loss of his beloved first wife and mother on the same day, Franklin's struggle to regain his health and resume a political career in the wake of polio and paralysis, or Eleanor's troubled childhood with a distant mother and alcoholic father, both of whom died before she was 10 years old. The Roosevelts' resilience in the face of these difficulties did not lead them to preach a political gospel of the importance of pulling oneself up by one's bootstraps and self-reliance, but rather invested them with an energy and sense of responsibility to work for what they saw as society's betterment, not merely through private charity but through public policy. The political and policy innovations charted by the Roosevelts would form the cornerstone of the 20th-century American state, and would chart a pathway for liberal policy in the United States for decades, inspiring future generations of progressive leaders to build on their legacy.

For the two Roosevelts who were elected president, the political moment upon which each came into office was perfectly timed for the transformation they would bring to the executive branch, government policy, and their respective political parties. President Theodore Roosevelt's tenure began as a wave of problems accompanying industrialization sparked calls for progressive

Roosevelt Political Dynasty Family Tree

Common Ancestors
1. Claes van Rosenvelt, unknown birth year–1659
   2. Son: Nicholas Roosevelt, 1658–1742
      3. Sons: Johannes Roosevelt, 1689–1750, Jacobus Roosevelt, 1692–1776

Oyster Bay Roosevelts
4. Theodore Roosevelt Sr., 1831–1878, great-great-grandson of Johannes Roosevelt

Married Martha Bulloch

Four children: Anna or "Bamie," Theodore, Elliott, and Corinne

5. Theodore Roosevelt Jr., 1858–1919
   Member of the New York State Assembly, 1882–1884
   President of New York City Board of Police Commissioners, 1895–1897
   Assistant secretary of the U.S. Navy, 1897–1898
   Governor of New York, 1899–1900
   Vice president of the United States, 1901
   President of the United States, 1901–1909

Married Alice Hathaway Lee

One child: Alice Lee Roosevelt

Married Edith Kermit Carrow

Five children: Theodore, Kermit, Ethel, Archibald "Archie," and Quentin

6. Theodore or "Ted" Roosevelt, 1887–1944
   Member of the New York State Assembly, 1920–1921
   Assistant secretary of the U.S. Navy, 1921–1924
   Governor of Puerto Rico, 1929–1932
   Governor general of the Philippines, 1932–1933

Married Eleanor Butler Alexander

Four children

Hyde Park Roosevelts
4. James "Rosey" Roosevelt, 1854–1927, great-great-great-grandson of Jacobus

Married Sara Ann Delano

One child: Franklin

(continued)

Roosevelt Political Dynasty Family Tree (*continued*)

5. Franklin Delano Roosevelt, 1882–1945
    Member of New York State Senate, 1911–1913
    Assistant secretary of the U.S. Navy, 1913–1920
    Governor of New York, 1929–1932
    32nd president of the United States, 1933–1945
Married Anna Eleanor Roosevelt, 1884–1962
    First lady of the United States, 1933–1945
    United Nations delegate, 1947–1953
    Chair of Presidential Commission on the Status of Women, 1961–1962
Five children: Anna, James, Elliot, Franklin Jr., and John

6. James, 1907–1991
    Chairman of the California Democratic Party, 1946–1948
    Member of U.S. House of Representatives, 1955–1965
Married four times
Seven children

6. Franklin Jr., 1914–1988
    U.S. House of Representatives, 1949–1955
Married five times
Five children

---

reform across the country. President Franklin Roosevelt's administration started off amid a catastrophic economic collapse, freeing his hand to orchestrate extraordinary federal government interventions in the economy and the creation of new social safety net programs. Both presidents served in eras when the stranglehold that local political party organizations held over politics, through machines and patronage, began to give way to more nationalized political interests and anticorruption movements. As the power of party bosses was challenged, the two Roosevelt presidents cultivated their own sources of influence, building public support for their preferred policies and helping launch the presidency as the dominant supplier of leadership in the American political system. In the years after Franklin's death in 1945, First Lady Eleanor Roosevelt became a more prominent politician in her own right, drawing attention to and advancing the humanitarian causes about which she had long been passionate. Her activism came at a time when women were gaining more power in government, human rights were becoming a global concern,

The Roosevelt Dynasty

and the United States increasingly sought to strengthen its influence on the international stage. Given the poor record of the two Roosevelt presidents on the civil rights issues of their time, Eleanor's accomplishments helped fill a glaring gap in the family's contributions to American politics. Overall, the enduring impact of the three pivotal Roosevelts was facilitated by more than just fortuitous historical circumstances, as each demonstrated enormous capacity to evolve in their careers, grow in their political beliefs, and master unexpected challenges, both political and personal.

Theodore Roosevelt's Road to Politics

Young Theodore Roosevelt's immediate family was rife with the political divides that defined the greater Roosevelt clan, with his parents on opposite sides of the most significant internal conflict in the history of the United States. During the Civil War, Roosevelt's mother Martha Bulloch, originally hailing from Georgia, supported the Confederacy, and his New Yorker father, Theodore Roosevelt Sr., backed the Union. Though Roosevelt Sr. found ways to

President Teddy Roosevelt and his family, c. 1903. (Library of Congress)

actively support the Union military effort, he did not fight in the war in deference to his wife, who had three brothers serving in the Confederate army. Wealthy from his family's plateglass importing business, Roosevelt Sr. was able to pay for a surrogate to serve in the army on his behalf, but for the rest of his life he was haunted by guilt for his failure to enlist. Those regrets were passed on to his son, Theodore, and helped inform the future president's zeal for interventionist politics and a strong desire to see military action firsthand.[1] Theodore Roosevelt idolized his father, who had an outsized influence on his young life. As an illness-plagued, asthmatic child, Teddy Roosevelt was advised by his father, "You have the mind but you have not the body. . . . You must make your body."[2] The young teenager thus set about a strenuous training regimen that transformed and toughened his physique and led to his lifelong pursuits of boxing, hunting, and outdoorsmanship.

Theodore Roosevelt Sr. was also a role model for his son when it came to reformist politics. In the wake of Ulysses S. Grant's presidency—a Republican administration rife with scandal—Roosevelt Sr. became part of an anti-corruption movement within the Republican Party. He was active in an effort at the 1876 Republican National Convention to prevent Roscoe Conkling, a machine man and obstacle to ending graft, from becoming the party's standard bearer. That endeavor resulted in Rutherford B. Hayes's placement at the top of the presidential ticket, and after winning the election, President Hayes sought to appoint Roosevelt Sr. as customs collector for the Port of New York. Although Roosevelt indicated he would accept this position, privately he was reluctant to do so because rooting out corruption in that venue seemed such an insurmountable task. The Republican machine in New York ultimately prevented Roosevelt from getting the job, probably to his great relief, but as with his failure to serve in the war, it created a sense in his son that the family had yet to complete its work.[3] While Roosevelt Sr. took tentative steps down the road toward government service, his son would race down this very same road at breakneck speed.

The high society world of the Roosevelts was changing as Theodore went to school and embarked on a career. The family was a part of New York's "Knickerbocker" elite, old money with a heritage that could be traced back for generations, bound by values of tradition, public service, and humility. This community was being supplanted by a new type of wealthy class, who chased the latest fashions and reveled in showing off what their money could buy.[4] Theodore Roosevelt had been raised to view a life of leisure and ostentatious consumption as morally repugnant, and his father had set a compelling example of the responsibility of the wealthy to care for the less fortunate. Roosevelt Sr. was heavily involved in charity work, helping to set up major relief organizations such as the Children's Aid Society and the Children's Orthopedic Hospital. When the senior Roosevelt gave money to a place like the Newsboys' Lodging House, he was not merely a distanced donor—he visited the newsboys regularly on Sunday nights with his own children, and many of the newsboys never forgot the personal connections they made with him.[5]

If the public service dimension of Theodore Roosevelt's decision to go into politics was in line with his father's values, that choice still defied norms for members of his class. When, as an adult, Teddy Roosevelt first began to forge relationships within local Republican organizations, many of his peers were appalled. Politics was not considered a proper vocation for a New York gentleman; that world was associated with shady backroom deals and a lower-class scrounging to enrich itself. In the era of party machines and patronage that had dominated American politics since the 1830s, holding public office was generally not perceived as an honorable profession. But Roosevelt, acting on the commitment his family had instilled in him to contribute to the greater good, which his father and his ilk had pursued through philanthropy, recast those values toward politics and government as the place where a person of his talents and resources could have the most impact.[6] Roosevelt's pioneering example was highly consequential within his own family, as his young cousin, Franklin, carefully followed—and would later emulate—his move into politics.

The Roosevelt family's social standing and wealth potentially made Theodore's claims to moral leadership and calls for progressive reform more resonant and convincing. As independently wealthy candidates often try to claim in the present day, Roosevelt could be seen as independent from the assumed sordid motivations of most men of his era for entering politics, as he stood to gain little in terms of fame and fortune. Ultimately, he was a key part of a new generation of upper-class men from the Northeast, educated at the most prestigious universities and connected to some of the country's most important businesses and law firms, that decided to enter politics around the turn of the 20th century.[7]

Personal tragedy also marked the beginning of Roosevelt's journey into politics: in February 1884, shortly after the birth of their first child, his wife Alice died of kidney failure. His mother had died just hours earlier in the same house. Roosevelt, devastated, asked his sister to care for his new baby daughter and threw himself into his work in the New York State Assembly. Two years later, he married his childhood friend, Edith Carrow, and they went on to have five children together.

Theodore Roosevelt and the Beginnings of the Dynasty

Emulating his father not only in values but actions, Theodore Roosevelt fought against the party establishment at the 1884 Republican National Convention to back James G. Blaine, who was dogged by accusations of corruption, as their nominee. Roosevelt stood out in urging fellow Republicans to reject graft and defy party bosses. His emerging popular persona as a reformer got him elected to the New York State Assembly for three terms, appointed to the federal Civil Service Commission by President Benjamin Harrison, and won him the position of police commissioner for New York City. In each of these roles, Roosevelt distinguished himself as a champion of good government, merit-based rather than patronage hiring, and an enemy of corruption and malfeasance.[8] After winning the presidency in 1896, Republican William McKinley appointed Roosevelt as assistant secretary of the navy. (An association with this position would prove important in the careers of two other Roosevelts in the future.) Teddy Roosevelt soon left the McKinley Administration, however, to command the 1st U.S. Volunteer Cavalry, also known as the Rough Riders, during the Spanish-American War (1898). Roosevelt's adventures and the Rough Riders' storming of San Juan Hill brought him popular glory and hero-status in America, and helped ease the familial regret produced by his father's failure to fight in the Union army. Teddy's widely regaled military exploits also led to his election as New York's governor in 1898. At this point, the New York state Republican party machine developed a strategy to get rid of troublesome, reform-minded Roosevelts, which they also sought to apply against his cousin Franklin years later. State party leaders pushed for Roosevelt as the vice presidential nominee in 1900, alongside incumbent President McKinley, in order to move him out of state politics.[9] The vice presidency at the time was typically more of a political black hole than the launching pad for the presidency that it would later become. Much to the chagrin of those who hoped the move would stall Roosevelt's political career, however, the assassination of President McKinley only six months after his 1901 inauguration made Theodore Roosevelt the president of the United States.

Roosevelt's forceful personality and strong commitment to reform, combined with the rising prominence of progressivism in the country's politics, resulted in a presidency that altered the office and national politics. Rapid industrialization and urbanization had led to economic growth and vast wealth for some, but also produced problems for many citizens that government had thus far proved ill-equipped to help. Into this historical moment, filled with opportunity, stepped Theodore Roosevelt. As political scientist Peri Arnold details, Roosevelt viewed the presidency as a venue for pursuing his policy preferences, identified new administrative resources to use toward reaching those goals, and embraced an approach to political leadership that was increasingly independent from the party organization. All of these developments were significant departures from most of his predecessors. The public's fascination with larger-than-life Teddy Roosevelt and the adventures of his wife and children, endlessly detailed in the press, made them beloved characters in a national storyline—they became "America's Family." Roosevelt also used a changing media to his advantage, as nonpartisan, mass circulation newspapers and magazines grew in popularity. He cultivated relationships with writers he called "muckrakers," who exposed corruption and wrongdoing in business and government, aiding Roosevelt in building public support for proposed solutions to those problems. The close relationship the president formed with the American people was built on his ability to use the "bully pulpit" of the presidency to persuade the public to support his policies, an innovation that scholars identify as the beginnings of the rhetorical presidency.[10]

Like Roosevelt's methods, his policy agenda was also innovative. He backed federal regulation of business and legislation to monitor the production of consumer products like food and drugs. He sponsored antitrust measures and pursued major infrastructure projects. He set aside millions of acres of national forests in the interest of conservation and pushed the United States toward a more interventionist international stance in a mostly isolationist era, especially in regard to Latin America. In the midst of a 1902 coal strike with potentially devastating effects for Americans with winter just ahead, Roosevelt brought industry owners and the head of the United Mine Workers together for an unprecedented meeting to hash out a solution. He became the first president to acknowledge labor rights in this manner, a stance his cousin Franklin would later help institutionalize with the passage of the National Labor Relations (or Wagner) Act of 1935 recognizing workers' rights to organize and engage in collective bargaining.[11] Roosevelt used executive orders to pursue his agenda unilaterally, issuing 1,091 over his two terms in office, hundreds more than any president before him. Roosevelt sought to legitimize this robust executive action as being necessitated by the broader public interest. His theory of presidential leadership identified the president, in his words, as "a steward of the people, bound actively and affirmatively to do all he could for the people. . . . My belief was that it was not only his right but his duty to do anything that the needs of the nation demanded unless such action was forbidden by the Constitution or by the laws."[12]

From a young age, Roosevelt's life was shaped by a desire for glory and a sense of obligation to work for the greater good. In office, this translated into his robust use of presidential power, enabled by a rapidly changing nation that called for a new level of activism by the federal government. Most Americans did not see President Roosevelt's expansive use of power as dangerous or nefarious, though his opponents made those charges. He was tremendously popular when he left office in 1908 and would likely have easily won another term had he not promised during the 1904 election that he would not run again.

Roosevelt's commitment to his political party, paired with his efforts to change it from within, reflected the ambivalent relationship he had with the Republican establishment throughout his career. During his presidency, the congressional Republican leadership was dominated by the more conservative (Roosevelt deemed them "reactionary") wing of the party, the "Old Guard." Though the two sides enjoyed common ground on a number of prominent issues, like the backing of currency and foreign policy, the president departed significantly from Republican orthodoxy in many of his domestic policy positions.[13] In such cases, Roosevelt would try to bypass these recalcitrant party members to get what he wanted: "Gradually . . . I was forced to abandon the effort to persuade them to come my way, and then I achieved results only by appealing over the heads of the Senate and House leaders to the people, who were the masters of both of us."[14] This charted a new trajectory for presidential leadership through establishing a personal relationship with the American people, a development that would be further solidified in the presidency of Franklin Roosevelt, linking the two cousins together in a true transformation of the presidency.

For most of his political career, Teddy Roosevelt was not at war with the Republican Party. Rather he valued the important constitutional role to be played by Congress, and his fellow party members therein, and wanted to see Republicans succeed, albeit on his terms. Though Secretary of War William Howard Taft was Roosevelt's handpicked successor to the presidency in 1908, Roosevelt found himself greatly disappointed in his former friend and the party regulars who backed him, viewing them as tools of the wealthy and special interests. After a failed attempt to wrest the 1912 Republican nomination away from Taft and the Old Guard that supported him, Roosevelt opted to fully break with the party, running as the Progressive—or "Bull Moose"—Party's candidate for president. The "New Nationalism" platform Roosevelt championed in this 1912 campaign—including suffrage for women, a minimum wage, unemployment insurance, and a powerful national government actively regulating the economy—was further to the left than policies he had supported as president.[15] The three-way race threw the election to Democrat Woodrow Wilson, as Taft and Roosevelt split the Republican vote, and despite the fact that Roosevelt won more popular and electoral votes than Taft. Roosevelt pondered another presidential run in 1920, but that possibility was foreclosed with his death in 1919, at the age of 60. Some of his early ideas for a 1920 platform included limiting working hours and social security insurance, which alongside his Bull Moose platform could be seen as a precursor to Franklin Roosevelt's New Deal agenda, another instance of a family member taking on the unfinished business of a forebear.[16]

When Theodore Roosevelt bolted from the Republicans in 1912, Franklin Roosevelt remained a Wilson supporter, a commitment to the Democrat he had made well before his cousin's Progressive entry into the race. Nevertheless, the Oyster Bay Roosevelts thought this a stunning and personal betrayal. In the years that followed, however, Franklin Roosevelt did not appear hurt in his own political prospects by standing with his party over his family. If Theodore Roosevelt harbored negative feelings about it, they were likely smoothed over by events in 1915, when New York State Republican Party Chairman William Barnes sued him for libel. The resulting trial, which the former president eventually won, lasted a grueling five weeks. Franklin was one of the few prominent figures willing to risk earning the ire of New York politicians by testifying on Theodore's behalf. When an attorney asked Franklin on the stand for his relation to the defendant, the witness declared, "Fifth cousin by blood and nephew by law!"—as proud as he had ever been of his relation to the 26th president.[17]

The Emergence of the Hyde Park Wing in the Roosevelt Dynasty

For the Roosevelts as a political dynasty, the dual party affiliation of the two wings of the family was hugely advantageous in allowing the family's legacy to continue to develop into the mid-20th century. Just as the post–Civil War, industrializing era of Republican Party dominance that allowed Theodore Roosevelt to rise to the presidency was coming to a close, another Roosevelt stood ready to usher in the start of the ascendency of the Democratic party.

Though Franklin Delano Roosevelt's father James came from money, when he married Sara Delano in 1880 he came into far greater wealth from her side of the family. Unlike the Oyster Bay Roosevelts, Franklin Roosevelt's father and grandfather were Democrats. Despite that partisan divide, Franklin was a great admirer of his cousin Theodore and in contrast to the election of 1912, he crossed party lines to support Teddy in the 1896 and 1904 elections. Franklin would later confess to a Democratic Party audience, "In 1904, when I cast my first vote for president, I voted for the Republican candidate, Theodore Roosevelt, because I thought he was a better Democrat than the Democratic candidates."[18] Perhaps intensified by his father's debilitating illness and death when Franklin was still a young man, Roosevelt looked to Theodore, from a distance, as a model for his own future career and political identity. Franklin recalled his elder cousin imparting to him that it was the obligation of people like the Roosevelts to be active in politics, lest government be overrun by those of lesser morals and dignity.[19]

Franklin Roosevelt's mother Sara was a formidable figure in his life, extremely close to him, even moving to Boston to be near him while he attended Harvard. Sara lavished her son with attention and unfailing support throughout his life. Indicative of their attachment, when Democratic Party leaders first approached Roosevelt about running for office, Franklin's immediate reaction was to say he would have to ask his mother. Sara's initial attitude toward her son's political aspirations reflected the upper class's disdainful view of politics that Theodore Roosevelt had also encountered and challenged. When a reporter once asked Sara if she had always wanted Franklin to be president, she replied in the negative, saying her greatest hope was that he would grow up to be just like his father.[20] There is no record of James Roosevelt serving in the Civil War, but also no indication that he had the painful regrets that Theodore Roosevelt Sr. did, and his son seemed spared Theodore's need to atone for the perceived sins of his father. James spent much of his time living the life of a gentleman farmer in the Hudson Valley, raising cattle and trotting horses. At times, Sara expressed a desire for Franklin to leave politics and follow this path, retiring to a life of leisure in Hyde Park, particularly when he was struck with polio. Like many of her peers, Sara believed that a gentleman's primary responsibility was to set a good example for less privileged men from afar, rather than by getting entangled in politics.[21] His mother would later recall about Roosevelt's move into government that "many of our friends said it was a shame for so fine a young man to associate with 'dirty' politicians. Some of them hoped he would be defeated for his own sake and learn a lesson. I knew only that I would always be proud of him."[22] The immense self-assurance that Sara instilled in her son, along with his cousin Theodore blazing the political trail, helped propel Franklin to explore and embrace the daunting challenges and enticing opportunities of a political career.

Franklin and Eleanor Roosevelt's Life in American Politics

Franklin Roosevelt's first move toward a life in politics came in 1910 when the Democratic Party in New York recruited him to run to represent Dutchess County, initially in the state Assembly and then in the state Senate. His candidacy appealed to party leaders for several reasons, primarily related to his family background. The great wealth on his mother's side could help finance the campaign, and Sara would indeed help bankroll many of her son's campaigns over the years. The Roosevelt name was also integral to their strategy—to win in Dutchess County, the Democrats would need to appeal to some Republicans, a prospect thought more likely with a Roosevelt on the ballot. Demonstrating his lifelong admiration for and deference to his older cousin, Franklin first sought Theodore's blessing. The former president relayed that though disappointed Franklin would run as a Democrat, he had faith that Franklin would challenge machine politics in whatever party he chose.[23] This proved accurate—after he became a state senator, Roosevelt positioned himself as a critic of the Tammany Hall political machine and led challenges to the party's leadership on key issues like their choice for New York's U.S. Senate seat in 1911. One prominent Democratic machine figure warned his colleagues that Franklin might lead to the same kind of internal party disruption as Theodore was creating for Republicans in 1912, remarking, "If we've caught a Roosevelt, we'd better take him down and drop him off the dock. The Roosevelts run true to form, and this kid is likely to do for us what the Colonel is going to do for the Republican Party, split it wide open."[24] Franklin's antigraft stance further connected the Roosevelt name with political reform and bucking the political establishment. As his career progressed however, the practical

President Franklin Roosevelt and Mrs. Roosevelt with members of their family leave the White House for church on Christmas, December 25, 1938. (Library of Congress)

politician in Roosevelt led him to reconcile with the Democratic Party machine, recognizing how essential its support was for reaching his goals. This was one of the key ways he deviated from Theodore Roosevelt's example, particularly at the end of his career. Franklin's personal wealth allowed him to concentrate on politics full-time from the outset. Although his state Senate position was technically part-time, he moved his family to the state capital in Albany, and did not have to leave throughout the year to pursue other endeavors as many of his fellow legislators did.

In his first years in politics, Roosevelt was quick to capitalize on his association with the reigning political giant in his family. At one early campaign event after Franklin was introduced, he told the crowd with a smile, "I'm not Teddy." Roosevelt continued, "A little shaver said to me the other day that he knew I wasn't Teddy—I asked him why, and he replied, 'Because you don't show your teeth,'" to the laughter of his audience.[25] When Woodrow Wilson tapped Roosevelt, with no background in the military, to be his assistant secretary of the navy in 1913, both the offer and Roosevelt's eagerness to accept could be traced to Theodore's conspicuous service in the same job. As the first Roosevelt to hold this position remained such a prominent public figure in those years, Franklin's role in the administration was also quite useful to President Wilson, particularly during his 1916 reelection campaign. As assistant secretary, Franklin was an advocate for preparedness and readying the navy for possible involvement in World War I. He thereby offered a symbolic Roosevelt counterpoint to Theodore's and the Republicans' assertions that Wilson, still firmly committed to neutrality, was weak and negligent in the face of the war in Europe.[26] Further parallels between the two Roosevelts' early careers emerged when Franklin was successfully elected governor of New York in 1928. Just as Theodore Roosevelt as governor dealt with matters that would later dominate his presidency, including labor laws, conservation, and regulation of corporations, so Franklin's gubernatorial stint anticipated his administration. Serving as governor when the Great Depression hit, Roosevelt initiated relief for the unemployed, public works programs, and labor reform within the state.[27]

Personal connections between the two wings of the Roosevelt family were also strengthened by various milestones in Franklin's life. Elliott Roosevelt, Theodore's brother, had been one of Franklin's godfathers at his baptism and had he not died in 1894, would have become Franklin's father-in-law after Franklin married his distant cousin Eleanor in 1905. This was among the many appeals of Eleanor to Franklin, that she brought him closer to one of his political idols. Uncle Theodore even gave Eleanor away at her wedding to Franklin in Manhattan, just after making a presidential appearance at the St. Patrick's Day parade in town. Eleanor's lineage, in some ways, was even more illustrious than Franklin's. Through her mother Anna Rebecca Hall's side, Eleanor's ancestry could be traced back to the Stuyvesants and Livingstons, both giants in New York's early history.[28]

At the same time, Franklin Roosevelt's emerging national political career widened a rift within his extended family. Theodore Roosevelt's children had never held their cousin Franklin in high esteem—they made fun of him during get-togethers as children and were dismissive of his actions in World War I.[29] Although all four of Theodore's sons had enlisted—two sustained serious injuries and the youngest, Quentin, was killed in combat—Franklin had originally sought to serve in uniform but was convinced otherwise by his superiors in the Wilson administration. Instead, he journeyed to Europe in his assistant secretary role to survey the troops and was never in harm's way.

The personal and partisan divides that Theodore helped contain during his lifetime were exacerbated following the ex-president's death. In 1920, when Franklin ran on the Democratic Party presidential ticket as James M. Cox's vice presidential nominee, he actively attached himself to his elder cousin, particularly when campaigning in western states where Theodore had been so popular. He worked into his speeches "bully," "strenuous," and other expressions associated with Theodore.[30] Some in the crowds he attracted incorrectly assumed he was Teddy's son. Meanwhile, one of Theodore's actual sons, Ted Jr., journeyed around the country attacking Franklin on behalf of his opponent, Republican candidate Warren G. Harding.

When Ted Jr. ran for governor of New York as a Republican in 1924, Eleanor returned the favor by following him around the state in a car with a giant teapot affixed to the top, giving speeches discrediting him and linking him to the Teapot Dome scandal that had plagued the Republican Harding administration.[31] When those scandals had unfolded, Ted Jr. was serving as Harding's assistant secretary of the navy, the position that had become nearly synonymous with Roosevelts. The 1924 opposition campaign seemed out of character for Eleanor, who later expressed regrets, but some speculate she may have been motivated by lingering bitterness over her troubled family history.[32] Her father, Elliott, was highly competitive throughout his life with his brother Theodore, eventually living largely in his shadow, and Elliott's last years before dying at 34 were marred by mental instability and alcoholism. At one point, in a lawsuit that generated embarrassing headlines for the family in New York City newspapers, Elliott's siblings, Theodore and Anna (or "Bamie"), sought to get a judge to deem him insane and have his assets placed in a trust for his wife and children, including Eleanor.

The rivalries between the next generation of Roosevelts were not meaningless or petty. Franklin Roosevelt's close adviser Louis Howe expressed more concern about Ted Jr. as a threat to Franklin's political rise than any other possible opponent.[33] Although a famous political name could empower a budding politician, there was a sense that a struggle over the legitimacy of claims to the family legacy, or the political field becoming crowded with squabbling Roosevelts, would deprive the name of some of its clout. The deteriorating relationship between the Oyster Bay and Hyde Park Roosevelts was the product of both political and personal forces. On the political side, the Oyster Bay Roosevelts believed that their father's celebrated legacy should be carried forward within the Republican Party by his own son Ted Jr. and not by Franklin, who had stuck with their father's political opponent, Woodrow Wilson, in 1912. Although the Hyde Park Roosevelts' inner circle saw the social and economic turmoil of the early 20th century as an open door for new kinds of leaders and policy solutions, the Oyster Bay Roosevelts remained committed to conservatism and the Republican Party.

The divide was also riddled with private grievances. The Oyster Bay Roosevelts were infuriated by what they saw as Franklin and Eleanor pretending that they could credibly take up Theodore Roosevelt's mantle. Eleanor recognized this source of irritation, writing to her aunt Corinne (Theodore's sister), "I do see how annoying it must be to have people saying and thinking Franklin is a near relation of Uncle Ted's and I do hope they realize we personally never sail under false colors."[34] Seeking to clear up any confusion, Ted Jr. told audiences in 1924 that Franklin was a "maverick" who "does not have the brand of our family."[35] Despite those efforts, when Franklin became the Democratic presidential nominee in 1932, Edith Roosevelt, Theodore's widow and Ted Jr.'s mother, received hundreds of messages congratulating her on her son's accomplishment. Her reaction to this widespread misconception was to publicly endorse Franklin D. Roosevelt's opponent, Herbert Hoover, even appearing at a Madison Square Garden rally to speak on behalf of the Republican candidate.

When Ted Jr. lost his 1924 race for governor and Franklin's star continued to rise, the most prominent political Roosevelt was now associated with left leaning politics and the Democratic Party, and the opportunities for the Roosevelt legacy to be carried forward by Theodore's own children diminished. Alone among the Oyster Bay contingent, Theodore's son Kermit made some shows of support for Franklin in the 1932 campaign, and when the president-elect and his cousin Kermit went on a cruise together it prompted *The New York Times* to write a headline declaring, "Rift between Roosevelt Families Bridged."[36] This was much to the consternation of the rest of Kermit's immediate family, however. Throughout Franklin's first term, Ted Jr. continued to attack the president and champion his own progressive Republicanism instead, seeking to undermine any sense that a direct line could be traced between the two Roosevelt administrations. But Ted Jr. was fighting an uphill battle. Franklin was building the same personal relationship and popularity with the American public as Theodore had as president, but in his own right, effectively remaking the political system even more fundamentally than his cousin and predecessor. Meanwhile, Ted Jr. was finding the brand of progressivism and reform that his father had carved out years earlier no longer had much of a home within the Republican Party of the 1930s.[37]

The Roosevelt dynasty reached its height when Franklin Roosevelt was elected president in 1932. Following the 1929 stock market crash, the United States was plunged into the worst economic crisis in its history, with nearly a quarter of the workforce unemployed. In response to the Great Depression, Roosevelt spearheaded a completely new ordering of American politics, creating a far more powerful federal government, establishing an institutionalized welfare state, and providing a wide-ranging array of emergency measures to respond to the economic dislocation of millions of Americans. Though both Roosevelt presidents championed progressive aims, the economic catastrophe that befell the nation after 1929 empowered Franklin Roosevelt to accomplish those goals in ways that Theodore never could. Political scientist Stephen Skowronek charts how Franklin Roosevelt came into office with the old Republican-dominated political order in complete disrepair, enabling him to shatter established political norms and institute a fresh approach to governing in its place. In so doing, he built a new and enduring coalition of supporters for the Democratic Party and his New Deal programs, an electoral coalition that would allow the party to dominate national politics for decades to come.

Although Theodore Roosevelt had also expanded the authority of the presidency, he had done so in less permanent ways; most of those who came after him, including Presidents Taft, Calvin Coolidge, and Harding, retreated from his robust exercise of executive power. In contrast, the changes Franklin Roosevelt brought to the presidency were permanent. The president now set the public policy agenda, garnered the lion's share of media attention, employed an expansive White House staff, and spoke directly to the American people via popular media (for FDR, it was radio). Every president to follow, Democrat or Republican, liberal or conservative, has grappled with the heightened expectations for presidential leadership that Franklin Roosevelt established.

What Roosevelt had pledged as a "new deal" for the American people was a series of innovative and experimental policies devised by the president and his advisers to address the Great Depression. The scale of federal government intervention in the U.S. economy was unprecedented, though economists and historians have debated the extent to which the New Deal led to the nation's economic recovery. The first 100 days of Franklin's first administration were historically productive; Congress immediately passed bills to stabilize the banking system and restore U.S. currency. The government committed millions of dollars to emergency relief, propped up agriculture, and created sprawling public works programs providing Americans with jobs and building the nation's infrastructure. Later phases of the New Deal included the landmark establishment of the U.S. welfare state with the 1935 Social Security Act; the aforementioned codification of workers' rights, including collective bargaining; and the creation of the empowering Executive Office of the Presidency (EOP).[38] This period marks the height of the Roosevelt dynasty as not only the pinnacle of Roosevelt's personal power and influence, but because his achievements, from Social Security to the Securities and Exchange Commission to fair labor standards, continue to be consequential to the country today.

Though the institutional presidency would ultimately grow under Roosevelt, in the early years of his first administration he pursued the New Deal's ambitious goals without the staff and resources his successors would enjoy. Here is where Franklin's personality and leadership style became so integral to the power he would ultimately wield. In the first of his fireside chats, radio addresses where he spoke directly to Americans as they listened in their homes, taking place just a week into his presidency, Roosevelt talked to the people about the banking crisis, urging them to remain calm and trust in the government's efforts to remedy the situation. When the banks reopened the next day, the public responded by depositing more money than they withdrew, which alleviated the emergency.[39] The personal relationship that Roosevelt built with the American public was transformative, a key element of an institutional change scholars refer to as the "modern presidency."[40]

Roosevelt's defining traits of self-assurance, a strong belief he was destined for leadership, and his enthusiasm for taking on challenges, could each be attributed to his upbringing and family history. He learned how to evolve and become a better politician over time. He later acknowledged, "I was an awfully mean cuss when I first went into politics."[41] Only eventually would Roosevelt assume the role of charismatic leader and master of the presidency, juggling ideas and advice and expertly soliciting support from politicians and the public alike. Roosevelt's late-in-life struggle with polio and the resulting paralysis of his legs in 1921 also built resilience in him, and made plain the central role played in his career by his immediate family and support system. Eleanor and Louis Howe, an aide and nearly honorary Roosevelt given his closeness to the couple, cared for Franklin during the darkest days of his illness and refused to allow him to give up on his future aspirations in politics.[42]

If the Roosevelt family unquestionably enjoyed elite status in the United States, Franklin's launch of the New Deal caused many in the upper-class and business world to cultivate a deep hatred for him, seeing him as a traitor.[43] But as in Theodore's case, Franklin viewed his privileged life as tied to obligatory public service and use of the levers of government to meet societal needs.

Franklin did at times seem to declare war on his own class. In his first inaugural address in 1933, Roosevelt employed one of his trademark biblical allusions and declared, "The money changers have fled from their high seats in the temple of our civilization. We may now restore that temple to the ancient truths. The measure of the restoration lies in the extent to which we apply social values more noble than mere monetary profit."[44] In 1935, addressing "gentlemen in well-warmed and well-stocked clubs" who charged that "a dole would be more economical than work relief," the president responded by chiding the isolationism of the upper class: "The men who tell me that have, unfortunately, too little contact with the true America to realize that . . . most Americans want to give something for what they get."[45] In a speech to the Democratic National Convention in 1936, the president exhorted a small segment of society who "had concentrated into their own hands an almost complete control over other people's property, other people's money, other people's labor—other people's lives. These economic royalists complain that we seek to overthrow the institutions of America. What they really complain of is that we seek to take away their power."[46]

As James MacGregor Burns and Susan Dunn put it, like Theodore Roosevelt, the 32nd president "exploded one of the most popular and deeply entrenched myths in America; he had disassociated the concept of wealth from the concept of virtue."[47] If this earned the ire of the wealthy and privileged in America as a betrayal, perhaps it also helps reveal why the Roosevelt message was not viewed with more apprehension by the general public, considering the radical changes Franklin Roosevelt proposed. Were a politician from an impoverished background to make this same case, potentially the message would have been interpreted, fairly or unfairly, as more extreme and dangerous, or even anti-American. But for a Roosevelt to make these claims, one who came from the very elite class he condemned, lent greater credibility to the idea that societal arrangements had been perverted and better justified a vigorous effort to restore core American values.

The Roosevelt tendency toward internal criticism of the political parties and craftsmanship of independent sources of popular support, key to both presidents' successes, also brought Franklin the same headaches as his cousin. Facing a Democratic Party in Congress with a powerfully positioned conservative southern wing, Franklin Roosevelt in his second term found himself enormously frustrated with their efforts to block crucial pieces of his reform agenda. Just as Theodore waged a battle in 1912 first within and then from outside the Republican Party when he decided it had moved too far from what he thought it should stand for, so Franklin embarked on an ill-fated effort to remake the Democratic Party in his own image. In 1938, he launched an unprecedented, wide-scale campaign in Democratic primary elections to purge the party of conservatives and replace them with loyal New Deal supporters. As was the case with Roosevelt's court-packing plan in 1937 to alter the Supreme Court after it dealt his legislative program a series of blows, this effort proved unsuccessful and politically costly. Beginning in his second term, Roosevelt could no longer count on the Democratic Party to support his agenda in lockstep; increasingly, conservative Democrats allied with Republicans against his priorities.[48] Here witness the liabilities of the seemingly limitless Rooseveltian self-confidence and reliance on personal popularity. In the case of both presidencies, their self-confidence led them to engage in ill-advised political campaigns in which entrenched party interests successfully resisted their will. Generally skilled at recognizing the limits of their authority and avoiding battles that could not be won, the Roosevelts overplayed their hand in these noteworthy instances.

The circumstances surrounding the United States' entry into World War II also revealed continuing clashes within the Roosevelt family over the essence of the dynasty. Though Theodore Roosevelt was associated with interventionist policies and had promoted a strong U.S. military presence around the globe, when Franklin as president began to push for greater American involvement in the growing conflict in Europe, Ted Jr., a World War I hero, publicly opposed him. Theodore's eldest son sought to bolster that stance by couching it in his father's beliefs, pointing to Theodore's opposition to the League of Nations as an indication he would have been against involving the United States in this new crisis. To many, this appeared to be an unconvincing interpretation of his father's legacy: Theodore Roosevelt had been highly critical of Wilson's delay in involving the United States in World War I and tried in vain to convince the Democratic president to let him organize a battalion of volunteer troops—an updated version of the Rough Riders—to fight in France.[49] Once America's involvement in World War II began, Ted Jr. faithfully returned to military action, and Franklin appointed him to the position of brigadier general at the onset of the conflict, perhaps trying to mend fences after many years of discord. Moreover, just as Theodore's sons had done during World War I, all four of Franklin and Eleanor Roosevelt's sons served in World War II, winning numerous military accolades between them.

When President Franklin Roosevelt died in office in 1945 after being elected to his fourth term, Roosevelts had served in the presidency for nearly half of the years thus far in the 20th century. Yet Roosevelt's death did not signal the abrupt end of this political dynasty. Although Eleanor Roosevelt in the early years of her husband's political career had played the traditional role of a dutiful politician's wife, making social calls and hosting parties, she gradually became a political force in her own right, providing her husband with advice and direction and pursuing her own political causes. This transformation began with the urging of Louis Howe, who solicited her ideas and encouraged her to give her opinion on Franklin's political moves.[50] Eleanor's passion for liberal crusades was further fueled by the close friendships she developed over the years with activists of her era. This dual personal and political evolution saw Roosevelt defying many norms for both women and her class—the intimate friends who helped transform her life included political rebels, lesbians, and highly independent women with whom the past Roosevelt matriarchs would never have socialized.[51]

Now, as the primary bearer of the Roosevelt mantle, Eleanor pushed the family's political legacy in new directions. President Harry Truman appointed her to represent the United States at the first United Nations General Assembly, making her the only woman serving in that delegation. She chaired the body's Human Rights Commission and became a major force in crafting the Universal Declaration of Human Rights, adopted in 1948, a new global standard for how human freedoms and dignity would be measured around the globe. She built a reputation for herself as she fought for the rights of refugees displaced by the war not to be forced back to their home countries against their will.[52] In this capacity and in those she would serve afterward for both the United Nations and organizations like the Peace Corps, Eleanor attached the family name to advocacy for humanitarian causes and the needs of vulnerable peoples on a global scale. In the last years of her life, President John F. Kennedy appointed Eleanor to chair his advisory Presidential Commission on the Status of Women. Given the poor record of both Roosevelt presidents on black civil rights, and the stain on Franklin Roosevelt's administration from ordering Japanese American internment during World War II, it was Eleanor Roosevelt who ultimately did the most to associate the family's contributions with efforts against discrimination and the respect for human rights, priorities that became a significant part of the Democratic Party's political identity in the mid-1960s and beyond.[53]

The End of the Roosevelt Dynasty

Dynasties inevitably come to a close if there is no future generation able to carry them forward. In the latter half of the 20th century, the Oyster Bay side of the family abandoned the project of carrying on the Roosevelt legacy by running for public office, though some of Theodore's grandsons served in government in less publicly visible roles, notably in the CIA. Their strong support for the Cold War in those intelligence positions put them in opposition to Eleanor Roosevelt's emphatic criticisms of that facet of U.S. foreign policy in the post–World War II period.[54] In the end, Theodore Roosevelt's children would be better known for their military rather than for their government service, perhaps reflecting their father's belief that it was on the battlefield where individuals could truly demonstrate character and bring honor to their family. As Theodore Roosevelt wrote later about his experiences with the Rough Riders during the Spanish-American War, "I would rather have led that charge and earned my colonelcy than served three terms in the United States Senate. It makes me feel as though I could now leave something to my children which will serve as an apology for my having existed."[55] In addition, Alice Roosevelt Longworth, Theodore's daughter, loved politics and was a mainstay of the Washington social scene for many years, but she herself never ran for office or drove policy.

Franklin and Eleanor's children, like their Long Island cousins, did make some forays into public office, but ultimately proved ill-equipped to follow in their parents' footsteps. Biographical accounts of Franklin and Eleanor Roosevelt chart that in their extraordinary reinvention of their personal lives over time, overcoming of major challenges, and joint project of remaking American politics, they were simultaneously less than impressive in their role as parents, unable to provide their children with the love and attention they craved.[56] The unusual arrangements surrounding their marriage after Eleanor discovered Roosevelt's affair with her social secretary Lucy Mercer in 1918, surely had an impact on their children. The Roosevelts subsequently forged a formidable political partnership that would endure for the remainder of their lives, but a loving marriage and romantic relationship no longer existed between them. As adults, their children accumulated a considerable number of failed marriages, unsuccessful career tracks, and assortment of personal problems. Some of the Roosevelt children used politics to rebel against their parents: Elliott Roosevelt used Texas radio stations he owned to broadcast opposition to a third term for his father and support the House Un-American Activities Committee, an arm of the Red Scare and McCarthyism that Eleanor despised. Their youngest son, John, officially became a Republican in 1952, seconding the nomination of Dwight D. Eisenhower at the Republican National Convention.[57] After Louis Howe died in 1936, Roosevelt brought his son, James, into the White House as his assistant, a rocky tenure marked by accusations that the younger Roosevelt was abusing his role for personal benefit, and culminating in James being forced to make his tax returns public in order to quell any further outcry. He left the administration soon afterward.[58]

Ventures into elected office similarly led to dead ends. Franklin Jr. was elected to Congress from New York in 1949, initially as a member of the Liberal Party and later as a Democrat, and his brother, James, followed his lead as a Democratic representative from California years later. But neither distinguished himself while serving in the legislative branch. Franklin Jr. was criticized by his fellow members for trying to skate by on his name alone, lazy and frequently absent; while James failed to demonstrate any leadership in Congress and was plagued by scandals in his personal life.[59] Though their father had certainly received benefits largely because of his name, such as being tapped for his first run for state Senate and the assistant secretary of the navy position, he made use of those opportunities to distinguish himself in his own right. That capacity was not evident among his children who tried out political careers, and it became clear the Roosevelt name alone could not continue to win them elections. Theodore Roosevelt's children, though they had eventually abandoned efforts to gain public office, remained extremely concerned about maintaining the dignity of the Roosevelt name, and frequently felt that the latest generation of the Hyde Park branch of the family was doing much to sully that hard-earned reputation.[60]

Further complicating the dynasty's future were the major changes stirring in the Democratic Party in the 1960s and beyond, as civil rights took on new importance in liberal politics. At the height of their presidencies, Theodore and Franklin Roosevelt had not embraced racial equality or worked toward addressing the racist policies of their respective eras. Though Theodore Roosevelt invited Booker T. Washington to dinner, the first president to host an African American in the White House for a meal, afterward he faced a great deal of criticism and never hosted another black guest. In a widely disparaged move in 1906 he also summarily dishonorably discharged an entire military regiment of black soldiers after the white residents of Brownsville, Texas, blamed the soldiers for the death of a local white man. This was particularly disconcerting because there was no substantiating evidence, and a local court had found the black soldiers innocent. One hundred and sixty-seven black men lost their jobs, pensions, and honors in an instant due to the President Roosevelt's actions.[61]

As president, Franklin Roosevelt worked with black leaders such as A. Philip Randolph and appointed African Americans to official positions within his administration. Black citizens gained access to jobs and government benefits under the New Deal for the first time, though some relief programs were marred by discrimination.[62] Despite his move further to the ideological left throughout his career, Roosevelt failed to champion meaningful policies to challenge segregation and racial discrimination. He refused even to publicly support antilynching legislation when it stood a chance of passing in Congress in the late 1930s, to avoid a backlash from his party's southern wing that might threaten the rest of his agenda.[63] Roosevelt gave in to racist hysteria when he issued executive orders to carry out the internment of Japanese Americans during World War II.[64] And some critics have charged that he failed to act quickly or proactively enough to combat Hitler's systematic extermination of the Jews in the Holocaust.[65]

Eleanor Roosevelt was responsible for many of the efforts to reach out to the black community during her husband's presidency: symbolically moving her seat between black and white delegations at a segregated conference and resigning her membership in the Daughters of the American Revolution after the group refused to allow acclaimed singer Marian Anderson to perform at Constitution Hall in the nation's capital, arranging for her to sing on the steps of the Lincoln Memorial instead.[66] As first lady, Eleanor forged connections with groups like the NAACP and the National Urban League. Though Roosevelt aligned herself with human rights causes throughout the world in her post–White House career, even she retained some of the lingering prejudices of her class and era; she privately expressed anti-Semitic and anti-Catholic views at various points in her life.[67]

In the mid-20th century, the Democratic Party began to make a slow move to embrace black civil rights and push for legislation to desegregate the South and ban discrimination. The party did this despite the opposition of its conservative southern members, who gradually abandoned the party over precisely this issue. But it would fall to later political figures like Presidents Kennedy and Lyndon B. Johnson to play the pivotal roles in pushing the Democratic Party in this direction; the Roosevelt dynasty would not be integral. Eleanor, as the last major Roosevelt politician standing, was reluctant to support some of the up-and-coming leaders in the Democratic Party. She hesitated to back John F. Kennedy in 1960 in part because she disliked his father so intensely, particularly his friendship with Joe McCarthy, a figure she loathed.[68] She did eventually come around to Kennedy, however, particularly after the young Democratic nominee promised to work closely with her preferred candidate, Senator Adlai Stevenson.

The pendulum swings back and forth ideologically in American politics, and so the Roosevelt legacy of ascendant liberal programs and government policy solutions to major public problems could not hold sway forever. Shifts in the political winds were apparent even during the second Roosevelt administration: it is unlikely Franklin Roosevelt would have won a third and fourth term without the international crisis of World War II. Before his third-term campaign, Franklin observed that he thought the country was probably sick and tired of Roosevelts, a sentiment Theodore had also expressed when third-term speculation bubbled up.

An early reaction against the prevailing progressivism of the Roosevelts was apparent in the sharp turn rightward among conservatives in the mid-20th century, most extremely evident in the rise of Senator Joe McCarthy and the Communist Scare of the 1950s. Later, the principal economic posture of both Roosevelt presidents—that the excesses of capitalism and inequalities produced by the free market must be curbed by a powerful and active federal government, regulation of the private sector, and expansive welfare programs—would begin to wane in popularity, particularly by the 1970s. A new age of conservatism, tax cuts, and deregulation would dominate American politics beginning under the Republican President Ronald Reagan in the 1980s. Yet, even in present-day U.S. politics, in policies that directly touch the lives of millions of Americans as far-ranging as the national park system, the role of the federal government in shaping the nation's economy, the widely supported social safety net programs like Social Security, and the public's expectations of strong leadership from the presidency, the Roosevelt dynasty's legacy continues to endure.

Notes

1. Peter Collier and David Horowitz, *The Roosevelts: An American Saga* (New York: Simon & Schuster, 1994), 34.
2. Corinne Roosevelt Robinson, *My Brother Theodore Roosevelt* (New York: Scribner's, 1921), 50.
3. Edward J. Renehan Jr., *The Lion's Pride: Theodore Roosevelt and His Family in Peace and War* (New York: Oxford University Press, 1998), 18–19.
4. James MacGregor Burns and Susan Dunn, *The Three Roosevelts: Patrician Leaders Who Transformed America* (New York: Grove Press, 2001), 17, 21.
5. Edward J. Renehan Jr., *The Lion's Pride*, 18.
6. James MacGregor Burns and Susan Dunn, *The Three Roosevelts*, 25–27.
7. Edward J. Renehan Jr., *The Lion's Pride*, 54.
8. Peter Collier and David Horowitz, *The Roosevelts*, 64.
9. Sidney M. Milkis and Michael Nelson, *The American Presidency, Origins and Development, 1776–2014* (Thousand Oaks, CA: CQ Press, 2016), 229.
10. For a more detailed discussion, see Jeffrey Tulis, *The Rhetorical Presidency* (Princeton, NJ: Princeton University Press, 1987).
11. Edmund Morris, *Theodore Rex* (New York: Random House, 2001), 157–169.
12. Theodore Roosevelt, *An Autobiography*, 357.
13. Daniel DiSalvo, *Engines of Change: Party Factions in American Politics, 1868–2010* (New York: Oxford University Press, 2012), 121–122.
14. Theodore Roosevelt, *An Autobiography*, 352.
15. Edward J. Renehan Jr., *The Lion's Pride*, 45.
16. Peter Collier and David Horowitz, *The Roosevelts*, 241.
17. Geoffrey C. Ward and Ken Burns, *The Roosevelts: An Intimate History* (New York: Random House, 2014), 193.
18. Jean Edward Smith, *FDR* (New York: Random House, 2008), 49.
19. Peter Collier and David Horowitz, *The Roosevelts*, 109.
20. Geoffrey C. Ward and Ken Burns, 53.
21. James MacGregor Burns and Susan Dunn, *The Three Roosevelts*, 174.
22. Jean Edward Smith, *FDR*, 63.
23. Geoffrey C. Ward and Ken Burns, *The Roosevelts*, 158.

24. Jean Edward Smith, *FDR*, 69.
25. Arthur M. Schlesinger, *The Crisis of the Old Order: 1919–1933, The Age of Roosevelt* (New York: Houghton Mifflin, 1957), 332.
26. Jean Edward Smith, *FDR*, 132.
27. Ibid., 250–252.
28. "Roosevelt Genealogy," Franklin D. Roosevelt Presidential Library and Museum, accessed September 20, 2017, http://www.fdrlibrary.marist.edu/archives/resources/genealogy.html#ermaternal.
29. James MacGregor Burns and Susan Dunn, *The Three Roosevelts*, 91.
30. Jean Edward Smith, *FDR*, 181.
31. The Teapot Dome scandal involved President Warren G. Harding's Secretary of the Interior Albert B. Fall taking bribes from oil companies and then giving them access to petroleum reserves intended for the government's use.
32. Peter Collier and David Horowitz, *The Roosevelts*, 298.
33. Ibid., 290.
34. Ibid., 259.
35. Geoffrey C. Ward and Ken Burns, *The Roosevelts*, 227.
36. Peter Collier and David Horowitz, *The Roosevelts*, 336.
37. Ibid., 388.
38. Sidney M. Milkis and Michael Nelson, *The American Presidency*, 305–312.
39. Jean Edward Smith, *FDR*, 315.
40. Fred Greenstein, "Change and Continuity in the Modern Presidency," *The New American Political System*, ed. Anthony King (Washington DC: American Enterprise Institute, 1979).
41. Arthur M. Schlesinger, *The Crisis of the Old Order*, 339.
42. Jean Edward Smith, *FDR*, 195–196.
43. James MacGregor Burns and Susan Dunn, *The Three Roosevelts*, 291, 309. See also H. W. Brands, *Traitor to His Class: The Privileged Life and Radical Presidency of Franklin Delano Roosevelt* (New York: Anchor Books, 2009).
44. "Franklin D. Roosevelt 1—Inaugural Address, March 4, 1933," The American Presidency Project, accessed September 16, 2017, http://www.presidency.ucsb.edu/ws/index.php?pid=14473.
45. "Franklin D. Roosevelt 190—Address at Atlanta, Georgia, November 29, 1935," The American Presidency Project, accessed September 16, 2017, http://www.presidency.ucsb.edu/ws/index.php?pid=14991.
46. "Franklin D. Roosevelt 82—Acceptance Speech for the Renomination for the Presidency, Philadelphia, PA, June 27, 1936," The American Presidency Project, accessed September 16, 2017, http://www.presidency.ucsb.edu/ws/?pid=15314.
47. James MacGregor Burns and Susan Dunn, *The Three Roosevelts*, 310.
48. Stephen Skowronek, *The Politics Presidents Make: Leadership from John Adams to Bill Clinton* (Cambridge, MA: Harvard University Press, 1997), 316.
49. Peter Collier and David Horowitz, *The Roosevelts*, 401.
50. Jean Edward Smith, *FDR*, 183–184.
51. James MacGregor Burns and Susan Dunn, *The Three Roosevelts*, 504.

52. "Eleanor Roosevelt and the United Nations," Franklin D. Roosevelt Presidential Library and Museum, accessed September 20, 2017, https://fdrlibrary.org/eleanor-roosevelt.

53. James MacGregor Burns and Susan Dunn, *The Three Roosevelts*, 542.

54. Peter Collier and David Horowitz, *The Roosevelts*, 445.

55. Theodore Roosevelt, *The Letters of Theodore Roosevelt: 1898–1903* (Cambridge, MA: Harvard University Press, 1951), 860.

56. Peter Collier and David Horowitz, *The Roosevelts*, 361.

57. James MacGregor Burns and Susan Dunn, *The Three Roosevelts*, 312.

58. Jean Edward Smith, *FDR*, 403.

59. Peter Collier and David Horowitz, *The Roosevelts*, 461.

60. Ibid., 378.

61. Edmund Morris, *Theodore Rex*, 467.

62. David Woolner, "African Americans and the New Deal: A Look Back in History," *Roosevelt Institute*, accessed September 20, 2017, http://rooseveltinstitute.org/african-americans-and-new-deal-look-back-history.

63. Jean Edward Smith, *FDR*, 400.

64. Greg Robinson, *By Order of the President: FDR and the Internment of Japanese Americans* (Cambridge, MA: Harvard University Press, 2003).

65. See, for instance, David S. Wyman, *The Abandonment of the Jews: America and the Holocaust, 1941–1945* (New York: Pantheon Books, 1984).

66. Jean Edward Smith, *FDR*, 401–402.

67. James MacGregor Burns and Susan Dunn, *The Three Roosevelts*, 396, 557.

68. Ibid., 557.

Further Reading

Burns, James MacGregor, and Susan Dunn. *The Three Roosevelts: Patrician Leaders Who Transformed America*. New York: Grove Press, 2001.

Morris, Edmund. *The Rise of Theodore Roosevelt*. New York: Random House, 1979.

Morris, Edmund. *Theodore Rex*. New York: Random House, 2001.

Smith, Jean Edward. *FDR*. New York: Random House, 2008.

CHAPTER TEN

The Taft Dynasty

Mindy Farmer

Alphonso Taft was an ambitious man, but even he could not have imagined the longevity of the political power of the Taft family name. Through fortune and fate, his descendants would grow to include a president and chief justice of the Supreme Court, two senators, a governor, and several local and state civil servants. The Taft family dominated Ohio politics at a time when the saying, "As Ohio goes, so goes the nation," came to be true. The family's journey bears witness to the evolution of the Republican Party and the meaning of conservatism in America.

Although it might seem obvious that the pinnacle of the Taft family dynasty's political power was reached by President William H. Taft, there is a strong case for the honor to go to his oldest son, Senator Robert Taft. Although William H. Taft is generally considered a passable president, Senator Taft was one of the most influential senators in U.S. history. Where his father struggled to balance law and politics, Senator Taft was an effective, if sometimes blunt and uncompromising politician. And, while his father labored to continue the progressive reforms of his presidential predecessor, Robert was a Republican leader who steered the Republican Party into new directions. Together, father and son built a reputation for integrity and steady, thoughtful leadership at home and abroad. What the Tafts lacked in charisma, they overcame with aptitude.

Later relatives would struggle to maintain the Taft family reputation. Most notably, in 2005, Governor Bob Taft was sanctioned for "Coingate," a scandal where public funds were invested in a series of unusual, high-risk funds managed by Republican supporters. At his lowest point, Governor Taft's approval rating dipped to a staggering 6.5 percent.¹ It was easily the most trying time for the Taft family dynasty.

The Taft family have yet to politically recover from the disastrous end of Bob Taft's governorship; however, it is very possible. In Ohio, the Tafts are as much an institution as they are family. And, they are adaptable. The progressive Republican Party of President William Taft is different from the conservative Republican Party that Senator Robert Taft worked to build in the 1930s and different still from the religious right of Governor Bob Taft's era in the late 20th century. As the Grand Old Party continues to change, it would not be surprising to see another Taft reflect new ideals—or even help shape them.

Alphonso Taft (1810–1891) inherited his ambition from his parents. The only child of Peter and Sylvia Taft, Alphonso was raised on the family's successful farm, known as Taft Hill, in Townsend, Vermont. As a child, he watched as his father served in several important local positions, including county surveyor, probate judge, and justice of the peace.² By all accounts, Alphonso was a gifted student who quickly learned that the way to success was through education. With his savings from odd jobs and help from his parents, he set out for college. In 1829, at the age of 19, he was accepted to Yale University. There he flourished both academically and socially. He was one of the first members of the secret Skull and Bones society and Phi Beta Kappa honor society, thus cementing bonds that would bind the Taft family for decades to come. Alphonso graduated in 1833, and after a brief period as a teacher and tutor, he returned to finish his law degree.

Following university, Alphonso was faced with a dilemma: where to start his young law career. Fueled by the expansion of the railroads and the changes brought about by the Industrial Revolution, the American landscape was evolving. People were moving from farms to cities, creating a vibrant metropolis in areas previously sparsely populated. Lacking the family connections that gave so many of his Yale colleagues a step-up, Alphonso sought a city full of economic and social opportunity where he could climb his own ladder. After stops in both New York City and Pittsburgh, eventually he settled in the "Queen City of the West," Cincinnati, Ohio, where he joined the law firm of fellow Vermonter, Nathaniel Wright. It is impossible to know, but interesting to consider, how differently the Taft family political dynasty might have developed had he settled somewhere else.³

While searching for a new home, Alphonso was also actively pursuing someone to share it with. During his visits to the Vermont family farm, Alphonso and his parents would often spend time with Charles Phelps, a local judge and landowner who traveled in many of the same social circles as Alphonso's father. Over many letters, Alphonso soon fell in love with Phelps's youngest daughter, Fanny. After passing the Ohio bar exam and settling in a new house in the heart of Cincinnati, Alphonso proposed to Fanny. She was 19 and he was 30 when they wed on August 29, 1841. Just a few months later,

The Taft Dynasty

Taft Political Dynasty Family Tree

1. Alphonso Taft, 1810–1891
    Secretary of war, 1876
    Attorney general, 1876–1877
    Minister to Austria-Hungary, 1882–1884
    Minister to Russia, 1884–1885
Married to Fanny Phelps
Two children: Charles Phelps and Peter Rawson
Married to Louise Maria Torrey
Three children: William Howard, Henry Waters, and Horace Dutton

2. William Howard Taft, 1857–1930
    Collector of internal revenue, 1881–1882
    Cincinnati superior court judge, 1887–1890
    Solicitor general of the United States, 1890–1892
    Federal circuit court judge, 1892–1900
    Chairman of the Second Philippines Commission, 1990–1901
    Governor of the Philippines, 1901–1904
    Secretary of war, 1904–1908
    27th president of the United States, 1908–1912
    Chief justice of the Supreme Court, 1921–1930
Married to Helen Herron
Three children: Charles Phelps II, Robert Alphonso, and Helen Herron

2. Charles Phelps Taft, 1843–1929
    U.S. House of Representatives, 1955–1957
Married to Annie Stinton
No children

3. Robert Alphonso Taft, 1889–1953
    Junior counsel, U.S. Food Administration, 1917–1918
    Legal adviser, American Relief Administration, 1919
    Ohio House of Representatives, 1920–1930
    Ohio Senate, 1930–1932
    U.S. Senate, 1938–1953
Married to Martha Wheaton Bowers
Four children including William Howard III and Robert Alphonso Taft Jr.

(continued)

Taft Political Dynasty Family Tree (*continued*)

3. Charles Phelps Taft II, 1897–1983
    Mayor of Cincinnati, 1955–1957
Married to Eleanor Kellogg Chase
Seven children

3. William Howard Taft III, 1915–1991
    Ambassador to Ireland, 1953–1957
Married to Barbara Bradfield
Four children

4. Robert Alphonso Taft Jr., 1917–1993
    Ohio House of Representatives, 1955–1952
    U.S. House of Representatives, 1962–1964
    U.S. House of Representatives, 1968–1970
    U.S. Senate, 1970–1976
Married Blanca Duncan Noel
Four children including Robert "Bob" Alphonso III
Married Katherine Longworth Whittaker
Married Joan McKelvy

5. Robert "Bob" Alphonso Taft III, 1943–
    Ohio House of Representatives, 1976–1981
    Ohio secretary of state, 1990–1998
    Governor of Ohio, 1999–2006
Married Hope
One child

Alphonso's family followed him to Cincinnati. Together the Tafts, old and new, settled into their new surroundings, some—like the Taft Museum of Art, Taft High School, and Taft Street—bear their family name today.

Helped by high-profile cases and newfound wealth, Alphonso moved quickly up the social and economic ranks. In 1847, he was elected to Cincinnati City Council, his first political post. There he led a bitter, public fight to annex metropolitan areas that had grown with the city but were officially outside the city lines and therefore free from expensive taxes.[4] While an independent councilman, he soon gravitated to the Whig political party. A chance connection to Whig leader Daniel Webster fortified Taft's allegiance.

While on the City Council, Alphonso presided over a local case that would have lasting ramifications. Having made his fortune in trading, resident Edward McMicken bequest his extensive property to the city he loved for the purpose of building an educational center. His heirs, who had different ideas on how to allocate the family fortune, opposed the move and promptly sued to stop the transfer of funds. Alphonso fought and won the case against the heirs, securing the land that would ultimately become home for the University of Cincinnati. Daniel Webster, having waged a similar battle himself, followed the case and the man behind it intently. Impressed by Taft's success, Webster wrote to him and the two become quick, though long-distance, friends. In 1848, Alphonso traveled to Washington to meet Webster in person. With Webster's help and Taft's own connections, Alphonso and Fanny met with President James K. Polk in the White House, unaware that it would be the first of many such visits.[5]

The railroads that drove Cincinnati's expansion would soon become vital to Alphonso's own growing influence. Legally, after becoming a superior court judge, he affirmed Cincinnati's constitutional right to build the Southern Railroad. On a personal level, he served as incorporator of the Ohio and Missouri Railroad; the Marietta and Cincinnati Railroad; and he was a longtime director of the Little Miami Railroad where he advocated for increased rail communication, subsidization, and expansion. Pleased with his success, Alphonso moved to a large home on Mount Auburn that would become the birthplace of a president. Unfortunately, the move was quickly followed by tragedy. Fanny fell ill after the birth of Alphonso Jr. and never truly recovered. She passed away in the summer of 1852, days before the death of newborn Alphonso. The senior Alphonso was left heartbroken with two young sons, Charles Phelps and Peter Rawson, in his sole charge.[6]

As he mourned his wife and infant, Alphonso learned of the death of his friend Daniel Webster and the subsequent dissolution of the Whig Party. Foreshadowing the Civil War only a decade in the distance, the Whig Party had split along sectional lines over the issue of slavery and expansion. The Whigs of the North could simply not find a suitable compromise with Whigs in the South or the West. Webster, a brilliant speaker, had used all his skill to hold the last factions together. Without him, the Whigs fell apart. Out of the political void, a new party—the Republican Party—emerged with a clearer focus and new leadership. In 1856, Alphonso received a letter inviting him to a Republican Convention in Pittsburgh where he and other influential men would "make a declaration of principles and nominate candidates for President and Vice-President of the United States to be supported in the election the coming fall."[7]

The birth of the Republican Party was followed shortly by the birth of the future Republican president, William H. Taft. Just over a year after Fanny's death, Alphonso returned to New England where he met his second wife, Louise. His social equal, Louise and Alphonso married in a quiet ceremony on

December 26, 1853—she was 26, he was 43. William was a hearty baby born in 1857, which was a relief after Alphonso and Louise's first son died of whooping cough at 14 months. Louise would give birth to three more children who lived into adulthood—Henry Waters, Horace Dutton, and Frances Louise.[8] If parents are judged by the success of their children, then few couples could be graded higher than the Taft's. Each of their children was remarkable in his or her own right. All of the boys would follow their father first to Yale and then into law, though not all would enter politics.

Alphonso's fortune grew with his family. In 1865, he was appointed to the superior court of Ohio where he developed a reputation for integrity that would follow him and his family. His reappointment as judge found support among Republicans and Democrats alike. However, in 1869 he fell sharply out of favor with some very influential people when he was asked to rule on an issue still important to the Republican Party: religious education in public schools. His decision would follow him throughout his career, as historian Jonathan Lurie observed, "the negative fallout from Taft's decisions may well have killed his chances for statewide political offices, even though he remained proud of it."[9]

The bible-reading case, as it would be called, pitted the Cincinnati public schools against the Protestant elite. As the city became more diverse, so too did the student body. Out of respect to the many different religions and customs practiced in their schools, the school board ended mandatory Bible readings and barred any and all religious instruction. Concerned citizens promptly filled a lawsuit questioning the school board's authority to enact such a ban. Alphonso argued that not only was it the board's right, it was their constitutional duty to prohibit such actions. Public schools, he argued, were subject to the separation of church and state. He was the only dissenting voice.[10] The Ohio Supreme Court ultimately agreed with his decision and overturned the lower court ruling, but it was of no matter. The damage had been done, and the ruling would forever follow not only Alphonso, but his heirs. It would also reinforce another early Taft family trait—the love of law over political expediency. Alphonso did what he believed was legally right even when it was not politically sound. His son and grandson would make similar stands and pay a similar price.

Although the bible-reading case stunted Alphonso's efforts to become governor of Ohio, his integrity and willingness to stand on principle were seen as a potential asset for a president battling scandals. In 1876, President Grant appointed Alphonso to the position of secretary of war following the resignation of the previous secretary, William W. Belknap, who was discovered to have profited from his position. After he cleaned up corruption at the War Department, Alphonso was appointed by Grant to an even more coveted position, attorney general. Alphonso's term as the nation's lawyer would prove short but momentous, when the contentious 1876 election between Republican Rutherford B. Hayes and Democrat Samuel B. Tilden ended in controversy.

The Taft Dynasty

After all of the votes were counted, both parties claimed victory. Eventually, Alphonso helped draft the bill that would create an electoral commission charged with settling the dispute.[11] The result, now known as the Hayes-Tilden Compromise, marked the end of the post–Civil War period of Reconstruction. It also marked the beginning of a series of discriminatory practices and laws that eventually formed the Jim Crow system. Although the Civil War ended slavery, it did not change the southern power structure or the hearts and minds of people who believed in the separation of the races. Alphonso could not have known that the Hayes-Tilden Compromise would have such long-term implications. As public figures, every member of the Taft political dynasty would have to grapple with issues of racial inequality and discrimination.

Alphonso's final call to national service came from President Chester A. Arthur. In acknowledgment of his lifetime of service to the still young Republican Party, Arthur appointed Alphonso as the ambassador to Austria-Hungary in 1882 and later Russia. Never exactly wealthy, the new position afforded the Taft family the chance to experience true opulence in the Austrian court of Emperor Franz Josef. From Vienna and St. Petersburg, Alphonso watched as his sons and daughter found their own paths.

Though talented in their own right, Alphonso's children with Fanny used their new family connections to advance their careers. After two years in the Ohio State legislature, where he helped reform the Ohio school system, Charles Phelps met and married his wife, Annie Stinton. She was from one of the most successful families in Ohio. With her financial assistance, Charles became a very successful businessman, profiting from the newspaper industry that would plague his brother as president. He was editor and publisher of the *Cincinnati Times-Star* and later the *Cincinnati Post*. He also invested in ranching, electric companies, railroads, real estate, and he even bought the Philadelphia Phillies and the Chicago Cubs baseball teams. Today, his home and personal art collection form the foundation for the Taft Art Museum in Cincinnati. During his life, Charles was very generous with his fortune, helping his parents in old age and augmenting his brother William's salary when he was offered the relatively low-paying position of solicitor general.[12] Peter Rawson's life was more difficult. He graduated at the top of his class at Yale, outperforming his brothers, but struggled after college. He worked briefly in his brother Charles's law firm and edited the Cincinnati superior court reports, but soon fell ill and struggled to recover. After a time in the sanitarium, he died of consumption at the age of 43.[13]

The three surviving children of Alphonso and his second wife, Louise, were born to parents on equal social footing. Henry, or Harry as he was known, was a famous antitrust lawyer and occasional real estate investor. He was a delegate to the Republican Convention in 1920 and 1924, but otherwise stayed out of politics. Horace abandoned law altogether, founding the Taft School in Watertown, Connecticut, and serving as headmaster for many years. The Taft

School's motto, "Not to be served, but to serve," is still taught to students today.[14] Fanny followed the path of so many Victorian women, marrying a wealthy surgeon and having a successful family of her own. In any other family, these accomplishments would earn their own spotlight. However, in a dynasty with so many early stars, William stole the attention. And, no other family member would benefit so much from being a Taft.

It was not always apparent that William was destined to serve in the nation's highest office. By all accounts, he was not the most ambitious or intellectually gifted of his brothers. Doris Kearns Goodwin, a Pulitzer Prize–winning historian, noted that even as he prepared to enter Cincinnati Law School after graduating as salutatorian of his Yale class, "Will's motivation continued to stem from his father's high expectations rather than any strong internal drive."[15] However, this easygoing nature was part of his charm. He was affable and eager to entertain. He was also a devoted and doting husband to his wife Nellie. After his father's death, Nellie would help push William into higher positions. Although she did not serve in politics in her own right, she was a major influence on her husband's political positions. As a young woman, she liked classical music, teaching, and writing as was expected of someone of her stature; however, unlike other women of her time, Nellie also loved smoking, drinking beer, betting on cards, and especially debating politics.[16] Although they grew up in the same town and their fathers knew each other from the courtroom, William and Nellie did not meet until they were 18.[17] Once they met, they were nearly inseparable. So much so, that observers would later wonder if some of William's difficulty as president was tied to Nellie's ill health at the time.

Although William had worked behind the scenes during his father's unsuccessful gubernatorial run, his own entry into politics was a surprise. In 1882, as his parents prepared to leave for Vienna, President Arthur offered William the position as tax collector in Cincinnati's federal district. Young and inexperienced, the reason for such an unusual appointment soon became clear. In the era before patronage laws were enacted to protect federal workers from partisan politics, William was expected to rid the office of workers with different political viewpoints. He refused, and when Republican losses in the next election opened a window for him to leave without suspicion, he promptly resigned. In total, he served less than a year.[18]

The bad taste of corrupt politics lingered in William's mouth for many years. Although he actively campaigned for Republicans—already an expected duty for a Taft—he often spoke ill of politics and redoubled his commitment to the law. It was this loyalty to his preferred profession that led him to join a sensational case against a corrupt colleague. In 1883, 17-year-old William Berner was accused of helping to beat his boss to death with a blacksmith's hammer and celebrating the crime at several saloons. The case against him was airtight—he had confessed to six different people. When the trial ended

The Taft Dynasty

in an innocent verdict after only 24 hours of deliberation, the city erupted in protest. Rumors soon circulated that Berner's wealthy, well-connected defense attorney, Thomas C. Campbell, had bribed some of the jurors. Eventually the rumors led to an indictment and an investigation by the Cincinnati Bar Association. William joined the investigation as junior counsel, where he traveled all over the state trying to piece together a pattern of Campbell's illegal behavior. When the matter went to court, William watched as more senior attorneys argued the case. Fatefully, however, on the day of the closing argument the original lead attorney fell ill and William was asked to take his place.[19]

His performance was praised in the press, and three years later when a judge on the superior court of Cincinnati suddenly stepped down, Governor Joseph Foraker considered William for the vacancy. A former captain of the Union army, Foraker had a well-developed sense of political tactics. He understood that William's appointment was a chance to both capitalize on the Taft family reputation for fairness while gaining a well-connected ally in a city that could help him secure a Senate seat in his next campaign. When Foraker made the offer, William quickly accepted just as his father had decades prior. He was only 29.[20]

Although a healthy bit of luck and strong family ties helped him get on the bench, William's competency kept him there. Although not necessarily a succinct writer—well-known biographer Henry Pringle brutally observed, "He had no flair whatever for the turning of a phrase, for brief analysis of a technical subject"—his opinions were thorough and well reasoned.[21] William ruled on some of the most pressing issues of the day, including labor relations, railways, and regulations. And, like his father, he occasionally took positions unfavorable to political party. In 1890, William wrote a ruling that would become a sore spot for the Republicans. The issue was simple: after a bitter dispute with the Parker Brothers, a contracting firm, the Bricklayers Union of Cincinnati demanded that all local businesses stop selling construction supplies to their rivals. If they refused, union members would not work with their materials. Moores & Company defied the union's request and suffered financially as a result. Rather than accept the loss, they sued the union for $2,250. A jury sided with the company. The case reached William and the superior court when the union made a request for a new trial.[22]

William, like many Republicans, was part of the Progressive movement who worked to remedy years of unregulated business and corrupt politics with state and local governmental reforms. As a progressive, he typically sided with workers as they fought to improve working conditions. However, in this case Taft ruled against the union. In his opinion, the union acted with malice—in the legal sense of intent to harm—when it ordered a "secondary boycott" of any institution that wished to do business with the Parker Brothers. That was a step too far, turning otherwise legal tactics into an illegal action.[23] Fortunately, his verbose prose shielded him against too much political harm. In describing the illegal action, he took great pains, and many pages, to extol the virtue of legal forms of protest. Unlike his father's blunt opinion in the bible-reading case, William's ruling left room for the prolabor Republicans to find some virtue. It was not until much later, when his son was in office, that the Democratic Party would become the party of unions.

When asked, William insisted that his ambition was the Supreme Court, not the presidency. It was with that goal in mind that he accepted President William Henry Harrison's offer to become solicitor general. He argued more than 18 cases before the Supreme Court, winning all but two. His most notable win was in a case between the United States and Great Britain. After the purchase of Alaska from Russia, the United States claimed jurisdiction of fishing rights over the entire Bering Sea. After several clashes between international fishermen and American revenue collectors, the United Kingdom petitioned the High Court for a writ of prohibition to block any more seizures. At the same time, President Harrison was working through diplomatic channels to resolve the issue. William argued that any action from the Supreme Court would undermine the efforts of the executive branch; the justices agreed with William.[24]

While he was solicitor general, William and Nellie made a favorable impression on the president and lots of friends within the capital, where they frequently threw elaborate parties. It was therefore little surprise when Harrison appointed Taft to be appellate judge for the 6th U.S. Circuit. There he continued to put precedent over politics, making rulings that rankled his progressive friends. For instance, he held firm in his opposition to "secondary boycotts" when he ruled that the American Railway Union (ARU) was responsible for the harm caused when it urged its members to boycott cars built by the Pullman Company. He openly worried that allowing such actions would give the ARU the power to shut down the nation's railways should it so choose. As before, however, the sheer volume of William's lengthy opinions worked to his advantage. In plenty of cases he sided with labor; and, whether intentional or not, he ruled with the Republican Party on the issue that would perhaps matter most to his future friendship with Teddy Roosevelt: antitrust laws. In what was heralded as a revival of the Sherman Antitrust Act, William and his fellow circuit judges ruled that the Addyston Pipe and Steel Company had in fact conspired to both fix prices and divide up territory with fellow companies.[25] It was a significant victory for Progressive era politicians trying to reform and regulate "big business."

The next stop for the future president was a move not even he could have foreseen. When President McKinley asked William to serve on the Philippines Commission, he wrote to his brother, "He might as well have told me that he wanted me to take a flying machine."[26] Despite his initial misgivings, for nearly four years William oversaw the commission, tasked with establishing a democracy in the United States' new territory. In the end, the reviews of his service

The Taft Dynasty

in the Philippines were generally favorable. The commission revised the tax code to lessen the load on the poor and built a series of schools employing recent U.S. graduates.[27] William himself, through many petitions to the secretary of war, effectively forced the U.S. military to put away their weapons and act with less aggression. Even more importantly, he forced the commission to treat the native population as relative equals, always welcoming them as guests at his many parties, even if his many letters suggest his personal opinions were not as kind.[28] His biggest takeaway from the Philippines, however, was his complicated friendship with Teddy Roosevelt. Roosevelt, who supervised William when he took over as secretary of war, was impressed with his work. William's time in the Philippines also left an impression on his young son and future U.S. senator, Robert Alphonso Taft. Robert eventually became a noninterventionist, which would be significant after World War I.

William returned from the Philippines ill but motivated. Even though President Theodore Roosevelt offered him a seat on the Supreme Court, William turned it down in hopes that the position of chief justice would become available. In the meantime, like his father before him, he accepted an appointment as secretary of war. There he could keep an eye on the Philippines and help Roosevelt with his reelection, in keeping with the tradition that presidents sent their surrogates to campaign instead of hitting the trail themselves. He also watched as President Roosevelt used his charm and celebrity to his advantage. Taft preferred a more steady, evenhanded approach that clashed with Roosevelt's "shoot from the hip" style. Nonetheless, as Roosevelt's time as president ended, it was clear that William was the natural successor. Even so, Roosevelt took his time in giving William his endorsement.[29]

The difference between the two men became apparent during Taft's campaign. Often called the first modern president, Roosevelt made some significant changes to the nation's highest office. For example, he used his whole family to improve his political image. His young, feisty daughter Alice, in particular, often stole the show and his wife hosted important soirees and cultural events. He also renovated the White House to create the now famous East and West Wings. In the new West Wing, he created a permanent home for the press where he would often interact directly with reporters. He also believed in the continuity of Republican policies, largely sticking to the principles of McKinley. He used the Sherman Antitrust Act to prevent monopolies, mediated on behalf of labor, created important regulatory agencies like the FDA, and he was an ardent conservationist. In foreign policy he expanded American power by annexing the Panama Canal Zone, mediating a settlement in the Russo-Japanese War, and promoting American naval power with a worldwide tour of the "Great White Fleet."[30] Most frustrating for William was his strong adherence to the principle of implied powers. Roosevelt believed that the president could, and should, do whatever was not explicitly prohibited by the Constitution. This prerogative often ran afoul of the courts, Congress, and even

William Howard Taft and his family, between 1910 and 1921. (Library of Congress)

his staff, who held tight to their traditions. He also was not afraid to attack reporters or staff who opposed his positions. His most famous saying, "Speak softly but carry a big stick," was more than a motto—it was his practice.

Following in Roosevelt's footsteps would be tough for anyone, but for a person as measured and careful as William Howard Taft, it was impossible. Taft was not the Roosevelt replica the voters thought they had elected. Lacking Roosevelt's charm, his attempts to address some of his problems only made him appear inactive and indifferent to public opinion. For instance, he created a commission on government efficiency and took the first steps in creating a modern federal budget, and while both initiatives had merit, they took so long that they were still ongoing when he left office. He also, unsurprisingly, believed in the boundaries of the law. While Roosevelt was willing to test the limits of presidential power, Taft opted to stay within the clearly defined lines of the Constitution and precedent. Despite his brother's connections as a newspaper owner and editor, President Taft also failed to foster a positive relationship with the press, a bond only made worse when he promoted a tariff that caused the duty on printed paper to rise. This contentious relationship ultimately hurt him more than his split with Roosevelt. After leaving office, Roosevelt was too young and active for retirement. When Taft proved to be an unwilling and sometimes boring subject, reporters turned to Roosevelt for color commentary. He obliged, and soon the rift between Roosevelt and his groomed successor was front page news. When Roosevelt

The Taft Dynasty

decided to run again as an independent candidate in 1912, Taft came in a distant third.[31] Although his administration was clean of any corruption, the Taft presidency was also not particularly effective. Although he continued some of Roosevelt's progressive reforms such as the prosecution of trusts, federal regulation of the railroads, and support for federal reforms to protect miners, scholars generally rank him in the middle of their rankings of past presidents.[32] Moreover, despite multiple attempts, no other member of the Taft family dynasty has secured the Republican presidential nomination.

After leaving office, Taft still campaigned. By mid-1918 he emerged as the Republican Party's most vocal supporter of Woodrow Wilson's League of Nations. Even though many in his party, including Teddy Roosevelt, opposed the League, Taft viewed it as an issue for humankind, not partisanship politics. After the horrors of World War I, Taft believed the league was the best mechanism to arbitrate international issues and, thereby, create lasting peace.[33] Not everyone in the Taft family dynasty shared this view.

Nine years after his presidency, Taft was finally appointed as chief justice to the U.S. Supreme Court. It was the position he truly desired, and it is little surprise that he excelled in the role. He streamlined the entire court system to speed up justice and, in 1925, he pushed Congress to pass the Judiciary Act, which gave the Supreme Court the power to only hear cases that poised important constitutional challenges.[34] Although tough on business, he was, in some ways, ahead of his time on individual rights, especially as they related to property and prosperity. For example, in *Meyer v. Nebraska*, the Taft Court overturned a law that forbade teachers from teaching any language other than English before eighth grade. The majority opinion based their decision in part on the rights of the parents to purchase their child's education. In *Adkins vs. Children's Hospital,* Taft wrote a very rare dissent against the court's decision to overrule legislation establishing a minimum wage for women. Although his colleagues viewed a guaranteed wage as violation of the freedom contract between and employee and employer, Taft argued that women were too often on unequal footing with their bosses and thus victims of abuse and greed.[35] He also secured federal funds to construct a separate building for the court; the nation's most powerful judges would no longer have to share a space with the Senate. In failing health, William resigned on February 3, 1930, and died a few weeks later.[36]

William left behind three children. In keeping with their family's tradition, each had remarkable careers. Helen Taft received a doctorate in history from Yale and served as dean, and temporary president, of Bryn Mawr College. Charles Phelps Taft II attended Yale, but left to serve in World War I. After an honorable discharge, he received his law degree and returned to Cincinnati to work in his older brother's law firm. Charles ran as county prosecutor, councilman, and mayor as a member of the Charter Party, a group of citizens nationally aligned with the Republican Party, but who put Cincinnati first in local matters. Deeply religious, he participated in a number of charities and was very active in his local church. During World War II, he worked in a series of federal agencies under the democratic leadership of Franklin Delano Roosevelt, putting him at odds with his older brother, Robert "Mr. Republican" Taft. This perceived lack of loyalty was also one of the frequent attacks lobbed by his opponents in his failed bid to become a Republican governor of Ohio.[37]

Robert Taft entered politics later in life than his grandfather or father, but once there, he was a fixture. As a young man, Robert was taught about the importance of service from his uncle Horace when he attended the Taft School. There he excelled as he would at Yale a few years later. Unlike his father, Robert won several academic awards and graduated as class valedictorian. After Yale, he attended Harvard Law School where he was named the editor of the prestigious *Harvard Law Review*.[38]

After law school, Robert returned to Cincinnati where his father helped him land a job at the firm of Lawrence Maxwell Jr., the solicitor general under President Grover Cleveland. While there, Robert struck up a remarkable friendship with Martha, the daughter of Lloyd Bowers, who had served as solicitor general under his father. The two wed on October 17, 1914, creating a union of American legal royalty. Martha Wheaton Bowers was herself well traveled and highly educated. She was also wealthy, which afforded them both the financial freedom to take jobs of their choosing.[39]

Robert was 27 when the United States joined World War I. Like his brother, he volunteered for service, but he was medically barred on account of poor eyesight. Unable to serve abroad, he supported the war effort on the home front. For 16 months, he worked as assistant counsel to the director of the U.S. Food Administration, Herbert C. Hoover, continuing the Taft family knack for working with future presidents. In 1919, Hoover took him to Paris as part of the American Relief Administration, where Taft learned importance of the free market in economic recovery from Hoover, who worked hard to loosen government regulations so that war-torn areas could resume trade and rebuild their economies.[40]

Following the World War I, Robert helped found the law firm Taft, Stettinius, and Hollister, which remains one of the most successful law firms in Cincinnati. Much to his father's chagrin, Robert did not seek national office until after his death. Instead, he rose to power in the Ohio General Assembly, serving in both the House and Senate. The bulk of his focus was on rewriting and reforming the state's taxation laws, but he was involved in several issues that both harkened to his past and pointed to his future. Like his grandfather, he voted against a bill that would have required teachers to begin their class with a Bible reading. Like his father, he opposed racism by supporting an initiative to force the Ku Klux Klan to submit their membership rolls to the state. And, over the objection of the powerful manufacturing lobby, he

The Taft Dynasty

supported a ban on child labor.[41] Like so many Republicans, Taft lost his seat to a Democrat opponent after President Hoover's very unpopular response to the Great Depression.

Franklin Delano Roosevelt's success had a push-pull effect on Robert. It both forced him out of office and convinced him to run for Senate. In 1939, Robert Taft was elected to the Senate seat he held until 1953. During that time, he made his opposition to FDR's expansive New Deal programs clear. As he explained to the Young Republicans of Lawrence, Ohio, in 1936, prior to his campaign, "The basis of the American business and constitutional system is political and economic liberty, with equal opportunity to improve one's condition by one's own effort. . . . Government is conceived as the keeper of the peace, a referee of controversies, and an adjuster of abuses; not as a regulator of the people, or their businesses and personal activities."[42] Robert Taft became one of the leaders of a new breed of conservatives who believed in some government intervention—unlike later Reagan Republicans who viewed large, federal government programs as the enemy—but thought Roosevelt's programs went too far in manipulating the market. These conservatives, including both Republicans and Democrats, gained influence with the post–World War II economic recovery. In 1946, congressional Republicans picked up dozens of seats with the slogan, "Had Enough Yet?" However, when asked to serve as party leader, Senator Taft declined. He preferred to spend his significant political capital elsewhere.

In a sharp break with Progressive era Republicans, in 1947, Senator Taft proposed his most famous piece of legislation, the Taft-Hartley Act. In keeping with his free market ideals, Senator Taft believed that there was a legal imbalance between management and labor unions. For decades, legislators had placed clear restrictions on the rights of employers. The Taft-Hartley Act placed similar regulations on the rights of unions. In doing so, it ended some of the most extreme tactics of major unions like closed shops, gave federal courts the ability to issue antistrike injunctions, and allowed the president to declare a national emergency to prevent striking workers from shutting down vital industries.[43] This final issue would have pleased President Taft, who openly worried about this issue in his rulings against secondary boycotts. The act passed over the veto of President Harry S. Truman.

In 1948, Taft failed for the second time to receive the Republican nomination for president, largely because of his conservative positions on foreign policy. Prior to the Cold War, the senator was part of small but vocal minority who favored noninterventionism. Not as extreme as isolationists, noninterventionists favored keeping diplomatic ties with countries, but were opposed to any treaties or alliances that might lead the nation into war. He vocally opposed entering World War II and, later, in one of his most polarizing positions, condemned the Nuremberg Trials. He believed that the trials violated the American principle of law that those harmed by the crime could not be trusted to issue justice.⁴⁴ At the same time, Taft was a staunch anti-Communist. As tensions between the USSR and United States intensified, his extreme view on anticommunism and noninterventionism grew increasingly incompatible. In a rare move for a politician, Taft changed his position. "By 1951, Taft's anti-statist and anti-interventionist arguments had taken a back seat to the requirements of a global Cold War, with the senator embracing balance-of-power theories that he denigrated in previous years."⁴⁵ In doing so, he became more aligned with his father, an ardent spokesman for the League of Nations.

Senator Taft failed to win the presidential nomination for the third and final time in 1952 when he lost to Dwight D. Eisenhower, a moderate Republican. After his defeat, he reluctantly agreed to serve as Senate majority leader. While initially foes, Eisenhower and Taft became close colleagues. The alliance, however, was short-lived. While on the golf course with the president, the senator felt a sharp pain in his hip. It was the start of a fast but vicious fight with cancer. He died on July 31, 1953, leaving behind an impressive legislative legacy and a family to continue the Taft family dynasty.

Even though their father fought against U.S. involvement in World War II, each of Senator Taft's four sons served in the military. And, in keeping with tradition, they each attended Yale. Two of the brothers stayed out of government: Horace Dwight stayed at Yale where he became a noted physics professor, and Lloyd B. Taft became an investment banker. Two of his sons followed in his footsteps. William Howard Taft III was an English professor turned diplomat. Having worked in Dublin for the Marshall Plan and having studied Celtic culture at Princeton, he was appointed ambassador to Ireland. He was the first U.S. ambassador who could speak Gaelic.⁴⁶ After a brief break, he returned to government to work for the State Department. In 1960 he was appointed the consul general in Mozambique.⁴⁷

Perhaps fittingly, it was his father's namesake, Robert Alphonso Taft Jr., who would carry the mantle of the Taft family dynasty. Although it was rumored that he might run for his father's Senate seat after his death, Robert Jr. decided instead to work his way up the political ranks. Like his father and uncle, in 1954, he was elected to the Ohio General Assembly where he served four terms before setting his eyes on a national office. In 1962, he handedly defeated his Democratic contender for the U.S. House of Representatives, after it was discovered that while he shared the Kennedy name, he was not a member of a political dynasty.

Unlike his father, Robert Taft Jr.'s time in office was not continuous. Rather than seek another term as representative in 1964, he unsuccessfully ran for his father's old Senate seat. This was a pattern of the "Young Bob," as he was known in his family. He would serve two more terms in the House of Representatives before serving six years in Senate. In 1976, he lost his reelection campaign. It was a clear sign that the Taft family name alone was no longer enough to ensure an election victory.

The Taft Dynasty

Robert Jr. idolized his conservative father, but struggled to move out of his shadow, especially away from his father's two biggest weaknesses: his isolationism and famously abrupt temperament. In a profile in the *Saturday Evening Post* just before his freshman year in Congress, he anticipated these challenges, noting, "I suppose my approach is a little different than my father's, I'm a bit more of an internationalist." He added, "I guess it's true when they say I meet people more easily. It's not that my father was not a warm person—he was—but he was a little preoccupied and a little shy."[48] There were other differences, too. On many issues, "Young Bob" was more moderate than his father. He supported amnesty for Vietnam draft dodgers, fought hard for the Civil Rights Act of 1964 in the House, and worked to extend the protections of the National Labor Relations Act to cover some health care workers. Like the Tafts before him, he believed in the liberty of the individual and the need to protect citizens from unnecessary government intervention and regulations.

One of Robert Taft Jr.'s most lasting legacies was his son, "Bob" Taft. He was finally able to achieve the position that had alluded the Tafts for generations: Ohio governor. In his inaugural address on in 1999, he noted, "The Taft family has worked hard to earn a reputation for common sense, for getting things done to help others, and for striving to live up to the highest standards of honesty and personal integrity. And that's the kind of administration I'll lead."[49] Unfortunately, this was a promise he did not keep. The Taft family's first state governor, he was also the first Taft politician convicted of illegal ethics violations during his tenure. After winning his reelection in a landslide, reporters uncovered that Thomas Noe, a Republican fund-raiser, was given $50 million from the Bureau of Workers Compensation to invest in high-risk rare coins. Taft defended his friend until more investigations uncovered that more than $10 million of those funds had disappeared. Soon, other illegal activities were uncovered. In the middle of these scandals, John Green, director of the Bliss Institute of Applied Politics at the University of Akron, observed, "The Taft name has always meant men who are conservative, even stodgy, but always ethical. These investigations are a blow to the magic of the great family name."[50] Taft was convicted and fined $4,000, the maximum amount allowed under law, for breaking Ohio's ethic laws.

Governor Taft's actions were indeed a blow to a political dynasty that has spanned more than a century. Although the Tafts were always Republicans, the Republican Party they served was not always the same. The Taft family evolved from progressives, to isolationists, and finally to Cold Warriors. And while, always conservative, they were never a part of the religious New Right. The standard that Alphonso Taft set for the separation of church and state was passed down through the generations.

It is also telling that the newspapers that so troubled President Taft would be the enemy of Governor Taft. The Tafts were solid leaders, though not great orators. As a family, they struggled to adapt to revolutions in communications. To repair the damage to their political names, future Tafts will have to make peace, rather than war, with the press. Given their adaptability, that is likely a surmountable problem.

Notes

1. Jim Tankersley, "Taft's Approval Ratings Sink into Single Digits," *The Blade* (November 29, 2005). Accessed June 17, 2017, http://www.toledoblade.com/Politics/2005/11/29/Taft-s-approval-ratings-sink-into-single-digits.html.

2. Ishbel Ross, *An American Family: The Tafts, 1678–1964* (Cleveland, OH: World Publishing, 1964), 4–5.

3. Ibid., 7–8.

4. Lewis Alexander Leonard, *Life of Alphonso Taft* (New York: Hawke Publishing, 1920), 47–48.

5. Ross, 11.

6. Ibid., 13–14.

7. Leonard, 105.

8. Ross, 26–27.

9. Jonathan Lurie, *William Howard Taft: The Travails of a Progressive Conservative* (New York: Cambridge University Press, 2012), 5.

10. Ibid.

11. Ross, 62–63.

12. Lurie, 25.

13. Doris Kerns Goodwin, *The Bully Pulpit: Theodore Roosevelt and the Golden Age of Journalism* (New York: Viking Books, 2013), 55.

14. "Mission," The Taft School, accessed January 21, 2017, http://www.taftschool.org/about/mission.aspx.

15. Goodwin, 33.

16. Ibid., 15.

17. Helen Herron Taft, *Recollections of Full Years* (New York: Dodd, Mead, 1914), 7.

18. Lurie, 11.

19. Goodwin, 60–61.

20. Ibid., 18–19.

21. Henry F. Pringle, *The Life and Times of William Howard Taft,* Vol. 1 (Norwalk, CT: Easton Press, 1967), 100.

22. Ibid., 103.

23. Ibid., 104–105.

24. Lurie, 26.

25. Ibid., 32–34.

26. Quoted in Pringle, 160.

27. Goodwin, 270.

28. Lurie, 50.
29. Ibid., 76–77.
30. Lewis L. Gould, *The Modern Presidency* (Lawrence: University Press of Kansas, 2003), 22–24.
31. Ibid., 31–33.
32. Clarence E. Wunderlin, *Robert A. Taft: Ideas, Tradition and Party in U.S. Foreign Policy* (New York: Rowman and Littlefield, 2005), 10.
33. Lurie, 187.
34. Peter G. Renstrom, *The Taft Court: Justices, Rulings, and Legacy* (ebook: Santa Barbara, CA: ABC-CLIO, 2003), EBSCOhost (accessed June 20, 2017), 184.
35. Ibid., 194–195.
36. Goodwin, 748–749.
37. Ross, 397.
38. Wunderlin, 14.
39. Ibid., 15.
40. Ibid., 18–20.
41. Ibid., 21.
42. Quoted in Russell Kirk and James McClellan, *The Political Principles of Robert A. Taft* (New Brunswick, NJ: Transaction, 2010), 17.
43. Wunderlin, 120.
44. Ibid., 112.
45. Ibid., 3.
46. Stephen Hess, *American Political Dynasties: From Adams to Clinton* (New York: Brookings Institution Press, 2015), 267.
47. Ross, 408.
48. Richard Armstrong, "Robert Taft Jr." *Saturday Evening Post* 236, no. 2 (January 19, 1963), 54. MasterFILE Premier, EBSCOhost (accessed January 29, 2017).
49. "Taft's Inaugural Address," *Cincinnati Enquirer* (January 12, 1999), http://enquirer.com/editions/1999/01/12/loc_tafts_inaugural.html (accessed January 30, 2017).
50. Dennis Cauchon, "Rare-Coin Deal Buys Scandal for Ohio Governor," *USA Today* (August 17, 2005), LexisNexis Academic (accessed January 29, 2017).

Further Reading

Burton, David. *William Howard Taft: Confident Peacemaker*. New York: Fordham University Press, 2004.
Gould, Lewis L. *Helen Taft: Our Musical First Lady*. Lawrence: University Press of Kansas, 2010.
Gould, Lewis L. *The William Howard Taft Presidency*. Lawrence: University Press of Kansas, 2009.
Patterson, James T. *Mr. Republican: A Biography of Robert A. Taft*. Boston: Houghton Mifflin, 1972.

PART TWO

State Political Dynasties

CHAPTER ELEVEN

The Brown Dynasty

Ethan Rarick

When Jerry Brown took to the rostrum of California's ornate Assembly chamber on January 2, 2015, to deliver his unprecedented fourth inaugural speech as governor, his address served not only as a statement of political goals for the four years to come, but also as a review of California history through the lens of his own family. He mentioned that his father, Pat, had been inaugurated as governor in 1959, 56 years before. He discussed his own first inauguration as governor, in 1975, 40 years earlier. He could have referenced his sister Kathleen's service as state treasurer and her bid for governor in 1994, 21 years earlier. He even noted that at his father's first inauguration, he sat next to his grandmother, Ida Schuckman Brown, then 81, whose father had been the first of the extended clan to arrive in California, in 1852, just two years after the state's admission to the Union.[1]

Such a deep intertwining of state and family history was possible because of the Browns' status as the preeminent family of California politics, in many respects the one true dynasty of the state's public life. In all, the Brown family has produced three two-term governorships spread over 60 years of California's modern history. So long a reign in so large and vibrant a state means that the Brown political dynasty has influenced, and has been influenced by, many of California's critical political, economic, and social developments over her history. These include California's growth from middling size to a nation-state with a role on the global stage; emergence as a harbinger of the broader American future, particularly through California's role as incubator and archetype of postwar optimism, 1960s rebellion, and conservative backlash; sequential shifts politically from Republican control to a competitive two-party state to near-total Democratic dominance; a growing fiscal conservatism that influenced the spread of antitax sentiment across the country, though which recently may have been overtaken by more liberal leanings; an increasing environmental awareness that challenged many of the state's postwar assumptions; and a sharply increasing ethnic diversity laden with partisan implications. In one way or another, a Governor Brown has been involved in almost all of these chapters of the state's history.

Such dynastic influence is unique in California, a state often seen as unfertile ground for the development of political dynasties. With weakened party structures and a tendency toward individualized campaigns as opposed to a more structured system in which party bosses can anoint the winners, the state lacks some qualities that seem conducive to passing down power from one generation to the next. Indeed, California has produced no major political dynasties other than the Browns. By contrast, New York has produced three dynastic families listed in this volume—the Roosevelts, the Rockefellers, and the Cuomos. Even Massachusetts, with a far smaller population, has produced both the Cabot Lodges and the Kennedys. And yet, the Browns have flourished in California's free-form electoral environment, both at the top of the ballot and lower down. In addition to the family's collective six terms in the governor's office, the Browns have produced another major-party nominee for governor and two other local officials. The dynasty has also played an indirect role in the development of two other major statewide politicians—one governor, one lieutenant governor—who are not members of the Brown family, but who have benefited from their proximity to the family's success and network. In short, no other family has had so great a degree of political success or influence in the nation's largest state.

Pat Brown

Unlike his children, Pat Brown entered politics with no established fame or connections. His subsequent climb up the political ladder required a long, gritty effort that his heirs could largely avoid. Perhaps this is typical of political dynasties in which the founder or founders lack family wealth or some particular notoriety that thrusts them into the public eye. In any event, Brown blazed his own trail, which in turn served as the foundation of such a long and successful dynasty.

Brown's father ran a string of small businesses in San Francisco—a cigar store, an arcade, a movie theater, photography shops, even small-time poker rooms—with varying degrees of success. He was a bit of a huckster, and his gambling ventures may even have occasionally skirted the edge of the law. While on his deathbed, a priest offered to take a last confession, and Brown summed up his life in his response, "Oh father, it would take too long."[2] Pat Brown's parents were not happy in their marriage. He remembered them actively disliking each other, living separate lives in the same household, and

Brown Political Dynasty Family Tree

1. Edmund Gerald "Pat" Brown, 1905–1996
    San Francisco district attorney, 1944–1951
    California attorney general, 1951–1959
    Governor of California, 1959–1967
Married Bernice Layne
Four children including Jerry and Kathleen

2. Edmund Gerald "Jerry" Brown Jr., 1938–
    Los Angeles Community College District Board of Trustees, 1969–1971
    California secretary of state, 1971–1975
    Governor of California, 1975–1983
    Chair, California Democratic Party, 1989–1991
    Mayor of Oakland, 1999–2007
    California attorney general, 2007–2011
    Governor of California, 2011–
Married Anne Gust
No children

2. Kathleen Brown, 1945–
    Los Angeles Board of Education, 1975–1983
    California treasurer, 1991–1995
Married George Rice
Three children
Married Van Gordon Sauter

2. Geoffrey F. "Jeff" Brown, 1943–
Nephew of Pat Brown (son of Pat's brother Frank Brown)
    San Francisco public defender, 1978–2001

2. Harold C. "Hal" Brown Jr., 1945–2012
Nephew of Pat Brown (son of Pat's brother Harold Brown)
    Marin County Board of Supervisors, 1982–2011

then eventually separating (though never divorcing), as Brown's father moved to a downtown hotel. Yet Brown took something from each of them—from his gregarious father an entrepreneur's energy, from his more studious mother an intellectual curiosity.

California governor Edmund "Pat" Brown meets with President Kennedy, April 20, 1961. (John F. Kennedy Presidential Library and Museum)

From the start, Brown was a glad-hander, not merely a member of every high school club but the leader of many. By 1928, he was still only 23 and less than a year out of night law school, but he revealed the extent of his ambition by running for the state Assembly. "I just had that political bug from the very, very beginning," he said later. "It was part of me."[3] He had no fixed ideology and ran as a Republican mostly because, strange as it may seem from a 21st-century perspective, California was a Republican state and San Francisco was a Republican town. Of the city's 20 seats in the state legislature, Republicans held 19. But Brown also had no real platform and no campaign, and thus he was trounced, taking just 15 percent of the vote and finishing third in a three-way field.

Brown regrouped and, at least as important, he transformed his politics. He built up his law practice and started a good-government civic reform movement, the New Order of Cincinnatus, which elected one candidate to the San Francisco Board of Supervisors. As the Great Depression dragged on, Brown found himself drawn to the activism of the New Deal, noting later with approval that in his view Democrats "wanted to do things for people and felt that the government had a part in it"[4]—a belief that would eventually define

The Brown Dynasty

his outlook for the rest of his career. By the time President Franklin Roosevelt sought a second term in 1936, Brown was a Democrat. In 1938 he attended the state Democratic Convention in Sacramento for the first time, working all the rooms tirelessly. The following year, he ran for San Francisco district attorney against Matthew Brady, a longtime incumbent widely thought to be both ineffective and dishonest. Brown lost but finished a strong second, positioning himself well for another bid. The second try came four years later, in 1943. Building on the publicity and connections he had developed in the preceding 10 years, Brown ran a far stronger and better publicized campaign than in either of his first two tries, and on election night he emerged with a fairly narrow but clear victory. At 38, he gained what he'd wanted for years—a firm grasp on the ladder of politics.

In office, Brown professionalized and strengthened the district attorney's staff and attracted attention for one especially high-profile prosecution that would today be viewed through a different ideological prism: he convicted Inez Burns, who ran an abortion clinic that a local newspaper once referred to as one of the city's "oldest and best-known institutions."[5] At the same time, he and his wife, Bernice, were busy raising the children who would one day carry on the family business. Daughters, Barbara and Cynthia, and son, Jerry, were born before Brown took office, and then their fourth child, a daughter named Kathleen, was born in 1945 while Brown was serving as district attorney. Perhaps befitting a parent who would spawn a political dynasty, Brown was unrepentant about mixing politics and parenting. Kathleen remembered that when she was a child, her father would sometimes suggest a trip for the day as if it were a fun excursion, though when they arrived it became clear they were attending a political rally. Although two of the Brown children would take to politics, the oldest daughter, Barbara, found the atmosphere a challenge. Family appearances at public events annoyed her, and she would later say that politics left her feeling as if she "had no identity." In time, she became a family therapist.[6]

By 1950, after seven years as district attorney, Pat Brown was ready for his next political step, and so he announced he was running for California attorney general. (He had sought the same office in 1946 and lost.) He won, and once in office proved himself a capable state administrator, issued a series of reliably moderate-to-liberal legal opinions, and gained some favorable press coverage by investigating and exposing deplorable conditions in the state's mental hospitals. Politically, he bided his time. He announced he would not run for governor in 1954 against Republican incumbent Earl Warren, then stuck with the decision even when Warren announced he would not seek a fourth term. (A few weeks after Warren's proclamation, President Dwight Eisenhower appointed him as chief justice of the United States, thus handing the California governorship to Lieutenant Governor Goodwin Knight.) But by 1958, Brown was ready to yet again move up the ladder and announced he was running for governor. The Republicans were in disarray. U.S. senator William Knowland had announced he would challenge incumbent Knight for the GOP nomination for governor. Buffaloed by Knowland's greater political profile, Knight dropped out of the governor's race and ran for Knowland's Senate seat, and this so-called "Big Switch" cast a suspect shadow that Democrats saw as an advantage. The year 1958 was also good for Democrats both statewide and nationally—the midterm election of President Eisenhower's second term—and that November, Brown led a landslide victory. He won the governorship by more than a million votes, carrying all but four of the state's 58 counties, while Democrats won Knowland's old Senate seat, took control of both houses of the state legislature, and swept all but one of the down-ticket statewide races.

From the perspective of the early 21st century, with California as one of the most Democratic states in the country, it is hard to realize what a shock the 1958 election outcome represented. Republicans had long dominated the state's politics; until the New Deal, most California voters had been registered Republicans—hence Brown's initial membership in the GOP. Even after the New Deal realignment gave Democrats a majority, Republicans were able to maintain almost continuous control of state government thanks to Governor Warren's popularity and a unique California political institution called "cross-filing," which allowed candidates to run in multiple-party primaries while shielding their true party affiliation from voters. As a result, GOP incumbents could use their advantage in name recognition to win both party primaries, as many Democratic voters never knew they were actually voting for a Republican. A reform of cross-filing that allowed voters to see a candidate's true party affiliation beginning with the 1954 election helped to build Democratic numbers in the legislature, but not a majority.[7] Before 1958, Democrats had never held unified control of the legislature during the 20th century and had elected only one governor to a single term. Brown's ability to win statewide—and to bring along other Democrats with him into office—was thus crucial to advancing Democratic fortunes. This was due both to his extraordinary retail political skills—he would affably accost almost anyone he met, even rolling down the window of his limousine to chat up pedestrians if the car was at a stoplight—and also to his natural tendency to espouse a broad message with bipartisan appeal. Sometimes his moderation frustrated more liberal activists, but it was necessary at the time to win statewide. "California was not and would not be a liberal state," his first gubernatorial chief of staff, Fred Dutton, said years later, "unless Pat got elected."[8] The 1958 landslide was important not merely for the period of Democratic hegemony it created, but also because it lent Brown—and perhaps by inheritance his dynastic heirs—a unique stature in the history of the party that would come to dominate the state.

Brown had run on a platform of bread-and-butter governmental activism that reflected his own faith in the New Deal, and once in office, he and the legislature's big new Democratic majorities delivered. The state had been running deficits for years, so during the first legislative session of Brown's tenure, taxes were raised, especially on rich people and corporations. In turn, the new revenue funded exactly the sort of muscular agenda the governor had promised. State aid to schools was increased, and health care for the poor was expanded. The state established new standards for air quality, including limits on pollution from cars. Consumer protections were strengthened. Disability benefits were raised. A new Fair Employment Practices Commission targeted discrimination. There were compromises on many of these items, befitting Brown's characteristic preference for the good over the perfect, but there was no question that the new governor had achieved great successes.

More major projects were yet in the works. To supply California's ever-widening thirst, the governor convinced voters to approve a massive bond measure to fund the new State Water Project, damming the Feather River in the northern part of the state and using canals, pipelines, reservoirs, and pumping plants to channel the water hundreds of miles to the south for San Joaquin Valley farms and Southern California cities. To provide for the state's baby boom crop of future college students, Brown encouraged the development of the state's Master Plan for Higher Education, laying out a rational scheme of growth for California's public colleges and universities that would provide a seat for each of the state's graduating high school seniors. Such accomplishments came with political rewards: a brief flirtation with a 1960 presidential bid; and then a successful 1962 reelection campaign against former vice president Richard Nixon, a man who had come within a hair's breadth of the White House and who initially so intimidated Brown that the governor considered dropping out of the contest. But if Brown's first term had proved a time of rich successes, his second was more difficult.

In the fall of 1964, voters approved a ballot measure to overturn a fair housing law that Brown had signed the year before, a personal blow to the governor. At the same time, California gave birth to two phenomena that would typify the 1960s in the public mind—student revolt and urban rebellion—and in the process gave to many voters an impression that the state was spiraling out of control on Brown's watch. First, students at the University of California's flagship Berkeley campus launched a protest against restrictions that prohibited political speech on the school's property. Intellectually, they had a sound case—that the First Amendment should apply as fully on campus as off—and ultimately the university capitulated to their demands. But the final chapter of a months-long series of protests involved the occupation of the university's main administrative building, and Brown was seen by conservative voters as the governor who had allowed student agitators to sully a prestigious campus. The following year, the Watts section of Los Angeles exploded in six days of rioting after a confrontation between white police officers and a black suspect. In the end, 34 people were killed, more than 1,000 were injured, and almost 4,000 were arrested. Brown called out the National Guard to quell the violence, but again was seen as the leader under whom turmoil had occurred.

Even as Brown's first term had typified booming postwar optimism in America, these events of the second term typified the emerging social unrest of the 1960s. Outside the civil rights movement, the Free Speech Movement (FSM) at Berkeley was the first major student protest of the era (FSM leaders drew inspiration from their experiences during civil rights Freedom Summer a few months earlier), and the Watts riots presaged similar urban rebellions in Newark and Detroit two years later. Such events were bound to have political consequences, and when Brown sought a third term as governor in 1966, Republican Ronald Reagan exploited the new social unrest brilliantly, announcing his candidacy by declaring that city streets had become "jungle paths," and that at Berkeley a great university had been "brought to its knees by a noisy, dissident minority" met only by "vacillation and weakness."[9] Reagan's landslide victory that fall hinted at the national political drama about to unfold two years later, when fellow California Republican Richard Nixon would appeal to a "silent majority" shaken by social instability, in his defeat of Hubert Humphrey, a politician not dissimilar to Pat Brown,[10] in the 1968 presidential race. Thus, Brown's political career embodied a period of time in which California moved to the central core of the American experience, when the state came to be perceived as predictive of the nation. This perception of California would only grow in the ensuing years of the Brown dynasty.

Jerry Brown

During Jerry Brown's long and extraordinary career in politics, he has at various times both embraced and resisted his dynastic inheritance, but he has never been so foolish as to deny its importance. The third of four children born to Pat and Bernice (and the only son), Jerry was a young child when his father first entered public office. He attended St. Ignatius High School in San Francisco while his father served as attorney general, then entered seminary and nearly became a Jesuit priest—surely a rejection of the back-slapping world of his politician father. But eventually Jerry opted against the priesthood and graduated from UC Berkeley and then Yale Law School, clerked for California Supreme Court Justice Mathew Tobriner (whom his father had appointed) before taking a job with a prestigious law firm in Los Angeles. In 1969, at the age of 31, he was elected to the Los Angeles Community College Board of Trustees, and the following year as California's secretary of state. Such a rapid rise owed much to the family dynasty, and indeed to his very name, for while in person his father was Pat and he was Jerry, on the ballot they were both Edmund Gerald Brown. "I want to thank my mother for naming me after my father," he said at his swearing-in as secretary of state. "I grew to like that name during the campaign."[11]

After just one term as secretary of state, he ran for governor in 1974, and, again undoubtedly benefiting from the family name, won a crowded Democratic primary that included candidates with far more experience, such as Assembly Speaker Bob Moretti and San Francisco mayor Joseph Alioto. With Election Day occurring just weeks after President Nixon's resignation in the wake of the Watergate scandal, 1974 was a very good year for Democrats, and Brown narrowly defeated Republican State Controller Houston Flournoy. Inaugurated almost eight years to the day after his father left the same office, Brown was just 36, the youngest California governor in more than a century. Jerry became a celebrity politician almost immediately, thanks to a combination of California's prominence, his iconoclastic intelligence, and his rock-star girlfriend, Linda Ronstadt. Barely more than a year into his first term, Brown succumbed to Presidential Fever—a malady that afflicts almost all California governors sooner or later—and made a late entry into the 1976 race for the White House. He won nearly every primary he seriously contested, but had made far too late a start to win the nomination. Nonetheless, he ultimately received more popular votes than any candidate save the eventual nominee, Governor Jimmy Carter of Georgia.

Back at home, Californians were contemplating a tax revolt that would set the stage for similar measures in other states, and to some degree would nurture a general antitax atmosphere across the country for decades to come.[12] Reforms to the state system of property value assessments had unintentionally shifted more of the tax burden from commercial to residential California property owners, just as home values spiked. The resulting increases in property-tax bills enraged voters, especially since the state government was sitting on a massive fiscal surplus. (Brown himself later acknowledged that he should have offered greater relief from rising property taxes: "I was too tight-fisted. I'm not a big spender."[13]) Taxpayer frustration provided the motivation for Proposition 13, a measure on the 1978 primary ballot that rolled back property assessments, limited future property-tax increases, and made it harder to enact tax increases in the state legislature.[14] The governor, displaying a tendency toward personal reinvention that has marked his entire career, opposed Proposition 13 with fervor—calling it "unworkable and crazy"[15]—but in the wake of its passage, declared himself a "born-again tax cutter." The following year, Brown proposed a cut in state income taxes even as the state was using much of its surplus to cushion local governments from the full impact of the lower property-tax revenues.

Reelected easily in 1978, Governor Brown ran again for president in 1980, challenging incumbent President Carter for the Democratic nomination. Four years before he had entered the race late and done well, but this time Brown entered early and did poorly. With polls showing that most Californians disapproved of their governor's failing presidential bid, Brown dropped out well before the end of the primary season. He could have run for a third term as governor in 1982, but, perhaps due to his father's disastrous third-term bid or perhaps just due to his own interests in national policy, he bypassed that idea and ran instead for the U.S. Senate seat being vacated by Senator S. I. Hayakawa. He won the Democratic primary easily (defeating, among others, the writer Gore Vidal), but in the general election lost to San Diego mayor Pete Wilson, who would go on to win the governorship in 1990 and then reelection in 1994 by defeating Jerry Brown's younger sister, Kathleen.

The loss in the Senate race meant that Brown, though not yet 50, was out of office with no immediate prospects to return. True to character, he indulged his intellectual and spiritual streaks as few other politicians would, spending six months in Japan studying Zen meditation and a month in Calcutta working with Mother Teresa. By 1988, however, the old political itch returned. He ran for chairman of the California Democratic Party, served one term, and then considered running for the Senate against his fellow Democrat Alan Cranston in 1992. Instead, Brown jumped into the presidential race as a bit of a Democratic insurgent, rejecting large campaign contributions, advocating term limits for members of Congress, and opposing the North American Free Trade Agreement. His campaign used what was then considered the cutting-edge fund-raising device of a toll-free number, and foresaw a coming era of political grievance with black-and-white placards reading "Take Back America." He did remarkably well, outlasting everyone save the eventual nominee, Governor Bill Clinton of Arkansas, but suffered a critical loss in the New York primary after saying he might pick Jesse Jackson as his running mate, angering many in the Jewish community. In the final wave of contested primaries in early June, Brown had to bank on a victory in his home state of California, but eventually lost to Clinton 47–40. Clinton had long been the choice of Democratic Party regulars, in part because of a perception that he was a more viable November candidate, in part because some of Brown's policy positions were unusual for a Democrat, such as his advocacy of a flat tax and his call to eliminate the U.S. Department of Education. Ultimately, Clinton received 52 percent of votes cast in primary states compared to only 20 percent for Brown, who had always been fighting an uphill battle against a more mainstream candidate.

Once again in the political wilderness, Brown began hosting a radio talk show and even dropped out of the Democratic Party, reregistering as an independent and openly declaring his alienation from both parties. His status as a has-been was so cemented in the popular culture that by 1995, the movie *Jade* used him as the butt of a joke: an ambitious young prosecutor is warned against pursuit of a controversial case "unless you want as much of a future in this state as Jerry Brown"; and the character responds, "Who's Jerry Brown?"[16] But sometimes even Hollywood gets it wrong. By 1998 Brown was writing the sequel to his own career, once again putting his name on the ballot to seek the open mayoralty of his adopted hometown of Oakland. He easily routed a field that included 10 other candidates. "The Brown name had worked its magic once again," wrote biographer Chuck McFadden, "only this time it was not because Pat Brown's son was on the ballot. This time it was because Jerry Brown, two-term celebrity governor, was running."[17] The victory launched a second career in elective office, and the pattern was almost eerily similar to Brown's rise in the late 1960s and 1970s: a local post, a down-ballot statewide victory, the governorship. This time, two terms as mayor led to a 2006 victory as California's attorney general, and then in 2010 Brown—who had rejoined the Democratic Party—took back his old job as governor, defeating former eBay CEO Meg Whitman.

The state's fiscal condition was by then disastrous with numerous issues coalescing to produce yawning fiscal shortfalls year after year. The Great Recession of 2008–2009 combined with California's volatile tax system, dependent on unstable income taxes rather than stable property taxes, to hinder the state's revenues. Legislative Republicans were able to effectively veto fiscal decisions even though they were in the minority due to the state's supermajority (two-thirds) requirement to pass a budget or raise taxes. In some years, the state resorted to issuing IOUs to pay its bills, and the resulting sense of dysfunction in governance produced a general sense that California was on the brink of collapse. National and even international news articles described a "failed state."[18] Brown shrewdly promised during his campaign that he would never raise taxes without voter approval, and once in office he put an initiative on the ballot to temporarily raise income and sales taxes, engineered its passage, and then watched as the resulting revenue and an improving economy eased the state back toward fiscal solvency.[19] The passage of Governor Brown's tax-hike initiative in 2010 may reflect a crucial turning point in the general ideological orientation of the California electorate, a reversal of the antitax fervor evident in the passage of Proposition 13. Indeed, the 2010 decision was reiterated by voters in 2016, when another initiative extended the income-tax increases for the wealthy for 12 more years. Reelection in 2014 proved an easy task, although after the 2018 election Brown's gubernatorial career will at last draw to a close, as California voters in 1990 amended the state Constitution to include a lifetime limit of two terms for governors. The measure included a grandfather clause that ignored past service. That clause allowed Brown to run again in 2010 and 2014 after being elected in 1974 and 1978, but obviously the term-limit law precludes any further bids for governor; however, the law also establishes Jerry Brown's place in California history. Barring a future constitutional amendment, he will stand alone as the only person in the state's history to be elected governor four times.

Throughout his political career, Brown's relationship with his family legacy has been complicated. His father yearned to provide sage advice almost from the moment Brown took office, but Jerry, understandably wanting to establish himself as his own man, was less interested in receiving such counsel. Pat's notes to his son during the first few months of the new gubernatorial administration in 1975 are an almost heartbreaking testimony to rejected entreaties. "I really think I can make some contributions. Please give your father a chance to meet with you alone." Then later: "My eight years as attorney general and eight years as governor have given me some insight into California government. . . . I still believe that you should discuss tough decisions with me."[20] Even Jerry's staff sometimes sympathized; the governor's appointments secretary eventually wrote to the first Governor Brown and apologized that more of his suggestions had not been met with approval by his son. All of this may reflect a truth about political dynasties, that the endless hours of a politician's career exact a cost on family relationships. Once, when an interviewer told Jerry Brown that some politicians successfully combine family and career, he responded, "Do they?"[21] Pat Brown died in 1996, making such dynastic issues irrelevant for Jerry Brown's second turn as governor, but there were occasional signs that the son had grown more comfortable with the father's legacy. In 1999 when Jerry Brown was inaugurated as mayor of Oakland, he held a meditation session for his close friends and in one corner displayed items dear to him, including a picture of his father.

Kathleen Brown

Kathleen Brown was the third family member to win election to a statewide office and the third to run for governor. The youngest of the four children born to Pat and Bernice, Kathleen never knew a life in which her father was not an elected official. She attended Stanford—much to the chagrin of a gubernatorial father proud of his role in helping to expand the University of California system—and then went to law school at Fordham. As an attorney, she began her own climb up the political ladder in 1975 with her election to the Los Angeles City Board of Education. She was reelected in 1979 and later appointed to the Los Angeles Board of Public Works. Then in 1990, Kathleen was elected treasurer of California, following her father and brother into statewide office. She was not as much a natural campaigner as her father, but neither was she as quirky as her brother, and after just one term, she ran for governor in 1994. She won the Democratic nomination and ran in the general election against Republican Pete Wilson, who had defeated her brother just eight years earlier for a seat in the U.S. Senate. With the state still recovering from a deep recession, Wilson trailed Brown badly early in the race, but crept closer over the summer and in September took his first lead in the state's well-respected Field Poll. In part, his growing popularity was because he tied his campaign to a popular ballot initiative, Proposition 187, that would have denied many public services to illegal immigrants. Though Wilson gained in the polls as he touted Proposition 187, in subsequent years many observers argued that this campaign played a role in alienating Latino voters from the Republican Party and contributing to rising Democratic fortunes in the state.[22]

At the time, however, Proposition 187 clearly aided Wilson's bid for governor, and Brown suffered her own problems, especially when her campaign almost completely ran out of money late in the race.[23] In the end, Brown lost by more than a million votes, ending her efforts at elective office, though she went on to a successful career in banking and the law.

The Brown Dynasty, Writ Large

Two of Pat Brown's nephews also entered politics and held local office. Jeff Brown served as the public defender of San Francisco, an elected post, for 22 years until 2001, when he was appointed to the California Public Utility Commission. Hal Brown was appointed to the Marin County Board of Supervisors by his cousin, Governor Jerry Brown, in 1982 to replace Barbara Boxer, who had just been elected to Congress and would eventually go on to a long career in the Senate. Hal Brown subsequently won election to the Board of Supervisors seven times, serving for 29 years. In 1998, he ran for California insurance commissioner, but lost in the Democratic primary.

Two other major California political careers deserve brief mention, for although the individuals are not members of the Brown family, both benefited (in different ways) from their proximity to the greater Brown political network. First, Gray Davis served as Jerry Brown's gubernatorial chief of staff during Brown's first term, and then went on to his own successful political career culminating in election as governor in 1998. Partly because one of his major opponents in the gubernatorial race was a business executive who had never held elective office, Davis's claim of extensive political experience, stretching back to his days as Brown's chief of staff, was a critical component of his victory. Second, Gavin Newsom, who served as a supervisor and mayor in San Francisco before being elected lieutenant governor in 2010, and who later led the early polls for the 2018 gubernatorial race, is from a family with long connections to the Browns—though Newsom and Jerry Brown are not close personally. Newsom's grandfather, William Newsom II, was a confidant of Pat Brown during the early days of Brown's political career, and his father, William Newsom III, was appointed to the Superior Court and then to the California Court of Appeal by Governor Jerry Brown.

The Brown Dynasty amid a Changing State and Nation

Any analysis of the Brown dynasty must focus on the three distinct high points of the family's power, and the extraordinary changes encompassed by the span of their political service. The Browns' collective tenure in the governor's office extends, albeit with significant interruptions, for 60 years—from the beginning of Pat Brown's first term in 1959 to the end of Jerry Brown's final term in 2019. Coming in three separate two-term tenures, the Brown dynasty touches on distinct eras in the history of both California and the nation: the postwar boom so loved by Pat Brown; the more tentative 1970s described by Jerry Brown as an "era of limits"; and the 2010s, still too contemporary for good historical perspective, but perhaps a period in which California is again portending the nation's future. A direct comparison of these eras and of the Browns' role in each throws into sharp relief two trends evident in the 1960s and 1970s—increasing fiscal conservatism combined with growing environmentalism—and a growing demographic diversity that is much more recent.

Pat Brown sought California's governorship at a high point in the postwar "New Deal consensus," when the two major political parties were far less polarized than they would later become, when they shared many beliefs about the importance of a mixed economy, and when broad economic growth was a hallmark of the American experience.[24] The era's relative enthusiasm for a robust public sector matched Pat Brown's personal philosophy that government could be a force for good. He described himself as a "big-government man," a phrase that would later be a death knell in politics. As he confided to his journal during the battle over his proposed tax increase, did not Brown have much tolerance for people who felt beleaguered by the costs of an activist government? "I have nothing but contempt," he wrote, "for those who say that no new taxes are necessary."[25] Jerry Brown, by contrast, has long evinced much greater skepticism about the public sector, and thus in practical terms has shown a far greater degree of fiscal conservatism. During his first term as governor, he boasted of his desire to "slow government down."[26] When he was sworn in as governor the second time, in 1979, he proposed a tax cut and spoke of the need for government to "live within limits."[27] In 2010, when he announced that he was running for a third term as governor, he vowed to oppose any tax increase not approved directly by the voters. None of this was mere rhetoric. During his first tenure as governor, his administration built a huge surplus, even as calls for property tax relief went unanswered. Throughout his second tenure, despite state fiscal surpluses, he consistently resisted the desires of legislative Democrats to spend more on social programs, insisting instead that the state bank more money in a "rainy day fund."

In this, the Brown dynasty reflects in miniature a change in the general American political landscape, as the country moved from a postwar period of relative consensus about the value of government's role in the economy (and, indeed, about the positive role of other large institutions) to a more recent period of skepticism about the public sector. A second aspect of the California postwar boom was a lack of environmental concern. Freeways were seen as the epitome of modern efficiency, and undammed rivers were said to be, in the phrase of the day, "wasting to the sea." Concern for environmental costs was largely in the future. By and large, Pat Brown was in this regard a creature of his era. To cite just one example, when San Francisco residents objected—uncharacteristically for the time—to plans for freeway construction right through their city, Brown chastised them for standing in the way of progress. When in 1964 the state celebrated surpassing New York in population and thus becoming the country's largest state, the governor was delighted. But the world began to change even as Pat Brown occupied the governor's office. In 1962 Rachel Carson published *Silent Spring*, a book often identified as a launch pad for the modern environmental movement. Other hallmarks soon followed, such as the first Earth Day in 1970 and the founding of Greenpeace in 1971.

Jerry Brown took office as governor in 1975, only eight years after his father left, but he embraced the new environmentalism in ways the older man never imagined. During his first tenure as governor, Brown eliminated a tax break for oil companies while creating one for solar panels, he opposed off-shore oil drilling, created energy-efficiency standards for buildings, and pushed President Carter to give federal protection to more California rivers. During Brown's second term, he continued his environmental advocacy, often in tune with the majority of the state's voters. In the wake of the 2016 presidential election and President Donald Trump's decision to withdraw from the Paris climate accords, Brown even took on an aggressively international role in environmental issues, traveling to China to discuss subnational agreements on such matters.

Perhaps no single moment better reflects the Brown dynasty's engagement with the changing ethos of these two issues—increasing fiscal conservatism and increasing environmental awareness—than the introduction to a television program aired by Pat Brown's campaign during his 1958 run for governor. On the program, Brown was to answer questions phoned in by voters about his proposed State Water Project. In introducing him, the announcer declared, "Should corporate interests and nature run their course at your expense, or should the government solve the water problem?"[28] Such language, portraying market forces and the natural world as harmful and the government as beneficial, is simply impossible to imagine from a campaign just a decade or two later, including a campaign for another Brown. Deeply reflective of its own era and sharply different from the one that followed, the viewpoint of the 1958 program reflects the wildly different worlds in which Pat Brown and Jerry Brown governed, and thus suggests that many of the policy differences between the two men were largely differences in time. The changing world around them would not have allowed the father and son to be the same kind of politician.

The long time span of the Brown dynasty also reflects the markedly different demography of the state and country. Pat Brown's California was, like the rest of the country, a largely homogenous place. Restrictive American immigration laws enacted in the 1920s meant that the vast majority of the population was native-born, and even among immigrants, a surprisingly high number were white. In the 1960 census, the most common native language of immigrant residents of California was English. Indeed, the census at that time did not even include a question as to Latino or Hispanic ethnicity. When in 1970—the census halfway between the departure of Governor Pat Brown and the arrival of Governor Jerry Brown—the census began to ask respondents if they were Hispanic, just 12 percent of California residents said yes.[29] But in 1965, as Pat Brown was finishing up his second term and launching his futile bid for a third, federal immigration reform legislation reoriented American policy away from national-origin quotas and toward family reunification.[30] The result, over the ensuing few decades, was a radical shift in American immigration, with far more people coming from Asia and Latin America than before the 1965 reform. For reasons of obvious geographical proximity, California became the leading destination for many of these new immigrant groups. Combined with the fact that California's Latino residents had a far higher birthrate than whites during the same decades, moved the state to the forefront of America's changing demography. By Jerry Brown's second gubernatorial tenure, the change in the state's population was dramatic. In the 2010 census almost 38 percent of Californians identified as Latino, and in 2014, as Brown was running for his fourth and final term, Latinos surpassed whites to become a plurality of the state's residents.

The Brown dynasty has long grappled with this changing demography, most often in ways that have attracted the state's growing Latino population to the Democratic Party. As early as 1959, Pat Brown sought to create a minimum wage for farmworkers, only to be rebuffed by a legislature still in the grip of rural and agricultural interests. Jerry Brown emphasized the appointment of minorities to important posts as no governor had before him, his father included. One study found that of Brown's early appointments, 10 percent were Latino, a high proportion for the time. Brown named Mario Obledo to lead the Health and Welfare Agency, the largest single department in state government. Only five months after taking office, Brown delivered on a campaign promise and signed the Agricultural Labor Relations Act, making California the first state in the nation to extend collective bargaining rights to farmworkers. He also signed legislation, previously vetoed by Ronald Reagan, that extended unemployment benefits to farmworkers.[31] Later, as noted above, Kathleen Brown's gubernatorial campaign was felled by a Republican who supported a measure to block many public services to illegal immigrants, a measure unpopular with many Latinos. More recently, during his second tenure as governor, Jerry Brown signed legislation allowing illegal immigrants to receive California driver's licenses.

Whether as a result of these initiatives or not—and there have surely been many factors at play—California Latinos have, on balance, been more likely than white voters to support Democrats. This has been one of the factors pushing the state ever more firmly into the Democratic column, a fact reflected in the political fortunes of the Browns. Pat Brown's first statewide victory came at a time when Republicans had long dominated California elections. Jerry Brown first served as governor when the state was competitive for both parties. His second tenure came in a period of Democratic dominance that has seemed only to grow during his two terms. By 2017, just 26 percent of California registered voters were Republicans, a mark that left the GOP in danger of falling behind independents.[32] Republicans had not won a single statewide election in a decade, and Democrats held all-powerful "supermajorities" in both houses of the legislature.[33] Numerous analysts have speculated that here too the state may set the pattern for the nation, with greater ethnic diversity spreading across the country and tilting the electoral map toward the Democrats.[34]

Conclusion

When Pat Brown first entered politics in 1928, California had fewer than 6 million residents and was the sixth largest state. During Brown's tenure as governor, California passed New York to become the nation's most populous state, and his policies played a major role in providing infrastructure for further growth. By 2016, as Jerry Brown served his fourth term as governor, California had nearly 40 million residents, was home to almost one of every eight Americans (the largest proportion for a single state since before the Civil War), and would possess, if it were an independent country, the sixth largest economy in the world.[35] The state's massive size elevated the Brown dynasty, affording its members national stature and granting plausibility to their presidential aspirations.[36] Perhaps more importantly, California provided the family with a dramatic and outsized backdrop. The Browns governed a state that served by turns as an embodiment of postwar growth, social turmoil, rising environmentalism, antitax zeal, and 21st century diversity. Although the dynasty may draw to a close with Jerry Brown's departure from the governor's office in January 2019, few political families—and perhaps none whose members do not include at least one president—have played a larger role on the American public stage.

Notes

1. Text of Governor Jerry Brown's 2015 inaugural address, https://www.gov.ca.gov/news.php?id=18828, accessed December 22, 2016.
2. Ethan Rarick, *California Rising: The Life and Times of Pat Brown* (Berkeley: University of California Press, 2005), 34.
3. Rarick, *California Rising*, 19.

4. Rarick, *California Rising*, 25.

5. Rarick, *California Rising*, 44.

6. Rarick, *California Rising*, 187.

7. Prior to 1954, candidates could run in multiple primaries, and the ballot contained no indication of their party affiliation. Beginning in 1954, candidates could still run in multiple- party primaries, but the ballot reflected each candidate's personal registration. Thus, voters for the first time could tell if, for example, a Republican candidate was running in the Democratic primary.

8. Rarick, *California Rising*, 106.

9. Rarick, *California Rising*, 344.

10. Like Brown, Humphrey was an establishment liberal sometimes attacked from the Left as well as the Right. Perhaps even more to the point, both men were believers in the power of government to do good. Humphrey biographer Carl Solberg described the Minnesota senator as an "unreconstructed believer in the power and duty of government to help widows, orphans, the handicapped, and the unemployed." It's a description that would have fit Brown well. Carl Solberg, *Hubert Humphrey: A Biography* (New York: Norton, 1984), 463.

11. Rarick, *California Rising*, 371.

12. For an assessment of the influence of Proposition 13 on other states, see Isaac William Martin, "Proposition 13 Fever: How California's Tax Limitation Spread," in Jack Citrin and Isaac William Martin, eds., *After the Tax Revolt: California's Proposition 13 Turns 30* (Berkeley, CA: Berkeley Public Policy Press, 2009), 33–49.

13. "The Once—and Future?—Governor Moonbeam," *GQ*, October 2010, http://www.gq.com/story/jerry-brown-interview-california-governor-election, accessed May 31, 2017.

14. For an excellent discussion of the background of Proposition 13, see Joe Mathews and Mark Paul, *California Crack-Up: How Reform Broke the Golden State and How We Can Fix It* (Berkeley: University of California Press, 2010), 35–57.

15. "Shades of Brown: The Once and Current Governor Reckons with His Own Legacy," *California Magazine*, Jerry Roberts, Fall 2012, https://alumni.berkeley.edu/california-magazine/fall-2012-politics-issue/shades-brown-once-and-current-governor-reckons-his-own, accessed May 31, 2017.

16. The mere fact of Brown's inclusion reflects his extraordinary presence in American life; most state-level politicians would be too obscure for such a reference, even in a state the size of California. Try, for example, to imagine a similar line about George Deukmejian. "How Jerry Brown Scared California Straight," *Bloomberg Businessweek,* April 25, 2013, https://www.bloomberg.com/news/articles/2013-04-25/how-jerry-brown-scared-california-straight, accessed May 31, 2017.

17. Chuck McFadden, *Trailblazer: A Biography of Jerry Brown* (Berkeley: University of California Press, 2013), 120.

18. For just one of many examples, see "Will California Become America's First Failed State?" *The Guardian,* October 3, 2009, https://www.theguardian.com/world/2009/oct/04/california-failing-state-debt, accessed May 31, 2017.

19. Also critical was voter approval of a measure to allow passage of the state budget with a simple majority vote in the legislature, rather than two-thirds.

20. Rarick, *California Rising*, 372.

21. Rarick, *California Rising*, 371.

22. Other scholars have been more skeptical of the role that Wilson's advocacy of Proposition 187 played in alienating Latino voters. For two competing treatments of this issue, see David Damore and Adrian Pantoja, "Anti-Immigrant Politics and Lessons for the GOP from California," http://www.latinodecisions.com/blog/wp-content/uploads/2016/11/Prop187Effect.pdf, accessed May 22, 2017, arguing that Proposition 187 was critical, and Morris P. Fiorina and Samuel J. Abrams, "Is California Really a Blue State?" in *The New Political Geography of California* (Berkeley, CA: Berkeley Public Policy Press, 2008), 291–308, arguing that the role of the Wilson campaign has been overstated.

23. For a thorough discussion of the 1994 campaign, see Gerald C. Lubenow, ed., *California Votes: The 1994 Governor's Race* (Berkeley, CA: Institute of Governmental Studies Press, 1995).

24. For recent discussions of this period, see the work of political scientists Jacob S. Hacker and Paul Pierson, especially *Winner-Take-All Politics: How Washington Makes the Rich Richer and Turned Its Back on the Middle Class* (New York: Simon & Schuster, 2010), and *American Amnesia: How the War on Government Led Us to Forget What Made America Prosper* (New York: Simon & Schuster, 2016).

25. Rarick, *California Rising*, 121.

26. Robert Pack, *Jerry Brown: The Philosopher-Prince* (New York: Stein and Day, 1978), 234.

27. Brown Second Inaugural Address, delivered January 8, 1979, http://governors.library.ca.gov/addresses/34-Jbrown02.html, accessed May 25, 2017.

28. Rarick, *California Rising*, 210.

29. "California's Population," Public Policy Institute of California, http://www.ppic.org/main/publication_show.asp?i=259, accessed May 26, 2017.

30. There are many sources for more information on the Immigration and Nationality Act of 1965. For a brief summary, see "Immigration Policy in the United States," Congressional Budget Office, February 2006, https://www.cbo.gov/sites/default/files/109th-congress-2005-2006/reports/02-28-immigration.pdf, accessed August 31, 2017.

31. McFadden, *Trailblazer*, 69–71.

32. "15 Day Report of Registration," Office of the California Secretary of State, http://www.sos.ca.gov/elections/voter-registration/voter-registration-statistics, accessed December 22, 2016.

33. In the five cycles from 2008 through 2016, Democrats won all 20 statewide candidate elections.

34. This was part of the argument made presciently, though perhaps a bit too early, by the authors John B. Judis and Ruy Teixeira in their book *The Emerging Democratic Majority* (New York: Scribner's, 2004).

35. State's population as a percentage of the nation from U.S. Census Bureau estimates for July 1, 2016, http://www.census.gov/data/tables/2016/demo/popest/nation-total.html, accessed December 22, 2016. State's economic size as reflected by California Department of Finance calculations of Gross State Product, http://www.dof.ca.gov/Forecasting/Economics/Indicators/Gross_State_Product, accessed December 22, 2016.

36. The early years of the 21st century provided a strange interlude in which California governors did not dream of the White House, precluded by Arnold Schwarzenegger's foreign birth and Jerry Brown's age (he was 72 when sworn in for his third term in 2011). But there is every reason to think that future California governors will once again be included on every short list of presidential contenders, the same situation that often applied to the Browns.

Further Reading

McFadden, Chuck. *Trailblazer: A Biography of Jerry Brown*. Berkeley: University of California Press, 2013.

Pack, Robert. *Jerry Brown: The Philosopher-Prince*. New York: Stein and Day, 1978.

Rapoport, Roger. *California Dreaming: The Political Odyssey of Pat and Jerry Brown*. Berkeley, CA: Nolo Press, 1982.

Rarick, Ethan. *California Rising: The Life and Times of Pat Brown*. Berkeley: University of California Press, 2005.

CHAPTER TWELVE

The Byrd Dynasty

Ted Ritter

The Byrd family of Virginia established a political dynasty in pre-Revolutionary America that would expand and grow during the Civil War era, become dominant during the Progressive era, and reach its zenith during the massive resistance movement to civil rights. The foundation of the dynasty can be traced to financial successes of early Byrd patriarchs as apple growers and a multigenerational political power base. The decline of the dynasty came with the death of the most notable members of the family, Henry F. Byrd Sr. and Jr., and with changing attitudes toward racial politics in their home state of Virginia.

Colonial Beginnings

The Virginia history of the Byrd family began in 1669/1670 with the emigration from England of the young 18-year-old William Byrd, son of John and Grace (Stegg) Byrd of London. Thomas Stegg, his maternal uncle, had become a prominent man in Virginia some years before and served as the first speaker of the Virginia House of Burgesses in 1643 after they began to meet as an independent body.

Stegg was possessed of considerable property but had no children. He convinced his nephew to come to Virginia and become his heir. Stegg died shortly after Byrd's arrival, and William Byrd found himself one of the landed gentry of the growing colony. Byrd settled on his uncle's lands and continued the planting operations and Indian trade begun by his uncle. He too served as a member of the Virginia House of Burgesses and was appointed to the Virginia

Council of State in 1681 by the king. Byrd was also appointed receiver-general of his majesty's revenues in 1687, a post he held until his death.

It is important to clarify the way the Virginia colony was governed so as to better understand the extent of the political power that Stegg and his nephew, William Byrd, held. Roughly a dozen of colonial Virginia's wealthiest and most prominent men comprised the Governor's Council (also known simply as the Council). Dating back to the 1630s—with a temporary exception from 1652 to 1660 when the General Assembly elected members to the Council—the British Crown appointed Council members for life. Until the outbreak of the American Revolution in 1775, the Council advised the royal governor and the lieutenant governor on all executive matters. Council members, together with the governor, also constituted the highest court in the colony. Furthermore, Council members served as members of the General Assembly. From the establishment of the assembly in 1619, the governor, Council members, and Burgesses all met in unicameral session until 1643. Thereafter, the Council met separately as an upper house of the General Assembly. In 1776, the new Virginia state constitution abolished the colonial Governor's Council.

One of Byrd's sons, William Byrd II, returned to England for his education. William was admitted to the English Bar in 1695 and returned to Virginia in 1696. He also served in the House of Burgesses and is credited with the founding of Virginia's capital city of Richmond.

Byrd was named as receiver-general upon his father's death and settled at Westover to lead the life of a prosperous planter. Efforts on his behalf at the same time to place him in his father's seat in the Council were unsuccessful. However, William Byrd was later appointed to the Council in 1708.

Colonel William Byrd III was born to William Byrd II and his second wife, Maria Taylor, on September 6, 1729. He went on to serve as a member of the House of Burgesses for Lunenburg County, Virginia. In 1754, William III was appointed a member of the Council. In 1758, he was commissioned as a colonel of the Second Virginia Regiment and served in active duty on the western frontier during the French and Indian War.

William Byrd III was 16 when his father died. He was formally educated in England, then returned to Virginia and married Elizabeth Carter—the only daughter of John Carter of Shirley Plantation. Shirley Plantation was the first plantation established in Virginia (1613) and is, today, considered the oldest family owned business in North America. Elizabeth died July 5, 1760. Within six months, Byrd married Mary Willing, daughter of Charles Willing, twice the mayor of Philadelphia.

Like his grandfather and father, William Byrd III's identity was intertwined with the political life of Virginia. He served a term in the House of Burgesses, and in 1754 he was appointed to the Council, where he served for over 20 years. Together with his status in Virginia politics, Byrd surpassed his father and grandfather in military achievement. Around 1754, during the

Byrd Political Dynasty Family Tree

1. William Byrd, 1652–1704
    Arrived in Virginia, 1669/1670
    Virginia House of Burgesses
    Virginia Council of State
  Married Mary Horsmanden
  Four children including William Byrd II

2. William Byrd II, 1674–1744
    Virginia House of Burgesses
    Founded the city of Richmond
  Married Lucy Parke, then Mary Taylor
  Three children

3. Richard Evelyn Byrd, 1800–1872, great-grandson of William Byrd II
    Virginia General Assembly, 1839–1851
    Served in Confederate army
  Married Anne Harrison
  Four children including William Byrd

4. William Byrd, 1828–1898
    Served in Confederate army
  Married Jennie Rivers Byrd
  Four children including Richard Evelyn Byrd II

5. Richard Evelyn Byrd II, 1860–1925
    Served on Democratic State Committee
    Virginia House of Delegates, 1906–1913
    Speaker of the House of Delegates, 1908–1913
    U.S. attorney for the Western District of Virginia, 1914–1920
  Married Eleanor Bolling Flood
    Bolling family traces their lineage back to Pocahontas
    Father, Major Joel Flood
      Served in Confederate army
      Virginia Assembly

(continued)

Byrd Political Dynasty Family Tree (*continued*)

    Maternal grandfather, Charles James Faulkner
        U.S. ambassador to France
        General Assembly
    Uncle, Charles James Faulkner Jr.
        U.S. Senate
    Brother, Henry D. Flood
        U.S. House of Representatives
Three children: Harry Flood, Richard, and Thomas Bolling

6. Harry Flood Byrd, 1887–1966
    Winchester City Council, 1909–1910
    Virginia State Senate, 1916–1926
    Governor of Virginia, 1926–1930
    U.S. Senate 1933–1965
    Received 15 electoral votes in 1960 presidential election
Married Anne Douglas Beverley
Four children including Harry F. Byrd Jr.

7. Harry Flood Byrd Jr., 1914–2013
    Virginia State Senate, 1948–1965
    U.S. Senate, 1965–1982

French and Indian War, Colonel William Byrd III served as justice of the peace and county-lieutenant of Halifax, the commanding officer of the military force of the county. He fathered 15 children by two wives. With his first wife, Elizabeth Carter, Byrd had five children: William, born 1749, lieutenant in an English regiment, who died while traveling in France in 1771; John Carter, born 1751; Thomas Taylor, born 1752; Elizabeth Hill, born 1754; and Francis Otway, born 1756.

Byrd and his second wife, Mary Willing, had 10 children: Maria, born 1761; Ann Willing, born 1763; Charles Willing, born 1765, died 1766; Evelyn Taylor, born 1766; Abby, born 1767; Dorothy, born and died 1769; Charles Willing II, born 1770, later U.S. district judge for Ohio; Jane, born 1773; Richard Willing, born 1774, member of Virginia House of Delegates, 1804–1806, died 1815; and William IV, born soon after his father's death.

Despite Byrd's political and financial successes, his gambling habits were so extravagant that during his lifetime he nearly wasted away the vast estate

The Byrd Dynasty

built up by his father and grandfathers. Despondent and heavily in debt, Byrd committed suicide in January 1777.

The 19th Century

Although the Byrd family would be a prominent part of Virginia politics for more than 200 years, the dynasty was the strongest during the political reign of Harry Flood Byrd. Byrd was born June 10, 1887, in Martinsburg, West Virginia. His father, Richard Evelyn Byrd, a lawyer, was Frederick County's Commonwealth's attorney and later speaker of the House of Delegates and an influential member of the emerging political organization led by U.S. senator Thomas S. Martin. His mother, Eleanor Bolling Flood, was sister of Congressman Henry "Hal" Flood, a leader of the Martin political machine (see below), and her uncle, Charles James Faulkner Jr., had been a U.S. senator from West Virginia. The Byrd name would be further illuminated by the exploits of Harry's brother, Richard Evelyn Byrd Jr. (1888–1957), a naval aviator who led an early expedition to the South Pole. His other brother, Thomas Bolling Byrd (1890–1968), was a lawyer and Harry's partner in the family's very prosperous apple business.

The Virginia Organization

Thomas Martin, a lawyer for the Chesapeake and Ohio Railroad, used railroad money to support candidates and thereby became a power in the state Democratic Party from the 1890s until his death in 1919. He used his influence to defeat incumbent Governor Fitzhugh Lee for an open seat in the U.S. Senate in 1893 and established himself as the leader of Virginia's Democratic Party. He was supported in his effort by a young lawyer from Appomattox in the House of Delegates, Hal Flood. Flood would become a key component of a political organization that would dominate Virginia politics for over 60 years.

As a leader in the "Martin Organization," Flood supported a state constitutional convention in 1901. Flood hoped to use the convention to disenfranchise black voters. His mission was accomplished through the imposition of a poll tax and other new constitutional restrictions. The convention also restructured state and local government and created a State Corporation Commission to regulate public utilities. This new constitution strengthened the Martin Organization by disenfranchising voters who were more likely to oppose the Martin machine candidates, undermined weaker parties and independent candidates, and placed a premium on patronage and election machinery.

The new constitution also created a circuit court system where judges would be appointed by the state legislature. The new judges would have the authority to select county electoral boards and other local officials. The combination of the organization's early political power, the appointment of new judges favorable to the Martin machine, and the resulting courthouse officials became the foundation of the Martin Organization's enduring political power.

Hal Flood was elected to Congress in 1900 and encouraged his brother-in-law, Richard Byrd, to become more active in politics. Byrd was elected to the House of Delegates in 1906 and was elected speaker two years later. He would remain speaker for six years and is generally regarded as a powerful and popular legislative leader.

In the presidential contest of 1912, Richard Byrd supported Woodrow Wilson in spite of the fact that his mentor—Martin—favored an unpledged delegation to the Democratic Convention. After Wilson's nomination, Byrd managed Wilson's presidential campaign in Virginia. President Wilson would later appoint Byrd as U.S. attorney for the Western District of Virginia (1914–1920) and as a special assistant to the U.S. attorney general at the end of Wilson's second term.

Harry F. Byrd and the Conservative Foundation

Harry Flood Byrd was born in Martinsville, West Virginia, in 1887, the son of Richard Byrd and Eleanor Bolling Flood, sister of Congressman Hal Flood. His family moved to Winchester, Virginia, the same year. His father would become a wealthy apple grower and publisher of a newspaper, the Winchester *Evening Star*. When the newspaper was near collapse, 15-year-old Harry asked to discontinue formal schooling to take over the failing paper. He thereby became one of many Americans during this era not to graduate from high school, much less college. Leaving high school was a decision Byrd never regretted, and it probably helped shape his later attitudes toward formal education. Throughout his political career, Byrd was never a strong supporter of higher education. He saw his own

Senator Harry Flood Byrd of Virginia. (Library of Congress)

success and attributed it to hard work and initiative. His lack of education might have also contributed to his unsophisticated attitudes—he possessed little appreciation for the arts or literature and notably lacked tolerance or empathy.

Byrd took to newspaper publishing with enthusiasm and determination. One of the problems facing his new business was its debts to the company that supplied the newsprint used to publish the paper. In order to acquire the newsprint to keep publishing, Byrd reached an agreement to pay for the newsprint upon delivery. He often struggled to get the last few dollars together to pay for a shipment. This experience and commitment to a "pay-as-you-go" financial policy would shape his philosophy for the rest of his life.

Once he got the newspaper on a sound financial foundation, Byrd expanded his small but growing commercial pursuits. He became local manager for the Southern Bell Telephone Company exchange at the age of 16 and a year later was elected president of the Valley Turnpike Company. His experience with the turnpike company gave him a solid understanding of road construction and maintenance. This knowledge would establish him as an expert in the field as he advanced in political office.

Byrd would also begin to engage in an apple growing business which would expand into an empire that made Byrd one of the largest apple producers in the country and a millionaire. As in his other business ventures, Byrd would be aggressively involved in all aspects of the apple business from land acquisition, orchard upkeep, and harvesting. This attention to detail and personal involvement was a trait that characterized every phase of his businesses and eventual entry into politics.

Harry Byrd received his political education through the lens of machine politics. He served a brief term on the Winchester City Council (1909–1910) but lost his bid for reelection. Even though he had received one of the party nominations, he did not campaign and finished last in a four-man contest. This rude awakening instilled a determination to never take any election lightly. He returned to his newspaper and concentrated on his growing apple business. In 1913, he married Anne Douglas Beverley, a childhood friend and member of another prominent Virginia family. They would have four children.

Byrd decided to run for the state Senate in 1915. His campaign focused on what would be the hallmarks of his political career: roads and governmental efficiency. During the campaign, Byrd proclaimed: "The State of Virginia is similar to a great business corporation . . . and should be conducted with the same efficiency and economy as any private business." His insistence on a pay-as-you-go system, learned through his struggles as a young newspaperman, would be the foundation of his approach to government. Byrd would win by a substantial majority and go to Richmond not as a political unknown, due his father's tenure as speaker and Uncle Hal Flood's position with the Martin Organization, but as someone who was immediately recognized as a potential legislative leader.

Byrd immediately attempted to reorganize the state highway department and improve the construction of roads but with limited success. The General Assembly session of 1916 would become known as the "Great Moral Reform Session" passing prohibition laws along with antigambling laws and laws attacking "houses of ill repute." Because he believed that a bill providing for criminal sanctions for owners of property used for immoral purposes might penalize innocent property owners, Byrd cast the only vote against it in the Senate, which would prove to be an embarrassment to him in his 1925 bid to be the Virginia governor. Although, throughout his career, Byrd continued supported prohibition.

Upon his Uncle Hal Flood's death in 1921, Harry Byrd was unanimously elected to succeed him as chairman of the Virginia Democratic Central Committee. Under Byrd's leadership the party performed well, and he coordinated a campaign to defeat a bond issue to build roads, preferring a pay-as-you-go policy. The referendum was defeated and talk started of a Byrd campaign for governor in 1925.

Byrd worked to build an organization that rivaled the old Martin Organization. His style of leadership was not to coerce but to reward supporters with praise, jobs, road projects in their electoral district, and favorable legislation. This hands-on leadership style would create a loyalty that gave Byrd wide latitude in selecting state candidates and policies. He would ascend to the U.S. Senate in 1933 and maintain control over a political organization that dominated Virginia politics for 40 years. In the Senate, Byrd proposed and became chairman of the new Joint Committee on Reduction of Non-Essential Federal Expenditures in 1941, and later he chaired the Finance Committee. Byrd also became active in national politics and attended the Democratic nominating conventions for several decades. However, his efforts to nominate a candidate were unsuccessful, and he never backed a candidate who went on to obtain the nomination.

After a spirited primary and an easy general election win, in January 1926, 38-year-old Harry Byrd became Virginia's youngest governor since Thomas Jefferson. Byrd's administration would be significant for frugality and government reorganization. But it was also noteworthy for other actions: defeating both the federal child labor amendment (which Byrd opposed) and a compulsory education bill that would have raised the required school attendance age from 12 to 14. More troubling was passage under Governor Byrd of the Public Assemblage Act that necessitated separate seating of the races at public gatherings. Governor Byrd, who had been urged privately to veto the bill, allowed it to become law without his signature, making Virginia the first and only state to require racial segregation in all places of public entertainment or assemblage. Limited to a single term by Virginia law, Byrd left the governorship in 1930 with a list of accomplishments that included industrial success, a $4 million treasury surplus, reorganization of the executive branch, more than 2,000 miles of new highways, and the creation of Shenandoah Park. He was generally praised for his administration.

Byrd's "retirement" would be short-lived as he was sworn in as a U.S. senator on March 4, 1933. He also flirted with the 1932 presidential nomination. Although he did not formally declare, he encouraged his selection as a Virginia "favorite son" and spoke to several organizations and legislative bodies outside Virginia. His hopes for a deadlocked nominating convention that might turn to him never materialized, and New York governor Franklin Roosevelt was nominated on the fourth ballot. Although Byrd never completely gave up on the idea of obtaining the presidency, Roosevelt's enormous popularity and the success of his New Deal prevented any realistic opportunity for a Byrd victory.

Although he would later condemn parts of the New Deal, Byrd was an early supporter and advocate for President Roosevelt's New Deal achievements in his first 100 days. Byrd's early support was probably due to the economic conditions confronting the nation, and Virginia in particular, but it also reflected his decision not to break with a enormously popular president with his own reelection in 1934 looming. Roosevelt's victory would also allow Byrd to control patronage in Virginia for a Democratic administration after 12 years of Republican control.

Still Byrd's support for the New Deal was not consistent, and he would break with the president's agenda on several fronts. Byrd would ultimately oppose the farm bill that extended the power of the secretary of agriculture and permitted stricter production controls. "We do not want," Byrd would proclaim, "a Hitler of American agriculture." He would later become a leading spokesman for conservative principles calling for economical, efficient, and limited government. Asserting "that government is best that governs least," Byrd feared that the growing power, cost, and what he perceived as wasteful bureaucracy of the federal government would threaten individual liberty. He refused to grasp the changing nature of American society—the decline of the family farm, the challenges of environmental pollution and poor farming practices, and the problems of long-term unemployment and an aging population without economic support. Byrd found it difficult to accept that a self-help ethic could no longer suffice for America in an industrial age, during the depression.

When Congress considered the Works Progress Administration (WPA) in 1935 that would emphasize work rather than simple distribution of benefits, Byrd strongly opposed the measure. Using language that would be repeated and rephrased for the next 30 years, Byrd called for the end of the "spending orgy at Washington" and asserted that he was opposed "to mortgaging the future welfare of our children, grandchildren, and even generations to come." Even though he opposed the legislation and tried to reduce the amount of money appropriated to the WPA, Byrd worked to capture as much funding as he could for projects in Virginia.

Byrd also opposed the Social Security Act, which established Social Security, unemployment insurance, and public assistance (welfare). He used his influence to stall its implementation in Virginia and, as a result, Virginians would not receive benefits under the law until three years after Congress enacted the measure. Byrd was one of only four Democratic senators to oppose the Wagner Labor Relations Act in May 1935, and he became a strident antilabor voice in the Senate. He opposed passage of the 1938 law that established a minimum wage, and he condemned workers' "sit-down" strikes.

Despite his opposition to much of the New Deal, Byrd endorsed President Roosevelt for reelection in 1936, stating that he voted for the proposals made by the administration when he believed them to be appropriate and voted against them when he thought they were wrong. Byrd campaigned for Roosevelt's reelection; however, this action was probably due more to Roosevelt's popularity in Virginia than any endorsement of his policies. Roosevelt would go on to win over 70 percent of the vote (90 percent in some rural counties). Despite his lukewarm support for Roosevelt, Byrd would oppose the president's court-packing plan and government reorganization efforts. Meanwhile, the citizens of Virginia seemed comfortable with supporting Roosevelt as president while at the same time supporting the Byrd Organization in state matters. Virginians would avail themselves of federal programs but would remain receptive to traditional platitudes of states' rights, individualism, economy, and efficiency. This permitted Byrd the freedom to attack the New Deal while maintaining personal control over Virginia politics.

Byrd solidified his power at home and in Washington through a series of challenges, including opposition to Roosevelt's nomination of a Judge Byrd opposed (the nomination would be defeated by a vote of 72–9) and an effort to undermine Byrd's rule in Virginia by Governor Price. The Byrd Organization met Price's challenge and elected Byrd supporters to the legislature. In 1940, Byrd was reelected to the Senate unopposed and solidified his control over Virginia politics. Meanwhile, Byrd's prominence as a spokesman for reduced federal spending and eliminating governmental waste contributed to a growing national reputation.

Growing tensions in Europe and America's ultimate entry in World War II presented Byrd with conflicting concerns. He understood what war could mean for the economy and government spending. He was not an isolationist but hated the thought of another war. He supported neutrality but would ultimately side with President Roosevelt's call to end the arms embargo for the Allied forces in Europe.

As Roosevelt's second term came to a close, Byrd and other conservatives were upset with the president's failed court-packing scheme and his attempt to purge Democratic opponents of the New Deal. They were also hesitant to endorse a third term for Roosevelt and favored adhering to the informal two-term limit that had been a presidential tradition since George Washington. Byrd may have had another reason to oppose Roosevelt's renomination:

his own growing national reputation provided some support for a Byrd presidential run. However, Byrd would accept the lack of any realistic success in 1940 and would, instead, concentrate on consolidating his power in Virginia.

As a member of the Resolutions Committee at the 1940 Democratic Convention in Chicago, Byrd favored a resolution to oppose a third term for Roosevelt and instead voted for John Nance Garner. After Roosevelt's nomination, Byrd was opposed to the convention's decision to replace Garner with Henry Wallace as vice president on the ticket. In the ensuing campaign, Byrd did very little on behalf of the national ticket. As for his reelection campaign, Byrd did not attend party rallies and had no campaign expenses. Still, he won with 95 percent of the vote.

As America moved closer to entry in World War II, Byrd criticized America's military readiness. When a new tax bill was proposed to finance increased military expenditures, Byrd recommended creation of a joint congressional committee to focus on ways to cut nondefense spending. The result was the creation of the Joint Committee on Reduction of Non-Essential Federal Expenditures. Byrd was selected as chair of the committee and would hold that seat for over 20 years. In time, the committee would become known as the Byrd Committee, and he used the platform to propose massive cuts in spending for social programs. After the Japanese attack at Pearl Harbor in December 1941, Byrd abandoned his call for neutrality and supported the declaration of war against Japan and, shortly thereafter, Germany. Byrd would, however, use the war effort to justify terminating major New Deal policies such as the Civilian Conservation Corps and the WPA.

Byrd's sons, Harry Jr., Beverly, and Dick, would all serve in the military during the war. Their well-being and his duties in the Senate kept Byrd occupied. He also was involved in the 1944 presidential campaign. Senator "Cotton Ed" Smith of South Carolina nominated Byrd for the presidency under the banner of a Southern Democratic Party. Byrd declined the nomination but was aware of the effort to promote a Byrd candidacy. In October 1943, a Byrd for President Committee was formed without his knowledge and began soliciting support. Few believed he could actually unseat President Roosevelt, and Byrd urged his avid supporters to be cautious. Byrd had always disavowed any interest in the presidency, but he did believe that some challenge to Roosevelt and his policies was warranted.

Byrd's name would be placed in nomination at the 1944 Democratic Convention more as a southern protest vote than anything. Roosevelt received 1,086 votes to Byrd's 89. Although Byrd never formally announced his candidacy for president, he became a lasting symbol of resistance within the Democratic Party. Byrd received 15 Electoral College votes in the 1960 presidential election from electors who refused to vote for either Democrat John F. Kennedy (the eventual winner) or Republican Richard M. Nixon: eight from Mississippi, six from Alabama, and one from Oklahoma.

Throughout his lifetime, Byrd was an ardent opponent of racial desegregation. This opposition led him to withhold support for Democratic presidential nominees Harry Truman (in 1948), Adlai Stevenson (in 1952 and 1956), and Kennedy (in 1960). The Byrd Organization in Virginia employed a a system of practices that limited voting by African Americans and poor whites, as a way to to maintain their hold on Virginia politics. Through the use of poll taxes and literacy tests, Byrd's organization monopolized the votes of white Viriginians and thereby continued to dominate state politics for decades.

Education funding had not been a priority for Byrd during his term as governor, and Virginia state spending for education would remain low through the 1960s. Much of Byrd's focus was to prevent the implementation of the U.S. Supreme Court's landmark *Brown v. Board of Education* decision of 1954, which unanimously overturned racial segregation as a violation of the U.S. Constitution. Byrd supported and signed the "Southern Manifesto" of the same year that condemned the decision as an "unwarranted exercise of power by the Court" and asserted that the Fourteenth Amendment was never intended to affect the system of education maintained by the states.

Byrd's anti-*Brown* strategy became known as "massive resistance," when other southern members of Congress joined with him in opposition to desegregation efforts. In 1956 the Virginia General Assembly, controlled by the Byrd Organization, passed a series of laws known as the Stanley Plan, after then governor Thomas Stanley. One of these laws denied state funding for any integrated schools and further authorized the governor to close any integrated schools. Other laws crated a three-member Pupil Placement Board to determine which school a student would attend and created tuition grant structures that would provide funds to students from closed schools so they could attend private, segregated schools of their choice. These massive resistance laws would ultimately be determined to be unconstitutional but not before several schools were closed for years. But attitudes regarding segregation in Virginia—and elsewhere in the South—were slowly beginning to change. In 1969, Virginia elected Republican A. Linwood Holton Jr. as governor. Holton had opposed massive resistance and placed his children in Richmond's public schools, which were mostly African American. One of his daughters, Anne Holton, would later serve as Virginia's first lady (as wife of Governor Tim Kaine) and state secretary of education. She is the wife of senator and 2016 Democratic vice presidential candidate Tim Kaine.

The Twilight of the Dynasty

Harry Byrd retired from the Senate in November 1965 and was replaced by his son, Harry F. Byrd Jr. After dominating Virginia politics for nearly 50 years, Byrd died one year later, on October 20, 1966. Harry F. Byrd Jr. was appointed to the Senate seat vacated by his father's retirement after serving

The Byrd Dynasty

17 years in the Virginia State Senate (1948–1965). While in the state Senate, Byrd would support the Byrd Organization and his father's massive resistance. After the Stanley Plan laws were ruled unconstitutional, a slow decline in the power of the Byrd Organization began. Byrd Jr. made no significant effort to prop up the political machine and seemed intent to forge his own professional path. In the state Senate, he authored the Automatic Income Reduction Act, which provided for tax rebates to citizens when the general fund surplus reached certain levels.

After his initial Senate appointment, Byrd Jr. won a special election in 1966 as a Democrat to serve out the remainder of this father's term. In 1970, Byrd Jr. broke with the Democratic Party when he was asked to sign an oath to support the party's presidential nominee in 1972. Since the nominee had yet to be chosen, Byrd said he could not and would not sign an oath to vote for a nominee whose policies and character he did not yet know. In 1970 Byrd Jr. ran for reelection as an independent and became the first such candidate to win a statewide election in Virginia—and the first independent to win a U.S. Senate seat by a majority vote. Byrd would continue to caucus with the Democrats in the Senate and won reelection in 1976 against Democrat Admiral Elmo R. Zumwalt. As a result of this election, he became the first senator to win election and reelection as an independent. Meanwhile, Republican President Gerald Ford would carry Virginia in the presidential election that same year.

Despite changing attitudes in Virginia, Byrd Jr., like his father, would remain steadfast in his opposition to school desegregation. In an interview with the *Washington Post* in 1982, Byrd stated that his support of the massive resistance policies, including the closure of schools rather than allowing them to be desegregated, was justified as it helped, in his view, to prevent racial violence. Byrd retired from the Senate in 1982. He died in 2013 at the age of 98.

Conclusion

The Byrd family came to prominence at the dawn of America. Influential members of colonial society, their political strength grew through the American Revolution and into the latter part of the 18th century. Despite economic setbacks, the family regained its footing and would remain a leading force in Virginia politics through the late 20th century. Through the efforts of Harry Flood Byrd, the family built an economic powerbase and assumed new heights in Virginia politics. Byrd and his son, Harry F. Byrd Jr., would serve in the U.S. Senate for a combined 50 years. The Byrd political organization would become synonymous with conservative pay-as-you-go fiscal policies and strident segregation policies. They played a major role in the massive resistance campaign engineered in response to court-ordered school desegregation in the 1950s that would cripple the state's educational system for years. The effort included the seizure by the state and closure of several schools to prevent their integration, a takeover eventually ruled illegal by state and federal courts. The legacy of the Byrd family is mixed as it includes strong, conservative fiscal restraint but also the stain of opposition to integration. Byrd Jr.'s decision to leave the Democratic Party and run as an independent opened the door for conservative Democrats to begin voting Republican. In 1952, Byrd Sr. announced he would not endorse a more socially liberal Democratic candidate, saying "silence is golden." Many Democrats took this as a sign it would be acceptable to vote for Eisenhower. From 1952 until 2004, Virginia voted Republican in every presidential race (except for Johnson's landslide victory in 1964). Obama would break that streak in 2008.

Perhaps symbolic of the changing view in Virginia of the Byrd legacy and its opposition to desegregation was the 2016 decision by the Henrico County School Board to change the name of Harry Flood Byrd Middle School to Quioccasin Middle School. Supporters of the name change asserted it was wrong for a school to be named after a man who had fought for so long to deny education to so many.

Further Reading

Hatch, Alden. *The Byrds of Virginia.* New York: Holt, Rinehart and Winston, 1969.

Heinemann, Ronald L. *Harry Byrd of Virginia.* Charlottesville: University Press of Virginia, 1996.

Kukla, Jon. *Speakers and Clerks of the Virginia House of Burgesses, 1643–1776.* Richmond: Virginia State Library, 1981.

Wilkinson, J. Harvie. *Harry Byrd and the Changing Face of Virginia Politics.* Charlottesville: University Press of Virginia, 1968.

CHAPTER THIRTEEN

The Cuomo Dynasty

Saladin Ambar

The Cuomo political dynasty began in 1982, with the election of Mario Cuomo as the first Italian American governor in the Empire State. Cuomo would go on to serve three terms (1983–1995), making him the longest-serving Democratic governor in New York history. Yet, unlike other famed New York political dynasties such as the Roosevelts and Rockefellers, the Cuomos were not nearly as well-heeled. Born in Brooklyn in 1932, Mario Cuomo came from a family of recent immigrants from the Campania region of southern Italy, and his early life was spent very much attached to the surroundings of his father's modest grocery store in the borough of Queens. Nevertheless, within several generations, the Cuomos would produce one of the most influential and recognized national politicians in Mario, and a rising, if somewhat less touted star, in Cuomo's eldest child, Andrew, who was elected to a second term in his own right in 2014.[1] Thus, a Cuomo has served as governor of New York longer than all previous Democratic governors combined, dating all the way back to Herbert Lehman's administration (1933–1942), which ended during World War II. It was a striking, if however unpredictable dynastic rise, one marked by very different approaches to politics by father and son. Although the senior Cuomo emphasized a liberal politics learned from the New Deal era into which he was born, Andrew Cuomo's tenure has hewed less closely to ideological commitments. Both approaches have been successful in their own ways.

Mario Cuomo was a successful lawyer, having graduated from St. Johns University School of Law in 1956, but he was not enamored with the legal profession—in part, because he had been rebuffed by the elite New York firms that barred Italian Americans from their practices. By the mid-to-late 1960s, Cuomo chose to take on an increasingly public career, first pushing back against the legendary and ruthless builder Robert Moses, who wanted to raze the many auto shops in Willet's Point, Queens, which he viewed as "eye sores," near the site of the 1964 World's Fair. Cuomo was hired to represent the many small shop owners and ultimately handed Moses one of his rare public defeats, preserving the right of the shop owners to keep their businesses. From there, Cuomo served again as a sort of public mediator, working for the self-described "Corona Fighting 69," a group of families, again in Queens, who were seeking to protect their homes from being destroyed in an effort to build a new public high school. Cuomo was again successful in his bid—another underdog story that got the attention of the city's tabloid press.

Finally, Cuomo came into some prominence in New York City politics, when in 1972, he mediated a third dispute—this one over an effort to build low-income housing for blacks in Forest Hills, Queens. The neighborhood's predominantly Jewish residents raised fears of crime, while many in the African American community saw the issue as one of plain housing discrimination. In the end, despite becoming one of the more racially charged political rows in the city politics at the time, Cuomo helped strike a deal to halve the number of residents moving into the neighborhood, while recognizing and supporting the need to integrate those patches of New York that were still almost exclusively white. At the time, Cuomo argued that the answer to white fears of integration—often couched in fears of crime—was to socially, and more importantly, economically integrate the lives of blacks into segregated neighborhoods.

It was Cuomo's well-reviewed *Forest Hills Diary*—a personal and honest look at the negotiating process in that neighborhood—that drew admiration from some of the city's most popular and better-connected journalists. Almost overnight, the book, published by Random House in 1974, helped Cuomo became fodder for mayoral consideration. In 1977, he took the dive into electoral politics, losing badly to Ed Koch in the Democratic primary. But Cuomo's rhetorical prowess, intellect, and dogged work ethic earned him the admiration of key state officials. He had put up a good, but ultimately losing, fight against Koch, who parlayed the city's increasing shift toward law and order into a campaign platform that favored the candidate "toughest" on crime (Cuomo had long been opposed to the death penalty, on religious grounds). But the mayoral defeat did not finish off Cuomo's political career. When Governor Hugh Carey's then lieutenant governor, Mary Anne Krupsak, suddenly resigned to challenge him in the 1978 gubernatorial race, Carey tapped Cuomo as her replacement. It was this critical break that fueled Cuomo's rise and put him on a path to prominence within the state. The truth is, Carey had his eyes on Cuomo for some time. Well before Cuomo joined him as his running mate, Carey had told those close to him, "I got a genius nobody knows

The Cuomo Dynasty

Cuomo Political Dynasty Family Tree

1. Mario Matthew Cuomo, 1932–2015
   Governor of New York, 1983–1994
Married Matilda Raffa
Five children including Andrew and Christopher

2. Andrew Mark Cuomo, 1957–
   U.S. Secretary of Housing and Urban Development, 1997–2001
   Attorney general, New York, 2007–2010
   Governor of New York, 2011–2019
Married Kerry Kennedy (divorced)
Three children

2. Christopher "Chris" Charles Cuomo, 1970–
   Journalist/News Anchor, ABC News and CNN
Married Cristina Greeven
Three children

---

about . . . Mario Cuomo. I begged him to run with me. Nobody knows him. The first time they ever hear of him, they'll be right there in his hands."[2] Carey's accolades aside, Cuomo was still somewhat of a latecomer, as he was 46 years old before he was elected to anything—and yet there were higher offices in sight. By 1981 when it became clear that Governor Carey would not seek a third term, Cuomo became the underdog candidate against his earlier political nemesis Ed Koch, who had a leading edge in money, organization, and name recognition in the Democratic primary.

One of Cuomo's advantages in the 1982 gubernatorial race came in the form of his campaign manager, his 24-year-old son, Andrew. Andrew, worked doggedly on his father's behalf, earning the reputation among some in the Koch camp (including the mayor himself) as a "dark lord of the political arts." Still, the younger Cuomo's deft political skills, along with critical errors made by Koch during the campaign, helped Mario Cuomo win the primary, all but assuring his victory in the November general election. Suddenly, at age 50, Mario Matthew Cuomo had gone from being a placeholder for the governor, and someone better known for overseeing internecine ethnic warfare in one of the city's lesser boroughs, to the most powerful elected official in perhaps the most powerful state in the country. And, in doing so, he also became the liberal standard-bearer for Democrats overnight, as his victory reflected the New Deal idealism into which he was born in 1932.

In his first inaugural address, Cuomo committed to the ideals that had won him the election and had been at the fore of his political thinking all of his adult life. Cuomo was in clear opposition to the rightward shift in American politics as best exemplified by the 1980 election of Ronald Reagan as president. Cuomo telegraphed his uneasiness with Reaganism from his first day in office. "Part of [our] program will be our message to Washington. We will say to our president and present administration that we have no intention of using Washington as a scapegoat for all of our failures and difficulties, or as an excuse for not doing for ourselves, as a state, everything we can," he said. But then, Cuomo left little room for doubt where he stood politically, in this new age. "On the other hand, we will not allow the national administration to escape responsibility for its policies. We will continue to point out what we believe, respectfully, is the massive inequity of the new redistribution of national wealth—a redistribution that moves our nation's resources from the vulnerable Northeast and Midwest to the affluent or at least less troubled parts of the nation." Cuomo saw himself from the beginning as a defender of liberal politics and the interests of his state and region. And it was this disposition to fight—rhetorically, and in governance—as best he could, that would make him in a few short years, the most prominent Democratic politician in the country, setting the stage for a possible future confrontation with the newly empowered forces of Reagan conservatism that he saw increasingly arrayed against his state, region, and New Deal liberal ideals.

Liberal Icon, 1983–1992

When Governor Mario Cuomo took office in January 1983, the nation's unemployment rate hovered above 10 percent, and New York's economy was moribund. Yet, he began his first term on a strong note, turning in a budget hailed for its combination of compassion and pragmatism. It was also turned in on time, something rare in New York State politics. Cuomo also oversaw a hostage crisis in Ossining, where after 53 hours, the standoff ended without bloodshed—all of that was just during his first week as governor. Early on, Cuomo sought to balance liberal desires for more government programs against conservative legislators' push to rein in the state's largesse. It was a delicate balance, and Cuomo frequently compromised; for example, he agreed to cut staff at state universities while approving the building of new prisons. Cuomo also backed AIDS research funding and earned plaudits for hiring more minorities and women in his administration than other governors in recent memory. He also defended his stance against the death penalty and a new restrictive immigration bill coming out of Congress. Meanwhile, he also supported and won new tax cuts that liberals opposed. With a strong Republican-led opposition in the legislature, Cuomo picked his battles for upholding his vision of liberalism—what he called "pragmatic progressivism."

The Cuomo Dynasty

He may have won the greatest increase in education funding in New York's history, but he also angered some of his Democratic base—particularly those in Albany—who wanted to do more with less.

Early in his administration, Cuomo was accused of running a very tightly controlled and top-down administration, with Andrew as the critical player in relationships with lawmakers in the state. Nevertheless, Cuomo's first year was widely hailed as a success, and politically speaking, he had moved from an afterthought in New York politics to a national figure. By the time Walter Mondale secured the Democratic nomination in the spring of 1984, Cuomo had been in office less than a year and a half but was already on Mondale's short list to become his running mate as vice president. Cuomo was uninterested, recalling his painful experience as Hugh Carey's number two as lieutenant governor; however, Cuomo did accept another Mondale invitation—to be his keynote speaker at the Democratic National Convention in San Francisco.

With much of the stagecraft of his speech brilliantly managed by Andrew, Cuomo gave one of the more memorable addresses at a political convention in modern times. His "Tale of Two Cities" speech carefully dismantled the Reagan record. It was a speech best remembered for Cuomo's attention to domestic affairs ("A shining city is perhaps all the president sees from the portico of the White House and the veranda of his ranch where everyone seems to be doing well"), but Cuomo was equally critical of Reagan's foreign policy. It was in short, an ode to the antipoverty and Social Gospel liberalism of the earlier part of the century, and Cuomo's skillful use of poignant examples of those in despair ran counter to the imagery of President Reagan's "Morning in America" campaign. Cuomo concluded his address, fittingly enough, by describing the "bleeding feet" of his father Andrea, who had worked so hard to provide for his family.[3] In the end, Cuomo's speech proved wildly successful, and it remains one regarded with deep emotional connection for those in attendance or who watched it live. More importantly, it made him an immediate favorite to become the Democratic nominee in 1988, in the aftermath of Mondale's disastrous defeat by Reagan in November 1984.

Cuomo's moment in the national spotlight was owed to his great talents as an orator. But his rhetoric raised expectations both nationally and within the state. He was now challenged to not only be a spokesman for progressive views (as he was in another powerful address on the subject of religion in politics delivered just 60 days after the DNC speech, at the University of Notre Dame); he was now also expected to deliver on policies that his base hungered for. This was especially difficult at a time of constrained economic resources and an ascendant conservatism. Cuomo was caught between a rock and hard place all the more because he seemed to promise so much. Yet, he remained popular in his state and nationally, and before he could formally declare himself to be a candidate for a second term in New York, he was already being asked about a 1988 run for the White House. Cuomo had famously quipped, "you campaign in poetry and govern in prose," a proverb that told one political truth while raising the question of whether or not it was possible to be equally effective at both. For Cuomo, the ancient ideal of the philosopher-king could only be met in distinct stages—first during the campaign, and then in office.

Cuomo fought in 1985 and 1986 to inoculate himself against the charge of being another northeastern, wild-eyed liberal. It seemed that his tax cuts, prison building, and budget cuts paled in comparison to the fruits of the Carey era, when that governor's building projects and liberal programs could be seen and felt by so many New Yorkers. Cuomo's terms were marked by fewer resources and a stronger Republican opposition. Nevertheless, Cuomo benefited from an economic rebound in the state, nurtured on his watch, and it placed him in the enviable position of being the Democratic Party's biggest fund-raiser as governor with reelection virtually assured. Cuomo dominated his Republican rival in 1986, besting businessman Andrew O'Rourke with 65 percent of the vote and winning 55 of New York's 62 counties. Cuomo was at the apex of his power and had two years to prepare for a shot at the presidency, if he so desired. Meanwhile, Andrew had moved on to his own career as a district attorney in New York City, and later as founder of a budding nonprofit agency, Housing Enterprise for the Less Privileged (HELP) in 1986. Andrew clearly had political ambitions beyond helping his father govern and get reelected. It was an opportune moment for Andrew to begin such a career for perhaps with the exception of Governor Bill Clinton of Arkansas, whose political career was just gaining some degree of national attention, there were few Democrats in the country enjoying the spotlight as much as Mario Cuomo.

Yet, as the presidential campaign season approached, Mario Cuomo prevaricated. He began to live up to an earlier political moniker given to him— "Hamlet on the Hudson." Cuomo hedged as to whether or not he would enter the 1988 race, at times seeming to keep the door open to an unlikely "Draft Cuomo" scenario at the Democratic convention. Ultimately, Cuomo reasoned that he could not run for the presidency while remaining governor—and he passed on what he would later call "the right" year" for him to run.[4] The long tease frustrated members of his own party, and it gave pause to Democratic Party leaders nationally, as Cuomo at once seemed to be preparing for a run, while later proving to be a reluctant political combatant. Speculation as to Cuomo's reasons for not entering the race ultimately dredged up old rumors about purported contacts or affiliations with organized crime—a baseless accusation rooted in a negative ethnic stereotype and one that drew Cuomo's frequent ire and, at times, poorly concealed contempt.

Perhaps all the talk of Cuomo's national political aspirations hurt him with voters back home, who wanted greater attention to their needs. Cuomo did his best to give them that attention, winning a well-earned reputation for scarcely leaving the state. Although Cuomo would go on to win a historic third term in 1990, his margin of victory was considerably smaller than in 1986—he garnered only 53 percent of the vote against an even weaker opponent. The most likely reason for Cuomo's weakened position was the simple fact that New York voters were growing more conservative, as voters had been nationally for some time. There was also a $2 billion shortfall in New York's budget, and the state's fiscal woes were bedeviling Cuomo at the start of his third term. They would do so for the next year.

With Andrew now working in the administration of New York City mayor David Dinkins as head of the Commission on the Homeless, Cuomo was without his chief political strategist and closest aid. Despite his woes in Albany, by the summer of 1991 he was still polling as the lead Democrat in a prospective race against other would-be presidential candidates. However, the timing seemed to be off for Mario—President George H. W. Bush looked invincible, with an approval rating of 72 percent and the nation euphoric over victory in the Persian Gulf War. Cuomo had deep troubles back home with a budget shortfall as well as growing voter disapproval in New York City. Others were better prepared: Arkansas governor Bill Clinton had been making the necessary connections among Democratic leaders required for a presidential run. But Cuomo's name still carried magic, dating back to his moment at the 1984 convention, and he had the ability to raise lots of money in a short time. The liberal base of the party idolized him. But the big question was: did he want it? The answer seemed to be an unequivocal no. Still, Cuomo never entirely dismissed a run out of hand, and so party members and voters alike were very much left as they were back in late 1987—waiting on Governor Cuomo to decide.

By late 1991, Cuomo acknowledged the obvious: that he was in fact considering a run at the White House. Polls showed him as the lead Democratic candidate were he to enter the race. His staff, including Andrew, were now making preparations for a run. And while even his closest aides seemed to not fully know his intent, the indications were that Cuomo was about to officially declare himself

New York governor Mario Cuomo (right) talks with Joseph P. Kennedy II (left), ca. 1984–1986. (City of Boston Archives, West Roxbury, MA)

a candidate. But New York State still did not have a budget, and Cuomo had long held the belief that he could not run successfully from a weakened position as governor. The state's Republicans were not eager to help, and so, even as Cuomo called a news conference in late December to finally announce his decision—a set piece straight out of Hollywood with two airplanes ready to fly him and his staff to New Hampshire to officially enter the primary—he was ensconced in the Executive Mansion, still trying to hammer out a budget deal.

It was not to be. Cuomo announced with evident disappointment in his voice that he could not run for the presidency while New York's budget was undecided and in a veritable state of emergency. And with that, the oxygen in Cuomo's national appeal dissipated, compelling Democrats to once again scramble for a candidate to take them out of the wilderness, after what had now been three consecutive stinging national defeats to Ronald Reagan and his chosen successor. Thus, Cuomo's power and influence within the state and around the nation fell into decline. He would only briefly command the national spotlight again, this time at another Democratic National Convention, where he delivered a masterful speech in support of Bill Clinton's nomination. But he would never go on to win another election, losing in a fourth term bid to a largely unknown state senator, George Pataki, in the historic Republican wave election year of 1994. Cuomo would have other opportunities for national prominence, turning down President Clinton's invitation to join the Supreme Court in 1993. In the end, he opted to let his record and legacy as governor stand, choosing to return to private legal practice rather than to continue in the world of politics. Whatever attention he would pay to that world, would now be directed toward his son, whose ambitions were clearly as great, if not greater, than his own.

A Dynasty Is Born: Andrew Cuomo's Rise to the Governorship

Andrew Cuomo was born in Queens, the oldest son of Mario and Matilda Cuomo. He attended Fordham University while serving as his father's campaign manager for mayor in 1977. He later attended Albany Law School, graduating in 1982, in time to work on his father's first gubernatorial campaign. None of the other Cuomo siblings would seek a political career, though Margaret, the eldest daughter, Maria, Madeline, and Chris—now a highly visible morning news anchor on CNN—would be highly successful in their own right. Much of this family success can be attributed to the steadfastness and work of Matilda Cuomo, who did the lion's share of the child-rearing as Mario was serving in elective office. Andrew's temperament proved to be very different from Mario's, and the two developed a deep but competitive bond, perhaps a result of Mario's frequent absences, a point, the senior Cuomo often acknowledged. Whatever antagonisms existed between father and son, Andrew proved to be a critical

The Cuomo Dynasty

New York governor Andrew Cuomo rides the subway, September 25, 2014. (Marc A. Hermann/MTA New York City Transit)

figure in shaping his father's campaigns, developing a tough and at times feared reputation as a no-holds-barred political combatant.

From Mario Cuomo's last day in office in 1995 until Andrew Cuomo took the reins as the 56th governor of New York in 2010, the state would have three governors. George Pataki would serve three terms in his own right before yielding to the two short-lived and scandal-ridden Democratic administrations of Eliot Spitzer and then David Patterson. The search for a liberal voice to match the elder Cuomo's among New York Democrats proved elusive, though the eyes of many party officials followed the career of Andrew Cuomo with more than passing interest.

Andrew Cuomo would later regret not being a significant part of his father's failed effort at a fourth term in 1994. At the time, he was mostly in Washington working in the Clinton administration as an assistant secretary of Community Planning in the Department of Housing and Urban Development (HUD). By 1997, Cuomo moved up to join the Clinton cabinet as secretary of HUD, improving his national profile as an up-and-coming political star in his own right. Before his election to the governorship in 2010, the *New York Times* reviewed Cuomo's time as HUD secretary, giving him "mixed reviews," mostly for his failure to address the looming subprime mortgage lending crisis and predatory lending practices of Fannie Mae and Freddie Mac. Nevertheless, the *Times* argued that blaming Cuomo for the subsequent economic recession that resulted from the housing crisis in 2008 was misplaced and "overblown."[5]

Andrew Cuomo more than survived his trials at HUD, and in 1990 he had further burnished his dynastic credentials by marrying Kerry Kennedy, one of Robert F. Kennedy's daughters—a fairytale political match if ever there was one. Thus, by the time Cuomo was weighing his run for the New York governorship in 2002, he had been the son of the most popular Democratic governor in generations, the youngest cabinet secretary since Robert F. Kennedy (Cuomo was appointed at 39), and now by marriage, an extended member of America's most renowned political family. The Cuomo family dynasty seemed ready to emerge in New York within a decade of Mario Cuomo leaving office. However high those hopes were heading into the 2002 campaign season, they were soon dashed with political and personal repercussions felt by Andrew.

Despite early leads in polls against Governor Pataki, Andrew Cuomo made what proved to be a colossal gaffe when he criticized Pataki's leadership during the aftermath of the tragic events of September 11, 2001. "He stood behind the leader," Cuomo said of Pataki, referencing Mayor Rudolph Giuliani, "he held the leader's coat."[6] Seldom has the political momentum of a campaign come to such an abrupt end. That remark, made in April 2002, compelled Cuomo to abandon the race even before the Democratic primary, which he lost to state treasurer Carl McCall, the highest ranking African American official in the state who went down to defeat in November. To make matters infinitely worse, Cuomo's marriage came apart shortly thereafter, and he and Kerry Kennedy divorced with all the public acrimony that New York's tabloids could muster. It was a low point for Andrew, and the future of any Cuomo dynastic claims seemed far-fetched at best.

Between the time of Andrew's defeat in 2002 and his election as New York attorney general in 2006, he methodically rebuilt his career. He became a visiting fellow at the Kennedy School of Government at Harvard. He earned large sums of money as a vice president at Island Capital, running interference for yacht owners looking for marinas. Both of these were logical if uninteresting endeavors for Cuomo, whose deepest longings were political in nature. When popular attorney general Eliot Spitzer announced in 2004 that he would run for governor, Cuomo immediately began thinking of the attorney general slot as his most natural reentry into state politics.[7] During Andrew's 2006 campaign for attorney general, Mario was there making calls to key leaders in New York on his son's behalf. It proved to be a decisive victory for Cuomo, whose time out of politics—or more precisely, time out of elected office—came to an end.

Andrew Cuomo's stint as state attorney general was mostly successful as he drew attention to corrupt lending practices that targeted students at state universities, and to the spread of child pornography through Internet service providers. These, among other issues, built up his résumé as a corruption fighter. By 2010, Governor Eliot Spitzer had resigned under a high-profile sex scandal, and his replacement, David Patterson, was also seriously weakened in office by personal scandal. Andrew Cuomo thus surfaced as the Democratic Party's preferred candidate in November, "using the infamous Tweed Courthouse in Manhattan as his backdrop" to announce his candidacy.[8] It was the reform governor Samuel J. Tilden, who fought against Tweed's political machine and corruption, ultimately working to arrest Tweed, who had fled to Spain. Although it was Tweed's funds that helped build the courthouse, it was the justice produced within the courthouse that Andrew Cuomo was interested in highlighting.

Once again popular, and with an enormous campaign war chest, Andrew Cuomo defeated Republican Carl Paladino, with over 62 percent of the vote. On New Year's Eve, 2010, Cuomo took the oath of office with his father present—an unparalleled moment in New York political history, one that cemented the Cuomo family dynasty into the lore of New York politics. Cuomo soon pushed to have his tenure remembered as one of accomplishments—not the rhetorical legacy left by his father, one he deemed short on substance.

For all their stylistic differences, Cuomo came into power like his father, facing a budgetary shortfall—this time estimated at $10 billion. Cuomo proposed harsh cuts to education, health care, and other beloved liberal programs. Despite initial struggles, in relatively short order Cuomo balanced the budget, passed an ethics-reform act, and began pushing for marriage equality in New York. Using all of his powers of persuasion and the inducements of the office, Cuomo won critical support from a handful of Republican legislators to help pass New York's Marriage Equality Act on June 11, 2011.[9] The feat made him an instant hero to millions of Americans who had long supported such a law, and Cuomo became a national symbol for change on one of the progressive movement's most desired public policies. As Cuomo said after the passage of the bill, "I think you're going to see this message resonate all across the country now. If New York can do it, it's OK for every other place to do it."[10] In mid-2011, approaching 30 years after his father's first campaign for governor, Andrew Cuomo had made his family name as widely hailed and significant as it had been since his father's time in office. And he had made himself in the process, as his father had before him, a figure whose national ambitions were the subject of enormous speculation.

The Cuomo Dynasty: A Work in Progress or Retreat?

"I do not mean we had enforced a civil right," Andrew Cuomo wrote in his autobiography, recalling the victory for marriage equality. "We had created one."[11] This was the sentiment he wanted left for posterity—but he had more time as governor before his 2014 reelection bid and broader political possibilities, if not expressed ambitions, still on the table. Cuomo would go on to pass a more progressive tax code in 2011, effectively manage the state's response to Hurricane Sandy, and in 2013 pass what was widely hailed as the country's toughest gun control law in the aftermath of the Sandy Hook Elementary School shooting massacre. Each of these achievements made him a more palatable figure for liberals in his party, and Cuomo was seen as having an outside shot at vying for the Democratic Party nomination for president in 2016. That possibility was rendered moot, when former first lady, New York's former senator, and then President Barack Obama's secretary of state, Hillary Clinton, became the clear front-runner. But in the aftermath of her shocking defeat, Cuomo remained as one of the few Democrats of national prominence with a record and name to give him a realistic chance in 2020. His reelection as New York governor in 2014 was not by as wide a margin as in 2010 (he won 54 percent of the vote), but he was nevertheless, well positioned—especially considering that 2014 saw the Republican Party regain a majority of seats in the U.S. Senate and President Obama's approval ratings drop below 50 percent.

For all of his successes, Andrew Cuomo has not escaped criticism as a purely calculating pol. He has been considered ruthless at times, and his ethics have been called into question going back to his father's 1977 run for mayor when he was blamed, albeit without evidence, of raising the issue of Koch's sexuality in the vilest of manners. He came under fire at HUD as well, with critics accusing him of using the office for personal political gain. Although Cuomo orchestrated clear reforms within the agency, there were also instances where HUD programs were targeted by the inspector general for abuse.[12] And, in early 2014, Governor Cuomo shut down the Moreland Commission, which he had launched just nine months earlier to investigate corrupt legislators in the state, when its investigatory powers were directed at those with whom he was trying to cut political deals.[13] As Jeffrey Toobin of the *New Yorker* wrote about the episode, "How could there ever be a legitimate reason, in a state long beset with corruption in its Legislature, for the governor to short-circuit his own marquee attempt to clean it up?"[14]

Aside from Andrew's disdain for the perceived power of rhetoric in politics, it is the question of personal ethics that most distinguishes the public perception of him from that of his father, who was viewed by many as statesmanlike and honest. Conversely, as Jimmy Vielkind put it, "[Progressives] see [Andrew] Cuomo's tenure through the lens of left-flank placation, with every marquee accomplishment shaded by sins committed inside the Albany bubble."[15] In thinking about a possible presidential bid, Cuomo's supporters will have to contend with a New York record that has at times inspired and yet frustrated liberals who see him as a fair-weather progressive.

With Mario Cuomo's passing on January 1, 2015, the day of Andrew's second inauguration, the Cuomo dynasty in New York was seen as largely the province of the senior Cuomo. Elected officials and dignitaries from New York and beyond attended Mario Cuomo's funeral. Almost all headlines and articles made reference to him as a "liberal icon" or standard-bearer. Before in life, and now in death, his governorship and political thought cast a large shadow over Andrew, who was poetic, ironically enough, in his remarks about his father. Before the many assembled at the Church of St. Ignatius of Loyola on New York's Park Avenue, Andrew Cuomo said his father "wasn't really a politician at all. At his core, at his best, he was a philosopher and he was a poet. And he was an advocate and a crusader. Mario Cuomo was the keynote speaker for our better angels."[16]

The lines were delivered with emotion, and they were well chosen. For Andrew, in the midst of a second term that not unlike his father's, well positioned him as a possible candidate for the nation's highest office down the road, it is far too early to speculate about what words might best describe his tenure as governor. He has already cemented one aspect of his legacy and that of the Cuomo dynasty—they are the only individuals to govern in New York State as father and son, each with at least two terms. And yet, part of the Cuomo legacy is that so much more seemed, and indeed, seems possible. Much has been written about the two Cuomos and their personal rivalries, be it on the basketball court or in politics. At times, the rivalry seemed beyond that of an ordinary father and son relationship. It has seemed fraught with pain and regret—largely for Mario Cuomo, who, like his own father, was not much of a physical presence in the lives of his children. But beyond regret, or feelings that can only be discerned by the public from a distance, there remains a greater sense of admiration. Mario and Andrew Cuomo saw different qualities in each other—ones they were lacking in themselves. The voters of New York have seen them as well, and have not seemed to mind in their voting decision to make both men governors of some historic proportion. How and under what circumstances will the Cuomo dynasty end—or perhaps be extended to further heights—remains to be seen. The prose is still being written.

Notes

1. Cuomo's five children are Andrew, Maria, Margaret, Madeline, and Christopher.

2. Mario Cuomo, *Forest Hills Diary* (New York: Random House, 1974), xii.

3. In his 1984 DNC address, Cuomo described how as a boy, he'd once seen his father return from work, collapse from exhaustion, and fall asleep with his feet bleeding. The quote was remembered in numerous newspaper obituaries of Cuomo. "What Made Mario Cuomo Such a Powerful Speaker," *Washington Post*, January 2, 2015.

4. "This was the right year," Cuomo told the *New York Times* after he made his decision. "If you wanted a made-to-order year, this was it." "Cuomo Cites Factors in Decision," *New York Times*, February 21, 1987.

5. "As HUD Chief, Cuomo Earns a Mixed Score," *New York Times*, August 23, 2010.

6. Jeffrey Toobin, "How Andrew Cuomo Gets His Way," *The New Yorker*, February 16, 2015.

7. Michael Shnayerson, *The Contender: Andrew Cuomo: A Biography* (New York: Hachette Book Group, 2015), 229.

8. Ibid., 283.

9. Cuomo said at the time, "I think New York sent a message to the nation and I think it is going to resonate and we are going to see real progress. The legacy of New York when it's at its best—New York is the progressive capital of the nation." The move proved significant as a flurry of other states soon followed. "Gay Pride Parade Marches through New York City; Gov. Cheered for Gay Marriage Law," *New York Daily News*, June 27, 2011.

10. Ibid., 319.

11. Andrew Cuomo, *All Things Possible: Setbacks and Success in Politics and Life* (New York: HarperCollins, 2014), 403.

12. "In Cuomo's Record as HUD Chief, Bold Steps and Missteps," *New York Times*, September 3, 2002.

13. Toobin, "How Andrew Cuomo Gets His Way."

14. Ibid.

15. Jeffrey Vielkind, "Cuomo Tiptoes toward 2020 Run," *Politico,* February 27, 2017. http://www.politico.com/story/2017/02/andrew-cuomo-new-york-2020-235403.

16. "At Funeral for Mario Cuomo, Praise for a Leader's Role as a Humanist," *New York Times*, January 6, 2015.

Further Reading

Ambar, Saladin. *American Cicero: Mario Cuomo and the Defense of American Liberalism.* Oxford: Oxford University Press, 2017.

Cuomo, Andrew. *All Things Possible: Setbacks and Success in Politics and Life.* New York: HarperCollins, 2014.

Cuomo, Mario. *More Than Words: The Speeches of Mario Cuomo.* New York: St. Martin's Press, 1993.

McElvaine, Robert S. *Mario Cuomo: A Biography.* New York: Scribner's, 1988.

Shnayerson, Michael. *The Contender: Andrew Cuomo: A Biography.* New York: Hachette Book Group, 2015.

CHAPTER FOURTEEN

The La Follette Dynasty

Nancy C. Unger

Arguably Wisconsin's most famous political family, two generations of La Follettes were synonymous with national progressive reform during the first half of the 20th century. Robert La Follette began the dynasty in earnest in 1906, when he was elected to the U.S. Senate and sought to implement nationwide the many programs and initiatives he had enacted successfully as three-term governor of Wisconsin. He spent 19 years in the Senate striving to end abuses of privilege and to return power to the people, becoming one of the most influential and best-known progressives. Although the La Follette sons carried on their parents' tradition of political activism, Phil La Follette failed to attain national office after serving three terms as Wisconsin's governor. Robert La Follette Jr. served in Congress even longer than his more famous and charismatic father, ultimately ending the family's 40-year service in the U.S. Senate when he was defeated by Joe McCarthy. The decline of the family's influence is attributed to widespread fatigue in the wake of decades of national reform and turmoil combined with La Follette Jr.'s distaste for campaigning. Beginning in the 1960s, however, the power of the La Follette name and tradition of facilitating meaningful reform helped a third-generation La Follette to serve as Wisconsin's attorney general for more than a decade. In the 21st century, a distant cousin—named La Follette—continues to hold state office in Wisconsin.

Before their marriage in 1881, Robert La Follette and Belle Case attended the University of Wisconsin, whose president impressed deeply upon them their obligation to serve the state. The couple dedicated their lives to providing remedies for Gilded Age problems that included corrupt politics, child labor, unsafe working conditions, environmental devastation, racism, and sexism, with the ultimate goal of more equitably redistributing the nation's wealth and power. Bob La Follette pursued this quest through various public offices. Belle La Follette was denied the right to vote as a woman until she was 61 years old; nevertheless, she successfully pursued other avenues to foster change—primarily public speaking and journalism.

The unfailing dedication of Bob and Belle La Follette led to state and national reforms, including women's suffrage, environmental and worker protections, tax reform, and the direct election of senators. Meanwhile, their refusal to compromise on matters of principle generated considerable controversy, as when they opposed the entry of the United States into World War I and supported civil rights for African Americans.

Although both Bob and Belle were lawyers capable of generating considerable income, they agreed to pursue the common good rather than personal wealth. The entire La Follette family paid a high financial price for Bob and Belle's altruism. Bob routinely incurred debt to promote his political goals, going so far as to create a magazine that was particularly burdensome, in terms of the time and energy, on his conscientious and frugal wife. Nevertheless, in Belle's biography of her husband, *Robert M. La Follette*, she approvingly quoted his assertion, "We have put by the chance to lay up anything for our children's future. . . . I wish to leave something to the state more lasting than bronze or marble and a better legacy to the state than mere wealth."[1]

The La Follette family was extraordinarily close, with the couple's four children—Flora (Fola), Robert Jr., Philip, and Mary—expected to remain, even as adults, personally and professionally involved in their parents' pursuits. Belle and Bob made clear their expectation that the children, especially their two sons, would also dedicate their lives to progressive reform. Although Phil was the more politically ambitious, only his brother Robert Jr. met the minimum age requirement to run for the U.S. Senate seat left vacant by their father's death in 1925. Bob La Follette Jr. held that seat and built on the family legacy of progressive reform throughout the Great Depression and World War II. Phil La Follette served three terms as Wisconsin's governor in the 1930s; however, the Wisconsin Progressive Party created by the two brothers during the Great Depression proved temporary. The family's influence in national politics came to a halt in 1946 when Robert La Follette Jr. lost the Republican primary to Joseph McCarthy. Although the many political achievements of the La Follette brothers continued the movement pioneered by their parents, the family's second generation was less path-breaking, passionate, and politically skilled than the first. Continuing this trend, although the La Follette name still generates recognition and votes in Wisconsin, the achievements of subsequent generation La Follettes who have entered public service pale in comparison to their progenitors.

The La Follette Dynasty

La Follette Political Dynasty Family Tree

1. Jesse La Follette, 1781–1843
Married Mary Lee
11 children including Josiah and Harvey

2. Harvey Marion La Follette, 1832–1865
Married Susan C. Fullenwider
Eight children including William LeRoy, Grant, and Harvey Marion

3. William LeRoy La Follette, 1860–1934
    Washington State House of Representatives, 1899–1901
    U.S. House of Representatives, 1911–1919
Seven children including Suzanne and William LeRoy Jr.

4. William LeRoy La Follette Jr., 1890–1950
    Washington State House of Representatives, 1937
Married Helen
Two children: Mimi and Mary Lee

4. Suzanne La Follette, 1893–1983
    Libertarian feminist, journalist

3. Harvey Marion La Follette, 1858–1929
    Indiana state superintendent of public instruction, 1887–1891
    Cofounder, city of La Follette, Tennessee, 1897
One child: Warner Marion

2. Josiah La Follette, 1817–1856
Married Mary Ferguson Buchanan
Four children: William, Marion, Josephine, and Robert

3. Robert M. La Follette, 1855–1925
    District attorney, Dane County, Wisconsin, 1880–1884
    U.S. House of Representatives, 1885–1891
    Governor of Wisconsin, 1901–1906
    U.S. senator, Wisconsin, 1906–1925

(continued)

La Follette Political Dynasty Family Tree (*continued*)

Married Belle Case, 1859–1931
    Journalist, woman suffrage advocate, peace activist
Four children: Flora (Fola), Robert Jr., Philip, and Mary

4. Flora La Follette, 1882–1970
    Woman suffrage advocate, labor activist, teacher
Married George Middleton

4. Robert La Follette Jr., 1895–1953
    U.S. senator, Wisconsin, 1925–1947
Married Rachel Wilson Young
Two children: Joseph and Bronson

5. Bronson La Follette, 1936–2018
    Attorney general, Wisconsin, 1965–1969, 1975–1987
Married Lynn Godwin
Two children: Robert and Deborah

4. Philip La Follette, 1897–1965
    District attorney, Dane County, Wisconsin, 1925–1927
    Governor of Wisconsin, 1931–1933, 1935–1939
Married Isabel Bacon
Three children: Robert, Judith, and Sherry

Distant relatives

Charles M. La Follette, 1898–1974
    Indiana House of Representatives, 1927–1929
    U.S. House of Representatives, 1943–1947

Doug La Follette, 1940–
    Wisconsin secretary of state, 1975–1979, 1983–

The Early Life of Robert M. La Follette

Robert "Fighting Bob" La Follette was born on June 14, 1855, to Mary Ferguson La Follette in Primrose, Wisconsin. His politically active father, farmer Josiah La Follette, came from a large, well-educated extended family of abolitionists, politically active in the newly formed Republican Party. Josiah La Follette served two terms as town clerk before being elected assessor. His political aspirations were cut short by his death at the age of 38, just eight months after Robert's birth. As Bob La Follette was growing up, his mother impressed deeply upon him his responsibility to never do anything to dishonor his father's name. As detailed in *Fighting Bob La Follette: The Righteous Reformer*,[2] Bob's longing to know more about this phantom father culminated with La Follette examining his father's remains in 1894 when the grave was exhumed to be transferred for reburial.

Organized religion played little role in Bob La Follette's lifelong dedication to doing right. As a child he resented the elderly, rigidly pious stepfather who preached that La Follette's beloved father's agnosticism condemned him to hell. Although Bob La Follette eschewed church attendance the rest of his life, his years as an undergraduate and law student at the University of Wisconsin honed his commitment to remedying the injustices plaguing society. As he noted in *La Follette's Autobiography*, even before his classes began, a speech by Edward G. Ryan influenced him profoundly. Wisconsin's future chief justice posed the challenge that his young listener recognized as moral as well as political and economic: "Which shall rule—wealth or man; which shall lead—money or intellect; who shall fill public stations—educated and patriotic free men, or the feudal serfs of corporate capital?"[3] The university's president, John Bascom, encouraged students to not only recognize the serious problems emerging from the nation's nascent industrialization and urbanization, but challenged them to translate their concerns and convictions into action. La Follette graduated from the University of Wisconsin in 1879 and from its law school the following year, honing his considerable talents as a public speaker.

Early Life of Belle Case

Bob La Follette met Belle Case at the university. They shared a love of public speaking and a desire to contribute to the greater good. As developed in *Belle La Follette: Progressive Era Reformer*, Belle Case grew up witnessing the camaraderie and sense of interdependence and partnership evidenced by her parents and other farming couples. Her childhood cemented her belief that culture, not ability, prohibited women from cultivating and sharing talents outside the domestic realm. Belle's feminist views were reinforced by her highly competent grandmother and by her mother, who had heard physician and minister Anna Howard Shaw promote women's suffrage. Two speakers visiting the university confirmed Case's confidence in women's potential: Olympia Brown, champion for women's educational, legal, economic, and political rights; and Annie Jeness Miller, who promoted women's mental and physical health through exercise and less restrictive clothing.

Bob pursued Belle avidly. At her insistence, she taught school for two years before the couple wed in 1881. At the bride's request, the word "obey" was omitted from the marriage vows. When their first child was still a baby, Belle La Follette joined her husband in the study of law, becoming the first woman to graduate with a law degree from the University of Wisconsin.

Robert La Follette's Early Political Career

Bob La Follette became district attorney of Dane County, Wisconsin, in 1881. Four years later, he entered the House of Representatives, where he was elected to serve three terms. In domestic affairs, La Follette's egalitarianism was already evident, which earned him the respect of leaders in the African American community and in the women's suffrage movement. He spoke passionately on behalf of Native Americans and established himself as a foe of pork-barrel legislation and of lumber companies and railroads seeking land grants and other special favors from Congress.

Following his failed congressional reelection bid in 1890, La Follette returned to private law practice in Wisconsin. He claimed that an effort to bribe him in 1891 forced the realization that the United States was fast being dominated by hostile forces thwarting the will of the people and menacing representative government. Previously he had seen the issues of the day,

Robert M. La Follette Jr. and his father, Robert M. La Follette Sr. (Library of Congress)

including the trusts, resource conservation, currency, and railroad regulation, as individual problems. Now he saw them as manifestations of one great struggle: "the encroachment of the powerful few upon the rights of the many."[4] He dedicated himself to breaking this corrupting influence through reforms of the nation's political and economic systems. La Follette sought the governor's chair in 1896. When the bribery of convention delegates cost him the Republican nomination, La Follette championed the destruction of the corrupt caucus and convention nominating systems operating nationwide in favor of the direct primary. Defeated again in 1898 by unscrupulous tactics including both sticks and carrots (threats of job loss as well as bribes to convention delegates totaling $8,300), he ran a third time in 1900, becoming the state's first Wisconsin-born governor.

As governor, La Follette sought to make the political machinery more directly responsive to the popular will—to promote equal rights over special privilege. He assured corporations that he was not against big business per se, but rather was against efforts to control prices, stifle competition, and create monopolies. To implement the primary election law and major tax reform, among other goals, he relied heavily on his alma mater, creating the famed "Wisconsin Idea." La Follette entrusted vast faith to faculty of the university as experts fit to advise, set standards, and administer Wisconsin's reform laws. The University of Wisconsin thereby became the state's unofficial fourth branch of government, and this so-called "Wisconsin Idea" made the state a nationally recognized progressive leader.

Governor La Follette's tenure was marked by the enactment of his direct primary plan (endorsed in in 1904, inaugurated in 1906), making Wisconsin the first state to require all candidates for public office be subject to direct election by the people. This and many other reforms, including railroad taxation legislation, increased the focus on Wisconsin as a national model for progressivism. When La Follette left the governor's office to join the U.S. Senate in 1906, his statewide achievements included thoroughgoing and efficient reform of railroads and other utilities, civil service reform for state officeholders, stringent rules for lobbyists, stronger provisions against corrupt government practices, environmental measures including a forest conservation program, and tax reforms. He sought next to implement such reforms on the national level.

La Follette was driven in the Senate by the same righteousness that had served as both an inspiration and an impediment during his gubernatorial years. Although it sparked many successes, his high-mindedness also kept him from making the compromises that are so crucial in the practice of politics. La Follette alienated many a potential ally, including Presidents Theodore Roosevelt and Woodrow Wilson. To detail and publicize his political ideas and goals, he began in 1909 *La Follette's Weekly Magazine*, which later became a monthly and remains in publication as *The Progressive*. His touted victories included the passage of a variety of national election reforms, the income tax, and La Follette Seaman's Bill, which ended the virtual enslavement of merchant sailors and improved safety for all ship passengers and crew members.

Belle La Follette: Combining Family with Progressive Reform

Belle La Follette rejected the popular early 20th-century assumption that being a proper mother precluded a woman from reaching her highest development personally or professionally. Indeed, she found raising her four children to be much less a strain on her time and talents than were the many needless practices middle-class women were virtually required by society to pursue. Privately and publicly in print, she railed against the complicated, uncomfortable, and expensive clothes designed for women, and the lavish, multicourse meals that women were expected to serve in overdecorated, unhygienic homes. She urged women to reject all such socially constructed barriers to their genuine health and happiness.

Although she shared her husband's commitment to progressive reforms, Belle grew weary of living in perpetual financial debt, and she viewed *La Follette's Magazine* as a particular strain on her husband's time and energy—and on the family's checkbook. The magazine nevertheless became one of the

Belle Case La Follette, Flora La Follette, and Robert M. La Follette on February 25, 1924. (Library of Congress)

prime arenas in which she could promote a wide range of reforms dear to her, including both suffrage and physical exercise for women, public health, the end of corporal and capital punishment, as well as a variety of political goals she shared with her husband, like direct democracy measures (initiative, referendum, and recall) and tax reform. She wrote columns to urge women to recognize that problems they viewed as personal (such as difficulties in household budgeting) were in fact political. She argued women needed to understand the tariff, tax structure, power of big business, and the need to regulate natural resources, private monopolies, and freight rates. Other journalists wrote admiringly of Belle's work, crediting her with taking seriously the intelligence of her women readers. In 1911, the North American Press Syndicate engaged La Follette to provide brief articles for syndication six days a week. Her "Thought for the Day" series appeared in 57 newspapers in more than 20 states. The publication of Olive Schreiner's *Woman and Labor*, also in 1911, confirmed Belle La Follette's belief that women's employment outside the home was to the benefit of both sexes and to society overall.

One of the largest barriers to women reaching their full potential, according to Belle La Follette, was their inability to vote. She termed the denial of suffrage to women antithetical to the democratic principles of the nation. Her many exhausting speaking campaigns in support of women's suffrage carried her throughout much of the country. In 1913, she was chosen to present the "pro" argument to the U.S. Senate Committee on Woman Suffrage, and she was part of a contingent of advocates who met with President Wilson at the White House. Feminist and leading women's suffrage strategist Alice Paul called her "the most consistent supporter of equal rights of all the women of her time."[5]

Support of Racial Equality and Opposition to U.S. Entry into World War I

The 1896 Supreme Court decision *Plessy v. Ferguson* upheld racial segregation under the doctrine of "separate but equal," yet the resulting Jim Crow laws mandating racial segregation doomed African Americans nationwide to decidedly inferior accommodations and opportunities, leading generations to suffer poverty, discrimination, shorter life spans, and acts of terrorism. Both La Follettes were committed to civil rights for African Americans. They rejected the "scientific" racism that guided the thinking of many white progressives at the time, and believed unequivocally in the complete equality of all citizens in a democracy. In more than one speech on the floor of the Senate, Bob La Follette scolded his colleagues, blaming their racism rather than African Americans, for the nation's racial disparities. Belle La Follette also believed that blacks were held back not by some inherent inferiority but by the prejudice of whites. She waged war, in speeches and in columns in *La Follette's Magazine*, on the efforts of the Wilson administration to racially segregate the federal government. She was bombarded with hate mail from racist whites, but grateful African Americans expressed their deep appreciation. For example,

African American educator and activist Nannie Helen Burroughs publicly hailed Belle La Follette as "the successor to Harriet Beecher Stowe."[6]

Although Bob did not share Belle's pacifism, the La Follettes had in common a deep aversion to war. Bob La Follette described war as "the money changer's opportunity, and the social reformer's doom." He dedicated himself to keep his country out of the war raging across Europe in 1914.[7] Belle La Follette was a founding member of the Women's Peace Party, later renamed the Women's International League for Peace and Freedom. As war in Europe raged, she sparred in the press with Theodore Roosevelt, declaring the former president "intoxicated with a false idea of war." She likewise insisted that her husband's opposition to U.S. entry in the war was the greatest service he could provide to his country. With Belle's staunch support, Bob led the Senate filibuster against President Wilson's Armed Ship Bill and was among the "little group of willful men" denounced by the president for rendering "the great Government of the United States helpless and contemptible."[8] In 1917, Bob was one of only six senators to vote against American entry into the war; his first cousin William La Follette, who represented Washington in the House of Representatives for nine years, also voted against entry into the war. Although Bob La Follette appeared publicly undeterred, he was privately shaken by opposition to his antiwar stance, which included being spat upon and burned in effigy. He answered calls for his expulsion from the Senate with an impassioned plea for the protection of constitutional rights and freedoms, including free speech during time of war. The entire La Follette family suffered intense public hostilities due to their pacifism during the war years, especially in their home state of Wisconsin.

Postwar Progressivism

Following World War I, Bob and Belle La Follette sought to shore up the faltering progressive movement. Belle devoted herself to universal disarmament and amnesty for political prisoners as well as more traditional progressive goals. Meanwhile, Bob spoke passionately against the Versailles Treaty, particularly against the proposed League of Nations, which he believed would involve Americans in foolhardy foreign entanglements at the price of progress at home. In addition to successfully keeping the United States out of the League of Nations, La Follette also won important natural resource protections in the Senate and demanded the investigation that culminated in the Teapot Dome oil reserve scandal and resignation of President Warren G. Harding's interior secretary, Albert Fall.

Bob La Follette's Final Battle and Legacy

Bob La Follette ran for president as an independent in 1924 with the planks in his platform reflecting his ongoing commitment to progressive goals.

Despite a tiny campaign chest, he received nearly 5 million votes, roughly 17 percent of the total number cast. He died of heart disease the following year at the age of 70. Throughout his career in public service spanning 45 years, farmers, laborers, and citizens from all walks of life in Wisconsin remained convinced that La Follette was sincerely dedicated to making their homes and workplaces safer; to reducing the disparity between the rich and the poor, and between the powerful and the powerless. These dedicated supporters remained faithful for the duration of his political career, and that loyalty, combined with name recognition, was crucial in launching the careers of the next generation of La Follettes.

Building the Foundation for a Dynasty

As parents, the La Follettes promoted among their children a family solidarity that journalist and family friend Elizabeth Glendower Evans called intense beyond any other she had ever encountered.[9] Both parents often appeared resentful of their children's attempts at privacy and jealous of diversions such as friends and outside interests. The children expressed their feelings of family loyalty toward each other as well as their parents. As young adults, the siblings exchanged unusually, even unsettlingly, strong declarations of love, approval, and admiration for one another; and such La Follette family solidarity was not disrupted even by the children's marriages. In-laws were incorporated into the family fold, which often meant joining the La Follette offspring in writing for *La Follette's Magazine* and taking part in various political campaigns.

Bob La Follette took his sons into his political confidence when they were still boys. Both parents made it clear to the boys that they expected their sons to follow in Bob's footsteps by attaining political office. Nonetheless, upon Bob La Follette's death, it was his widow who was petitioned by members of the Wisconsin legislature to complete her husband's term. According to Phil La Follette, his mother rejected the opportunity to become the first female senator because she recognized that her service would be granted more as a tribute to her husband than as a serious political investment—once her term expired, Wisconsin would turn elsewhere for its political leadership. By virtue of his sex as well as his age, Robert La Follette Jr., was far more likely than his mother to be repeatedly reelected and could thereby lead the La Follette progressive movement for years to come and further cement its legacy. Belle La Follette served as her son's campaign manager for the Senate. Despite her support of civil service reform intended to eliminate cronyism, Belle did not hesitate to promote her son as the best man to fill his father's seat, even though the only elected position Bob Jr. had ever held was president of his freshman class in college. She also ignored her son's lack of a college degree and dearth of passion for politics, citing instead his experience gained in six years as his father's private secretary. Belle La Follette also advised her son Phil, who was politically ambitious but too young to become a senator, in his initial run for governor of Wisconsin in 1930. Upon their elections to office, Belle La Follette served as closest adviser and political confidante to both of her sons. Only her death in 1931 brought a halt to her ceaseless dedication to ensuring the La Follette political dynasty.

The Second Generation of La Follette Women

Of Bob and Belle La Follette's four children, only one did not dedicate a large portion of adulthood to building the family legacy. Although Mary, the youngest, did contribute to the family magazine and worked in her father's Senate office in her youth, she did not—like her older sister and brothers—make a career in the family business of progressivism. Fola, the older daughter, shared her father's love for theater and the commitment to social justice lived out by both her parents. Fola originally pursued a career on the stage, with brief success on Broadway in 1911, the same years that she married playwright George Middleton (yet retained the La Follette name). She acted in a number of productions promoting women's suffrage and supported the women garment workers' strike in New York City in 1913. Following her mother's death, Fola La Follette edited what Belle had written into what became roughly the first fourth of her father's biography. It took Fola 22 years more to write the more than 1,000 additional pages needed to complete the two-volume study. Critics complained that the work's unblinking focus on Bob La Follette allowed little room for historical context and perspective, but praised the authors for comprehensive coverage and dramatic flair. With a permanent record of her parents' progressivism assured, Fola then began cataloging and organizing the more than 400,000 documents that today make up the La Follette collection in the Library of Congress, work that would occupy her until her death in 1970 at the age of 87.

The Second Generation of La Follette Men

In his work *The La Follettes of Wisconsin*,[10] author Bernard Weisberger provides an overview of the political careers of the second generation of La Follette men in a chapter aptly titled "The Succession That Wasn't." Both sons shared their father's commitment to reform and, with other key La Follette supporters, joined forces with President Franklin D. Roosevelt, bringing many of Bob and Belle La Follette's goals to fruition in the New Deal. In her jointly authored work *Belle: The Biography of Belle Case La Follette*, Phil La Follette's younger daughter Sherry describes the feelings of inadequacy felt by La Follette descendants. As an example she recounts how her uncle, Robert La Follette Jr., was taunted during the special election campaign for his father's Senate seat, "You ain't as good as your pa and you never will be." He tellingly replied, "No one knows that better than I, my friend. No one knows that better than I."[11]

La Follette Jr. undertook the duty of completing his father's Senate term in 1925 with a deep sense of obligation and a determination to maintain the principles to which his father dedicated his life. Patrick Maney's *Young Bob: A Biography of Robert M. La Follette, Jr.,* argues that La Follette Jr. was one of the best senators in history but also one of the most tragic. At the age of 30, as the youngest senator since Henry Clay a century before, La Follette Jr. embarked on the service that would last 21 years—nearly the rest of his life cut short by suicide. He spent his first few years in the Senate as an able but rather unimaginative successor to his father, but by the end of 1928 he became more self-assured. He served as a transitional figure in the history of modern reform movements; he achieved national attention during the Great Depression as one of the first to develop a coherent plan for combating declining purchasing power. As detailed in Jerold S. Auerbach's *Labor and Liberty: The La Follette Committee and the New Deal*,[12] the height of La Follette Jr.'s prominence occurred between 1936 and 1940 when he served as chairman of the Senate Civil Liberties Committee investigating unionists' civil liberties' violations by industrialists.

Despite his occasional brilliant successes, La Follette Jr. endured rather than enjoyed public life and grew to resent the intrusions on his privacy over time. The specter of his father always loomed large, and the fears of failing his father's memory were constant. Considered a superior senator but a weak political leader, La Follette Jr. left the Republican Party in 1934 to create the Progressive Party of Wisconsin; however, he did not provide firm leadership for the party and devoted less and less time to Wisconsin affairs. In 1946, he decided to return to the GOP but was beaten in the Senate primary by political newcomer Joseph R. McCarthy. Following his defeat by a man who embodied the antithesis of his family's progressive values and unable to take satisfaction from his own considerable achievements, Robert La Follette Jr. retired from politics, preoccupied by the poor state of his health and suffering from depression and anxiety attacks. On February 24, 1953, La Follette Jr. committed suicide; he left behind his wife, Rachel, and two sons, Joseph and Bronson. Just days before shooting himself, Robert Jr. expressed to his friend Senator J. Lister Hill (D-AL), "how he never should have let McCarthy beat him, how he had let his father down."[13]

As noted in Jonathan Kasparek's *Fighting Son: A Biography of Philip F. La Follette*,[14] the La Follette's second son, Philip, proved to be an aggressive, flamboyant, controversial, and influential leader whose political style was reminiscent of his father's. Despite his ambition and dedication, as governor of Wisconsin Phil La Follette was unable to master a dependable political majority in his attempt to have Wisconsin provide leadership during the Great

Depression. Defeated after his initial term as governor from 1931 to 1933, Phil went on to serve two more terms from 1935 to 1939; however, the last was plagued by controversy, especially after his creation of the National Progressives of America (NPA) in 1938. For example, even among Governor La Follette's supporters, many people found his design choice for the NPA's logo to be disconcertingly similar to the Nazi Party's swastika logo. La Follette strove to create a new national party while simultaneously running for a fourth term as governor, and he failed at both. He was only 41 when he left office for the final time in 1939 and returned to the practice of law.

During World War II, Phil served on the staff of General Douglas MacArthur, then returned to his law practice at the war's end. Increasingly diverging from the family's liberalism, in the 1940s and 1950s he promoted the presidential campaigns of MacArthur, Earl Warren, and Dwight Eisenhower. Although Phil struggled with depression and alcohol abuse, he served as president of Hazeltine Electronics in New York from 1955 to 1959 before returning to Wisconsin. In the midst of writing his political memoirs, Phil died in 1965. He was survived by his wife, Isabel, and three children—Robert, Judith, and Sherry.

Subsequent Generations and the Family Legacy

Bronson La Follette was 16 when his father, Robert Jr., took his own life. Amid five terms as Wisconsin's attorney general from 1965 to 1969 and again from 1975 to 1987, Bronson made an unsuccessful run for the governor's chair in 1968. He was reelected as Wisconsin attorney general in 1982, despite a drunk driving conviction the previous year; but after an ethics investigation earned him a reprimand, he failed to earn reelection in 1986. Bronson retired from public service, but to date appears occasionally at events honoring his famous predecessors. He has two children, Robert and Deborah.

The only family member to remain active in politics is Doug La Follette, Robert La Follette's first cousin twice removed. Although name recognition likely contributed to his early success in local politics, a steadfast dedication to some of the progressive goals associated with that name, especially environmental protection, has led to his constant reelection as Wisconsin's secretary of state, a position he has held since 1983. Doug La Follette's multiple efforts at other positions, including two runs for federal office, have not been successful.

Despite meaningful contributions to the La Follette's progressive reform agenda by subsequent generations, the dynasty's originator, Robert La Follette, remains by far the most well-known and celebrated politician. In 1982, the National Governors Association ranked Robert first on its list of 10 outstanding governors of the 20th century; and in 2000, a Senate resolution recognized him as one of the seven greatest senators in American history. Each of the 50 states is allowed up to two symbolic statues in the rotunda of the nation's capitol, and they sometimes update their choices: to this day, a statue of Robert La Follette represents Wisconsin. The La Follette political dynasty was intense but short-lived—blazing brightly but then virtually burning out, suffocated by its own shadow before the end of a second generation.

Notes

1. Belle Case La Follette and Fola La Follette, *Robert M. La Follette* (New York: Macmillan, 1953), 184.

2. Nancy Unger, *Fighting Bob La Follette: The Righteous Reformer* (Chapel Hill: University of North Carolina Press, 2000); (Madison: Wisconsin Historical Society Press, 2008).

3. Robert M. La Follette, *La Follette's Autobiography: A Personal Narrative of Political Experiences* (Madison, WI: Robert M. La Follette, 1911, 1913), 24.

4. Ibid., 760.

5. Dee Ann Montgomery, "An Intellectual Profile of Belle La Follette: Progressive Editor, Political Strategist, and Feminist" (PhD dissertation, Indiana University, 1975), 225.

6. James H. Hayes to Belle Case La Follette, February 18, 1914, La Follette Family Papers, D-13, Library of Congress, quoted in Nancy C. Unger, *Belle La Follette: Progressive Reformer* (New York: Routledge, 2016), 89.

7. Robert M. La Follette, "War and Reform," *La Follette's Magazine* 1, no. 16, April 24, 1909, 4.

8. Wilson asked Congress for authority to arm merchant ships so that they could fire upon their attackers. Critics of the Armed Ship Bill, including La Follette, argued that this move would almost certainly bring about an exchange of fire that would inexorably lead to a declaration of war. Wilson's "willful men" charge against those who organized and participated in the filibuster that kept the bill from coming to a vote was part of an indignant formal statement that was widely circulated. See "Sharp Words by Wilson," *New York Times*, March 5, 1917, 1.

9. Elizabeth Glendower Evans, *Springfield Republican*, April 15, 1931, reprinted in *Robert M. La Follette*, 281.

10. Bernard Weisberger, *The La Follettes of Wisconsin: Love and Politics in Progressive America* (Madison: University of Wisconsin Press, 1994).

11. Lucy Freeman, Sherry La Follette, and George Zabriskie, *Belle: The Biography of Belle Case La Follette* (New York: Beaufort, 1986), 242.

12. Jerold S. Auerbach, *Labor and Liberty: The La Follette Committee and the New Deal* (Indianapolis: Bobbs-Merrill, 1966).

13. Drew Pearson, "'Young Bob' Felt He'd Failed Dad," *Washington Post*, March 4, 1953, 33, quoted in Patrick Maney, *Young Bob: A Biography of Robert M. La Follette, Jr.* (Madison: Wisconsin Historical Society Press, 1978), 314.

14. Jonathan Kasparek, *Fighting Son: A Biography of Philip La Follette* (Madison: Wisconsin Historical Society Press, 2006).

Further Reading

Drake, Richard Drake. *The Education of an Anti-Imperialist: Robert La Follette and U.S. Expansion.* Madison: University of Wisconsin Press, 2013.

Henningsen, Kate. "A History of her Own: The Transformation of Belle Case La Follette, 1859–1914." Senior Honors Thesis, Georgetown University, 2004.

La Follette, Philip. *Adventures in Politics.* New York: Holt, 1970.

Thelen, David. *The Early Life of Robert M. La Follette.* Chicago: Loyola University Press, 1966.

Thelen, David. *Robert M. La Follette and the Insurgent Spirit.* Boston: Little, Brown, 1976; Madison: University of Wisconsin Press, 1986.

Unger, Nancy C. "The Burden of a Great Name: Robert M. La Follette, Jr." *The Psychohistory Review* 23, no. 2 (Winter 1995): 167–191.

Unger, Nancy C. "The Two Worlds of Belle Case La Follette." *Wisconsin Magazine of History* 83, no. 2 (Winter 1999–2000): 82–110.

Wiesberger, Bernard. "Changes and Choices: Two and a Half Generations of La Follette Women." *Wisconsin Magazine of History* 76, no. 4 (1993): 248–270.

CHAPTER FIFTEEN

The Roberts Dynasty

Richard A. Clucas and Skyler Brocker-Knapp

The Roberts family of Oregon was an unconventional political dynasty. Emerging during the heart of what many political observers consider the golden era in Oregon politics, the dynasty centered around Frank Roberts, with the other members joined together under a common last name. Yet what made the dynasty unconventional was that it was based more on legal unions than on blood. The cornerstone of the Roberts dynasty was Frank Roberts's three marriages, which created ties among several of the state's leading political actors during the latter part of the 20th century. While relatively short-lived in comparison to other American political dynasties, the Roberts family presented a concentrated political power, reaching up to the state's highest elected offices.

Over the years, Oregon has developed a reputation for progressive politics and maverick politicians. The reputation is not entirely accurate, but there is a kernel of truth to it. In the years after World War II, Oregonians elected a series of Republican and Democratic politicians who pursued progressive policies and became known for their political independence. These include Wayne Morse (U.S. senator), Mark Hatfield (governor, U.S. senator), Robert Straub (treasurer, governor), and Tom McCall (secretary of state, governor). It was during the latter part of this period that the Roberts family rose to political prominence. The Robertses were among the progressive leaders of the state, helping to create some of the state's most innovative policies and build Oregon's distinctive reputation. Along with Frank, the primary members of the political dynasty were Mary Wendy Roberts, Roberts's eldest daughter from his first marriage to Mary Louise Charleson; Betty Roberts, his second wife; and Barbara Roberts, his third wife. Barbara Roberts likened the Oregon dynasty to the quintessential American political family: "It was a very solid, well-recognized political name in our part of the state. I laughingly compared the Robertses of Oregon to the Kennedys of Massachusetts . . . without the money!"[1]

Although the dynasty may have centered around Frank Roberts, it was the political careers of two of his wives, Oregon Supreme Court Justice Betty Roberts and Governor Barbara Roberts, which made the family surname prominent and the dynasty significant in Oregon's history.[2] The unusual character of the dynasty meant that it was not a well-oiled political machine or a close-knit family; rather, the tensions and distances between the Robertses were obvious during certain points at the dynasty's peak. One revealing story about the relationships within the dynasty is that Mary Wendy only met Betty when they were both serving in the Oregon legislature, several years after Frank and Betty had already divorced.[3] An *Oregonian* newspaper reporter wrote, "Sen. Betty Roberts and Rep. Mary Roberts agree that their closest tie is membership in the Democratic Party."[4] Indeed, progressive Democratic politics and a deep-seated commitment to the state, more than personal ties or blood relationships, are the legacies of the Roberts dynasty of Oregon.

Frank Roberts

Frank Roberts was a college professor, Oregon state legislator, and avid sailor. Born in Boise, Idaho, he grew up in a modest home in Oregon with three siblings. Frank's father abandoned the family when Frank was young, leaving Frank's mother the responsibility for raising the four children on her own. Roberts received a bachelor's degree from Pacific University (1938), a master's degree from the University of Wisconsin (1943), and a doctorate from Stanford (1954). In 1946, after returning from Germany as an army officer, Roberts began his 38-year career as a speech professor at Vanport College (now called Portland State University).[5] His career in politics began in 1960 when he became chair of the Multnomah County Democratic Party. Roberts was elected to the Oregon House of Representatives in 1966 and to the Senate in 1974. He remained in the Senate from 1975 until terminal cancer prompted him to retire in September 1993.[6] Roberts also ran twice for Senate president, but was unable to secure enough votes among conservative Senate Democrats to be put forward as the party's nominee.[7]

Unlike members of some political dynasties who are drawn to politics because of their elite status within the community or a sense of civic duty, Frank was motivated by a sincere concern for the public, as well as by a love of politics.[8] A traditional liberal Democrat, Roberts was particularly successful in using his seat on the Ways and Means Committee to shape policy through the appropriations process.[9] Roberts redirected Oregon's social services agenda in an effort to assist working families and those most in need. His legacies include expanding medical coverage for more Oregonians, increasing

Roberts Political Dynasty Family Tree

1. Frank Roberts, 1915–1993
    Oregon House of Representatives, 1967–1971
    Oregon Senate, 1975–1993
Married Mary Louise Charleson
Two children: Mary Wendy and Leslie
Married Betty (Cantrell) Rice
Married Barbara (Hughey) Sanders

1. Betty Cantrell Roberts, 1923–2011
    Oregon House of Representatives, 1965–1969
    Oregon Senate, 1969–1977
    Oregon Court of Appeals, 1977–1982
    Oregon Supreme Court, 1982–1986
Married Bill Rice
Four children
Married Frank Roberts
Married Keith Skelton

1. Barbara Hughey Roberts, 1936–
    Oregon House of Representatives, 1981–1985
    Oregon secretary of state, 1985–1991
    Governor of Oregon, 1991–1995
Married Neal Sanders
Two children
Married Frank Roberts

2. Mary Wendy Roberts, 1944–
    Oregon House of Representatives, 1973–1975
    Oregon Senate, 1975–1979
    Oregon commissioner of labor and industries, 1979–1995
Married Richard Bullock
One child
Married Edward E. Simpson

2. Leslie Roberts, 1948–
    Multnomah County Circuit Court, 2007–
Married Rex Armstrong
14 children

government funding for Head Start programs and prenatal care, and protecting those who were unable to advocate for themselves. He was also considered a pioneer in advocating for Death with Dignity, a progressive reform allowing terminally ill patients to end their lives voluntarily with medication prescribed by a physician.[10]

Members of both parties admired Roberts's unwavering determination, naturally self-effacing demeanor, and strong speaking skills.[11] His dedication to progressive politics, civil rights, human rights, higher education, and children was perceived by his capitol colleagues, the media, and other political observers in the state to be unmatched during his tenure; indeed, he was sometimes referred to as the "conscience of the Senate."[12] Former Oregon governor Neil Goldschmidt said of Frank, "If there was ever an anchor to the wind in terms of both conscience and effort, an absolute stopper against those who would run over the little guy, he's been it."[13]

Betty Roberts

Although Frank may have been the lynchpin in the Roberts dynasty, Betty Cantrell Roberts was the first to hold state legislative office, capturing a seat in the House in 1964. Born in Kansas and reared in Texas, Roberts moved to Oregon in 1945 with her first husband Bill Rice, with whom she had four children. Betty initially attended Texas Wesleyan College but left school at the start of her first marriage.[14] She returned to college in her early thirties over her first husband's objections, signing up for courses first at Eastern Oregon College in LaGrande, Oregon, and then at Portland State College (University), from which she graduated in 1958.[15] She taught social studies at a local high school and then completed a master's degree in political science at the University of Oregon in 1962.[16] After her divorce from Bill Rice, Betty married Frank Roberts in 1960, a union that would last until 1966. Like Frank, she was drawn to politics out of a desire to address social problems. In later years, Betty described her marriage to Frank as being "more of convenience than romance." What they had in common was that they "both liked politics and . . . to be around other politicians."[17]

Growing up in poverty during the Great Depression, Betty Roberts overcame considerable adversity to pursue her education and professional goals. One of the key challenges she faced in her chosen career was that she chose an occupation dominated by men. Denied admission to the doctoral program in political science at the University of Oregon allegedly because of her age, Roberts attributed it to the department's history of being unsupportive of women.[18] Roberts decided to pursue a law degree instead, applying to the Northwestern College of Law (Lewis and Clark Law School), where neither her age nor gender prevented her from being admitted. Roberts completed her juris doctorate degree in 1965.[19]

Roberts first became interested in politics at Portland State, where she took a course from Marko Haggard, a political science professor who inspired many of his students to embark on successful political careers.[20] She soon became involved in Democratic Party activities, including service on the local precinct committee. Her first bid for political office came in May 1960, when she was elected to a local elementary school district board. It was soon after the election that she and Frank began to develop a romantic relationship. Near the end of November, they were married.[21]

Living in a house filled with political talk, both Betty and Frank began to set their sights on running for the legislature. Betty first ran unsuccessfully for the Oregon House in 1962, but was then elected in 1964 from a three-person multimember district just beyond the eastern edge of Portland. She was reelected in 1966. After her divorce from Frank, she married Keith Skelton, another member of the House, in 1968. Later that year, she won election to the Oregon Senate, defeating a long-term conservative incumbent from her own party. After the election, she was the lone female senator in a building that did not have a bathroom for women senators.[22]

In 1973, Roberts announced her candidacy for governor. Here too she experienced the challenges confronting women in politics at the time, especially in being taken seriously as a candidate for an office in which nationwide only three women had ever served and none in Oregon.[23] When a reporter asked her whether Oregon was ready for a woman governor, she responded, "The question should not be, is Oregon ready for a woman governor, but is this person ready?"[24] The problem of being taken seriously is certainly not confined to Oregon; scholars have found that the public is more likely to question the credentials of women candidates.[25] It is hard to know whether gender played a decisive role in the election. Betty was defeated in the primary by former state Treasurer Robert Straub, who was the most prominent Democrat in the state at the time, with a well-known record of accomplishments and a broad network of support.

Following the loss, Roberts was named by the state Democratic Party Central Committee to be the party's candidate for the U.S. Senate in 1974 after Wayne Morse, the former senator and the party's 1974 nominee, unexpectedly passed away. Roberts lost the election to the incumbent, Bob Packwood. Ultimately, Roberts ended up serving a total of 13 years in the Oregon state legislature, beginning in the state House in 1965 and moving to the Oregon Senate in 1969. Throughout her career as a legislator, Roberts championed progressive causes, including protections for women and minorities. She was considered essential to Oregon's ratification of the 1973 Equal Rights Amendment to the U.S. Constitution.[26] She stepped aside from the legislature in 1977 when she was appointed to the Oregon Court of Appeals. She was then appointed to the Oregon Supreme Court in 1982. Her most prominent achievement as a member of the Supreme Court is that she wrote the opinion in *Hewitt v.*

SAIF (1982), a landmark case which established equal rights for men and women under the Oregon Constitution.[27] As the first woman to serve on both courts, Roberts broke significant gender barriers, but it was not always easy. When she served on the appellate court, she faced a workplace environment that was not accepting of a woman judge, one which was so hostile that even some of the female clerks working in the court offices were afraid to associate with Roberts because of the animosity of other judges toward having a female colleague.[28] She decided to step down from the Supreme Court in 1986, citing her third husband's retirement and her long commute as the reasons, though underlying it was a feeling of burnout after more than two decades of demanding and stressful work.[29]

Betty Roberts is considered a pioneer among women political leaders in Oregon. Her successes in gaining office and in championing women's rights are considered to have helped open the door not only for Barbara Roberts but for other Oregon women, including many of whom she personally mentored.[30]

The Roberts Sisters

The most politically successful Roberts among Frank's blood relations was his daughter Mary Wendy (1944–). Mary Wendy served one term in the Oregon House of Representatives (1973–1975) before being elected to the state Senate and serving from 1975 to 1979. When Betty Roberts was appointed to the Court of Appeals in 1977, Mary Wendy Roberts became the only woman in the Senate for the next two years. She vacated her seat in January 1979 after she was elected commissioner of labor and industries, a position she held until 1995.[31] Mary Wendy's decision to run for commissioner helped bring another family member into the legislature, and in so doing, created controversy. Mary Wendy filed to run for labor commissioner at the very last minute, which enabled her husband, Richard Bullock, to be the only candidate to file for her Senate seat.[32]

The labor commissioner is a statewide executive office, which was originally created in the early 20th century to protect workers and enforce labor laws. Over time, the responsibilities of the office expanded to include other workplace and business-related duties, including overseeing the state's apprenticeship program. Under Roberts's prominent leadership, the bureau became more vigorously involved in civil rights cases, and in protecting workers against discrimination, establishing family and parental leave, and improving the conditions of farmworkers.[33]

The dual election of Mary Wendy and Frank Roberts to the Senate in 1974, along with the continued presence of Betty Roberts in that body, helped attract the public's attention to the emerging dynasty. It also made it confusing at times during the 1975 legislative session, especially with Barbara Roberts also working in the chamber as Frank's legislative aide. Reporters and even fellow legislators were often uncertain of the connections between the three senators and staff member, all with the same last name. One of the most repeated stories from that session about the extended family is recounted in Barbara's memoirs. She describes one day during the session when all four Robertses gathered at Frank's desk for the opening prayer because Betty and Mary Wendy did not have time to reach their own desks once the prayer had begun. As the prayer concluded, Betty leaned over and whispered to Frank, "The family that prays together, stays together."[34] The story may give the impression that it was a close-knit clan. Yet the gathering was more a matter of happenstance than warm familial bonds.

Mary Wendy was not the only blood relative to enter politics in Oregon. Her younger sister, Leslie Roberts (1948–), graduated from Yale Law School in 1972, began practicing law in Multnomah County two years later, and was then elected to the Multnomah County Circuit Court in 2006.[35] She was reelected for her third six-year term in 2018. In addition, Leslie's husband, Rex Armstrong (1950–), has served as an Oregon Court of Appeals judge since 1994.[36]

Barbara Roberts

Barbara Hughey Roberts (1936–) was the first woman to serve as governor of Oregon. Raised in a small town in western Oregon, Roberts came from a family with deep roots in the state. Her ancestors arrived over the Oregon Trail. Her parents met when they were working in a logging camp.[37] Barbara was drawn to politics, as with others in the Roberts's dynasty, by a desire to address social ills. Roberts began her political career as a citizen advocate, seeking to get the 1971 legislature to pay attention to the educational needs of one of her two sons who had autism. She pushed the legislature to enact legislation requiring school districts to provide special education for emotionally handicapped children.[38] Like Leslie, Barbara became actively involved in Democratic Party politics, including serving as a precinct committee member. It was through her work as a Democratic Party activist that she met Frank Roberts, who would soon become her political mentor and second husband. They married in 1974. After their marriage, Barbara served on Frank's staff in the Oregon Senate for six years. She then ran successfully for her own seat in the Oregon House of Representatives in 1980.[39]

Roberts became the first woman to serve as the Oregon House majority leader (1983–1984).[40] In 1984, she was elected secretary of state, the first Democrat to hold that office in 110 years and only the second female secretary of state in Oregon's history.[41] Halfway through her second term, Roberts ran for governor, following a path that had been attempted previously by Betty Roberts in 1974 and Norma Paulus in 1986. Yet the result for Barbara was different from her two female predecessors, as she squeezed out a victory in the four-candidate race with less than 50 percent of the vote, defeating her major opponent, Oregon attorney general David Frohnmayer.[42] Roberts was sworn in as Oregon's first female governor on January 14, 1991. The only other female governor in the state has been Kate Brown, who as secretary of state succeeded to the office in 2015 after the sitting governor resigned. Brown was then reelected in a special election in 2016.

During her tenure, Governor Roberts was hailed for her commitment to families and children, and her support for environmental protections, human rights, and civil rights. Roberts also received acclaim for her innovative approach to government redesign and reinvention.[43] Yet Roberts had the unlucky situation of being elected in the same year that the federal government listed the spotted owl as an endangered species and state voters passed strict limits on property taxes (Measure 5), two events that profoundly transformed Oregon politics; the state divided politically along urban-rural and partisan lines, while voters made it difficult for the state to make ends meet. The passage of the property tax measure forced Governor Roberts to find almost $2 billion in additional funds over the course of her term when the biennial budget was only $6 billion.[44] She fought unsuccessfully to get the legislature to place a major tax reform bill on the state ballot to address the fiscal problems created by the measure. The tax reform measured failed in the legislature by two votes, never reaching state voters.[45]

Of all the conflicts that took place within the Roberts dynasty, the most visible occurred soon after Barbara Roberts was elected governor. After being sworn into office, Barbara had the responsibility of appointing someone to fill her former position as secretary of state. She appointed Phil Keisling, an up-and-coming leader in the Democratic Party, to the office. In making that selection, Roberts rejected Mary Wendy Roberts, Oregon's commissioner of labor and industries. Later, Barbara Roberts acknowledged that she should have considered her stepdaughter. In her memoir, Barbara wrote, "She had the political experience, the intelligence, the wish to hold the office, but she had the handicap of being my stepdaughter."[46] Two years later, Mary Wendy Roberts challenged Keisling in the Democratic primary for the secretary of state position; he defeated her 46 percent to 39 percent and went on to win reelection. Barbara Roberts later recalled that "the race was an awkward one for our family, with Frank supporting his daughter and my endorsement going to my appointee."[47]

The Roberts dynasty reached its zenith in the 1980s and 1990s with Betty in the state courts, Mary Wendy as labor commissioner, and Barbara serving as House majority leader, secretary of state, and then governor. Yet by the mid-1990s, the family's position in Oregon politics had changed. Barbara served only one term as governor. Confronting a variety of serious health problems among close family members, and a difficult primary challenge from John

Kitzhaber, the state senate president, Roberts decided to withdraw from the 1994 race for governor. Frank Roberts died in October 1993. During that same 1994 election cycle, Mary Wendy Roberts was defeated in her efforts to be reelected as labor commissioner. With these departures from elected office, the Roberts dynasty had all but come to an end. After 1995, the sole immediate family member of the Roberts clan to remain in office was Leslie, who continues to serve as a judge in Multnomah County Circuit Court. No one in the next generation has to date followed a political career path.

In many ways, calling the family a dynasty may not be precise. Power was not handed down from one generation to the next. They were not bound together by blood. Rather, each family member made his or her own individual mark on the state around the same period. Despite the limited number of blood relations, the members of the Roberts family came from similar stock and shared similar experiences. The four main family members were all liberal Democrats. They were not part of Oregon's social and economic elite, but a group of individuals who were passionate about politics and making the state a better place. Throughout their careers, they all championed progressive policies to help the disadvantaged, protect individual rights, and improve the quality of life in the state. Betty, Mary Wendy, and Barbara were also trailblazers, opening doors that had previously been closed to women. In so doing, they forged paths for later women to follow. It was these political values, more than familial relations, which bound the dynasty together. Frank may have been at the center of the dynasty, but all four Robertses played a critical role in Oregon politics in the latter half of the 20th century.

Notes

1. Barbara Roberts, *Up the Capitol Steps: A Woman's March to the Governorship* (Corvallis: Oregon State University Press, 2011), 85.

2. "Roberts 'Dynasty' Ends after 30 Years," *Register-Guard* (Eugene, OR), January 10, 1995.

3. Betty Roberts and Gail Wells, *With Grit and by Grace: Breaking Trails in Politics and Law, a Memoir* (Corvallis: Oregon State University Press, 2008), 148

4. Roberts and Wells, *With Grit*.

5. Brent Walth, "Roberts Succumbs to Cancer," *Register-Guard* (Eugene, OR), November 1, 1993.

6. Barbara Coombs Lee, "A Pioneer for Death with Dignity," *New York Times*, March 18, 2015.

7. Walth, "Roberts Succumbs"; Stan Federman, "Robert Fights on, Despite Loss to Boe," *Oregonian*, May 10, 1977.

8. Leslie Roberts, interviewed by Katherine O'Neil, October 24, 2005, Oregon U.S. District Court Historical Society Oral History Program, https://usdchs.files.wordpress.com/2016/05/betty-roberts-usdchs-oral-history.pdf, 40.

9. Walth, "Roberts Succumbs."
10. Lee, "A Pioneer."
11. Walth, "Roberts Succumbs."
12. Roberts, *Capitol Steps*, 323.
13. Walth, "Roberts Succumbs."
14. Roberts and Wells, *With Grit*, 22.
15. Gail Wells, "Betty Roberts (1923–2011)," *The Oregon Encyclopedia*, Oregon Historical Society, https://oregonencyclopedia.org/articles/roberts_betty_1923_2011_/#.WIEBO7GZPow.
16. Wells, "Betty Roberts."
17. Leslie Roberts, interviewed by Katherine O'Neil, 40.
18. Roberts and Wells, *With Grit*, 52.
19. Wells, "Betty Roberts."
20. Roberts and Wells, *With Grit*, 39; David Yaden, interviewed by Ernie Bonner, August 20, 2001, Ernie Bonner's PlanPDX.org oral history program.
21. Roberts and Wells, *With Grit*, 48.
22. Leslie Roberts, interviewed by Katherine O'Neil, 52–53.
23. Susan J. Carroll, "Women in State Government: Historical Overview and Current Trends," *The Book of the States* (Lexington, KY: Council of State Governments, 2007).
24. Roberts and Gail Wells, *With Grit*, 177.
25. Denise Baer and Heidi Hartmann, *Shifting Gears: How Women Navigate the Road to Higher Office* (Cambridge, MA: Political Parity, 2014).
26. Wells, "Betty Roberts."
27. Janice Dilg, "From Coverture to Supreme Court Justice: Women Lawyers and Judges in Oregon History," *Oregon Historical Quarterly* 113 (2012): 368.
28. Wells, "Betty Roberts"; Leslie Roberts, interviewed by Katherine O'Neil, 97–109.
29. James Mayer, "Betty Roberts, First Woman on the Oregon Supreme Court and Trailblazer in Politics, Dies," *Oregonian*, June 25, 2011.
30. Tara Watson and Melody Rose, "She Flies with Her Own Wings: Women in the 1973 Oregon Legislative Session," *Oregon Historical Quarterly* 111 (2010): 58.
31. William G. Robbins, "Oregon Politics—Women, Natural Resources, and Social Change," *Oregon History Project*, Oregon Historical Society, 2002, https://oregonhistoryproject.org/articles/oregon-politicswomen-natural-resources-and-social-change/pdf.
32. Roberts, *Capitol Steps*, 81.
33. Oregon Bureau of Labor and Industries, *Centennial Anniversary Book* (Salem, OR: Bureau of Labor and Industries, 2003), 54–66.
34. Roberts, *Capitol Steps*, 64–65.
35. "Judge Leslie Roberts," Multnomah Bar Association, 2012, https://www.mbabar.org/Resources/LeslieRoberts.html.
36. "The Honorable Rex Armstrong," Court of Appeals, Oregon Judicial Department, 2014, http://courts.oregon.gov/COA/judgebios/pages/armstrongbio.aspx.
37. Roberts, *Capitol Steps*, 5–6.

38. Roberts, *Capitol Steps*, 42.
39. Roberts, *Capitol Steps*, 83–84, 89.
40. Roberts, *Capitol Steps*, 98.
41. Roberts, *Capitol Steps*, 130.
42. Roberts, *Capitol Steps*, 172, 214.
43. "Barbara Roberts," Democratic Party of Oregon, http://dpo.org/people/barbara-roberts.
44. Alan Rosenthal, *The Best Job in Politics: Exploring How Governors Succeed as Policy Leaders* (Thousand Oaks, CA: CQ Press, 2013), 24.
45. Roberts, *Capitol Steps*, 274–277, 314–315.
46. Roberts, *Capitol Steps*, 226–227.
47. Roberts, *Capitol Steps*, 227.

Further Reading

Dilg, Janice. "From Coverture to Supreme Court Justice: Women Lawyers and Judges in Oregon History." *Oregon Historical Quarterly* 113 (2012): 360–81.

Roberts, Barbara. *Up the Capitol Steps: A Woman's March to the Governorship*. Corvallis: Oregon State University Press, 2011.

Roberts, Betty, and Gail Wells. *With Grit and by Grace: Breaking Trails in Politics and Law, a Memoir*. Corvallis: Oregon State University Press, 2008.

Watson, Tara, and Melody Rose. "She Flies with Her Own Wings: Women in the 1973 Oregon Legislative Session." *Oregon Historical Quarterly* 111 (2010): 38–63.

CHAPTER SIXTEEN

The Simpson Dynasty

Cody J. Foster

The Simpson political dynasty in Wyoming spans about a century in length. Different from political dynasties that have relied on the accumulation of wealth and influence over several generations in order to grasp and maintain power, the Simpsons rose to political prominence through deep social connections made primarily through their legal occupations. However, in the late 20th century, the rising tide of conservatism swept over Wyoming and left the future of the Simpson dynasty in crisis as they continued to defend the more moderate beliefs of the Republican Party. The dynasty soon crumbled when the family struggled to challenge and unseat more conservative Republican incumbents. It is uncertain whether the era of the Simpson dynasty has come to a close or whether the patriarch's great-great-grandchildren will one day, too, enter the political arena.

The Simpson family has long pursued opportunities despite the possible damage that might occur by taking such risks. Robert and Nancy Simpson first saw opportunity in the days of westward expansion and soon moved with their young son John Porter Simpson (1835–1921) from Huntingdon, Pennsylvania, to Bear Creek, Colorado, in the 1860s. John found opportunity as a ranch hand in Wyoming where he met his wife, Margaret Susan Sullivan (1846–1922). After the arrival of their firstborn son, William "Billy" Simpson (1868–1940), they traveled around the region before settling in an area of Wyoming in 1893 where both husband and wife would design and name the town: Jackson. A rather uneducated Billy would soon marry his Latin instructor, Margaret Burnett (1874–1974), while studying for law school before having three kids of his own. The marriage of their middle child, Milward Lee

Simpson (1897–1993), to Lorna Hellen Kooi (1900–1995) would be the main influx of a vast amount of wealth into the family, as her father, businessman Peter Kooi (1866–1935), had negotiated the sale of his coal-mining properties to the Sheridan-Wyoming Coal Company. Kooi passed on his knowledge of politics, learned as a Wyoming state senator, to Milward, who would later become a state representative, U.S. senator, and Wyoming governor. This interest in politics would be passed down through the next generation through Peter (1930–) and Alan (1931–), and even later, through Colin (1959–), as each groomed the next for careers as attorneys and politicians.

Unfortunately, some of the family's youthful dalliances and their moderate Republican ideology would come to taint their political potential, as stories from the past clouded the political present. Billy Simpson's penchant for drinking and gambling soon gave way to a level of impulsivity that frequently resulted in both personal and family misfortunes. As a young man, Billy's grandson Alan participated in thievery, played dangerous shooting games with his friends, and once was found guilty of arson on federal property. These stories followed the family onto the campaign trail long after both men had sought repentance. Meanwhile, their moderate Republicanism eventually clashed with the party's embrace of far right conservatism in Wyoming. While the Simpsons embraced moderate views on abortion, gay rights, and equality, the Wyoming public began to vote for Republicans who espoused a more conservative ideology toward such controversial social issues. For this reason, the Simpson dynasty struggled to compete in congressional and gubernatorial elections in ways that appear, as of 2017, to be the downfall of the dynasty.

Milward Lee Simpson: Wyoming's One-Term Leader

Born the middle child to Billy and Margaret, Milward Simpson first glimpsed the world through the slits of his parent's log cabin in Jackson, Wyoming, on November 12, 1897. Although his father chaired Park County's Democratic Party, his father's many vices prevented him from achieving elected political office. In 1905, Billy entered Hays and Company Bank with a pistol in hand and nearly blew a bank teller's ear off for having bounced the Democratic Party's check on multiple occasions. He was not charged with a crime but paid the price by losing his bid for Park County attorney. In 1922, he got into a brawl with Edward Uriah Raines, a barber involved in a property ownership lawsuit. A furious Raines attacked Billy on the streets of Cody, Wyoming, slamming a rock into the side of his head to the point where one of Billy's eyes became partially dislodged. Angered and seeking retribution, Billy left his medical examination, found Raines, and twice shot him; one bullet was blocked by a silver dollar in Raines's pocket, but the other pierced his abdomen. A long and arduous trial followed before a hung jury allowed the judge

Simpson Political Dynasty Family Tree

1. William "Billy" Simpson, 1868–1940
    Attorney in Cody, Wyoming
Married Margaret Burnett, 1874–1974
Three children including Milward Lee Simpson

2. Milward Lee Simpson, 1897–1993
    Wyoming House of Representatives, 1927–1929
    Governor of Wyoming, 1955–1959
    U.S. senator, 1963–1969
Married Lorna Hellen Kooi, 1900–1995
Two children including Peter Kooi Simpson Sr. and Alan Kooi Simpson

3. Peter Kooi Simpson, 1930–
    Wyoming state representative from Sheridan County, 1981–1984
Married Lynne Alice Livingston, c. 1941–
Three children

3. Alan Kooi Simpson, 1931–
    Wyoming House of Representatives, 1965–1977
    U.S. senator, 1978–1996
Married to Susan Ann Schroll, c. 1932–
Three children including Colin Simpson

4. Colin Mackenzie Simpson, 1959–
    Wyoming House of Representatives, 1998–2011
Married to Deborah Oakley
Two children

---

to dismiss the case. Billy's life may not have impacted his son's political future, but it certainly influenced the young Milward to pursue a more cautious path toward a legal career, before he entered a life in politics.

In between his father's violent exhibitions, Milward left for the Tome Prep School in Port Deposit, Maryland, where he lived in a rigid environment structured by rules and decorum. This strict educational experience translated easily into military service where he assumed command of a unit as second lieutenant in the infantry during World War I. With the war behind him, he attended the University of Wyoming and thereafter Harvard University Law

School before returning to Cody to set up practice as an attorney in 1926. Three years later he married Lorna Helen Kooi, the daughter of a wealthy businessman from Chicago, Illinois, who, in 1922, was appointed by Wyoming governor Frank C. Emerson as a member of the State Department of Commerce and Industry. As an influential businessman and civic leader, Peter Kooi shared with his new son-in-law the importance of political networking as an opportunity to frequent the company of esteemed government officials.

Under the tutelage of Peter Kooi, Milward first cast his hat into the ring in 1926 to become a state representative, a position he held for only one term from 1927 to 1929. Although he gave politics a break in the intervening years after having failed to properly prepare himself for the frequent failures that can accompany life in politics, Milward finally reentered the political scene in 1940 to compete for a U.S. Senate seat against incumbent New Deal Democrat Joseph O'Mahoney. On the campaign trail, Simpson showcased strong anti-Communist credentials at a time in which the Soviets were still Allies with the United States in their fight to defeat Hitler. Having jumped the gun prior to the rise of a powerful anti-Communist Cold War ideology, Wyomingites overwhelmingly voted for O'Mahoney out of fear that Simpson was too radical in his views. After another hiatus from politics, Simpson finally returned in 1955 when he was elected as governor of Wyoming for yet another single term. Disappointed and tired, Milward returned to his law practice and promised himself to stay out of the electoral process and only to serve on the University of Wyoming Board of Trustees and the National Association of Governing Boards of State Universities and Allied Institutions. That promise held until 1967 when Senator-elect Keith Thomson died suddenly of a heart attack taking the oath of office. In a special election on November 6, 1962, Wyoming residents elected Milward to the vacated office, allowing him to serve as U.S. senator until the end of the term in 1967. Thereafter, he avoided electoral politics until he died in 1993.

The Simpson Brothers: Wyoming's Rightward Turn and the Struggle to Keep Up

Peter Kooi Simpson and Alan Kooi Simpson were born to Milward and Lorna a mere year apart in Cody, Wyoming. Although the former tried his hand at politics on several occasions, he found his talents best suited to university administration and the professional study of history. Each graduated from the University of Wyoming, where each were members of Alpha Tau Omega fraternity. Moreover, each dedicated years of service in the military.

Peter Simpson's path into politics was unconventional and differed from the trail left by his father, grandfather, and brother. Forgoing the family's tendency to attend law school, Peter followed his passion for history to achieve both a master's and doctoral degree, writing two regional studies: the first a history of the initial Wyoming legislature, the second a history of the cattle industry in southern Oregon. He finished his doctoral dissertation in 1973 and enlisted in the U.S. Navy at the tail end of the Vietnam War, in which he served overseas for four years. Unsure of his professional future, he moved to Billings, Montana, where he created a local television program and wrote and performed folk music. He finally returned to Wyoming in the late 1970s where he climbed the academic ladder as an administrator at several local colleges before deciding to try his hand at politics. He was elected to the State House of Representatives in 1981; however, having a predilection toward the arts and education, Peter felt unsatisfied as a career politician and only served until 1984. Although he attempted to secure the governorship in 1986, Peter lost to Democrat Mike Sullivan. Some historians have attributed the loss to the fact that his brother, Alan, had been elected to the U.S. Senate where he quickly became known for outspoken, brash opinions.

Like their father, Alan spent a postgraduate year after high school at a specialized school in Bloomfield Hills, Michigan, before returning to the University of Wyoming in 1950 to pursue his bachelor of science and his law degree. While Peter enrolled in the U.S. Navy for four years, Alan joined the U.S. Army and served in Germany between 1955 and 1956. He practiced law for nearly a decade after he returned from military duty before jumping into politics in 1965. He became a representative of Park Country in the Wyoming House of Representatives, serving over a decade until 1977. Looking to continue up the political ladder, Alan soon eyed a vulnerable seat in the U.S. Senate. Reminiscent of other moments in his family's history, Alan gained an advantage in election for the U.S. Senate after the incumbent, Clifford P. Hansen, resigned his seat only three days prior to his term ending in order to give Alan a boost. Clifford felt that Alan deserved the seat because Alan's father, Milward, had occupied the seat prior to Hansen.

Alan Simpson finally had an opportunity to express his national political views after he secured a seat in the U.S. Senate. Throughout his senatorial tenure between 1978 and 1996, Simpson served as Republican whip, chair of the Veterans' Affairs Committee, chair of the Immigration and Refugee Subcommittee of Judiciary, and participated in the Nuclear Regulation Subcommittee, the Social Security Subcommittee, and the Committee on Aging. In these committees, in Congress, and in town halls, Alan had the chance to express his moderate Republican views toward key conservative issues such as abortion, gay and lesbian rights, and social equality. Although he sided with his more conservative colleagues on the role of entitlements in society as a source of economic strain on future generations, he expressed more moderate— even libertarian—views toward key social issues. As much of the country took a rightward turn after the Vietnam War and, in particular, during the years of Ronald Reagan's presidency, Alan Simpson and his family maintained a more moderate approach toward critical social issues. Although he agreed with most Reagan conservatives that the federal government should have a less intrusive role in the private lives of American citizens, Simpson then argued that social issues like abortion and gay and lesbian rights therefore should not be political issues. Although he was a fiscal conservative, Simpson broke with the government-enforced social conservatism that was embraced by much of the Republican Party. As George H. W. Bush became the Republican presidential nominee in 1988, he offered his good friend Alan the vice presidential position. Alan, however, declined out of fear that his moderate political views would hinder the party's chances for victory.

Years after Simpson retired from the Senate, President Barack Obama appointed him as cochair of the National Commission on Fiscal Responsibility and Reform in 2010, with the mission to reassess the 2008 economic crisis and recommend reforms to both Congress and the president. In this setting, Simpson advanced his views that differed from his Republican colleagues and their core constituents when he said that Congress should eliminate private contractors from Department of Defense spending, reduce Medicare and Medicaid expenditures, cut Social Security spending, and slice the deficit. He made national headlines when newspapers across the country reported that he criticized the elderly for relying so heavily on Social Security, calling them "greedy geezers," a phrase that surely hampered his son's political aspirations.

Colin M. Simpson: The Fall of the House of Simpson

Born in 1969 in Cheyenne, Wyoming, Alan Simpson's oldest son, Colin, followed the path forged by his father, grandfather, and great-grandfather. Colin received his law degree from the University of Wyoming in order to practice law alongside his father and brother, William, at two firms: Simpson, Kepler and Edwards in Cody, Wyoming; and Burg, Simpson, Eldredge, Hersh, and Jardine in Englewood, Colorado, where the firm focused on plaintiff practice against pharmaceutical companies.

Like his father, Alan, Colin Simpson expressed interest in holding political office to continue the family tradition. He began in state politics when he ran for and won a seat in the Wyoming House of Representatives in 1998. He served six terms, moving from House majority leader to speaker pro temp, speaker of the House, and chairman of several committees. Unfortunately, a series of election losses convinced Colin to remove himself from the political arena by 2011 and to focus on his legal career instead. Beginning in 2007, he campaigned to replace Republican Craig Thomas in the U.S. Senate, after Thomas's sudden death from leukemia. Under Wyoming law, an open seat can only be filled by the appointment of a new member from the same party by the sitting governor, after reviewing nominations made by the incumbent's party. Having campaigned to become a nominee, Peter did not appear on the Republican Party's list when it hit the desk of Governor David Freudenthal in June 2007, suggesting that the Simpson dynasty's strength in the Wyoming

Republican Party had drastically diminished since Alan Simpson left political office.

The Simpson dynasty would again suffer defeat in 2008 when Colin announced that he would challenge Republican Congresswoman Barbara Cubin for her seat in the U.S. House of Representatives. For reasons unknown (beyond his citing of family reasons), Peter dropped out of the race without any indication of whether he would again try to run for office at a later time. In 2010, Peter began to campaign for the governorship of Wyoming, a plan that probably influenced his decision to stop running for Cubin's seat in 2008. Although once seen as a front-runner for governor in 2010, Peter placed fourth in the election. Defeated and unsure of his political future, Colin left the Wyoming legislature in 2011 and retired to practice law.

Unlike some states further east in the United States, long been recognized for harboring well-known political dynasties, Wyoming is not nationally known for its political families. University of Wyoming Phil Roberts agrees that family names in politics have long been less important in Wyoming than in other states. Perhaps for this very reason, the Simpson family entered the political game later than other American dynasties and held power for far less time. Still, the rise of the Simpson political dynasty shows how tumultuous the struggle can be to grasp and maintain power over multiple generations. Changing demographics only made the situation more difficult for the Simpsons as their more moderate brand of conservatism increasingly clashed with their fellow Wyomingites.

In 1984, Alaska finally overtook Wyoming in population and left the state as the least populated in the United States with a total population of just 584,153 residents. A 2009 Gallup Poll showed the state with a "solid Republican" base and growing more conservative by the year. The Simpson dynasty failed to keep up with these changing political demographics, remaining moderate toward social issues during the culture wars of the 1980s, 1990s, and 2000s. Although Milward Simpson might have represented a more moderate wing of the Republican Party in the state, nationally, his son, Alan Simpson, was unable to consistently represent the growing conservative base in Wyoming. This made the dynasty's political future uncertain in turn for Alan's son, Colin, who encountered a base that had already transitioned toward more conservative members of the Wyoming Republican Party. As such, Colin failed to be able to maintain the strength of the dynasty. Today, the future of the Simpson political dynasty remains uncertain given that Colin still has a campaign webpage and has not yet admitted his retirement from politics despite leaving office in 2011. Today, Wisconsin elected officials at the local, state, and national level are overwhelmingly conservative. Even during the presidential election cycles, the state has cast its electoral votes for conservative Republican candidates since 1967. This might also explain the Simpson family dynasty's political decline given their moderate views toward capital punishment, abortion, and LBGTQ issues clash with the predominant views of the conservative wing of the Republican Party. As such, the future of the Simpson family dynasty remains uncertain.

Further Reading

American Heritage Center. Alan K. Simpson Papers, Collection 10449, University of Wyoming.
American Heritage Center. Milward L. Simpson Papers, Collection 00026, University of Wyoming.
American Heritage Center. Peter K. Simpson Papers, Collection 10702, University of Wyoming.
Hardy, Donald Loren. *Shooting from the Lip: The Life of Senator Al Simpson*. Norman, OK: University of Oklahoma Press, 2011.
James, Frank. "Alan Simpson: Cut Entitlements, Defense; Not Aid to Poor." *NPR*. February 16, 2011. http://www.npr.org/sections/itsallpolitics/2011/02/16/133801977/alan-simpson-cut-entitlements-defense-dont-touch-help-to-poor. Accessed February 25, 2017.
Jones, Jeffrey M. "State of the Union: Political Party Affiliation." *Gallup*. January 28, 2009. http://www.gallup.com/poll/114016/state-states-political-party-affiliation.aspx. Accessed February 25, 2017.
Mark, David. "Simpson Family Faces Dynastic Break." *Politico*. December 4, 2007. http://www.politico.com/story/2007/12/simpson-family-faces-dynastic-break-007191. Accessed February 25, 2017.
Mitrovich, George. "The Return of Alan Simpson." *The Huffington Post*. May 25, 2011. http://www.huffingtonpost.com/george-mitrovich/the-return-of-alan-simpso_b_482857.html. Accessed July 1, 2017.
Pelzer, Jeremy. "Wyoming's Simpson Family Out of Public Office, But Probably Not for Long." *Casper Star-Tribune*. January 1, 2011. http://trib.com/news/state-and-regional/govt-and-politics/wyoming-s-simpson-family-out-of-public-office-but-probably/article_20cb1170-cac9-52e2-9f69-3087d5cfbb87.html. Accessed February 25, 2017.
Simpson, Alan K. *Right in the Old Gazoo: A Lifetime of Scrapping with the Press*. New York: William Morrow/HarperCollins, 1997.
United States Congress. *Tributes to Milward L. Simpson of Wyoming*. 89th Congress, 2nd Session. 1966. Washington, DC: Government Printing Office, 1966.
Wakefield, Robert. *Milward L. Simpson: The Fiery Petrel*. Sheridan, WY: Willington Press, 2005.
Wyoming PBS, "Alan K. Simpson—Nothing Else Matters," Documentary, PBS, 2011.

PART THREE

Regional and Metropolitan Political Dynasties

CHAPTER SEVENTEEN

The Daley Dynasty

Larry Bennett

In late 1993, Mayor Richard M. Daley and his wife Maggie moved from the Bridgeport neighborhood on Chicago's near Southwest Side to Central Station, an upscale residential enclave rising on repurposed, former railroad property at the edge of Chicago's downtown "Loop" business district. The Daleys' move was in most respects conventional, reflecting a successful middle-aged couple's preference for a conveniently located, newly built townhouse after having lived for many years in a neighborhood characterized by journalist Edward Walsh as a "ramshackle collection of bungalows, two flats and small frame houses with tiny front yards." Yet for many Chicagoans, Bridgeport was much more than a successful politician's residential steppingstone. Across the 20th century it was the wellspring of Chicago mayors: Edward Kelly, Martin Kennelly, Michael Bilandic, Richard M. Daley, and most conspicuously, Richard M.'s father, Richard J. Daley.

Bridgeport once adjoined Chicago's Union Stockyards, and until shortly before the Daleys' move, remained the home of one of the city's iconic sports venues, Comiskey Park. Dating from 1910, Comiskey Park still attracted a working-class White Sox fan base, and as such, evoked a vanishing Chicago of heavy industry and laconic working men. A headline in the *Chicago Tribune* referred to the Daleys' move as the "Bridgeport Bomb," and reporters John Kass and Richard Jones built their story on the comments of Bridgeporters who were distressed by the mayor's abandonment of their neighborhood. Richard M. Daley was accused of "acting big," with Kass and Jones observing that he was "leaving his tribe to live with the Yuppies."

Soon enough the Daley family's move lost its news value. Over the next decade as mayor, Richard M. Daley presided over a seemingly reinvented city. Long gone was the Chicago of belching smokestacks and "broad shoulders"; in its place emerged a metropolis noted for its concentration of "business services" firms, leading cultural institutions such as the Art Institute of Chicago and Chicago Symphony Orchestra, highly regarded research universities, and even culinary excellence, the "foody" domain of chef Charlie Trotter and other gastronomic innovators. Although inconsequential by itself, the Daleys' move paralleled Chicago's transition from the industrial core of the American heartland to global city. More subtly, Richard M. Daley's change of residence marked his personal evolution from ethnic politician vocalizing the concerns of working-class voters to pillar of a new Democratic Party whose fundamental instincts were business-friendly and whose voter base was at once demographically diverse and increasingly prosperous.

The Daleys and Chicago

The stature and political reach of the Daleys has been intimately joined to the fortunes of their hometown. Although Richard J. Daley, the dynasty's founder, was elected mayor of Chicago at a time of widespread prosperity and substantial local harmony, Chicago of 1955 was also the insular, not-quite-ready-for-midcentury place skewered in A. J. Liebling's *Chicago: The Second City*. During the first decade of his two-decade mayoralty, Richard J. Daley presided over a city that was physically transformed; yet even this remade "city that worked" was a place that journalist Mike Royko could proudly differentiate from America's bastions of hip urbanity, New York and San Francisco. Richard J. Daley's Chicago was at its core working class and workaday. In the second half of his long mayoralty, not only did Richard J. Daley's political stock plummet, but his city's national reputation was also badly damaged. At about the time that Richard M. and Maggie Daley made their move from Bridgeport to Central Station, their city was finally emerging from the long shadow cast by Richard J. Daley's declining years. Chicago's resurgence served to fuse the reputations of the two Mayor Daleys. Just as Richard J. Daley was heralded as a pragmatic political insider who modernized midcentury Chicago, Richard M. Daley earned an international reputation as a "hands-on," forward-thinking municipal chief executive. For Richard M., "Daley of Chicago" was a descriptor just as evocative in the late 1990s and early 2000s as it had been for his father in the late 1950s and early 1960s.

Both Mayor Daleys have been associated with a particular brand of urban politics—machine politics—but this seeming affinity is really a matter of image lag. Richard J. Daley was indeed one of the great practitioners of machine "bossdom," whereas Richard M. Daley's approach to local governance reflected the changed conditions that, at the end of the 20th century, had rendered ward-based, ethnically inflected politicking largely obsolete, and instead

Daley Political Dynasty Family Tree

1. Richard J. Daley, 1902–1976
    Illinois House of Representatives
    Illinois Senate
    Illinois director of revenue
    Mayor of Chicago, 1955–1976
Married Eleanor "Sis" Guilfoyle
Seven children including Richard M., William, John, and Patricia

2. Richard Michael Daley, 1942–
    Illinois Senate, 1973–
    State attorney, Cook County, Illinois, 1981–1989
    Mayor of Chicago, 1989–2011
Married Margaret Ann Corbett
Four children

2. John Patrick Daley, 1946–
    Illinois House of Representatives, 1985–1989
    Illinois Senate, 1989–1992
    Cook County Board of Commissioners, 1992–
Married Mary Lou Briatta
Three children

2. William "Bill" Michael Daley, 1948–
    U.S. secretary of commerce, 1997–2000
    President Obama's chief of staff, 2011–2012
Married Loretta Aukstik
Four children

3. Patrick Daley, 1975–, son of Patricia Daley Thompson
    Chicago City Council, 2015–
Married with three children

expressed a decidedly contemporary, globally conscious approach to civic identity formation, local coalition building, and policy development. It is likely that Richard J. and Richard M. Daley will be eternally linked by name, city, public-speaking infelicity, and political pedigree, but in fact, they sought to govern Chicago in decidedly different ways.

One other idiosyncratically Chicago aspect of the Daley dynasty is worth noting: the Daleys are the most prominent political dynasty in a city awash in such dynasties. There are the Madigans—Lisa (daughter) and Michael (father)—of Chicago, concurrently occupying the positions of Illinois secretary of state and speaker of the Illinois House of Representatives; the three Burkes of contemporary Chicago—currently a city alderman (of the 14th ward, and successor to his father in that post), state representative, and Illinois Supreme Court judge—and possibly most notoriously, the Mells, who by marriage include Rod Blagojevich, the impeached former governor of Illinois. These political families are the most substantial remnant of the Cook County Democratic machine, maintaining electoral footholds in various sections of the city, as well as coteries of funders and loyal election workers. These are also political dynasties for which "public service" is *not* the first term that would come to mind for most Chicagoans if asked to characterize them. Rather, politics at some point in time became the family business, and the family has retained that business interest across the generations. Local judgment of the Daleys is shaped both negatively and in a way positively by this context. Like the Madigans, Burkes, and Mells, the Daleys are widely viewed as the self-interested proprietors of a family political firm, though as such, very few would deny that they have clearly outperformed the competition.

Richard J. Daley: Ascent, Triumph, and Undoing

Richard J. Daley was born on May 15, 1902. His parents, Michael and Lillian, were each descended from Irish immigrants of the potato famine generation. Daley's biographers agree that Lillian, eight years her metalworker husband's senior, was the principal parental influence on young Richard. By his teenage years, Daley's political career was launched, first as a member of a politically connected neighborhood youth organization, the Hamburg Athletic Club, and second, as protégé of 11th ward Alderman Joseph McDonough. McDonough hired Daley as his personal assistant, an appointment that was the first in a series of political and governmental positions that Daley would hold: Chicago City Council clerk, state representative, state senator, Illinois director of revenue, and Cook County clerk. For a portion of the decade that Daley served in the state legislature in Springfield, he also held the position of deputy Cook County controller, a practice known as double-dipping that at the time was one of the prized material rewards available to Illinois political insiders. In his biography of Daley, *Boss*, journalist Mike Royko reports this interpretation of Richard J. Daley's rise, as offered by rival Benjamin Adamowski: "He made it through sheer luck and by attaching himself to one guy after another and then stepping over them."

In 1953 Richard J. Daley won the chairmanship of the Cook County Democratic Party. Within two years he was slated as the party's preferred

Mayor Richard J. Daley welcomes President Richard Nixon to Chicago on February 6, 1970. (National Archives)

A young Richard M. Daley served as an Illinois delegate to the Democratic National Convention held in Chicago while his father was mayor, August 28, 1968. (Library of Congress)

candidate for mayor of Chicago, and in early 1955 Daley won first the Democratic Party primary election, followed by a triumph in the general election. In the latter campaign, Daley's vote count was 708,222, a figure that for the remainder of his life was commemorated on his limousine's license plate.

Though Daley had been associated with the Democratic machine's more progressive, New Deal–friendly faction, his election as mayor was widely expected to signal a return to the ward boss-dominated, Mafia tolerant ethos of Mayor Ed Kelly's regime during the 1930s and 1940s. Daley's general election opponent in 1955, Robert Merriam, predicted that a Daley victory would produce a "wide open city": "Every syndicate operation is going to open up in Chicago: open up for high stake, high pressure gambling, crooked dice games and all the rest." Seemingly concurring, at a Daley victory celebration 43rd ward alderman and Daley supporter Paddy Bauler roared that "Chicago ain't ready for reform." Nevertheless, the campaign also revealed one of the primary sources of Daley's long-term popularity. Reflecting on the ambivalent stance toward Daley adopted by even the city's Republican-leaning newspapers, journalist and Daley biographer Len O'Connor recalled that:

> Even an antagonistic press finds it is unseemly to be vicious toward to a church-going candidate, father of seven, who is untouched by scandal and whose only fault appears to be his injudicious surrender to a consuming political ambition. The anti-Daley newspapers could not bring themselves to the point of attacking him personally.

In fact, though the newly elected mayor adopted a public persona that was cautious to a fault, from the start he was determined to take both his office and his city in a new direction. From the standpoint of the mayoralty, Daley took advantage of a newly imposed executive budget process to wrest control of municipal appropriations from the City Council. The mayor's amplified budget power gave him more control over the operations of city's various service delivering agencies, and further, permitted him to exercise substantial influence over their hiring decisions. Thus, a tweak to Chicago's municipal charter enabled the mustering of a centralized patronage army. Daley also used the resources at his command as party leader—for instance, his ability to support the electoral ambitions of favored individuals—to undermine the power of South Side African American congressman William Dawson by winning over several of Dawson's ward-level protégés.

Richard J. Daley's Chicago of the late 1950s and early 1960s was a city on the move. This was a period of generous federal government support for urban rebuilding, and Daley aggressively sought funding to construct public housing, initiate neighborhood urban renewal projects, and following the passage of the Federal-Aid Highway Act of 1956, build a network of expressways linking Chicago to its suburban periphery and beyond. Daley's redevelopment efforts, moreover, were not simply a helter-skelter campaign to import funds and host ribbon-cutting ceremonies. In 1956 Chicago enacted an updated zoning ordinance, and two years later Daley's newly formed Department of City Planning issued the *Development Plan for the Central Area of Chicago*. The *Development Plan* imagined a remarkably transformed downtown Chicago: Chicago riverfront, lakefront, and parks improvements; home to a substantially increased residential population; and largely purged of the manufacturers that had once crowded around the Loop and the interregional rail network converging at central Chicago. During this golden era, Daley never shed the reputation of powerful political boss, but he became a boss who sported a halo. Though renowned as a cagey political operative, he recruited highly respected professionals to run many of his city agencies. It was during this period that Chicago earned the widely circulated moniker "the city that works."

As the 1950s rolled into the 1960s, Richard J. Daley's political reach extended well beyond Chicago. As chair of the Cook County Democratic Party—and equally, as a popular mayor and powerful local vote-getter—Daley was able to exercise substantial control over the Democrats of the Illinois congressional delegation. As the journalist Nicholas Lemann observes in Daley's film biography, *The Last Boss*, if a president wanted to corral the largest single bloc of votes for an upcoming congressional action, the man to call was Richard J. Daley. Among national Democratic luminaries, Daley was on especially good terms with the Kennedy family. In 1945 Joseph Kennedy had purchased a huge commercial property in downtown Chicago, the Merchandise Mart, and for the next several decades Kennedy representatives such as R. Sargent Shriver were a noteworthy presence among Chicago's business elite. In 1954, recently elected Massachusetts senator John F. Kennedy addressed a Daley fund-raiser at Chicago's Conrad Hilton Hotel.

The Richard J. Daley–Kennedy family bond was sealed by the 1960 presidential election. Democractic nominee John F. Kennedy's razor-thin victory over Republican Richard Nixon was ensured by Kennedy's narrow pluralities in Texas and Illinois, the latter, in effect, determined by the huge majorities Kennedy racked up in Chicago and Cook County. In the years to follow, Richard J. Daley became a frequent visitor to Washington, DC, sometimes as tribune for Chicago, on other occasions joining delegations sponsored by groups such as the U.S. Conference of Mayors. In 1960, Daley served as president of the mayors' conference. Before the calamitous local events of 1968—first the April civil disturbances in the wake of Martin Luther King's assassination, then the tumultuous Democratic National Convention during August—Daley, widely hailed as an accomplished mayor and expert on cities, was a frequent subject of press profiles and a source for countless newspaper, magazine, radio, and television reports.

At home in Chicago, however, Richard J. Daley's halo had begun to shrink. Following a landslide reelection victory in 1959, Daley encountered a far more determined opponent in the 1963 mayoral campaign, Benjamin Adamowski, a one-time Democrat and more recently Cook County state's attorney. Adamowski overtly courted Chicagoans of Polish descent—a much larger demographic group than the city's Irish, but far less entitled within the ranks of the Democratic Party. Adamowski portrayed Daley as a free-spending, high-tax mayor who was overly beholden to African Americans. Although Daley defeated Adamowski by more than 100,000 votes—a plurality that was largely due to overwhelming African American support—the 1963 mayoral campaign stiffened Daley's resolve to solidify his presumably natural electoral base, Chicago's "ethnic" working class. At the same time, Daley began to feel intense pressure from civil rights activists. In 1962 a citywide civil rights coalition, the Coordinating Council of Community Organizations (CCCO), was formed. By the fall of 1963, just months after Daley's triumph over Adamowski, the CCCO organized a one-day boycott that drew more than 200,000 schoolchildren from the Chicago Public Schools, with many attending impromptu "freedom schools" in local churches and at other neighborhood sites. Over the next several years the CCCO sought the removal of school superintendent Benjamin Willis, who had persistently resisted calls to integrate Chicago's public schools, and lobbied city council members to pass a binding open housing ordinance. In 1966 the CCCO brought Martin Luther King Jr. to Chicago to spearhead a final push to remove the barriers preventing African Americans from settling in neighborhoods across the city.

Much of Richard J. Daley's energy in 1966 was devoted to a prolonged sparring match with Reverend King, who worked with the CCCO to organize a series of marches—several through outlying Chicago neighborhoods and nearby suburbs. The marches brought out hectoring white mobs prepared, if given the opportunity, to physically clash with both civil rights marchers and their police escorts. In August of 1966, Daley and King signed a largely symbolic compact committing the city of Chicago and local realtors to a series of measures intended to end local residential segregation. The Daley/King agreement was unenforceable, but its signing permitted Reverend King to claim victory and move on from Chicago. Still, the impression of Richard J. Daley as an intransigent racist was now fixed. This impression was reinforced by subsequent events such as his famous "shoot to kill" order to Chicago police officers patrolling the riot-torn West Side in the days after the April 1968 murder of Reverend King, and the 1969 police raid and fatal shooting of Chicago Black Panther leader Fred Hampton.

During the 1960s Richard J. Daley had ready access to both Presidents Kennedy and Johnson, but nonetheless, his relationship with these Democratic Party colleagues was complicated. Daley was, for example, extremely skeptical of the Kennedy administration's anti–juvenile delinquency projects, as well as the Johnson administration's similarly participatory War on Poverty initiative, the Community Action Program (CAP). Indeed, Daley's centralized implementation of the CAP, which excluded grassroots organizations from any program oversight, generated intense local criticism. Administrators in the Office of Economic Opportunity, the federal agency overseeing CAP, repeatedly sought to pressure Daley into bringing Chicago's CAP structure and programs in line with the national initiative's specification of "bottom-up" implementation, but to little effect. Daley repeatedly went over the adminstrators' heads, directly appealing to President Johnson, who acquiesced to his ally's approach. On a very different matter, the Vietnam War, Daley also communicated his views directly to LBJ, in this instance opposing increased U.S. force commitments. Not recognized as a foreign policy expert, Daley's advice seems to have carried little weight. However, the overreaction of Daley's Chicago Police Department to antiwar protests directed at the 1968 Democratic National Convention in Chicago was the misstep that most critically undermined his national reputation and influence among Democratic Party leaders. In that fall's general election, Democratic presidential nominee Hubert Humphrey was narrowly defeated by Republican Richard Nixon, and more than a few Democrats assigned a good portion of the blame for Humphrey's loss to Richard J. Daley, who had been President Johnson's personal choice to host the Democratic Convention. Daley was held responsible for sullying the image of the party and validating Nixon's claim that the United States had descended into a state of chaotic lawlessness.

The lion of Chicago politics to the end of his life, even after the catastrophes of 1968, Richard J. Daley was never seriously challenged as municipal chief executive. In both 1971 and 1975 he handily won reelection, though it is clear that some combination of Cook County Democratic machine unraveling and voter alienation was at work. In the 1975 general election, Daley's vote total was 536,413, nearly 175,000 fewer votes than he had won in his first mayoral campaign; and for the first time since 1931 the total number of votes cast in a Chicago mayoral election fell short of 1 million. In these final years of his mayoralty, several of Daley's close allies were prosecuted and convicted on criminal charges related to their political activities, most notably, Daley's long-time city council floor leader Tom Keane. Subject to incessant interrogation by Chicago's press corps, the elderly Daley fell into the habit of public crankiness that became his enduring image. On December 20, 1976, Richard J. Daley—still on the job, having dedicated a new Chicago Park District gymnasium in the morning—succumbed to heart failure. The following day, not far from Daley's home in Bridgeport, approximately 25,000 Chicagoans braved subfreezing temperatures to pass his coffin, lying in state at Nativity of Our Lord Church. Across the United States, journalists and political analysts characterized Richard J. Daley's death as the end of an era.

The Second Coming, but Not Exactly

The youth and early political career of Richard J. Daley's eldest son, Richard M. Daley, was a classic case of a noteworthy lineage's mixed blessing. Like his father, an undistinguished scholar, Richard M. Daley began his postsecondary education at Providence College in Rhode Island, left Providence to return to Chicago and complete a bachelor's degree at DePaul University, and ultimately earned a law degree at DePaul. Richard M. Daley twice failed the Illinois Bar Examination, missteps that were noted by the Chicago press and became grist for the widely circulated proposition that the younger Daley *was not* the equal of his father. Richard M.'s first significant electoral triumph, at the age of 27 in 1969, earned him delegate status at the convention that rewrote the Illinois State Constitution in 1970. Richard M. Daley was not a key player at the state's constitutional convention, but the selection of delegates yielded a train of events with great consequence for Chicago politics. One of the losers in the delegates' election, a young attorney named Michael Shakman, subsequently filed a federal law suit claiming his First and Fourteenth Amendment constitutional rights had been violated by the practice of political patronage workers campaigning on behalf of Cook County Democratic machine-backed candidates. This practice substantially tilted local elections toward party-sponsored candidates. Shakman's petition led to an initial federal district court–approved consent decree in 1972, and over the following decades a series of follow-up "Shakman Decrees" greatly diminished the influence of politics in the hiring and firing decisions of the city of Chicago and other local jurisdictions such as the Chicago Park District.

In 1972 Richard M. Daley won a seat in the Illinois State Senate, and following his father's death, he became the 11th ward Democratic committeeman. The latter position, which had been held by the senior Daley for many decades, would pass on to Richard M.'s brother John in 1980. In that same year, Richard M. Daley won an interdynastic contest for the post of Cook County state's attorney. His opponent was Edward Burke, 14th ward alderman and ally of then mayor, Jane Byrne. Byrne, who expected Daley to enter the upcoming mayoral race in 1983, persuaded Burke to seek the state's attorney post, calculating that a Burke victory would impede her prospective mayoral challenger. However, Byrne bet on the wrong horse, and the recently elected State's Attorney Richard M. Daley would indeed seek to unseat her in 1983. When Congressman Harold Washington entered the Democratic mayoral primary that year, however, the contest became a three-way race that was narrowly won by Washington, who went on to win two general elections.

From 1981 until Chicago's special election for mayor in 1989 (following Washington's death due to heart failure in late 1987), Richard M. Daley retained his position as state's attorney, Cook County's chief public prosecutor. During that period, Daley rewrote his life narrative as the privileged, underperforming son of a great man. Press accounts characterized him as a detail-oriented executive who ran a largely apolitical agency. And further, during the racially charged mayoralty of Harold Washington, Chicago's first African American chief executive, Daley resolutely avoided taking sides. He never became an outright Washington partisan, but he also refused to endorse Washington critics such as Aldermen Edward Vrdolyak and Edward Burke. Ironically, as state's attorney Daley was evidently less detail-oriented than was widely supposed, and his failure to act on a simmering, racially tinged Chicago Police Department scandal became a blot on his long-term reputation.

During this period, police detective John Burge was routinely extracting confessions from detained African Americans by pressing them against heated radiator units, subjecting them to electric shocks, and otherwise abusing them. Complaints about these practices reached Chicago's superintendent of police, who in turn forwarded the information to the state's attorney office. During Daley's eight years as state's attorney he never authorized an investigation of these charges. Many years later, John Burge was fired by the Chicago Police Department, and a series of in-house and external investigations revealed hundreds of instances of police brutality committed at his direction.

Richard M. Daley handily won Chicago's mayoralty in the special election of 1989. In the Democratic Party primary, he defeated incumbent Eugene Sawyer, who had been selected mayor by the Chicago City Council following Washington's death. In the general election, Daley successfully competed in a three-way race that pitted him against Edward Vrydolak—now the nominee of the Republican Party—and Washington loyalist, Alderman Timothy Evans, running as the nominee of the short-lived Harold Washington Party. Richard M. Daley won both elections by comfortable margins, largely attributable to his success in projecting the image of a steady-handed chief executive who would pull Chicago back from the racially inflected policy disputes that plagued the Washington administration.

In fact, Richard M. Daley's approach to municipal governance was a work in progress. Like many incoming municipal chief executives, Daley's inclination was to advocate for major public works projects. In Daley's case, these included promoting a new airport to be developed in Chicago's economically declining far South Side, a downtown tram line, and a near-Loop gambling casino. However, none of these proposals bore fruit, in large part due to the absence of plausible funding sources and Daley's frosty relationship with Illinois governor Jim Edgar. As well, during Daley's first years as mayor, he remained widely suspect among Chicago African Americans, a constituency that had held the late Harold Washington in great esteem, and who viewed Richard M. Daley as an upstart determined to turn back the clock of Chicago politics. As late as the 1999 mayoral election, when he was challenged by U.S. 1st congressional district Representative Bobby Rush, Daley struggled to build a base of support among Chicago's African American voters. Nevertheless, by reaching out to African American pastors and taking pains to bring African American notables into his administration, by the early 2000s Richard M. had won over a sizable share of the city's African American electorate.

The 1990s were a noteworthy decade for Richard M. Daley, due in part to astute decision making and in part due to serendipity. In 1995, Daley supported state legislation overhauling the Chicago Public Schools, which permitted him to appoint a new school board and chief administrator. To fill the latter position, Daley chose a school policy novice, Paul Vallas, previously his budget director at City Hall. Over the next several years Vallas pursued a policy redirection that centralized public school operations, instituted a rigorous standardized testing regime, and aggressively reorganized or even closed underperforming schools. Actual improvement in Chicago public school student performance was slow to materialize, but Mayor Daley was given credit for taking decisive action to address a longstanding governmental problem. At the end of the decade, Daley was likewise praised for inaugurating the "Plan for Transformation," an ambitious program of high-rise public housing demolition, "mixed-income community" redevelopment, and privatized management. Again, the longer term impacts of the "Plan for Transformation" have been mixed, but Richard M. Daley once more earned plaudits for directly confronting the deficiencies of the much-maligned Chicago Housing Authority.

At the end of 1997 the public affairs journal *Governing* named Richard M. Daley as its Public Official of the Year, proposing that "he has been patient and skillful in mastering the details of local government, and remarkably creative in devising pragmatic solutions to the most complex problems." A few years before, a Springfield, Illinois–based publication, *Illinois Issues*, described Daley as "a mayor who keeps track of potholes and burned-out streetlights from the back seat of his city car, who familiarizes himself with arcane Building Department procedures . . ." Chicago's second Mayor Daley, at least in the eyes of national and local media, was comporting himself in a fashion that was highly reminiscent of his legendary father. Richard M. Daley, like his father, was neither master of the spoken word nor commanding policy wonk, but again, like his father, he was a determined practitioner of "mayoring."

However, as is the case with any governmental executive, some part of Richard M. Daley's success during the 1990s was a matter of chance. For example, Chicago was offered two notable "hosting opportunities" in the mid-1990s: in the summer of 1994, several early round matches of international soccer's World Cup—a competition held in the United States for the first time—were contested at the lakefront Soldier Field; and in 1996, the United Center, just west of downtown Chicago, hosted the Democratic Party's National Convention. In both instances the proceedings were executed without incident, and both national and international media representatives commented very favorably on Chicago's downtown vitality, architecture, and noteworthy cultural institutions. The 1990s were also a decade in which residential gentrification pushed into previously forlorn areas such as Wicker Park and Logan Square to the northwest of the Loop, the near West Side, and South Side Kenwood. In the latter case, Chicago for the first time witnessed a neighborhood gentrification process in which African Americans constituted the majority of newcomers. As a capstone to Richard M. Daley's great decade, 2000 U.S. Census tabulations revealed that for the first time since the decade of the 1940s the city of Chicago had added population.

The second half of Richard M. Daley's mayoralty was considerably less auspicious than the first. Ironically, Daley's single greatest success during the latter years of his administration also revealed him to be less the hard-nosed manager than many had supposed. In 1997 the mayor announced that the city planned to develop a new public space on the eastern edge of the Loop between Michigan Avenue and Lakeshore Drive, directly north of the Art Institute of Chicago. The new project, which was dubbed Millennium Park, would commemorate the coming turn of the millennia. The construction of Millennium Park was a very complicated process, both physically, due to its location above a commuter rail line and subterranean parking garages, and organizationally, due to the involvement of a small army of engineers, contractors, architects, sculptors, and landscapers. Millennium Park's opening ceremony missed the arrival of the new millennium by four years; its budget ballooned from $150 to $500 million. For the mayor, there was an initial godsend: Millennium Park was wildly popular with the public and much praised by architectural critics. Nonetheless, Mayor Daley was only saved from a likely tempest of criticism over cost overruns thanks to an aggressive private fund-raising campaign that generated approximately $200 million in donations. Even so, his reputation for fiscal prowess and attention to detail was sullied. This became especially apparent when, several years later, a *Chicago Tribune* reporter discovered that day-to-day Millennium Park operations were not funded via a conventional Chicago Park District line-item appropriation, but rather by issuing bonds.

By the early 2000s, Richard M. Daley was widely touted as among America's most innovative mayors, the proponent of a physical improvement agenda that emphasized both beautification and environmental sustainability, and an astute manipulator of emerging fiscal management tools. As examples of the latter, between 2006 and 2008 Daley's administration negotiated long-term leasing deals with private interests that took over the management of a South Side toll highway, city-owned parking garages, and streetside parking meters. The presumed benefit for the city government was the immediate payout of billions of dollars by the contracting organizations, which were to be set aside by the city as a "rainy day fund" and in anticipation of major public works initiatives. Each of the ordinances authorizing these privatization deals was rushed through the Chicago City Council, but when the actual takeover of the parking meters was executed by a company spun off from the Morgan

Stanley investment bank, public outrage likewise accelerated. Parking meter charges increased substantially, and there was widespread confusion regarding the monitoring of meters and the issuing of parking tickets. Moreover, by the end of Mayor Daley's tenure in 2011, press accounts revealed that a large portion of the so-called rainy day fund had actually been spent to fill holes in the city's operating budget. Similarly troubling was the revelation that during the same period, several public employee pension funds had been underfunded.

In 2004 another of Daley's innovative management projects blew up, in this instance revealing that political insiders continued to play a part in lubricating local politics and governance. In what came to be known as the "Hired Truck" scandal, *Chicago Sun-Times* reporters discovered that a program to scale back city government costs associated with vehicle purchase and maintenance—by using private vendors to service public works sites and the like—involved the recruitment of the vendors' employees to work on political campaigns and the owners of the trucking firms making campaign contributions to leading Chicago area Democratic Party politicians. Then, two years later, a major figure in the Daley administration, Robert Sorich, head of the Office of Intergovernmental Affairs, was convicted on criminal charges involving preferential hiring—barely disguised patronage hiring—within city government. Though Richard M. Daley was not directly connected to either of these scandals, his reputation as a scrupulous public manager was further tarnished.

In his final years as mayor, a large portion of Richard M. Daley's energy was spent promoting a Chicago bid to host the 2016 Olympics, an idea that was spawned by the city's civic elite. Mayor Daley initially dismissed the Olympics as a "construction industry," but was soon won over to the local quest for the games and accepted the post as bid committee cochair. Chicago's Olympic committee raised more than $70 million, won the support of the U.S. Olympic Committee, and in early 2009 was selected by the International Olympic Committee (IOC) as one of the four finalists in the 2016 Olympic host competition. However, by the summer of 2009 it was evident that local support for the Olympic proposal was shaky. The usually compliant city council had to be cajoled by Mayor Daley to pass an ordinance committing the city to absorb Olympic cost overruns. In a series of neighborhood hearings, local residents voiced concerns running the spectrum from Olympic-generated neighborhood gentrification to Olympic-induced tax increases. In any event, Chicago was saved from any such peril by the IOC, which in October 2009 rejected Chicago's bid in the first round of the host city "final four" voting.

Richard M. Daley—by this point in time Chicago's mayor for two decades—was clearly deflated by the Olympic defeat. He, along with many Chicagoans, had come to believe that the IOC's choice to host the 2016 Olympics *had to be* Chicago. Coincidentally, his wife Maggie suffered a recurrence of a previously treated cancerous condition, which ultimately led to her death on Thanksgiving Day 2010. By then, Richard M. Daley had announced that he would not seek reelection in 2011. Nevertheless, Daley's decision to retire caught both the public and press by surprise: Daleys don't walk away from positions of power, do they? In this case, the sources of Daley's decision were easy enough to discern: concern over his spouse's deteriorating health, frustration at Chicago's resounding failure in the Olympic host city competition, and the exhaustion that results from governing a large, complex city for more than two decades.

The Remaining Second Generation, and Beyond

At the time of her death in 2010, Richard M. Daley's wife, Maggie (née Margaret Ann Corbett), was a respected and long-serving member of Chicago's philanthropic elite. Maggie Daley had served on the boards of several Chicago cultural institutions, had been president of Pathways Awareness—a group advocating for children with disabilities—and had founded "After School Matters," an organization offering arts training to impoverished young people. Interestingly, After School Matters also achieved some notoriety for reasons that were highly emblematic of the shifting contours of Chicago politics and public policy. In the fall of 2011, Chicago's municipal inspector general issued a report documenting that major sources of funding for After School Matters were firms that had received city government fiscal support via the neighborhood development tool known as tax increment financing (TIF). Maggie Daley was not linked in any way to possible quid pro quos involving TIF subsidies and After School Matters contributions, but the presumption that government/private sector "partnership" could yield such arrangements was typical of Chicago's political climate in the early 2000s. Though few observable vestiges of the old Democratic machine remained, because of the Daley family's long domination of the city's government and politics, many observers presumed that a carryover culture of clientelistic political dealmaking persisted. In the future, Maggie Daley may be best remembered in the designation of a carefully planned public space dedicated to young persons—Maggie Daley Park—which opened in 2014 just east of Millennium Park.

Two of Richard M. Daley's brothers, William and John, have also had political careers of note, though they followed very different tracks. William "Bill" Daley served as secretary of commerce under President Clinton, and for a year he was President Obama's White House chief of staff. His other political jobs have included managing electoral campaigns—early in his career for his brother Richard, the near-miss presidential candidacy of Al Gore in 2000—and working on the Clinton administration team that lobbied Congress on behalf of the North America Free Trade Agreement. On several occasions, Bill Daley has contemplated running for elected office, in particular for Illinois governor in 2002 and 2014, but he did not formally enter either of these elections. When not working in government, or on Democratic Party matters, Daley has held influential corporate positions at Mayer, Brown & Platt (the law firm now known as Mayer Brown), SBC (corporate descendant of Southwestern Bell Telephone), and J. P. Morgan Chase. In each instance, Bill Daley's role focused on "outreach," both to private sector clients and governmental entities.

John Daley, in contrast, has been a longtime officeholder and power wielder at the local level. Like his father and brother Richard, John's political career began in Springfield, Illinois, holding seats in the state legislature. Since 1992 John Daley has served on the Cook County board of commissioners, the unit overseeing nonmunicipal governmental operations in Cook County outside the city of Chicago. For many years, the local press characterized John Daley as the "power behind the throne" of Cook County Board President John Stroger. Since 1980, Daley has held that most iconic of local Chicago political positions, 11th ward Democratic Party committeeman. His predecessors in that position were, of course, Richard J. and Richard M. Daley. Journalists frequently note that John is the only second-generation Daley to remain a Bridgeport neighborhood resident.

In Chicago's 2015 city council elections, a *third* generation Daley, Patrick Daley Thompson, was elected alderman from the 11th ward. Patrick Thompson is the son of Richard M. Daley's sister, Patricia, who—after her divorce from her husband, William Thompson—returned to Bridgeport to raise her children. Patrick Thompson is thus another Daley from the old neighborhood. Prior to his election to the Chicago City Council, Patrick had served as an elected commissioner on one of Chicago's arcane special purpose governments, the Metropolitan Water Reclamation District. In his brief tenure on the city council, Patrick Thompson has not emerged as an especially commanding figure, but given his pedigree, some expect he will seek higher office. For example, at the time of his election to the city council, a *Chicago Magazine* article profiling Thompson was titled "Could Patrick Daley Thompson Be Chicago's Mayor in 2019?"

The "Honorary" Daleys

Like the Kennedy family dynasty of Massachusetts, the Daleys have cultivated numerous allied and in some cases very accomplished political figures: honorary Daleys. In his study of race and politics in Chicago, *Bitter Fruit*, political scientist William Grimshaw identified a group of "loyalist" African American politicians whose careers were advanced by Richard J. Daley. This group included two aldermen, Eugene Sawyer and John Stroger, who would go on to serve as Chicago's mayor and Cook County Board of Commissioners president, respectively. Stroger clearly entertained his own dynastic ambitions. After he suffered a stroke in 2006, his political allies—including fellow commissioner, John Daley—executed a behind-the-scenes maneuver that permitted Stroger's son, Todd, to succeed him as president of the Cook County Board. Other honorary Daleys indebted to Richard J. Daley include Michael Bilandic, his successor as mayor, and Jane Byrne, Daley's figurehead "cochair" of the Cook County Democrats, longshot victor in the 1979 mayoral contest, and the municipality's first female chief executive. The most notable first-generation honorary Daley was, without question, Congressman Dan Rostenkowski, known for many years as "Daley's man in Washington," who served for more than a decade as chair of the House of Representatives' powerful Ways and Means Committee. The son of a Chicago alderman, Rostenkowski's most notable congressional achievement was his collaboration with the Reagan administration in the passage of the 1986 tax reform bill.

Second-generation honorary Daleys have also achieved national prominence, most notably David Axelrod and Rahm Emanuel. Axelrod was a political reporter who shifted to political consulting in the late 1980s. Among his early clients was Richard M. Daley, but Axelrod's great claim to fame is his political communications work for Barack Obama, both as candidate and as president. Early in his career Emanuel was a Richard M. Daley staffer. His subsequent political positions have included aide to President Bill Clinton, U.S. congressman, White House chief of staff for the first two years of Obama's presidency, and from 2011, mayor of Chicago.

The Daleys and American Politics

The "two-plus" generation Daley political dynasty has been rooted in successfully adapting to and in turn shaping the rules of Chicago politics. The Daleys' influence, however, has extended beyond Chicago, and the evolution of the Daley political worldview—as expressed on the one hand by Richard J. Daley, and on the other by sons Richard M. and Bill—very closely tracks the shifting identity of Democrats nationally since the mid-20th century. Richard J. Daley was an immigrant-descended politician whose local Democratic Party organization thrived in an environment of ethnically inflected neighborhood-level mobilization that was largely free of ideology but determinedly clientelistic in practice. Individuals who involved themselves in politics did so out of perceived self-interest, and the mutual bonds that cemented collective action were largely matters of interpersonal exchange: campaign workers expected to be rewarded; campaign victors used their public positions to cement the loyalty of their supporters.

This form of political activism coexisted uncomfortably with the more ideologically and programmatically driven politics of Franklin Roosevelt's New Deal. Nevertheless, through the 1950s and into the 1960s, local Chicago Democrats like Richard J. Daley offered constituents a local government that provided expansive day-to-day services and even economic stimulus through federal programs such as urban renewal, public housing, and highway construction. These were initiatives that presidential administrations and the Congress defined as important not only to cities, but also in the national interest. As late as Lyndon Johnson's War on Poverty, these programs put millions of Americans to work either directly or indirectly, and were indeed affordable, given an expanding postwar economy and a citizenry still tolerant of taxation dedicated to widely popular public purposes.

In the early 1970s, however, the functional, if awkward alliance of Roosevelt and Daley-style Democrats collapsed. Civil rights activism discredited the white privilege that was intrinsic to big city ethnic machine politics. A slow growth economic era followed the oil embargo of 1973, and the American citizenry's tolerance of large-scale public initiatives funded by their hard-earned dollars began its downward slide. The conservative critique of federal social welfare and urban-focused spending fueled the 1968 election of President Nixon, and peaked with Ronald Reagan's triumph in 1980. In response, "New Democrats" such as Arkansas governor Bill Clinton nudged their party toward the perceived center of the ideological spectrum. By the time Richard M. Daley became the master of Chicago in the early 1990s, his mayoral program tracked very closely the New Democratic agenda of President Clinton: government could be "good," but to do so it needed to collaborate with business; for Democrats to flourish, special outreach to women, racial minorities, and other marginalized constituencies was mandatory, but "standing up for the working class" was no longer a priority. As a much-praised mayor and effective political campaigner, Richard M. Daley was as free of ideology as his father, but his political methods departed substantially from his father's, and the groups that he attempted to reach were even further afield. The city of Chicago remains a heavily Democratic city in much the same way as Boston, Los Angeles, New York, and San Francisco. As such, it is unclear what particular local genius upcoming Daleys might bring to the politics of their city. The Daley brand is largely indistinguishable from the Democratic brand across the United States. Whether or not the most recent generation of Democrats can craft a more compelling narrative of the American future, and build a coalition that includes a substantial portion of the American suburban and rural populations—a vision and movement strong enough to once more become the shaping force in American politics—remains to be seen. Considered within this broader context, the Daley-style politics of Richard M., Bill, and John does not appear to be the likeliest of seedbeds for reinvigorating the Democratic Party.

Further Reading

Bennett, Larry. *The Third City: Chicago and American Urbanism*. Chicago: University of Chicago Press, 2010.

Carlson, Peter. "Dan Rostenkowski Goes Down in History," *Washington Post*, October 17, 1993. Accessed May 27, 2017, at https://www.washingtonpost.com/archive/lifestyle/magazine/1993/10/17/dan-rostenkowski-goes-down-in-history/d620fee1-5367-4213-a754-2b8c46d6873d/?utm_term=.8b71217d875f.

Cohen, Adam, and Elizabeth Taylor. *American Pharaoh: Mayor Richard J. Daley: His Battle for Chicago and the Nation*. Boston: Back Bay Books, 2001.

Dardick, Hal. "Millennium Park Built 'the Chicago Way,'" *Chicago Tribune*, July 14, 2014, pp. 1, 6.

Ehrenhalt, Alan. "Master of Detail," *Governing*, December 1997, p. 22.

Felsenthal, Carol. "Brother Bill: A Look at William Daley," *Chicago Magazine*, February 2005. Accessed May 27, 2017, at http://www.chicagomag.com/Chicago-Magazine/February-2005/Brother-Bill-A-Look-at-William-Daley/index.php?cparticle=2&siarticle=1#artanc.

Gilfoyle, Timothy J. *Millennium Park: Creating a Chicago Landmark*. Chicago: University of Chicago Press, 2006.

Goodman, Barak, Dir. "Daley: The Last Boss," *American Experience*, Season 8, Episode 5, January 22, 1996.

Grimshaw, William J. *Bitter Fruit: Black Politics and the Chicago Machine, 1931–1991*. Chicago: University of Chicago Press, 1992.

Kass, John, and Richard Jones. "Bridgeport Bomb: Daleys Housing Hunting," *Chicago Tribune*, April 1, 1993. Accessed March 27, 2017, at http://www.upi.com/Archives/1993/04/01/No-April-fool-Daley-may-leave-Bridgeport/5359733640400.

Koeneman, Keith. *First Son: The Biography of Richard M. Daley*. Chicago: University of Chicago Press, 2013.

Liebling, A. J. *Chicago: The Second City*. New York: Knopf, 1952.

O'Connor, Len. *Clout: Mayor Daley and His City*. Chicago: Contemporary Books, 1984.

Office of Inspector General, City of Chicago. "Report of the Inspector General's Office: Review of TIF Public Benefits Clauses and Charitable Donations." Chicago, 2011. Accessed May 27, 2017, at http://www.chicagobusiness.com/assets/downloads/TIF.pdf.

"Remembering Richard J. Daley," Special Collection at the University of Illinois at Chicago Library: http://rjd.library.uic.edu.

Rivlin, Gary. *Fire of the Prairie: Harold Washington, Chicago Politics, and the Roots of the Obama Presidency*. Philadelphia: Temple University Press, 2013.

Rivlin, Gary. "San-Fran-York on the Lake," in *I May Be Wrong, But I Doubt It*. Chicago: Henry Regnery, 1967, pp. 3–6.

Roeder, David H. "Mayor Daley as Conciliator," *Illinois Issues*, April 1994, pp. 23–27.

Royko, Mike. *Boss: Richard J. Daley of Chicago.* New York: Signet, 1971.
Spirou, Costas, and Dennis R. Judd. *Building the City of Spectacle: Mayor Richard M. Daley and the Remaking of Chicago.* Ithaca, NY: Cornell University Press, 2016.
Walsh, Edward. "Letter from Bridgeport," *Washington Post,* December 26 1993. Accessed March 27, 2017, at https://www.washingtonpost.com/archive/politics/1993/12/26/letter-from-bridgeport/66003fa0-2ad6-4c16-818c-d85ee2f43c64/?utm_term=.853001d0fb45.

CHAPTER EIGHTEEN

The Dingell Dynasty

Julio L. Borquez

Based on the definition of a political dynasty as "one or a small number of families who dominate the power distribution in a particular geographic region," the Dingell family neatly fits the bill. A member of the Dingell family has served in the U.S. House of Representatives continuously since 1933, representing a district in southeastern Michigan. John D. Dingell Sr. was first elected to the House in 1932 and served until his death in September 1955. His son, John D. Dingell Jr., won a special election to succeed his father and served in the House from December 1955 until his retirement in January 2015, making him the longest serving member in the history of the institution. John Dingell Jr.'s wife, Debbie Dingell, was elected to the House in 2014 and was reelected in 2016.

One of John Dingell Jr.'s sons, Christopher Dingell, has pursued a different career path. Christopher Dingell studied metallurgy in college before earning a law degree. He served in the Michigan State Senate from 1987 to 2003. Christopher Dingell's focus turned toward Michigan state judicial politics, and since 2003 he has served as a judge for the 3rd Circuit Court in Wayne County.

The Dingell dynasty lacks the celebrity and drama of some of the other dynasties covered in this volume. There are no sibling rivalries or competing ambitions, no intergenerational tensions, no presidential aspirations. But the Dingell dynasty is instructive in illustrating the interplay between (1) family ambition and political enterprise, and (2) institutional developments in American politics.

The Dingell dynasty is rooted principally in the U.S. House of Representatives, and that will be the focus of this chapter. Because the Dingell name is so closely associated with the House, the profile and influence of the Dingells over time have been tied to developments in the House as an institution, as well as the ebb and flow of American party politics. The eight decades (and counting) in which a Dingell has served in the House have seen changes in the importance of seniority as well as the power of committees and committee chairs, the advent of daunting incumbent advantage in congressional elections, switches in party control of the House, and a sharp increase in partisan polarization in the House. Over time, these considerations have both enhanced and limited the scope of the Dingell dynasty. At the same time, the dynasty has been sustained by the initiative and political savvy of successive generations of Dingells.

John D. Dingell Sr.

John D. Dingell Sr. was born in Detroit in 1894 as John Dzieglewicz. He worked in a variety of occupations, including construction, wholesale pork and beef, and newspaper printing. While working as a printer for the *Detroit Free Press*, he became a union organizer.

Michigan gained five House seats after the 1930 Census. By this time, John Dzieglewicz had changed his name to John Dingell, and he ran as a Democrat in the newly created 15th congressional district. At the time, the district encompassed western Detroit.

Congressman John D. Dingell of Michigan in January 1939. (Library of Congress)

Dingell Political Dynasty Family Tree

1. John D. Dingell Sr., 1894–1955
   U.S. House of Representatives, 1933–1955
   Married Grace Bigler
   Three children including John D. Dingell Jr.

2. John D. Dingell Jr., 1926–
   U.S. House of Representatives, 1955–2015
   Married Helen Henebry, 1952–1972
   Four children including Christopher Dingell
   Married Debbie Insley, 1981–

3. Christopher Dingell, 1957–
   Michigan State Senate, 1987–2003
   Judge, 3rd Circuit Court, Wayne County, Michigan, 2003–

Debbie Dingell (formerly Insley), 1953–
   U.S. House of Representatives, 2015–

During his tenure in the House, Dingell was a reliable New Deal Democrat and was a sponsor of the legislation that created Social Security. The most notable legacy of his career was his support for national health insurance. He introduced a national health insurance bill at the beginning of every congressional session, a practice that was maintained by his son. But Dingell's New Deal liberalism on economic and social welfare issues was tempered by less liberal positions on other matters; in August 1941, he suggested that 10,000 Japanese-Hawaiian Americans be held by the federal government in order to ensure "good behavior" on the part of Japan.

John Dingell Sr. pursued a particular strain of liberal Democratic politics—unfailing support for concrete social welfare initiatives, balanced by more cautious positions on other issues, such as racial equality—that became a template for his descendants. Both John Dingell Jr. and Debbie Dingell developed their own versions of this approach.

John D. Dingell Jr.

John D. Dingell Jr. was born in Colorado in 1926, where the family was seeking a cure for his father's tuberculosis. Dingell moved with his family to Washington, DC, when his father was first elected to the U.S. House of

Congressman John D. Dingell Jr. of Michigan in September 1981. (Library of Congress)

Representatives, and the House became a focal point of his youth. Dingell attended Georgetown Preparatory School and worked as a page on the floor of the House from 1938 to 1943. Following service in the U.S. Army from 1944 to 1946, Dingell returned to Washington and enrolled at Georgetown University, where he earned his bachelor's degree and his law degree. After law school in 1952, Dingell worked briefly in private practice and as a research assistant to a U.S. circuit judge. He then moved back to Michigan and served as an assistant prosecutor for Wayne County.

When his father died in 1955, Dingell Jr. won a special election to finish his congressional term. At the time, the congressional district still covered western Detroit. Dingell won his first full term in 1956 with 77 percent of the vote. What followed was a remarkable record of electoral success. Including the 1955 special election, Dingell was elected to the U.S. House 30 times. In his 29 campaigns for full terms (1956–2012), Dingell twice ran unopposed, received at least 70 percent of the vote on 18 occasions, received less than 60 percent of the vote only once, and always won by double-digit margins (Office of the House Clerk). Over the years, Dingell deftly used all of the tools that have contributed to incumbent advantage in modern congressional campaigns: superior name recognition and fund-raising capacity, an ability to shape local media coverage, and attention to casework and constituency service.

Dingell's only serious electoral challenges came in two Democratic primaries, when he was forced to run against fellow Democratic incumbents due to redistricting and consolidation of the district boundaries. In 1966, much of Dingell's 15th district was merged with the neighboring 16th district, represented by Democrat John Lesinski Jr. It was at this point that Dingell first campaigned in the Detroit suburb Dearborn, which later became recognized as his political home base. After defeating Lesinski in the Democratic primary, Dingell easily won the general election. Similarly in 2002, Dingell found much

The Dingell Dynasty

of his existing 16th district merged with an adjacent district, the 13th district, held by Democrat Lynn Rivers. Facing voters in the liberal university community of Ann Arbor (home of the University of Michigan main campus) for the first time, Dingell defeated Rivers in the Democratic primary with 59 percent of the vote, and went on to win the general election with 72 percent of the vote.[1]

The political importance of the Dingell family is based in no small part on the longevity of John Dingell Jr., but the more critical foundation for the dynasty is the clout and influence that Dingell Jr. developed during his long career. As a House colleague summarized, "His strength comes because he takes the skill he has and combines it with good staff work, a thorough knowledge of the issues and a bulldog determination not to let go. He is the most tenacious member of Congress."[2]

Overall, Dingell's political and policy outlook was much like his father's. He was reliably liberal on bread-and-butter social welfare issues like health care and Social Security. Of course, this was not simply a matter of family influence; it was also a product of his congressional district. Throughout his career, Dingell's congressional district had a strong manufacturing base. The district was (and still is) home to Ford Motor Company's corporate headquarters as well as its engineering and manufacturing facilities. Early iterations of the district included Ford's massive Rouge assembly plant. The blue-collar character of his district motivated Dingell's focus on economic social welfare concerns.

The importance of the auto industry in southeastern Michigan set boundaries on Dingell's liberalism, especially on environmental policy. An avid hunter, Dingell enjoyed the outdoors and helped establish some popular recreation areas in his district. But he generally received higher marks from "conservationist" groups than from "environmentalist" groups. Organizations like the Sierra Club often took issue with Dingell's efforts to balance clean air and fuel mileage standards with concerns for the well-being of the auto manufacturers and auto factory jobs. Dingell was also a supporter of gun rights, receiving A+ ratings from the National Rifle Association. Dingell's stances on the environment and guns put him at odds with some of his liberal colleagues in the Democratic caucus, but these positions resonated with many of his working-class Democratic constituents back in Michigan.

The most important factor in Dingell's ascension to congressional influence, and to his later decline from his leadership role in the institution, was his chairmanship of the House Energy and Commerce Committee. Dingell entered the House at a time when committee chairs had more independent authority than they do today. He assumed the chairmanship of the Energy and Commerce Committee in 1981 and didn't relinquish that post until 1995, after Republicans took majority control of the House. However, Dingell still served as the ranking Democrat on the committee until 2007, when he regained the chairmanship following the Democrats' retaking of House control. Dingell's second stint as committee chair was short-lived, as he lost the position to California congressman Henry Waxman in a Democratic caucus meeting in November 2008.

During the 1980s, the Energy and Commerce Committee handled approximately 40 percent of all House bills, giving Dingell tremendous visibility and clout. At the time, the *Almanac of American Politics* described him as "one of the three or four most powerful Members of the House." Even more succinctly, *Washington Monthly* singled out Dingell as "the best congressman."

The Energy and Commerce Committee provided an effective mechanism by which Dingell could shape policy critical to southeastern Michigan. This was vividly illustrated by his work on clean air legislation during the 1980s. In the early part of the decade, the Reagan White House pushed regulatory changes in an attempt to weaken the Clean Air Act of 1970 and its 1977 follow-up. Dingell, conscious of the impact of the bills' requirements on an already ailing auto industry, attempted to work with the Reagan administration, framing his approach as a path to protecting jobs. Unfortunately for Dingell, his early 1980s effort was stymied by proenvironment Democrats in the House, primarily Henry Waxman of California.

Dingell and Waxman would go on to have a rocky, though at times productive, relationship over the years. The tension between Dingell and Waxman was due partially to ideological and personality differences, but it was also driven by their perceptions of each other's districts, and their instincts to protect their own constituents. For his part, Dingell sometimes expressed annoyance about Californians who loved their cars but were unconcerned about the midwesterners who built them.[3]

By the late 1980s, the new administration of President George H. W. Bush began work on new clean air legislation, with a special focus on dealing with acid rain. Dingell realized that new legislation could place new burdens on the automobile industry. But he also realized that some kind of bill was likely to pass; the Bush White House wanted a bill, and proenvironment Democrats in Congress wanted a bill. Dingell used his position on the Energy and Commerce Committee not so much to try to stop legislation but rather to shape a bill that would limit harm to the auto industry. That would require working with Waxman, who was aggressively pushing for more stringent environmental standards. And it would require reassuring the auto industry, who at times worried that their ally, who was looking for paths toward compromise and accommodation, was backing down. The resulting Clean Air Act of 1990 did indeed impose stiffer emissions standards on the auto industry, but Dingell was able to engineer some key concessions at critical stages in the legislative process. Even though Dingell was facing stiff political headwinds, he made effective use of his institutional resources as committee chair to keep a place at the policy-making table, maintain his own stature in the House, and achieve useful policy outcomes for his constituents.

Another key development in Congress during Dingell's career was the increased emphasis on congressional oversight.[4] Once thought to be a secondary function, congressional committees in the 1970s and 1980s began to devote more time and attention to monitoring the implementation of policies by executive branch agencies. The broad jurisdiction of the Energy and Commerce Committee gave Dingell ample opportunity to hold hearings, issue subpoenas, and conduct investigations. Dingell was known for his aggressive questioning of executive agency officials. His efforts uncovered wrongdoing at the Environmental Protection Agency and the Food and Drug Administration, leading to resignations, and in some cases, jail time. His committee famously exposed a Defense Department contract to purchase $600 toilet seats.[5] Other high-profile investigations targeted scientific fraud by researchers who had received government grants.

Dingell's influence in the House was significantly diminished when Republicans took control of the chamber following the 1994 election. In his new role as ranking Democrat on the Energy and Commerce Committee, he was no longer in a position to shape the legislative agenda or spearhead investigations. The 2006 election returned the House control to the Democrats, and Dingell briefly stepped back into his role as Energy and Commerce Committee chair; however, the previous Republican leadership had pared down the committee's jurisdiction, leaving Dingell with less reach over policy. Moreover, Dingell did not regain his position as chair of the subcommittee for oversight, so he no longer had that high-profile platform.

Back in the 1980s, there were already hints that House party leadership was trying to limit the autonomy of committees and committee chairs. These efforts intensified under Republican leadership during the 1990s, and the shift toward more centralized party control continued under the Democrats after 2006. This further constrained Dingell's previous levels of influence. Another critical blow to Dingell's clout came in 2009, when Henry Waxman challenged him for the chairmanship of the Energy and Commerce Committee. House Speaker Nancy Pelosi, a longtime political ally of Waxman, backed the move, and he defeated Dingell 137–122 in a Democratic caucus vote.

In February 2014, Dingell announced his intention to retire from Congress at the end of his term. By then, he felt an acute frustration with the House as an institution. He saw it driven increasingly by polarization and acrimony rather than bipartisanship and collegiality. "I find serving in the House to be obnoxious," was one of his final observations.[6]

Debbie Dingell

Within a week of his retirement announcement, John Dingell's wife, Debbie Dingell, announced her candidacy to succeed him in the U.S. House of Representatives. That sparked a round of media commentary decrying the prospect of a continued Dingell dynasty. Interestingly, that commentary came from across the political spectrum. The conservative *Weekly Standard* opined "two generations of Dingells is more than enough." In their view, John Dingell's career encapsulated failed Democratic Party policies, which would only be continued by Debbie Dingell. The more progressive *Huffington Post* compared the Dingells to the British aristocrats portrayed on "Downton Abbey." Much of the commentary argued that after John Dingell's 59 years in the House, the institution needed new blood and new perspectives, things that Debbie Dingell presumably could not provide. The unstated assumption of much of the writing seemed to be that Debbie Dingell would be a political carbon copy of her husband. The reality is a bit more complicated.

Debbie Dingell was born Deborah Insley in 1953. She grew up in a prominent Michigan automotive family, the Fishers, who founded Fisher Body, a longtime division of General Motors (GM). Deborah Insley grew up a Republican, and her interest in public affairs was reflected in her studies at Georgetown University, where she graduated from its School of Foreign Service. She embarked on a career as a lobbyist for General Motors, rising to the position of executive director for Global Community Relations and Government Relations.

Deborah Insley married John Dingell Jr. in 1981 (he and his first wife divorced in 1972), at which time she switched her party affiliation from Republican to Democrat and moved to a less expressly political job at GM, eventually serving as president of the General Motors Foundation. Some liberal political watchdog groups expressed concerns about possible conflicts of interest due to John Dingell's marriage to a high-level GM employee. But as one wiseacre put it, "John Dingell was married to General Motors long before he was married to Debbie."[7]

Before she entered electoral politics herself in 2014, Debbie Dingell's career enabled her to cultivate a broad-based network of contacts and working relationships, a good deal of it independent of her husband. In addition to her work for GM, Debbie Dingell had been a consultant to the American Automobile Policy Council, president of the consulting firm D2 Strategies, a member of the Democratic National Committee, and a regular commentator for national and regional media, such as Fox News Channel, MSNBC, and Detroit Public Television. She regularly organized bipartisan congressional retreats and hosted an annual women's "friendship luncheon" in Washington.

Debbie Dingell's policy preferences parallel John Dingell's in many ways, though she differs from him on some key matters. Despite her Republican upbringing, she espouses traditionally liberal Democratic positions on social welfare issues like health care and Social Security. She also shares John Dingell's priorities for supporting the automobile industry and manufacturing jobs in southeastern Michigan. In that sense, Debbie Dingell has carried on the legacy of a distinct, balanced variety of Democratic liberalism. At the same time, she is more liberal (or at least more eloquent) than John Dingell on gender equity concerns, and she is more open to gun safety proposals.

The Dingell Dynasty

Debbie Dingell easily won election to the House in 2014 and faced only token opposition in 2016. The long-term electoral outlook for Debbie Dingell is very positive. In its current configuration, the 12th congressional district is solidly Democratic. Yet the district is home to two contrasting sets of Democratic voters. Monroe County, south of Detroit, is still built largely around manufacturing and other blue-collar employment. The Democrats there resemble the Reagan Democrats made famous by Stanley Greenberg's focus group research in nearby Macomb County.[8] These Democrats place a high priority on jobs and basic economic security. By contrast, Washtenaw County, west of Detroit, is characterized by a more "postmaterial" liberalism.[9] The economic and political hub of Washtenaw County is Ann Arbor, a quintessential liberal college town. The Democrats in Ann Arbor tend to be well educated and affluent, and therefore they assign more weight to issues concerning the environment, education, and gender equity, and are less concerned with basic economic security.

The Dingell dynasty is undoubtedly a campaign asset to Debbie Dingell. She entered electoral politics as a Dingell, not as a product of either Ann Arbor or Monroe County politics. That, as well as her distinct brand of Dingell liberalism, allows her to appeal to disparate sets of Democratic voters. Her traditional liberal views on bread-and-butter economic issues and her attention to auto industry concerns—in the mold of both John Dingell Sr. and Jr.—play well in Monroe County. And her more progressive approach to postmaterial issues resonates in Ann Arbor.

Just as John Dingell sometimes found himself out of sync with the leftward drift of the Democratic caucus, Debbie Dingell has expressed concerns about finding her niche in Democratic House politics. And like her husband, she has pointed to tensions between the auto industry and environmentalists as especially vexing.[10] Although her status as a Dingell can certainly be beneficial on election day, it can also complicate her relationships on Capitol Hill, notably with the Democratic leadership in the House. Minority Leader Nancy Pelosi butted heads with John Dingell more than once; in 2002 she endorsed Lynn Rivers over Dingell in the Democratic primary, and she supported Henry Waxman's efforts to unseat Dingell as chair of the Energy and Commerce Committee. Debbie Dingell and Nancy Pelosi both state that their own working relationship is amicable, but they also acknowledge its awkward history.

When defined by campaign success, Debbie Dingell enjoys a clear path to maintaining a Dingell dynasty; but when it comes to continuing a legacy of influence in policy making, the path is more challenging. As a Democrat, Debbie Dingell is part of the House minority. Thus, she has no clear leverage in shaping the legislative agenda or congressional oversight efforts. The partisan polarization that left John Dingell so dismayed has not diminished, so opportunities for bipartisan policy making are quite limited.

Based on this outlook, it might be tempting to conclude that the Dingell dynasty is entering its twilight as a political force in the House and in the

Democratic Party. The Dingell style of Democratic party liberalism, which still has firm roots in the New Deal, might seem outdated in the current Democratic Party. Back in the 1990s, John Dingell Jr. served as a bridge between "old bull" New Deal–style Democrats and Clinton-era New Democrats, as well as more conservative Blue Dog Democrats. His tenacity, pragmatism, and tempered liberalism enabled him to communicate and collaborate with disparate party factions. By now, of course, the Blue Dogs are extinct, the New Democrat movement (and its primary infrastructure, the Democratic Leadership Council) is defunct, and the Democratic House caucus is decidedly, and more uniformly, liberal.[11]

But as the Democrats try to come to grips with Donald Trump's victory in the 2016 presidential election, there might still be a place in the party for the Dingell brand of liberalism. During the 2016 campaign, Debbie Dingell warned that her Monroe County constituents might break for Trump (Dingell, 2016). Unlike most of her Democratic colleagues, she has direct experience in balancing outreach to working-class Democrats with appeals to more upper-income progressive Democrats. Her district poses many of the challenges that vexed Democrats in Michigan, Wisconsin, and Pennsylvania during the 2016 campaign. Perhaps the next chapter in the Dingell dynasty will be to provide an example of how to repair the Democrat's industrial state "blue wall." It would not be the first time the Dingell dynasty had set an example for Democrats in other parts of the country.

The Dingell dynasty has been important not only for Michigan politics but in the Democratic Party nationally. In particular, the Dingell family embodied a middle-of-the-road liberalism that allowed the Democratic Party to maintain long-term dominance in central Michigan, despite the conservative views of many working-class Michiganders. As new left activists of the 1960s increasingly challenged the Democratic Party's old-style economic liberalism of the New Deal, John Dingell Jr. adeptly maneuvered the divide; but more than simply survive politically, he held to anchor the party in the 1970s to its New Deal roots in ways vital to its strength nationally, in spite of only four years with a Democratic president in nearly two decades.

Notes

1. Barone, Michael, and Richard E. Cohen. *The Almanac of American Politics, 2004*. Washington, DC: National Journal, 2003.

2. Cohen, Richard E. *Washington at Work: Back Rooms and Clean Air*, 2nd ed. Boston: Allyn and Bacon, 1995, p. 33.

3. Ibid.

4. Aberbach, Joel. *Keeping a Watchful Eye: The Politics of Congressional Oversight*. Washington, DC: Brookings, 1991.

5. Barone, Michael, and Grant Ujifusa. *The Almanac of American Politics, 1996*. Washington, DC: National Journal, 1995.

6. Hulse, Carl, and Ashley Parker. "John Dingell to Retire after Nearly 60 Years in House." *New York Times*, February 24, 2014.

7. Cohen, Richard E. *Washington at Work: Back Rooms and Clean Air*, 2nd ed. Boston: Allyn and Bacon, 1995, p. 23.

8. Greenberg, Stanley B. *Middle Class Dreams*. New York: Times Books, 1995.

9. Ingelhart, Ronald D. *The Silent Revolution: Changing Values and Political Styles among Western Publics*. Princeton, NJ: Princeton University Press, 1977.

10. Capehart, Jonathan. "One Democrat Knew Trump Would Win. Now She Struggles to Find a Place in Her Own Party." *Washington Post*, June 20, 2017.

11. Baer, Kenneth S. *Reinventing Democrats: The Politics of Liberalism from Reagan to Clinton*. Lawrence: University Press of Kansas Press, 2000.

Further Reading

Borquez, Julio, and Donna Wasserman. "Press Coverage of the Lynn Rivers–John Dingell Congressional Primary Campaign: Patterns of Incumbent Advantage in an Incumbent-versus-Incumbent Contest." *Harvard International Journal of Press/Politics*, vol. 9, no. 1, 60–74.
Bruni, Frank. "Public Lives: The Whirlwind Life of (Not Just) a Political Wife." *New York Times*, March 22, 1999.
Crawford, Craig. "The Dingell Dynasty." *Huffington Post*, February 26, 2014.
Davidson, Roger H., Walter J. Oleszek, Francis E. Lee, and Eric Schickler. *Congress and Its Members*, 15th ed. Washington, DC: CQ Press, 2015.
Dingell, John David, and David Bender. *The Dean: The Best Seat in the House, from FDR to Obama*. New York: HarperCollins, 2018.
Jacobson, Gary C. *The Politics of Congressional Elections*, 8th ed. Boston: Pearson, 2012.
King, David C. *Turf Wars: How Congressional Committees Claim Jurisdiction*. Chicago: University of Chicago Press, 1997.
Mann, Thomas E., and Norman J. Ornstein. *It's Even Worse Than It Looks*. New York: Basic Books, 2012.
Mataconis, Doug. "Debbie Dingell, Political Dynasties, and the Problem with Long-Term Incumbency." *Outside the Beltway*, August 7, 2014.
McCarty, Nolan, Keith T. Poole, and Howard Rosenthal. *Polarized America: The Dance of Ideology and Unequal Riches*. Cambridge, MA: MIT Press, 2006.
Palmer, Anna. "Dingell Hat Trick: Debbie to Run." *Politico*, February 25, 2014.
Shea, Bill. "Debbie Dingell: 'Way beyond' Other Political Wives." *Crain's Detroit Business*, December 12, 2010.
Sinclair, Barbara. *Party Wars: Polarization and the Politics of National Policymaking*. Norman: University of Oklahoma Press, 2006.
Stolberg, Sheryl Gay. "Debbie Dingell Ready for Spotlight as Her Husband, the 'Dean' of Congress, Steps Aside." *New York Times*, November 23, 2014.
Warren, Michael. "Dynasty on the Hill." *Weekly Standard*, March 10, 2014.

CHAPTER NINETEEN

The Udall Dynasty

Zachary A. Smith and Molly E. Thrash

In any discussion of politicians in the American southwest involved with environmental and natural resource law and policy, one family name stands out: Udall. The Udall family political legacy stretches across Arizona, Colorado, New Mexico, and Utah, and reaches back through multiple agencies and administrations for over 100 years. The dynasty also looks toward the future through two foundations—one federal and one educational—that continue to work in the family name for progressive research in environmental and natural resource policy education and development, and in related outreach efforts. Moreover, although the name Udall is no longer as prominent in public affairs as it was in the mid-20th century, the families of the Udall daughters include contemporary elected officeholders in the southwest region, the Smiths of Oregon, and the Lees of Utah.

The Udall family political dynasty cannot be separated from the family's history as early members of The Church of Jesus Christ of Latter-day Saints (the Church). Gordon Smith, during his term as U.S. senator from Oregon, stated at a Church function that his religious appointments within the Church were more important than his election certificate.[1] The same personal qualities that result in winning local elections also result in gaining appointments in the Church across the southwest. In a speech in Arizona in 1971, Morris Udall reflected on the qualities of his family as being talented in the public service arena: "And we've had others in the family who've been in Congress, who've held judicial offices and county offices, and all the rest. I guess I should say that the voters have been very kind and good to us. But a lot of it comes, as I said at the beginning, from this deep feeling and belief that if you have talent for public service you owe it to the public, that it's an honorable calling, there's nothing cheap or dishonest or disgraceful about serving the public, and this all came down to us as young men."[2] Mormon pioneers were early ranchers and farmers in the American west, working with the land and on the land to develop irrigation systems, establish crop and livestock operations, and expand their settlements as the western boundaries of the new country expanded.

Origins of Udall Family's Political Legacy

The patriarch of the Udall political family in the American southwest was David King Udall (1851–1938). David was the oldest child of English immigrants who were converts to the relatively new Mormon faith. After David was born in St Louis, Missouri, the Udall family settled in Nephi, Utah.[3] Just after marrying Eliza Luella Stuart (aka Ella), David Udall's faith would take him to his parents' homeland in 1875 for his first Mormon mission. After returning to Utah from this two-year mission in England, Udall expected to be sent to Arizona, but instead he remained in Utah for two years, in Nephi briefly, and then Kanab. It was there that he began his life of public service: both within The Church of Jesus Christ of Latter-day Saints and in local, state, and federal office. While in Kanab, Udall's first elected positions were as justice of the peace and water master. As stated in the history of The Church of Jesus Christ of Latter-day Saints: "The [male] Udall descendants have all followed in David's footsteps, with sons and grandsons working as county attorneys, judges, mayors, congressmen, and teachers"[4]

In 1880, Udall was called by the Church to lead a group of recent (referred to as Saints) converts to Mormonism to St. Johns in the Arizona Territory, where pioneer Mormons were establishing a settlement among local Hispanics and other pioneers from the east. He left Kanab on his 29th birthday with his wife Ella and daughter Pearl, for a 340-mile month-long journey by wagon through what was largely untamed land to St. Johns, in the Arizona Territory. He was named bishop of St. Johns Ward in the Arizona Territory, his first Church position of leadership and authority, and was the first Mormon bishop in the Territory. As bishop, Udall was responsible for development of the Church and the town, including the irrigation works, a school, stores, and a meeting house. After seven years, Udall became president of the St. Johns Stake (a Stake is a collection of Wards, which is a small unit of congregational organizations within the Church), a position he would hold for 35 years. During his years as president of the Stake, Udall assisted in the construction of Lyman Dam south of St. Johns, which irrigated thousands of previously untilled acres, and was the founder and early leader of the St. Johns Stake Academy—the only secondary school in Apache County until 1921.[5]

The Udall Dynasty

Udall Political Dynasty Family Tree

1. David King Udall, 1851–1938
    Arizona Territorial Senate, 1899–1900
   Married Eliza "Ella" Luella Stuart, Ida Frances Hunt, and Mary Ann Linton
   15 children with first two wives including David K. Udall Jr., John Hunt, Levi Stewart, Jesse Addison, and Don Taylor

2. John Hunt Udall, 1889–1959
    Arizona House of Representatives, 1921–1924
    Mayor of Phoenix, 1936–1938
    Federal prohibition director, Arizona, 1936–1938
   Married Ruth Kimball
   Children including John Nicholas

3. John Nicholas "Nick" Udall, 1913–2005
    Mayor of Phoenix, 1948–1952
    Superior Court judge, Maricopa County, Arizona, 1953–1958
   Married Sybil Webb, then Joan Romney
   Seven children

2. Levi Stewart Udall, 1891–1960
    Apache County attorney, Arizona, 1923–1924, 1927–1928
    Judge, Apache County Superior Court, Arizona, 1931–1947
    Justice, Supreme Court of Arizona, 1947–1960
   Married Louisa Lee
   Children including Stewart Lee and Morris King

3. Stewart Lee Udall, 1920–2010
    U.S. House of Representatives (Arizona), 1955–1960
    U.S. secretary of the interior, 1961–1968
   Married Ermalee Webb
   Six children including Thomas Stewart

3. Morris "Mo" King Udall, 1922–1998
    U.S. House of Representatives (Arizona), 1961–1990
   Married and widowed three times
   Five children including Mark Emery

(continued)

Udall Political Dynasty Family Tree (*continued*)

4. Mark Emery Udall, 1950–
    Colorado House of Representatives, 1996–1998
    U.S. House of Representatives (Colorado), 1999–2009
    U.S. senator (Colorado), 2009–2015
Married Maggie Fox
Two children

2. Jesse Addison Udall, 1893–1980
    Graham County attorney, Arizona, 1924–1925
    Arizona House of Representatives, 1930–1938
    Superior Court judge, Graham County, Arizona, 1939–1947, 1953–1958
    Justice, Supreme Court of Arizona, 1960–1972
Married Lula Lee (sister of Louisa Lee, married to Levi Stewart Udall)
Children including Stewart Levi and Jessica (Smith)

3. Milan Smith Jr., 1942–, son of Jessica Udall Smith
    Judge, U.S. Court of Appeals

3. Gordon Smith, 1952–, son of Jessica Udall Smith
    U.S. Senate (Oregon), 1997–2009

4. Thomas Stewart, 1948–, son of Stewart Levi Udall
    Assistant U.S. attorney general, District of New Mexico, 1978–1981
    Attorney general, New Mexico, 1990–1998
    U.S. House of Representatives (New Mexico), 1999–2008
    U.S. Senate (New Mexico), 2008–

2. Don Taylor Udall, 1897–1976
    Arizona House of Representatives, 1941–1942
    Superior Court judge, Navajo County, Arizona, 1946

3. David Udall, 1963–, son of David K. Udall Jr.
    Superior Court judge, Maricopa County, Arizona, 2001–

4. Michael Shumway Lee, 1971–, grandson of Rex Lee, brother of Louisa and Lula Lee
    U.S. Senate (Utah), 2011–
Married Sharon Burr
Three children

In 1882, before the Church changed its position on polygamy but before the enforcement of the Edmunds Act effectively outlawing plural marriages, Udall took a second wife, Ida Frances Hunt. In 1884, he was indicted on charges of polygamy, but Ida had been quietly relocated to Utah to avoid being called to testify against her husband. While she awaited word that it was safe to return, she bore her first child to David (PBS, 2001). The following year, Udall was convicted of perjury. Sources differ in regard to the substance of the case in which he perjured himself[6]; it is thought that either the case involved a land claim or the polygamy trial for another Mormon—usually acknowledged to be Miles P. Romney, great-grandfather of Mitt Romney. Nevertheless, Udall was convicted and freed on bail before his trial. Bail was posted by a merchant from Prescott, Arizona, Michel Goldwater—grandfather of future U.S. senator and presidential candidate Barry M. Goldwater. Udall was pardoned by President Grover Cleveland in 1885, just the first year of his three-year prison sentence, and his next son was named Grover Cleveland Udall.[7]

In 1899, Udall was elected as the senator to represent Apache County in the 20th Arizona Territorial Legislature, the legislative body for the Arizona Territory before statehood. (Arizona gained statehood on February 14, 1912.) He served in this capacity for a single year. His Senate colleagues included Michel Goldwater (who had previously posted his bail—see above), future Arizona senator Henry F. Ashurst, and future Arizona governor Sidney P. Osborn.[8]

Udall fathered a total of 15 children with his two wives. By Ella, the children were: David Stewart Udall (1878–1878—dies in infancy before the family traveled west); Pearl Udall [Nelson] (1880–1950); Erma Udall [Sherwood] (1882–1966); Mary Udall (1884–1885); Luella Udall [Pace] (1886–1952); David King Udall Jr. (1878–1960); Levi Stewart Udall (1890–1960); Paul Drawbridge Udall (1894–1896); and Rebecca May Udall (1897–1898). By Ida, the children were: Pauline Udall [Smith] (1884–1968); Grover Cleveland Udall (1887–1950); John Hunt Udall (1889–1959); Jesse Addison Udall (1893–1980); Gilbert Douglas Udall (1895–1981); and Don Taylor Udall (1897–1976). The Church banned polygamy as a practice in 1890, just months after the Edmunds Act of 1882 was in full enforcement. However, while not often reported, in 1903, Udall married a third wife, Mary Ann Linton, the widow of a friend. There is little known of this union other than Udall supported Linton's children by her previous husband until they attained adulthood.[9]

Times were often hard for the Udall family in St. Johns. Other Mormon families would come and go, not being suited to the hardships that the town and climate brought. The non-Mormon settlers and ranchers were often less than neighborly, but the Udalls stayed nonetheless[10] (PBS, 2001). The Udall men delivered mail, a job initially taken to supplement their meager farm incomes. Meanwhile, the Udall daughters taught at the St. Johns Stake

Academy and ran an ice-cream parlor for a brief period, all in an effort to get the family and their father out of debt (Adams, 1993). Ida Udall died of complications following a series of strokes in 1915, just after the family had finally bought property and completed construction of a house large enough for the whole family (Adams, 1993). In 1922, David Udall was released from his position as president of the Stake. Five years later, David and Ella Udall were called to be the first president and matron of the new Arizona Temple, and at 75, Udall again moved his family—this time to Mesa. The Udall family resided in Mesa until 1934, when Udall was again released from service to the Church. He and Ella returned to their home in St. Johns, where Ella died three years later. David King Udall died following a short illness less than one year after Ella (Carson and Johnson, 2004). David Udall's lasting influence on the state of Arizona is seen in the political careers of his sons, grandsons, and great-grandsons. Of Udall's 11 children that survived to adulthood, seven sons and four daughters, four of his sons went on to hold public offices. Of those sons, five of Udall's grandsons would hold office, and two of his great-grandsons.

Political Careers of David King Udall's Descendants

According to the Arizona State Library Archives and Public Records, and as recorded as a "death resolution" memorializing departed former legislators of the 24th Legislature in 1960, John Hunt Udall (1889–1959) was the clerk of the Apache County Superior Court in 1914, after which he was elected as a Republican to the Arizona House of Representatives representing Apache County from statehood in 1921 through 1924 (Burke, 2010). Other biographical information appears to conflict with this, stating that in 1922, John Hunt Udall won the election for the clerk of the Court for an Arizona Superior Court as a Republican. According to those sources, John Hunt Udall filed to run immediately after his half-brother Levi—who had held the position from 1919 until the 1922 election—filed to run as a Democrat.[11] Sources, however, agree that John Hunt Udall was elected mayor of Phoenix 1936–1938, prior to which he served as a magistrate for the city. Additionally, from 1926 until 1933, John Hunt Udall was the federal prohibition director for the state of Arizona, supervising state-level prohibition efforts to enforce the 18th[h] Amendment. Federal prohibition directors were responsible for all "permissive and enforcement work connected with the national prohibition act."[12] John Hunt Udall remained active in the Church as bishop of the Phoenix First Ward from 1928 to 1939. In 1948, he ran for the Republican nomination for governor of Arizona, but did not make it to the primaries. That same year, he also lost the race for the U.S. House of Representatives from the Arizona 1st District.

According to biographical information compiled by the University of Arizona, Levi Stewart Udall (1891–1960) lost the position of clerk of the Court for the Arizona Superior Court to his older half-brother John in 1922. However, as

The Udall Dynasty

a Democrat, Levi went on to be the Apache County attorney for two terms (1923–1924 and 1927–1928). In 1931, he was elected judge of the Apache County Superior Court, and in 1947 he was elected judge of the Supreme Court of Arizona. He would hold this position until his death from a heart attack in 1960.[13] Levi Stewart Udall married Louisa Lee, whose sister Lela Lee married Levi's paternal half-brother, Jesse Addison Udall.

One of David King Udall's younger sons, Jesse Addison Udall (1893–1980) (R) served in a multitude of legislative and elected judicial positions and was an army officer and veteran of both world wars. He also served as a bishop, Stake president, and missionary president in the Church. Jesse graduated from the University of Arizona law school in 1924; in 1925, he was elected the county attorney for Graham County, Arizona. In 1930, he was elected to the Arizona House of Representatives to represent Graham County for the 10th and 11th Legislatures. In 1939, he was elected as the Graham County Superior Court judge, a position from which he resigned in 1942 to serve in the Judge Advocate Department for the army for World War II (Elsberry, 2010).[14]

After the war, from 1953 through 1958, Jesse again served as the Graham County Superior judge, until he left to accept an appointment with the Church as president of the Southern California Mission. Jesse had previously been president of the St. Johns Stake and patriarch of the Tempe Stake. Upon the unexpected death of his older half-brother Levi in 1960, Jesse was appointed as justice of the Arizona Supreme Court. Jesse held that position by reelection until his resignation in 1972. It was from this position in 1948 that Judge Udall penned the majority opinion allowing Native Americans living on reservations in Arizona the right to vote. On March 29, 1976, Arizona governor Jack Williams proclaimed Justice Jesse A. Udall Day in recognition of Jesse's lifetime of state service.[15]

Don Taylor Udall (1897–1976) was the youngest son of David King Udall. Unlike most of the Udall men in law, Don graduated from Georgetown University in 1923. Don served as a Democrat representing Navajo County in the Arizona House of Representatives in 1941 and 1942, a position from which he resigned before joining the Judge Advocates Department of the U.S. Army for World War II like his brother, Jesse. After his military service during the war, Don Taylor Udall returned to the bench in Arizona as judge of the Navajo County Superior Court through 1946. By the end of Don and Jesse's careers in public service, the next generation of Udall men began to enter local politics as well. Five grandsons of David King Udall would be elected to office in Arizona, and one would campaign to be the Democratic nominee for president in 1976.[16]

John Nicholas Udall (Nick) (1913–2005) was born to John Hunt Udall and Ruth Kimball Udall. A Republican, Nick Udall served as mayor of Phoenix for three terms, from 1948 until 1952. Following his time as mayor, he served as a judge of the Maricopa County Superior Court for five years. Like the other

Udall men in politics, Nick Udall was also very active in the Church. He presided as a bishop in Arizona's 3rd Ward and was a Stake patriarch after being released as bishop.[17]

Stewart Lee Udall (1920–2010), son of Levi Stewart Udall, served as a Democrat in the U.S. House of Representatives representing Arizona's 2nd District from 1955 to 1960. During this time, Udall also campaigned heavily for Kennedy, and won Arizona's delegates for Kennedy, taking them away from Johnson in the 1960 Democratic Convention.[18] In 1961, President John Kennedy appointed him as the 37th secretary of the interior, and he continued to serve throughout the administration of President Lyndon Johnson. Prior to his life in politics, Stewart served in World War II as a gunner on a U.S. Army Air Corps bomber before completing his studies at the University of Arizona. In 1963, Stewart Lee Udall published his first book, *The Quiet Crisis*, in which he examined American environmental activities, attitudes, and policies.[19]

Stewart Udall's many contributions as secretary of the interior are captured in the establishment of six national monuments, including Marble Canyon, which was later incorporated into the Grand Canyon National Park; four national parks, including the Redwoods National Park; four national seashores, including the Padre Island National Seashore; and two of the four lesser-known national lakeshores. He was also instrumental in the passage of five environmental protection acts and the signing of the Central Arizona Project. On September 21, 2010, Secretary of the Interior Ken Salazar dedicated the Main Interior Building in Washington, DC, to Udall following legislation signed by President Barack Obama.[20]

Morris King Udall (1922–1998) or Mo was the younger brother of Stewart Udall, and like his brother, he graduated from the University of Arizona law school (1947) and served in the U.S. Army Air Corps during World War II. During this period, he commanded an all-black squadron from Louisiana; it was this experience that led to his inactivity in the Church. (The Church changed its policy on black membership in the priesthood in 1976.) Mo was the only member of the Udall family to ever run for president and made it further in that ambition than any other Mormon, prior to Mitt Romney's run for president in the 2012 election. Mo Udall lost the Democratic nomination in 1976 to Jimmy Carter, who went on to become the 39th U.S. president. Mo was also the only member of the Udall family to become a professional athlete: he was a basketball guard for the NBA Denver Nuggets in the 1948–1949 season. When his brother Stewart Udall was appointed the secretary of the interior in 1961, Mo was elected to fill his seat in the U.S. House of Representatives. He served in Congress until his resignation in 1991.[21]

During Mo's tenure representing Arizona's 2nd congressional district, he served as the chair of the House Committee on Interior and Insular Affairs from 1977 until his retirement in 1991. During this time, his liberal ideology and environmental ethics, perhaps in step with those of his brother as the

The Udall Dynasty

secretary of the interior, gave him a key role in legislation regarding environmental protections and congressional support for national parks and public lands. In 1964, Mo was the floor whip for the1964 Civil Rights Act, and he spoke in Congress against the Vietnam War. He also led the inquiry that led to the uncovering of the My Lai massacre of civilians by American soldiers. Mo also sponsored legislation in every term in support of Native American rights and protections and was an advocate of the termination-by-assimilation policy of the mid-20th century. He supported Indian education, gaming rights, land and water claims, health policies, and self-determination, but like Secretary Stewart, did nothing to increase or encourage Indian participation in creating Indian policy.[22]

Although two other grandsons of David King Udall also served in local politics in Arizona, little is traceable about them in the public record. David K. Udall was a councilman for the city of Mesa for eight years. Little other information on him is available. Lee Kenyon Udall (1952–2009) served as mayor of Gilbert, Arizona, from 1956 to 1959; Lee was also president of the Mesa Arizona Temple of the Church from 1997 to 2000.

The Third Generation of Udall's Descendants

Thomas Stewart Udall, son of Stewart Levi Udall (1948–), is the current senior U.S. senator from New Mexico. His grandmother, Lula Lee, was from

Congressman Morris "Mo" Udall of Arizona meets with President Jimmy Carter, January 17, 1978. (National Archives)

New Mexico, and Tom graduated from the University of New Mexico law school in 1977. His Senate term ends in January 2021, and he is eligible for reelection; he is a registered Democrat. Senator Udall was elected to the U.S. Senate in 2008 following his tenure in the U.S. House of Representatives from New Mexico's 3rd congressional district for 10 years. Prior to his election to Congress, Udall was New Mexico's attorney general from 1990 to 1998 and assistant U.S. attorney general for the District of New Mexico from 1978 through 1981. He has always been a strong supporter of health and environmental causes in New Mexico, and as senator, founded the Congressional Conservation Caucus, which he still cochairs.

Meanwhile, Mo Udall's son and Tom's cousin, Mark Emery Udall (1950–), served as U.S. senator (D) from Colorado in 2009–2015. His first elected position was one term in the Colorado House of Representatives for 1996–1998. Prior to his election to the Senate, he served for five terms in the U.S. House of Representatives for Colorado's 2nd district, from 1999 to 2009. During his tenure in office Tom championed sustainable and renewable energy development, and helped pass legislation to address the well-known threats to the Colorado mountain environments—wildfire and bark beetles. Prior to entering politics, from 1985 through 1995, Mark Udall was the executive director of Outward Bound, based in Boulder, Colorado.

David Udall (son of David K. Udall) has been a sitting judge in the Maricopa County Superior Court of Arizona since 2001. He has served in various departments and is currently in the Civil Department of the Superior Court of Maricopa County.

Michael Lee (1971–) is the junior U.S. senator (R) from Utah. He is a 1997 graduate from the Brigham Young University law school and the son of Rex E. Lee, U.S. solicitor general appointed by President Ronald Reagan from 1981 to 1985. He is the grandnephew of Mo and Stewart Udall. Michael Lee's grandfather, Rex Lee, was also a graduate of Brigham Young University, but received his law degree from the University of Chicago[23] (The Washington Post, 1987). He was the brother of sisters Lela and Louisa Lee, who married Jesse Addison Udall and Levi Stewart Udall, respectively.

Gordon Smith (1952–) was the junior U.S. senator (R) from Oregon from 1997 to 2009. His older brother, Milan Smith Jr. (1942–), is a federal judge of the U.S. Court of Appeals for the Ninth Circuit. They are sons of Jessica Udall Smith and Milan Smith, a former assistant secretary of agriculture under President Dwight D. Eisenhower, who also revolutionized the frozen food industry.[24] Jessica Udall was the daughter of Lela Lee and Jesse Addison Udall.

The Udall Foundation and the Udall Center

The Udall Foundation is a federal agency of the executive branch, located in Washington, DC, and Tucson, Arizona. It was established by Congress in

1992 to honor the legacy of Morris Udall. In 2009, President Obama signed into law the Morris K. Udall Scholarship and Excellence in National Environmental Policy Amendments Act, which included honoring the legacy of Stewart Udall as well. "The Udall Foundation became the Morris K. Udall and Stewart L. Udall Foundation in recognition of the historic Interior Secretary's contributions to the United States. The Udall brothers worked together on many environmental and American Indian initiatives while Stewart was Secretary of the Interior and Morris was a member of Congress."[25]

The work of the Udall Foundation carries on the work of the Udall brothers in environmental policy and guidance, support for indigenous nations and their development and sovereignty, and environmental conflict management and resolution. The Udall Foundation also sponsors congressional internships for Native American and Alaskan native students and approximately 50 undergraduate scholarships for students who are focused on the environment, tribal policy, or Native American health care. Current programs of the Udall Foundation are housed in the Native Nations Institute for Leadership, Management and Policy, the U.S. Institute for Environmental Conflict Resolution, and the Udall Center for Studies in Public Policy. The Udall Center is part of the University of Arizona and was founded in honor of both Mo and Stewart Udall having attended the University of Arizona law school. It is closely and permanently affiliated with the Udall Foundation, which provides some of its funding. "Founded in 1989, the Udall Center specializes in issues related to environmental policy and Indigenous nations policy."[26]

The Udall Political Dynasty

The peak of the Udall family's political power was the period from 1961 until 1991, from when Morris was elected to fill his brother Stewart's seat in the U.S. House of Representatives and Stewart was appointed secretary of the interior, until Mo's resignation from Congress for health reasons. The accomplishments and influence of these two brothers on initiatives and policies especially regarding the environment and treatment of Native Americans cannot be overstated. Although first cousins Tom and Mark Udall would both serve in Congress from 1998 to 2008 along with their cousin Gordon Smith (grandson of Jesse Udall)—a rare occurrence of three members of the same family serving simultaneously—the family's political influence had already peaked.

The March 20, 2010, *New York Times* obituary of Stewart Lee Udall summed up the peak of the Udall family in American politics:

> At his death, Mr. Udall was a senior member of one of the nation's last and largest political dynasties—in the West it was often said there were "oodles of Udalls" in politics. His grandfather David King Udall served in the Arizona Territorial legislature; his father, Levi Udall, was for decades an elected

judge in the Arizona Superior Court and later a justice and chief justice of the Arizona Supreme Court; Morris Udall was followed to Washington by his son Mark Udall, elected in 2008 as a senator from Colorado, the same year that Tom Udall was elected.[27]

As these brief biological sketches show, the Udall men active in American politics are or were also active in their church organizations. They also were very fond of and comfortable in the outdoors. An attachment to the land of the West can be seen in the Udall men in public office over the last seven decades. They have been avid hikers, river rafters, and mountain climbers, activities from which they draw their love of the American western outdoors.[28] They bring that passion into their offices as well, where they have associated the family name with environmentalism, conservationism, and public policy that supports the environment and Native Americans.

Notes

1. Canham, M., and Burr, T. (2016, October 30). Piety before politics? Mormon politicians defend ex-Sen. Gordon Smith after video leak. http://archive.sltrib.com/article.php?id=4428075&itype=CMSID.

2. Udall, M. K. (1998, December 22). "Mormon Settlement in Arizona," Heard Museum, Phoenix, Arizona, February 18, 1971. http://dizzy.library.arizona.edu/branches/spc/udall/mormon.html.

3. Adams, K. R. (1993, August). David King Udall, Arizona Pioneer. https://www.lds.org/ensign/1993/08/david-king-udall-arizona-pioneer?lang=eng&clang=ase=.

4. Adams.

5. PBS. (2001). New Perspectives on the West. https://www.pbs.org/weta/thewest/people/s_z/udall.htm.

6. Lucas, R. (2011, May 21). St. Johns: Town of Friendly Neighbors Had Unfriendly Start. http://arizona100.blogspot.com/2011/05/st.html.

7. Carson, D. W., and Johnson, J. W. (2004). *Mo: The Life and Times of Morris K. Udall*. Tucson, AZ: University of Arizona Press.

8. Carson.

9. Carson.

10. PBS.

11. Myers, R. (1990). The University of Arizona Universities Library. http://www.library.arizona.edu/exhibits/lsudall/ms293.html.

12. U.S. Congress, House Appropriations Committee. (1921). Treasury Department Appropriation Bill, 1923: Hearing before the Subcommittee of House Committee on Appropriations. Washington, DC: U.S. Government Printing Office.

13. Myers.

14. Elsberry, F. (2010, December 27). Arizona Legislators: Then and Now. http://apps.azlibrary.gov/officials/Legislators/Person/1389.

15. Steere, P., and Whitten, M. (1994). The University of Arizona Universities Library. http://www.library.arizona.edu/exhibits/jaudall/homepage.html.

16. Udall (1998).

17. The Arizona Republic. (2005, June 19). http://www.legacy.com/obituaries/azcentral/obituary.aspx?n=john-nicholas-udall&pid=14324354.

18. Clarkin, T. (2001). *Federal Indian Policy in the Kennedy and Johnson Administrations: 1961–1969*. Albuquerque: University of New Mexico Press.

19. Schudel, M. (2010, March 21). *The Washington Post*. http://www.washingtonpost.com/wp-dyn/content/article/2010/03/20/AR2010032003261.htm.

20. U.S. Department of the Interior. (2010, September 21). Secretary Salazar Honors Stewart Lee Udall at Interior Building Dedication Ceremony. https://www.doi.gov/news/pressreleases/Secretary-Salazar-Honors-Stewart-Lee-Udall-at-Interior-Building-Dedication-Ceremony.

21. University of Arizona Library Manuscript Collection MS 325. (n.d.). http://www.library.arizona.edu/exhibits/udall/index.html.

22. Clarkin.

23. The Washington Post. (1987, October 23). Milan A. Smith, Mormon Leader in Area, Dies. Retrieved from *The Washington Post*.

24. The Washington Post. (1987, October 23).

25. The Udall Foundation. (n.d.). The Udall Foundation. https://udall.gov.

26. The Udall Center for Studies in Public Policy. (2017, July 24). http//udallcenter.arizona.edu/about-us.

27. Schneider, K., and Dean, C. (2010, March 20). Stewart L. Udall, Conservationist in Kennedy and Johnson Cabinets, Dies at 90. http://www.nytimes.com/2010/03/21/nyregion/21udall.html?emc=eta1.

28. Gifford, B. (2013, November 23). Mark Udall's Toughest Climb. http://www.mensjournal.com/magazine/mark-udalls-toughest-climb-20131127.

Further Reading

Smith, Thomas G. *Stewart L. Udall: Steward of the Land*. Albuquerque: University of New Mexico Press, 2017.

Udall, Stewart L. *The Quiet Crisis* (Classic Reprint). London: Forgotten Books, 2017.

Conclusion: American Democracy and Hereditary Power in the 21st Century

Scott J. Spitzer

It is worthwhile to restate the obvious impetus for this study: how can the United States, the oldest continuously active democratic nation, still continue to have powerful, familial political dynasties? Political dynasties seem inherently undemocratic. Indeed, as I stated in the Introduction, the American Revolution was aimed at dissolving forever the connection between birthright and political power. We might expect families to pass power down to their children in authoritarian regimes, such as North Korea, but democracies were designed precisely to open up positions of authority in government for all citizens, to be filled through the collective will of the majority via the electoral process.[1] Yet, as a number of scholars have shown, the prevalence of hereditary advantage in electoral politics in the United States continues to be a small, but significant, component of Congress.[2] Moreover, as Stephen Hess's pioneering work on American political dynasties illustrates, and as the chapters that fill this volume corroborate, it's not just the numerical significance of political dynasties that suggests their importance: these political dynasties have often had a powerful impact on the development of the nation, of large regions of the country, of various states, and even of important cities.[3] It would not be too much to argue that despite efforts to replace hereditary privilege with democratic process, America has been indelibly shaped by the continued relevance of family political dynasties, into the 21st century.

Moreover, the most memorable of these families are not so much unusual exceptions to the practice of democracy as they are interwoven with the development of America's politics and governance. The Roosevelts, Kennedys, Bushes, Clintons—these families, and each of the others considered in this volume—were integral in the shaping of contemporary American politics, or of the regions, states, or cities that they, for a period, dominated politically. In reading through these studies, the powerful themes of America's political development in the 20th century emerge time and time again, differently in each case, but repeatedly across each one. In other words, the stories of America's modern political dynasties tell the story of American democracy.

Replacing Privilege with Merit

Early in the history of the nation, a system of political patronage was established, whereby government jobs were commonly provided to partisan supporters of winning candidates. The "spoils system" that emerged hand in hand with the mass-based political parties that President Andrew Jackson and his vice president, Martin Van Buren, created was a response to the "patrician" governments run by federalist elites. Aside from functioning as a political mechanism for ensuring the loyalty of voters and for stabilizing the established power of party "machines," the spoils system was also an effort to democratize—to ensure that government was not reserved for the wealthy, highly educated elites, but that new immigrants such as the Dutch (Van Buren's people) and Irish would have access. In a sense, such party machine patronage was the direct opposite of dynastic politics, whereby power was held by a wealthy, powerful few and passed down as a family inheritance—as with the second president John Adams and his son, the sixth President John Quincy Adams.

After the Civil War, however, a reform movement targeted the corruption and governing incompetence that the political machines created. Reformers sought a civil service that would hire and reward merit and that would reduce the importance of political favors in shaping the character of government. With the signing of the Pendleton Act of 1883—the first Civil Service Act—a system of competitive exams was established and other reforms followed, transforming American government from a source of political patronage to a merit-based, union-protected workforce. This was a transformation of American governance with profound implications.[4]

From the perspective of this study, this emergence of the spoils system was a rejection of political privilege generally and a rejection of the legitimacy of a family political dynasty, such as the Adams family represented. How fitting it was, then, that the progressive reforms of the late 19th and early 20th centuries, which aimed to limit the excesses of democracy and of immigrant political power, were led nationally by Theodore Roosevelt, a leading member of perhaps the most powerful family political dynasty of the 20th century.[5]

Conclusion

Nepotism and American Political Dynasties

Still, even while the civil service reform movement was enormously successful in ensuring that federal, state, and local government jobs would be awarded based on merit—through civil service examinations or based on educational qualifications rather than partisan ties—there was nothing at all that barred political leaders from using their positions to benefit their family members directly. Nepotism—defined as "favoritism based on kinship"[6]—was perhaps considered so far outside legitimate political practice that there was no legislation passed to outlaw the practice until 1967.

The Federal Anti-Nepotism Statute, section 3110 of a larger postal service reform, was passed just six years after President John F. Kennedy's controversial appointment of his brother Robert F. Kennedy (RFK) to be attorney general of the United States. President Kennedy was roundly criticized in the press for the appointment, but nonetheless his brother became a powerful attorney general and the president's closest adviser. Meanwhile, a "mutual contempt" emerged between RFK and President Kennedy's vice president, Lyndon B. Johnson (LBJ), which only grew more hostile after President Kennedy's assassination and Johnson's ascent to the presidency.[7] Many historians have thought, without confirmation, that President Johnson personally sought passage of this law aimed at his nemesis, RFK. Therefore, although the anti-nepotism law was added as a rider to a seemingly innocuous and unrelated piece of legislation by the act's sponsor (Representative Neal Simpson, D-IA), the rider became known as the "Bobby Kennedy Law."[8] According to the statute:

> A public official may not appoint, employ, promote, advance, or advocate for appointment, employment, promotion, or advancement, in or to a civilian position in the agency in which he is serving or over which he exercises jurisdiction or control any individual who is a relative of the public official.[9]

Since passage of this law, there have been only two instances involving the presidency where concerns have arisen: first, when President Bill Clinton appointed First Lady Hillary to head his task force on health care reform: and second, when President Trump appointed his son-in-law, Jared Kushner, his daughter, Ivanka, and his sons, Donald Jr. and Eric, as part of his transition team. Trump then appointed both Jared and Ivanka as White House advisers. In the Clintons' case, a federal lawsuit was brought challenging her role, and the judge ruled that Hillary wasn't a "government employee," and that as long as some of the Clinton task-force meetings were held in public, her appointment was not a violation of the antinepotism statute.[10] Similar arguments have been levied on behalf of President Trump's family members serving in his transition team and in advisory positions within the White House—that they are neither on the federal payroll nor formal appointments to the White House staff. Some legal scholars have even argued that the law cannot be used to limit the president's appointment power, which is provided for by the Constitution in Article II.[11] In any case, it is highly unusual to have family members appointed to powerful positions in presidential administrations in the 21st century, and the roles of the Trump appointees suggest that a potential Trump family dynasty may emerge in unorthodox fashion from anomalous arrangements.

American Political Dynasties: Common Patterns

As noted in the Introduction, at the beginning of this project we asked our invited authors to consider several broad questions concerning the formation, peak, and decline in the power of the family dynasty they studied, as well as any important conflicts among members of the family. Although each family dynasty was/is unique, the hope was to identify patterns in the interactions between democracy and the hereditary transmission of political power in America. It became clear that four major themes in 20th-century American political development (APD) were prevalent throughout these chapters: (1) the importance of party machines and the reforms that ended their dominance of state and local politics; (2) racial segregation in the Jim Crow South and the civil rights movement's successes in dismantling its formal institutional power; (3) the conservative movement's transformation of the Republican Party in the Reagan era and since; and (4) the efforts of the liberal coalition to redefine itself and remain politically relevant into the later decades of the 20th century and the early decades of the 21st.

Tables 1 to 3 summarize patterns for each of the political dynasties considered in this volume, along these lines. For each table, the primary factors explaining the emergence and perseverance of each dynasty are listed first. Second, the peak of each dynasty's power is summarized, by political office held and years. Third, the period of the dynasty's decline is identified, along with the chief factor(s) explaining that decline. Fourth, the moment that the dynasty ended is identified, and the primary reason for that end is summarized. Of course, there are some dynasties that are still a powerful influence, and in those cases I have simply indicated that identifying its end is not applicable. Finally, for each case, one of the four APD themes that emerged from these studies is highlighted. Each of these dynasties rose to power and lost power under one of two possibilities. Some emerged out of a stable set of institutional politics at a specific time, and then lost power as those arrangements were destabilized or were gradually eroded in significance. Others found opportunity to obtain power as previously powerful institutional politics became destabilized, and were able to rise as new ways of governing were established (and eventually lost power as these new, stable, institutional relationships were destabilized). In the tables, each of these APD themes is listed.

Some general observations are warranted based on these summary tables. First, it is clear that in every case the ambitions and successes of the originator of the political dynasty were of great importance. For the nationally significant dynasties, a combination of wealth, social standing, and business success were also key. At the state level, we can add that a quality of perseverance and marriage ties were also significant. At the regional and local level, the availability of widespread networks was also important. To sustain all these dynasties once they were established, the key factors have been wealth, networks, and name recognition. At the state, regional, and local levels, there was a greater variety of factors in the long-term viability of these political dynasties, including marriage ties, family loyalty, incumbency advantage, and the state's importance in the regional and/or national life. In looking at the peaks of the families' political power, at the national level this was largely achieved through the attainment of the presidency (or a major-party nomination and near win at the presidency). At the state level, it was achieved with a family member elected to be governor or U.S. senator. At the regional and/or local level, the peak of the dynasty's power came through the House of Representatives or mayoralty of a major city.

The decline and end of the political dynasties occurred in different ways depending on the level of government: for national dynasties, it was generally because of a major shift in the stable governing arrangements that had defined the era in which that family's dynasty emerged. At the state, regional, and local levels, there was more variation, but it generally had much more to do with the ending of an individual's term in office or hold on political power, and less to do with general shifts in the governing arrangements that dominated the nation's politics.

Finally, in looking at the major themes of American political development that were prominent across these studies, a few patterns are noticeable. For the national political dynasties, major changes in the underlying organization of the dominant party were fundamental to the rise, peak, and decline of these dynasties. Whether it was the decline in the power of political machines and the spoils system, or the shift in the Republican Party from the fiscal conservatism of the Eisenhower years to the cultural conservatism of the late 1990s and beyond, these shifts in the organizing principles of the party with which the family dynasty was affiliated were of great consequence for their capacity to sustain political power. For the state-based political dynasties, sometimes the regional or even the state party system itself underwent great change, again altering the basis for the family's political dynasty. The civil rights revolution led to a long-term decline in the Democratic Party's power in the South, as white southern democrats turned away from their party's embrace of civil rights legislation under Presidents Kennedy and Johnson, and eventually

Table 1a National Political Dynasties, Summary Comparison

	Bush	Cabot-Lodge	Clinton	Gore	Kennedy
Emergence	Business success; ambition, risk-taking, resilience	Social standing; wealth; ambition	Education; ambition	Business success; ambition	Business success; wealth
Sustaining	Wealth; resilience; family loyalty; networks; name recognition	Wealth; name recognition; networks; education	Networks; name recognition; fund-raising acumen	Networks; name recognition	Wealth; networks; name recognition
Peak	Presidencies: 1988–1992; 2000–2008	Mid-20th century	Presidency: 1992–2000	Presidential nomination: 2000	Presidency: 1960–1963
Decline	Early 21st century	1960s	2016	2000—after loss of campaign	1963 on (after assassination)
End	TBD; possibly 2016 Jeb Bush's loss for Republican nomination	1974—end of Vietnam; Nixon resigns	2016—Hillary Clinton's losing bid for president	2000—but signs of reemerging in 2016	Still relevant in 2017
American Political Development Theme	Republican Party shifts: from "old" to "new" wealth; from traditional politics to populism; fiscal conservatism to cultural conservatism	Rise of immigrant party machines: replacement of patrician class political leadership	Democratic Party shifts: from Great Society liberalism to "third way" politics; rise of conservative populism	Civil rights movement and racial change: shift in South from Democratic to Republican Party dominance	Democratic Party shifts: from New Deal liberalism to post-civil rights era liberalism

Table 1b National Political Dynasties, Summary Comparison

	Paul	Rockefeller	Romney	Roosevelt	Taft
Emergence	Ambition; commitment to ideology	Wealth, Social Standing	Wealth; industrial success	Wealth; social standing	Wealth, ambition, talent
Sustaining	Networks; name; strong political ideals	Wealth, Social Standing, Network	Wealth; education; network; name recognition	Wealth; name recognition; networks	Wealth, networks; name
Peak	Presidential candidate: 2008	1968–1976—Nelson Rockefeller's presidential campaigns and Vice Presidency.	Presidential nomination: 2012	Presidencies: 1901–1909; 1933–1945	Presidency: 1907–1912
Decline	2014—rise of populism over libertarianism in Republican Party	1976, Ford's loses election	2012—Mitt Romney's presidential loss	Post–World War II	2005–2006: Governor Bob Taft's scandal
End	Still relevant in 2017	2013, with Senator "Jay" Rockefeller's retirement	2016—election of Donald Trump	1945—FDR's presidency ends	2007—Governor Taft leaves office
American Political Development Theme	Republican Party shifts—fragmenting of party, and increased importance of libertarians (along with other factions)	Rise of social conservatism and demise of liberal wing of Republican Party	Republican Party shift toward populism; social conservatism	Democratic Party shifts: emergence of powerful New Deal coalition and politics	Rise and fall of Republican Party in Progressive era; and in populist 2000s.

Table 2 State Political Dynasties, Summary Comparison

	Brown	Byrd	Cuomo	La Follette	Roberts	Simpson
Emergence	Ambition; perseverance	Business success; networks	Ambition; education; idealism	Wealth; institutional position (university)	Ambition; perseverance	Marriage; network
Sustaining	Networks; name recognition; California's increasing national significance	Networks; name recognition; wealth	Networks; name recognition	Networks; name recognition; strong political ideals; family unity	Marriage; networks; name recognition	Name recognition; networking
Peak	Governors: 1959–1967; 1975–1983; 2011–2019	Senators: 1933–1965; 1965–1982	Governors: 1983–1995; 2011–2019	Senate: early New Deal era—1930s	Governor: 1991–1995	Senator: 1979–1997
Decline	21st century	Post–civil rights era	n/a	Cold War; McCarthyism	1995—end of Barbara Roberts's term as governor	2000s—rise in cultural conservatism
End	TBD—possibly will continue with heirs to Brown legacy	1982—last year of Senate term	Still relevant in 2017	1950s	1995	1997—Alan Simpson retires from Senate career
American Political Development Theme	Democratic Party shifts: progessivism in west moving from Republican to New Deal Democratic Party; to post–New Deal Democratic liberalism	Civil rights movement and racial change: reconfigures bases of power in South	Democratic Party shifts: from New Deal liberalism to nonideological progressivism	Republican Party shift—decline of progressive republicans	Marriage as an important pathway for women to executive office	Republican Party shift, from fiscal to cultural conservatism

Table 3 Regional and Metropolitan Political Dynasties, Summary Comparison

	Daley	Dingell	Udall
Emergence	Ambition, persistence	Ambition; labor organizing; New Deal	Ambition; network (Mormon church)
Sustaining	Networks; rise of Chicago's significance nationally	Incumbency advantage; networks; name recognition	Network (Mormon church); commitment to public service
Peak	Mayors: 1955–1976; 1989–2011	House of Representatives: 1932–1955; 1955–2014; 2014–	House of Representatives; presidential candidate: 1976 (Mo Udall)
Decline	1968; but reinvigorated in 1990s	2006–2014; but reinvigorated in 2014–	n/a
End	2011—end of Richard Daley Jr.'s mayoralty	Still relevant in 2017	Still relevant in 2017
American Political Development Theme	End of party machine era; rise of business-oriented liberal urban leadership	Institutional change in the House of Representatives in 1970s; Democrat Party shift: from labor focus to civil rights	Progressivism and Republican Party of the West; conservation politics and progressive Republicans in West

brought the Republican Party into power in the South. This shift in the partisan balance in the South was critical for a number of these family dynasties. Finally, for several of these dynasties, the changes were regional or local, but again focused on the character of the party system. For example, the rise of progressive reforms and the importance of environmental sustainability in the West and Southwest were important factors in the emergence and rise to power of the Udall family.

It is fitting that the less formal components of America's politics, those that were never written into the Constitution but which shaped the nation as powerfully as that formal document nonetheless, connect most strongly with the rise, sustenance, peaking of power, decline, and end of these powerful, family political dynasties. These include the powerful force of political parties in

American politics; the heavy toll of race in the shaping of the American South, and of national politics more generally; and the variability in the political, economic, and social life in states and regions across the nation. The effort, more than 200 years ago, to establish a republic, based on popular sovereignty and elite leadership simultaneously, created natural tensions for the long-term governance of the nation. Informal institutional developments emerged to fill the gaps between the formal Constitution and the lived democratic experience of the nation. These have been well documented by historians and political scientists. The role of these hereditary family political dynasties, however, remains underappreciated by scholars. Since Stephen Hess's pioneering work on the subject, and his recent update, there have been few efforts to explore the influence of these families on America's development and politics. This study, and the clear patterns identified here, suggest that there is far more to be learned about the nation's political character through the study of intergenerational political families than we have previously acknowledged.

Notes

1. President Kim Jong-un of North Korea inherited his authoritarian power from his father, Kim Jong-il, in 2011, who inherited his position from his father, Kim Il Sung, in 1994. Daniel M. Smith, *Dynasties and Democracy: The Inherited Incumbency Advantage in Japan* (Stanford, CA: Stanford University Press, 2018), p. 2.

2. Ernesto Dal Bo, Pedro Dal Bo, and Jason Snyder, "Political Dynasties," *The Review of Economic Studies* (2009) 76: 115–142; Brian D. Feinstein, "The Dynasty Advantage: Family Ties in Congressional Elections." *Legislative Studies Quarterly* (2010) 35(4): 571–598.

3. Stephen Hess, *America's Political Dynasties: From Adams to Clinton* (Washington, DC: Brookings Institution Press, 2016).

4. Stephen Skowronek, *Building a New American State: The Expansion of National Administrative Capacities: 1877–1920* (New York: Cambridge University Press, 1982), Chapters 3 and 6.

5. Sidney M. Milkis, *Theodore Roosevelt, the Progressive Party, and the Transformation of American Democracy* (Lawrence: University Press of Kansas, 2009).

6. Webster's dictionary, online, at https://www.merriam-webster.com/dictionary/nepotism, accessed on April 13, 2018.

7. Jeff Shesol, *Mutual Contempt: Lyndon Johnson, Robert Kennedy, and the Feud That Defined a Decade* (New York: Norton, 1997).

8. Olivia B. Waxman, "Behind the Law That May Keep Donald Trump's Children from White House Jobs." *Time* (2016) (online version) at time.com/4574971, accessed on October 25, 2017.

9. U.S. Code, Title 5, Part III, Subpart B, Chapter 31, Subchapter I, 3110. "Employment of Relatives; Restrictions." December 16, 1967, 81 Stat. 640;

amended Pub. L. 95-454, title IX, 906(a)(2), October 13, 1978, 92 Stat. 1224. *Legal Information Institute.* https://www.law.cornell.edu, accessed on September 10, 2017.

10. Scott Bomboy, "Presidential Nepotism Debate Goes Back to the Founders' Time." *Constitution Daily (/blog)* (2016) *National Constitution Center.* http://constitutioncenter.org/blog/feed, accessed on September 10, 2017.

11. Bomboy, "Presidential Nepotism Debate."

About the Editors and Contributors

Editors

Kathleen A. Gronnerud is an associate faculty member of the history department at Saddleback College and an author specializing in American political history. A graduate of UC Berkeley, Northwestern University and California State University, Fullerton, she holds master's degrees in both journalism and history with early training as a television and radio reporter in Washington, DC.

Scott J. Spitzer is an associate professor of political science at California State University, Fullerton. He earned his PhD in political science at Columbia University in 2000. Spitzer's research focuses on the U.S. presidency, racial politics, and social welfare policymaking, particularly in the 1960s and 1970s. His work has been published in *Presidential Studies Quarterly* and *The Sixties: A Journal of History, Politics and Culture*.

Contributors

Saladin Ambar is an associate professor of political science and senior scholar at the Center on the American Governor, Eagleton Institute of Politics, Rutgers University–New Brunswick.

Larry Bennett retired from DePaul University's political science department in 2017 and became executive director of North Branch Works, a Chicago-based neighborhood economic development organization. Professor Bennett's most recent book is *Neoliberal Chicago* (University of Illinois Press, 2016), coedited with Roberta Garner and Euan Hague. Professor Bennett continues to coedit Temple University Press's Urban Life, Landscape, and Policy book series.

About the Editors and Contributors

Julio L. Borquez is an associate professor of political science, department of social sciences at the University of Michigan–Dearborn.

Skyler Brocker-Knapp is a graduate student in the political science department at Portland State University and a native Oregonian.

Richard A. Clucas is a professor of political science at Portland State University. He is the editor and author of several works on Oregon politics.

William Cunion is the associate dean of liberal arts at Cuyahoga Community College in Cleveland, Ohio. Previously, he was the associate academic dean and an associate professor of political science at the University of Mount Union in Alliance, Ohio.

Mindy Farmer is the director of the May 4 Visitors Center and an assistant professor of history at Kent State University. Previously, she served as the founding education specialist at the federal nonpartisan Richard Nixon Presidential Library and Museum where she oversaw the library's education and public programming. She holds a doctorate from The Ohio State University.

Michael R. Fitzgerald is a professor of political science at the University of Tennessee–Knoxville.

Cody J. Foster is a presidential fellow and PhD candidate at the University of Kentucky where he specializes in 20th-century American political history and U.S. foreign relations.

Jennifer Hopper is the author of the book *Presidential Framing in the 21st Century News Media: The Politics of the Affordable Care Act* (Routledge, 2017). She is an assistant professor of political science at Southern Connecticut State University.

Dean J. Kotlowski is a professor of history at Salisbury University in Maryland. He is the author of *Paul V. McNutt and the Age of FDR* (Indiana University Press, 2015) and *Nixon's Civil Rights: Politics, Principle, and Policy* (Harvard University Press, 2001) and the editor of *The European Union: From Jean Monnet to the Euro* (Ohio University Press, 2000).

Scott Lasley is a professor and head of the department of political science at Western Kentucky University.

Barbara A. Perry is the Gerald L. Bailes professor and presidential studies director at the University of Virginia's Miller Center, where she cochairs the

Presidential Oral History Program and directs the Edward M. Kennedy Oral History Project. She is the author of *Rose Kennedy: The Life and Times of a Political Matriarch* and *Jacqueline Kennedy: First Lady of the New Frontier.*

Ethan Rarick is the director of the Robert T. Matsui Center for Politics and Public Service and a lecturer in the department of political science at the University of California, Berkeley. He is the managing editor of the *California Journal of Politics and Policy* and is the author or editor of several books, including *California Rising: The Life and Times of Pat Brown* and *Governing California: Politics, Government, and Public Policy in the Golden State.*

Ted Ritter is an assistant professor of political science and chair of the department of history, political science, and religious studies at Virginia Union University.

Margaret E. Scranton is a professor of political science at the School of Public Affairs at UA Little Rock. Her specialties are the American presidency and first ladies. She participated in planning the Clinton School of Public Service, taught their course on international public service, and taught the 15-week "Clinton Presidency" course on C-SPAN during 2003.

Richard Skinner teaches government in advanced academic programs at the Johns Hopkins University. He is the author of *More Than Money: Interest Group Action in Congressional Elections* (Rowman & Littlefield, 2007), as well as numerous articles and book chapters in both academic and nonacademic venues, and a contributor to blogs maintained by Vox.com, the Brookings Institution, and the R Street Institute.

Zachary A. Smith is a regents' professor, politics and international affairs at Northern Arizona University. He is an internationally recognized expert of environmental and natural resources policy and administration.

Molly E. Thrash is a PhD candidate, politics and international affairs at Northern Arizona University.

Joel F. Turner is an associate professor and director of SSRC in the department of political science at Western Kentucky University.

Nancy C. Unger is a professor and chair, department of history at Santa Clara University. Her work on the La Follette family includes the prize-winning biographies *Fighting Bob La Follette: The Righteous Reformer* (University of North Carolina, 2000) and *Belle La Follette: Progressive Era Reformer* (Routledge, 2016).

Index

Agnew, Spiro, 139–140, 142–143
Arthur, Chester A., 197

Brown family, 211–227
   Brown, Edmund Gerald "Jerry," Jr., 211, 213, 218–222, 223–227
   Brown, Edmund Gerald "Pat," 212–218, 222–227
   Brown, Kathleen, 213, 222–223
Bush family, 3–22
   Bush, George H.W., 3, 5, 6, 13–17, 50, 52, 53, 54, 74, 75, 322
   Bush, George W., 3, 5, 6, 17–20, 52, 54, 60, 75
   Bush, Jeb, 3, 5, 6, 60, 75
   Bush, Prescott, 3, 5, 6, 11–13
Byrd family, 231–244
   Byrd, Harry Flood, 236–242
   Byrd, Harry Flood, Jr., 242–244
   and the Virginia "Martin Organization," 235–236

Cabot family, 25–38
   Cabot, George, 26–29, 30, 35
   See also Lodge family
Carter, Jimmy, 46, 48, 50, 54, 101
Church of Jesus Christ of Latter-day Saints (LDS Church)
   and Romney family, 152–154, 157
   and Udall family, 329–330

Civil Rights
   in Arkansas, 144–145
   Civil Rights Act of 1964, 13, 71
   civil rights movement, 132
   George and Mitt Romney's support for, 154, 157
   Internment of Japanese, 184
   and Roosevelt, Eleanor, 182, 185
   Theodore and Franklin Roosevelt's poor records on, 184
Clinton family, 39–61
   Clinton, Bill, 39–61, 101, 253, 314
   Clinton, Chelsea, 41, 43, 55, 56–59, 61
   Clinton, Hillary, 39–61
   Clinton Foundation, 42, 54, 58
Cuomo family, 245–257
   Cuomo, Andrew, 245, 247, 251, 252–257
   Cuomo, Mario, 245–252, 256

Daley family, 297–314
   Daley, John Patrick, 299, 312
   Daley, Richard J., 297–299, 300–305
   Daley, Richard M., 297–299, 301, 306–311
   Daley, William "Bill," 299, 311–312

Democratic Party
  in Arkansas, 46
  and Civil Rights, 135
  and the Clintons, 49
  and FDR, 173
  in New Jersey, 9
Dingell family, 317–326
  Dingell, Christopher, 317, 318
  Dingell, Debbie, 317, 318, 323–326
  Dingell, John D., 317, 318–319
  Dingell, John D., Jr., 317, 318, 319–323
Dulles, John Foster, 128

Eisenhower, Dwight D., 12, 16, 34, 35, 70, 125
  and Rockefeller, Nelson, 127–130, 131, 132, 135, 143–144
  and Romney, George, 154
  and Taft, Robert, 204

Fitzgerald, John Francis "Honey Fitz," 30, 81, 84, 87, 91
Ford, Gerald D., 15, 16, 19, 36, 143
Foreign Relations Committee (U.S. Senate), 30, 31, 42, 92

Garfield, James, 122
Goldwater, Barry, 135–138
  and Rockefeller, Nelson, 139–143
Gore family, 67–77
  Gore, Albert, 67–72
  Gore, Albert, Jr., 4, 54, 67, 69, 72–77
Grant, Ulysses S., 168, 195

Harrison, Benjamin, 170, 198
Harvard University, 18, 26, 29–30, 33, 35, 36, 37, 45, 72, 76, 79, 84, 85, 99
Hoover, Herbert, 202

Johnson, Lyndon B., 36, 51, 59, 68, 71, 93, 100, 101, 102, 125, 138, 140, 185

Kennedy family, 79–103
  Kennedy, Edward "Ted," 37, 38, 82, 95, 99–103
  Kennedy, John F., 36, 38, 39, 42, 81, 87–94, 95, 125, 134–135, 182, 185, 379
  Kennedy, Joseph P., 36, 72
  Kennedy, Robert F., 38, 82, 94–99, 100, 140–141, 254
  See also Fitzgerald, John Francis "Honey Fitz"
King, Martin Luther, Jr., 44, 97, 98, 134
Kissinger, Henry, 125, 141, 142
Koch Brothers/Americans for Prosperity, 110
Kooi, Peter, 288, 289, 290–292

La Follette family, 259–273
  La Follette, Belle Case, 259, 262, 263–270
  La Follette, Flora (Fola), 260, 262, 266, 270
  La Follette, Phil, 260, 262, 269, 271–272
  La Follette, Robert, 259, 261, 262–270, 272–273
  La Follette, Robert, Jr., 260, 262, 269, 270–271
Lincoln, Abraham, 120
Lodge family, 25–38
  Lodge, Henry Cabot, 27, 29–33
  Lodge, Henry Cabot, Jr., 28, 33–37, 135–136
  Lodge, John Davis, 28, 33–37
  See also Cabot family

McCain, John, 20, 111
McConnell, Mitch, 113, 114, 115
McKinley, William, 122
  and Roosevelt, Theodore, 170
  and Taft, William H., 199

Index

National Bureau for Economic Research, 123
Nixon, Richard M., 35, 36, 44, 46, 71
  and Goldwater, 136–137
  and 1972 election, 143
  and 1968 election, 139–142
  and Rockefeller, Nelson, 129, 132–134, 135, 140–143
  and Romney, George, 154–155

Obama, Barack, 114
  and "Obamacare," 116

Paul family, 109–116
  and the Campaign for Liberty, 111–112
  and Citizens for a Sound Economy (CSE), 110
  and the Foundation of Rational Economics and Education (FREE), 110, 112
  and Institute for Peace and Prosperity, 112
  and Kentucky Taxpayers United, 112
  Paul, Rand, 112–115
  Paul, Ron, 109–111
Presidential elections
  and Iowa Caucuses and New Hampshire Primary, 110, 112, 114
  of 1936, 37
  of 1960, 132–133
  of 1964, 43, 134–139
  of 1968, 44, 139–143
  of 2000, 3, 54, 75–77
  of 2008, 110
  of 2012, 112, 114
  of 2016, 40, 56, 59

Reagan, Ronald, 139–141, 143
Republican Party
  and Bush, George H. W., 15
  and Bush, Prescott, 12

Roberts family, 275–283
  Roberts, Barbara, 275, 277, 281–283
  Roberts, Betty, 275, 277, 278–280
  Roberts, Frank, 275, 277–278, 283
  Roberts, Mary Wendy, 275, 277, 280–283
Rockefeller family, 119–148
  Rockefeller, David, 145–146
  Rockefeller, John D., 120–123; and the Rockefeller Foundation, 122–123, 146; and Standard Oil, 120, 122
  Rockefeller, John D. IV, 146–147
  Rockefeller, John D., Jr., 123
  Rockefeller, John D. III, 124, 146
  Rockefeller, Nelson, 13, 124, 129–144
  Rockefeller, Winthrop, 124, 144–145
  Rockefeller, Winthrop Paul, 148
  Rockefeller Brothers Fund, 124
  Rockefeller Plaza, 125
Romney family, 151–160
  McDaniel, Ronna Romney, 151, 153, 160
  Romney, George, 135, 138, 151–156
  Romney, Lenore, 155–156
  Romney, Mitt, 101, 114, 151, 156–160
Roosevelt family, 163–186
  Roosevelt, Franklin D., 35, 37, 40, 67, 68, 80, 83, 84, 86, 87, 126, 129, 176, 178–180, 181–184, 270, 314
  Roosevelt, Theodore "Teddy" (Teddy), 26, 30, 31, 84, 103, 122, 168–174, 183, 199–201

Simpson family, 287–294
  Simpson, Alan, 288, 289, 290–292, 293
  Simpson, Colin, 288, 289, 290, 292–293

Simpson, Milward Lee, 288–290, 293
See also Kooi, Peter
Stewart, Thomas, 332, 337

Taft family, 189–206
    Taft, "Bob," 189–190, 205
    Taft, Robert, 189, 202–204
    Taft, Robert Alphonso, Jr., 189, 204–205
    Taft, William Howard, 31, 36, 122, 189, 196–202
Tea Party movement, 110, 113–114
Truman, Harry, 68, 127, 182
Trump, Donald, 40, 56, 61, 114, 115, 159–160

Udall family, 329–340
    Udall, David King, 330, 332
    Udall, Mark Emery, 332, 338
    Udall, Morris "Mo" King, 331, 336–337
    Udall, Stewart Lee, 332, 336, 339
    Udall Center, 339
    Udall Foundation, 327, 338–339
See also Stewart, Thomas
United Nations, 15, 35, 127

Vietnam/Vietnam War, 36, 42, 54, 88, 92, 139

Watergate, 54–55
World War II, 14, 34, 35, 53, 86

Yale University, 8, 11, 13, 14, 18, 43, 45

www.ingramcontent.com/pod-product-compliance
Lightning Source LLC
Chambersburg PA
CBHW070009010526
44117CB00011B/1486